THE PATTERN OF HUMAN CONCERNS

Other Books by Hadley Cantril

Human Nature and Political Systems

The Morning Notes of Adelbert Ames, Jr. (editor)

Soviet Leaders and Mastery over Man

Reflections on the Human Venture (with Charles H. Bumstead)

The Politics of Despair

How Nations See Each Other (with William Buchanan)

Public Opinion 1935–46 (editor)

The "Why" of Man's Experience

Tensions that Cause Wars (editor)

Understanding Man's Social Behavior

The Psychology of Ego-Involvements (with M. Sherif)

Gauging Public Opinion (contributing editor)

The Psychology of Social Movements

The Invasion from Mars

The Psychology of Radio (with G. W. Allport)

The
Pattern
of
Human
Concerns

HADLEY CANTRIL

Rutgers University Press
New Brunswick · New Jersey

To Lloyd

Preface

There has been a great deal of discussion about the "revolution of expectations," but solid data from representative samples of people from all parts of the world are hard to come by. Any superimposing of preconceived ideas which forces patterns upon people's reports loses the richness, the uniqueness, the flavor, or the authenticity of what they are trying to say about themselves. What is needed is information which transmits reliably, in people's own terms, what they are feeling. The data contained in this book represent an attempt to fill this need, providing as they do, information about the aspirations and fears of people in various stages of development within their own culture and in a wide variety of countries which are themselves in different phases of development.

The book attempts to provide a systematic psychological study to complement those made by political scientists and sociologists. It tries to find common ground in a unitary psychological system for the diversities of mankind as they are revealed in the varied nations into which people are grouped at this point of human history.

Surveys of representative samples of the adult populations in the many nations studied were made by native interviewers who used a device especially invented to get information in the people's own terms, without forcing their replies into arbitrary categories. The scope of the study is necessarily an ambitious one: it took six years to accumulate the data presented here. Nearly 20,000 people have been interviewed, including 600 members of the legislative bodies of some of the countries studied. My research partner, Lloyd Free, and I have traveled more than 250,000 miles to organize and supervise the work in the thirteen different countries studied: Brazil, Cuba, the Dominican Republic, Egypt, India, Israel, Nigeria, Panama, the Philippines, Poland, the United States, West Germany, and Yugoslavia. The results of a study in Japan, conducted by their Central Research Agency, are also included here, as an addendum. Mr. Free or I conducted the first such national surveys made in Brazil, Cuba, and Yugoslavia and managed the first nongovernment survey ever made in Egypt (after obtaining the permission of two cabinet ministers). In Yugoslavia, where permission to go ahead with the work was also obtained, cooperation was complete and enthusiastic. In Israel, the special sampling of members of the Kibbutzim was also a pioneer venture. Except for the study done in Cuba Mr. Free and I worked openly, and with the full cooperation of any government officials involved. And, in all cases, any of the individuals or organizations who cooperated were sent the complete tabulations of results if they wished them. Along with the data went the full privilege of analyzing them, and the recipients were wholly free to publish their own findings and interpretations independently. In addition to gathering quantitative material, I have read thousands of interviews and have tried, through them, to learn more precisely what the figures mean in the concrete contexts of the daily lives of the many people interviewed. The costs of all operations involved in this study were met by the Institute for International Social Research, established in 1955 with an endowment from the Rockefeller Brothers Fund.

In the researches discussed and analyzed here, literally several million figures were accumulated, along with several thousand tables processed from sorting machines and an IBM 7090 computer. There is, indeed, almost no limit to the number of tabulations and cross-tabulations the data might yield. Thus, the main task in writing this book has proved to be one of presenting the rich data in a fashion not too complicated for general grasp and use, yet with sufficient detail to satisfy the expert. It would have been easier simply to report the material descriptively, country by country, and let it go at that. I have tried, as far as possible, to group and compare data so as to reveal significant patterns of human concerns. This goal was paramount. For the use of qualified research scholars, most of the raw quantitative data have been duplicated in the Roper Public Opinion Research Center at Williamstown, Massachusetts, where they are available for work on specialized problems.

This study was emphatically not undertaken for the purpose of providing up-to-the-minute information on the state of mind of people in any country, even though certain special reports, prepared on some of the studies conducted during the past few years, have been of acknowledged value to high governmental officials in various countries. Above all else, the purpose is to understand the effects of circumstances on the outlooks which people hold for themselves and their nations. And, as a psychologist, I hoped to learn something more about the forces which propel and frustrate people in various social and economic situations. Obviously, repeat studies utilizing the same technique reported here could provide valuable data about social change and social forces at work. It would be important if future periodic checks were made in the countries here studied. In addition, base lines in other nations and regions are more than needed.

I hope this book will be of value not only to the layman and the social scientist in terms of increasing their understanding and demonstrating the potentialities of a method of research in social and political psychology, but also that it will be helpful to those people in governments who are responsible for major decisions. For sound policy should be determined only on the basis of needs and attitudes of the people for whom institutions and governments are designed. Yet, all too often, decisions are being made on the basis of what J. K. Galbraith terms "conventional wisdom," without taking account of facts that can become readily available through well-directed, well-timed "policy research."

Acknowledgments

The list of acknowledgments for a work of this sort is a long one. Many organizations and individuals cooperated in different parts of the world. In Brazil, the work both on the public and parliamentary surveys was done by the Instituto de Estudos Sociais e Economicos, Ltda., directed by Dr. Octavio da Costa Eduardo. In Cuba, identification has perforce to be omitted, but the men and women who did the work were most reliable. They have long since left that unhappy country. The Cuban data were processed by the Bureau of Social Science Research, directed by Dr. Robert T. Bower with Mrs. Laure Sharp as supervisor. In the Dominican Republic the International Research Associates of Mexico City were directed by Mr. George M. Gaither. In Egypt, data were gathered under the direction of Professor Abdo Elkholy. In India, the Indian Institute of Public Opinion, Ltd., did both the public and parliamentary studies, and I am indebted to Mr. Eric da Costa and Mr. J. S. Yogie. In Israel, my thanks go to Dr. Aaron Antonovsky and Dr. Louis Guttman of the Israel Institute of Applied Social Research. In Japan, I am grateful to the Central Research Agency of Tokyo, the only organization mentioned here that was not commissioned to do the research but utilized the Institute's methods for its own agency purposes and kindly provided the ladder ratings obtained. Unfortunately, the questionnaires were destroyed before I learned the survey had been done, and therefore the coding scheme could not be applied to the full data. In Nigeria, both the public and parliamentary studies were conducted by the Market Research (Nigeria) Limited, directed by Dr. Gordon Wilson, with the work directly supervised by Mr. James R. Wilson and Mr. M. A. Giwa Osagie. Coding here was handled under arrangement with Dr. Henry Durant of Social Surveys (Gallup Poll) Ltd., in London and supervised by Mrs. Naomi McIntosh.

In Panama the research was done by International Research Associates of Mexico City. In the Philippines the public survey was made by The Psychological Center under the direction of Dr. George H. Hodel, while the parliamentary survey was conducted by Robot Statistics, under the direction of Mr. George Cohen. In Poland, I am especially indebted to Dr. Adam Sarapata, director of the Department of Sociology of the Work Institute of the Polish Academy of Sciences, for so competently handling all phases of the survey, and to Dr. Adam Schaff, Director of the Institute of Philosophy and Sociology of the Academy of Sciences, for his assistance in making arrangements with us for the survey to be done. Also in Poland I am indebted to Krzysztof Hirszel and Irena Woźniakowska for coding, to Stanisława Walkowska for statistical work, and to the interviewers from the Public Opinion Research Center at the Polish Radio. In the United States, all field work was done by the American Institute of Public Opinion and I am grateful to Dr. George Gallup, Mr. Paul Perry, and Mr. Emery Ruby. In West Germany, both the parliamentary and public studies were conducted by DIVO, with Herr Peter Schmitt in charge. In Yugoslavia, I am indebted to the Hon. Dr. Radivoj Uvalić, then Director of the Institute of Social Sciences at Belgrade and presently his country's Ambassador to India; to Professor Ilija Stanojčić, Voyna Milovanovic, Sveta Culibrk, Zlata Grebo, Mira Balen, and to Dr. Dančika Nikolić, of the Institute of Statistics, who prepared the sample.

For statistical advice, I am indebted to the late Professor Samuel S. Wilks of the Department of Mathematics, Princeton University. For advice in computing a socioeconomic developmental index of the different countries, I am indebted to Professor Everett Hagen, Department of Economics at The Massachusetts Institute of Technology. Dr. Peter Janicki worked out the tables of significance for differences in ladder ratings when he was a research associate with the Institute and also analyzed the American data. Dr. Janicki also traveled to Poland and India and helped work out sampling details. Drs. Carl Helm and Roald Buhler of the Princeton Computer Center programmed and processed our data on the IBM 7090 computer, and Mr. Lou Vexler of The Gallup Organization made hundreds of tabulations for the study. Mr. Barry Margolin of Harvard kindly wrote some explanatory text to aid in the interpretation of certain charts in Appendix C.

In the Institute's own office I am grateful to Mrs. Pauline Smith and Miss Nynke Ytsje Witteveen for their assistance, but most of all to Mrs. Carol O'Brien Desmond and Mrs. Alice Anne Navin who prepared nearly all the tables and got data in shape for the computers. Mrs. Navin has furthermore checked and double-checked the figures in the manuscript. My son, Tad, calculated the economic indices, did many correlations, prepared the background material for the different countries, and helped me organize some of the data. I am indebted to the late Adelbert Ames, Jr., for discussions we had concerning many of the concepts developed here.

Most of all, I owe my deepest gratitude to my colleague, Lloyd A. Free, who is responsible for all the parliamentary studies as well as for the gathering of data on the public surveys in Brazil, Cuba, the Dominican Republic, Nigeria, Panama, the Philippines, and West Germany. In addition, Mr. Free and I worked out the final coding schemes together. Throughout the study, he has contributed insights based on his rich background of experience in studying the political dynamics at work in many different countries. I am also most grateful to him for his helpful comments on the manuscript. He is, then, essentially a collaborator in this book.

A few of the passages in Chapters I and II have been taken from previously published material: "Toward a Humanistic Psychology" in *ETC: A Review of General Semantics; The Politics of Despair* (Basic Books); "The Concept of Transaction in Psychology and Neurology," with W. K. Livingston, in *The Journal of Individual Psychology;* "Hopes and Fears for Self and Country," with Lloyd Free, in *The American Behavioral Scientist;* and "A Transactional Inquiry Concerning Mind," in *Theories of the Mind,* edited by Jordan Scher (Free Press).

H. C.

Institute for International Social Research
Princeton, N.J.

Contents

Part One

THE PSYCHOLOGICAL APPROACH

CHAPTER I

What the Problem Is

One major obligation of the social psychologist is to provide his own discipline, the other social sciences, and interested laymen with conceptual tools that will increase the range and the reliability of their understanding of social phenomena. Beyond that, responsible government officials are today turning more frequently to the social scientist for insights into the nature and solution of the problems with which they are confronted.

New problems require new solutions. And new problems arise with new populations and new technologies. The solutions of these problems require new institutions, new political, economic, and social mechanisms. Yet institutions and political and economic arrangements grow slowly and die slowly. Information about what people want and will accept is vital if new institutions are to be devised to meet new needs and conditions. Because old institutions die hard, new institutions should be given every chance of success. And in this process, social scientists, including psychologists, should be able to help. By means of research findings, decisions based on opinions and guesswork should be lessened while decisions based on knowledge and understanding should be enlarged. More reliable predictions of what people want or do not want, believe or do not believe, will accept or will not accept, should aid the process of creating new forms of economic, social, and political institutions.

On balance, I believe the psychologist has so far not been markedly helpful. In many important areas, the social scientist finds a dearth of psychological concepts appropriate to the level on which he is working and from which he might pick and choose. Thus, knowingly or unknowingly, he is too often left to settle for concepts that may have been satisfactory for their times, or for the particular situations they were created to deal with, but which become strained beyond the boundaries of adequacy, validity, or plausibility when they must be utilized to account for ongoing, complex problems. So, the political scientist sometimes

3

feels he must invent his own system of psychology, since none of those worked out so far by psychologists themselves seems to fill the bill.

I do not mean to imply that nothing useful has yet been provided. The young discipline of social psychology has already developed some most helpful conceptual tools.[1] But in this field of psychology, as in so many branches of the subject, the tendency has been to proliferate sidewards instead of going forward. There is a great need to pull together in some systematic way the most important general specifications for a sound social psychology that will, among other things, enable people doing research in the field to formulate new inquiries that will constantly add to understanding.

THE SEARCH FOR AN APPROPRIATE LEVEL OF ACCOUNTING

Just what the nature of these conceptual tools will be depends upon the investigator's conception of what constitutes "explanation." Because of the different types of problems and situations with which different disciplines deal, what is "explanation" for one discipline is merely "description" for another. What the psychologist may think is explanation may be mere description for the physiologist. And what the sociologist or political scientist may call explanation may be description for the psychologist. Thus, the political scientist may appeal to concepts such as "symbols" and "loyalties" as explanations, while the psychologist will want to understand how and why symbols and loyalties are formed and what they refer to in the experience of individuals. There is a sort of hierarchy here: from mathematics, to physics, to chemistry, to physiology, to psychology, to sociology, to political science, and finally to philosophy which in a sense subsumes them all. Within psychology itself, some psychologists put their faith in the conditioned response and all of its ramifications; others posit various needs that are manifest or latent in the human individual and build their systems accordingly; others stretch Freudian concepts to an almost absurd degree in ferreting out motives for people's social behavior. The final justification for any accounting or explanatory concepts must be the extent to which they enable a person to understand the problems with which he is dealing in all their full-bodied, ongoing complexity, without distorting them to fit some preconceived model he may have.

Psychologists, among others, often shy away from a functionally integrated, "organismic" view of process and real-life situations, finding it difficult to handle the interdependence of all the variables involved. The point was made by Henry A. Murray in 1948 when he wrote: "The main body of psychology started its career by putting the wrong foot forward and it has been out of step with the march of science much of the time. Instead of beginning with studies of the whole person adjusting to a natural environment, it began with studies of a segment of a person responding to a physical stimulus in an unnatural laboratory environment." [2] There is a tendency to resort to model building and the like which leave out variables that may be disturbing, such as those of needs, wants and valuing. An eminent scientist-philosopher, Michael Polanyi, has reminded us:

> The higher level relies for its workings on the laws governing the particulars of the lower level, and these laws also limit the range of the operations on the higher level and account for its failures. But the operations of the higher level cannot be accounted for in terms of the laws which govern the lower level, since the examination of the particulars of the lower level does not reveal the laws of the upper level. The higher level is unaccountable in terms of its particulars. . . . Since the workings of the mind form such a physiognomy, the behaviourist programme of attending to the particulars controlled by the mind, instead of to the mind, is in itself impossible and indeed absurd. [3]

It may be helpful in pointing to the level of accounting I am using and in setting the stage for my study if I differentiate four different ways in which human experience may be viewed, four different areas of complexity and quality.

First, there is *ongoing, naïve* experience. Here I refer to the level of immediate "pure" experience—unanalyzed, unconceptualized, unmediated, and with no concern on the part of the experiencing individual to describe, analyze, conceptualize, or communicate this experience. This ongoing, naïve experience is what Korzybski called "first-order" or "unspeakable" experience. It is the kind of experience the poet Wordsworth had in mind when he said that "we murder to dissect."

As has frequently been pointed out, any attempt to describe or analyze experience immediately alters that experience. When a person tries to describe or analyze experience or any aspect of it, he is functionally organized quite differently than at the times when he is participating in a process of living and not describing or analyzing it. Experiences in the occasions of living are dependent upon and characterized by processes involving, for example, overtones of satisfaction or dissatisfaction, a sense of involvement or responsibility, a sense of intent or aim, commitment through activity, a sense of worry, frustration, or urgency, a sense of despair, hope, or faith, depending upon the particular orchestration going on in a particular unique occasion of living.

A second level of experience is that of *description*. Verbalization and communication must be distinguished methodologically from naïve experience itself. For in describing, a person focuses on selected aspects of experience. It is as if with any such focusing, awareness is shifted from the full orchestration as a whole to the role of a particular instrument in the orchestra. Hence, reports of experience are not to be equated with experience itself. Such descriptive data, however, do, of course, provide the psychologist with some of his most valuable raw material and may be about as close as he can get to ongoing, naïve experience itself.

A third variety of experience is that concerned with *analysis* and *conceptualization*. Here, instead of focusing on a selected phenomenon in an experience of living, one may, in the midst of that living, try to "figure out" conceptually what is going on. This is done for some purpose. Perhaps one is trying to resolve some personal problem, or perhaps he is delving into his own experience or his own observation in the hope of discovering hunches or clues that will provide him with some hypothesis. Analysis of any occurrence for whatever purpose is very different from purposive behavior itself or focused aspects of it.

This area of complexity described as "focused analysis and conceptualization" also includes one person's attempt to understand the behavior and purposes of other people as he tries to carry out his own purposes in social situations. Such understanding will usually be successful insofar as he is able to bring to an occasion appropriate abstractions derived from his own experience. The ability to put oneself into another's position and share his experience vicariously seems generally to depend on similarity of experiential backgrounds, purposes, standards for sensing satisfaction, values. Thus it is difficult for people in highly developed nations to understand the problems faced by underdeveloped people; it is difficult for those living in Communist lands to understand non-Communists and vice versa. But no matter how close the correspondence may be between all the factors involved in giving one person an awareness of another person's experience under certain circumstances, he still has to interpret their experience in terms of his own experience.

The fourth and final level of experience is that of *abstracting* for scientific speculation, a level closely interrelated to analysis and conceptualization but useful to isolate. The scientist's attempt to understand the nature of human living is ultimately an attempt to distinguish components, to choose those by means of which he will be able to define and interpret the significance of any process of living, and to describe the variables on which the singularity of any process depends. If the scientist can effectively relate his abstracting to his presuppositions, then he will have an instrument to render communication more accurate and to enable him to understand the abstraction without reference to any particular item of behavior that might illustrate it.

Such scientific abstractions are not affected by individual behavior and are not altered when conceptualized from the point of view of different persons. If they were so affected or altered, they would prove useless;

it is their static quality that gives them the utility they have in understanding the significance of concrete behavioral situations. This does not mean, of course, that such scientific abstractions never change. They are constantly evolving, being modified by new ones created by scientists themselves. On the basis of the study reported here, some tentative abstractions have been created which seem to bring the data together in plausible fashion. The creative scientist tests his abstractions by their performance, not by their consistency, realizing that any abstraction is man-made and highly tentative. What I mean by "the static quality" of an abstraction is simply that scientific abstractions would be operationally useless if their significances were not fixed. The point was made, in a sense, by Marshal Foch, Chief of the High Command of the Allied Armies in World War I, who is reputed to have said, "When historians of the future tell posterity what the World War was about, they will agree upon a cause that nobody who fought it ever suspected."

There is the very great danger that the psychologist, as well as others who study different aspects of human behavior, will confuse the level of experience with which he is dealing and begin to think that the abstractions he has created actually are the reality, when, in fact, they are several steps removed from the ongoing process of experience itself. This tendency to mistake the levels of abstraction for ongoing experience itself can lead to the most dangerous bifurcations. Since abstractions are brought about and communicated by the nouns or adjectives man himself has devised, they often provide a static rather than a moving picture, leaving out the genesis or process-of-becoming, with its irreversible sequence, which seems to be a major characterization of personal, social, and political life.

The task I have undertaken in this study was to try to discover from the point of view of the individual participants in social and national life just what the dimensions and qualities of their reality worlds were. I have tried to conduct this inquiry always with the aim of learning about a person's own unique behavioral center, with "center" defined by Webster as "a point or source from which a force, influence, process or the like, takes its origin; as, Niagara, a power center." I have tried to minimize as much as possible any point of view brought to the people of a nation by an outside observer, especially a self-righteous or condescending observer. I have tried to understand people in their own terms.

CHAPTER II

The Genesis of Aspirations

WHAT WE START WITH

In trying to account for the genesis of aspirations, of what a person wants and longs for, one of course lands squarely in the area loosely called "motivation." In their effort to conceptualize this important subject, psychologists have proposed a variety of theories and posited different needs, instincts, and drives. A basic difficulty is that since motives cannot be directly observed, the psychologist can only infer what such motives might be and then create abstractions which seem to him best to conform to behavioral evidence.

One way of explaining the concept of motivation is to search for some physiological equivalents without sacrificing the subtlety, complexity and development of purposive behavior as we observe it. While neourophysiologists still cannot give clear-cut answers, they are now finding basic systems within the nervous system itself which do apparently propel the organism toward or away from certain situations, and which may well turn out to be the original substratum or matrix within which and from which aspirations are derived. The two systems that neurophysiologists have demonstrated as "existing" within the most primitive parts of the brain have been variously called the pleasure or "I like" system and the aversive or "I dislike" system. The former, when electrically stimulated by electrodes implanted in certain parts of the brain, clearly produces experiences the experimental animal likes and wants more of; the latter clearly produces experiences the animal wants to get away from.

The problem of finding an appropriate name for these two systems is complicated by the fact that behavior may change while a single area in the brain is being stimulated, and also by the fact that the two systems are not invariably in opposition to one another in any simple yes-no relationship. Although the exact anatomical limits of these two systems have not yet been established and the study of their functions is yet in its early stages, the mere fact of their existence is important here.

It is likely that as research progresses the systems will lose much of their vagueness.[1]

For want of a better designation, the two built-in systems may be thought of as appetitive, in the way Aristotle used this term. He wrote: "Where sensation is found, there is pleasure and pain and that which causes pleasure and pain; and where these are, there also is desire, desire being appetite for what is pleasurable." [2] Webster's New International Dictionary defines "appetite" as "an inherent or habitual desire or propensity for some personal gratification, either of body or mind." I like this inclusion of mind in the definition, because, as will be seen, perceptual events as well as behavior are modified by desires and purposes, most of which have their origin in influences derived from past experience and learned values as well as from bodily appetites. What I am describing here has been called by Michael Polanyi "the appetitive-perceptive agency" of organisms.[3]

The word *genesis* as used by the ancient Greeks meant the "process of becoming" or "becomingness," a noun that sounds strange to modern ears. There is no proper word in the English language to express satisfactorily the ongoing changes exhibited by all forms of life in their progress from birth, through growth and maturation, to old age and death. This ongoing change in life, which apparently exists in certain inorganic material as well as in human beings and societies, is not a haphazard process but moves in a discernible direction, conforming to the progressive outlines determined by the constituents involved as these all play their role in the orchestration of living.

In the course of development, and without any intent or awareness that might be called "thought," the child is impelled toward objects and people that give it comfort and satisfaction, and away from objects, people, and situations that cause it distress. The traces left by these early experiences lead to an association between certain objects, persons, and situations and the feelings they elicit. These associations, in turn, lead to intelligent recognition of objects, persons, and situations and to selective behavior in relation to them as information is transformed into useful knowledge. The research reported in this volume provides abundant evidence of this fact.

It is at this point, I think, that "mind" is born, establishing its own identity as definitely as did the first mass of living protoplasm originating from the chemicals of the sea. And once mind arrives on the scene in an individual's life, the apparent fact cannot be sidestepped that consciousness, an aspect of mind, has the capacity to act as a first cause, to initiate behavior, to imagine, create, invent, and to choose.

Every human being has to learn what to desire, what to want, has to learn to channel his behavior and his intentions. I do not believe this is by any means a matter of the displacement or rationalization of a few innate appetites, instincts, or impulses: desires and purposes function in their own right when the individual discovers they will maximize satisfaction or protect him not only from physical harm but from losing the satisfaction derived from whatever gains he has made.

The guiding star for the individual in this process is a capacity unique to the human being as a species; namely, the capacity to experience satisfactions that are permeated with value overtones. *As human beings, we seem to seek a quality of experience far different from that sought by any other type of organism we know. Man's capacity to experience value satisfactions propels him to learn and to devise new ways of behaving that will enable him both to extend the range and heighten the quality of value satisfactions and to insure the repeatability of those value satisfactions already experienced.*[4]

While the principle of homeostasis and the notion of a drive to reduce "cognitive dissonance" are useful in describing certain limited phases of human behavior, I think both of these accounting models fall far short of the mark by overlooking the larger context of this more enduring, overriding characteristic of man. What Polanyi observes as the "desire for tension," the "craving for mental dissatisfaction," and the "essential restlessness of the human mind, which calls ever again in question any satisfaction that it may have previously achieved"[5] are, I believe, fundamentally due to the fact that this tension, dissatisfaction, and restlessness are by-products of the built-in desire of man to enrich the value satisfaction of living and are instrumented by man's inventive and creative capacities.

It is because of man's desire to enrich the value satisfactions of his life that human motives have the great variety, subtlety, depth, and complexity they do. And, of course, this is one of the reasons that human beings are so difficult to understand. It is because of the myriad forms value satisfaction can take that the studies here were conducted as they were and reveal as they do the varieties of patterns in the strivings of people who are in different circumstances. For the nature of the situations that hold out some possibility for the experiencing of value satisfactions varies with the life history, the capacities, and the involvements of every individual. In order to understand the multifarious aspirations people acquire and exhibit, it is essential to be clear on a crucial interrelated and interdependent problem: how human beings learn what is significant to pay attention to anyway, and how they do this more, or less, effectively in order to carry out their purposes.

LEARNING WHAT IS SIGNIFICANT

An accumulating body of evidence—much of it from experimental psychology—justifies the statement that the world any individual experiences is in part the creation of his perception and not the whole cause of it. While this statement may disturb those who are "stimulus-bound" and who think in terms of the concept of interaction between an environment out there and an insulated reacting individual, the point of view is also attested to by eminent men in the so-called hard sciences. For example, the physicist P. W. Bridgman wrote that "naked sense impressions simply do not occur, and the traditional analysis of our conscious experience into naked sensations as building blocks is palpably bad description." [6] The biologist J. Z. Young writes that "The form we give to this world is a construct of our brains, using such observations as they have been able to make. Only in that sense does it exist." [7] Polanyi believes "that into every act of knowing there enters a tacit and passionate contribution of the person knowing what is being known." [8] And the distinguished neurologist Sir Russel Brain says that "The scientific account of perception . . . teaches us that the objects which we perceive outside our brains are not as independent of us as they appear to be: they have qualities which are generated by our brains and which have no other existence." [9]

The significances and meanings a person assigns to all aspects of the environment within which he attempts to carry out his purposes are learned in the course of experience. Essentially a person tries from infancy on to construct for himself a pattern of assumptions that will increase the correspondence between what he perceives in the environment around him and what this environment turns out to be when he acts within it to experience some intended consequences. And he generally does this, of course, without being aware of the processes involved in the creation of patterns of assumptions.

Here are some of the varieties of assumptions a person learns that give him his conceptions of what is significant: [10]

1. *Assumptions concerning the significance of objects.* The objects in the world around us have the meaning they do because we attribute to them certain characteristics, sizes, shapes, or properties. All of us have built up these significances in the course of our dealings with these objects. For example, even though we see only the head of a horse projecting from behind the barn, we report that we are seeing a horse because we have learned to take for granted that the rest of the horse is there. We have learned to assume that things are wholes. We learn to regard objects as large or small, as far or near, as moving fast or slowly because of the experiences we have become used to relative to these objects.

2. *Assumptions concerning the significance of people.* When a situation in which a person is participating or intends to participate involves other people, the assumptions that guide his action include new and different aspects. He must guess and understand the purposes of other people, and in the process he must realize that their purposes are just

as "real" as any physical characteristics of objects. He must predict upon the basis of his assumptions what effect his intended behavior will have on others' purposes, how others will see him, and how their participation with him in turn will affect his own subsequent action in the endless chain of events in which he is involved. Particular significances are attributed to certain individuals because of learned assumptions about the meaning of the roles they play, their vocations, their place in the status hierarchy, the neighborhood, the group, the nation, or the race they represent. All of these personal attributes are often thought of as fixed characteristics of people according to the particular purpose any such grouping may serve us.

3. *Assumptions concerning the significance of sequential happenings.*
Obviously the world of objects and people does not remain passive and static. Things keep moving. There is the ceaseless flow of happenings around us. Day follows night; our lives follow certain rhythms; our hunger stops when we eat; the motor of our automobile comes to life when we turn on the starter; the traffic policeman stops us if we disobey his signal. In the course of living, a whole host of sequential significances are built up in us as we carry on in a world that is in continual flux.

In order to make more certain that a particular event can be counted on to follow another event, man has devised a whole host of artifacts with built-in specifications. Many of the tools, instruments, machines, buildings, power systems, communication devices—in fact, the whole bewildering variety of man-made equipment that characterizes modern life —have been devised to insure that certain events or satisfactions will follow each other in predictable and reliable ways. Often this standardization is at considerable cost to the richness of experience if one looks at aspects other than efficiency.

When the combinations of assumptions concerning people and sequential significance are pondered, one begins to get some insight into the complexities of understanding other people and their understanding us in a social world, which, like the physical world, is constantly changing. For example, the quality of the relationship a person has with other people depends in part on his capacity to comprehend simultaneously the sequential significances they are experiencing in a chain of events, together with the sequential significances he himself is experiencing in the same phase of this chain of events. A person is able to share the same experience of what is significant in his participation with other people only insofar as he and they experience the same significances simultaneously in a chain of events in which all are involved. Many allegiances and loyalties come about because people have learned to share sequential events—such as a parade, a church service, a wedding—and have experienced a particular quality of value satisfaction from joint participation in what they are therefore able to call the "same" event.

4. *Assumptions concerning the significance of actions.* Each of us eventually learns, sometimes gradually, sometimes suddenly, what the probable significance of certain of our actions will be. We learn what we are likely to experience if we initiate a certain chain of behavior. The child learns that a rubber ball will bounce if he throws it on the floor, that the cat will scratch him if he pulls its tail, that he has a better chance of getting the cooperation he desires if he says the right thing in the right way at the right time to his parents or friends. Each individual, according to his purposes, learns through the repeated testing of his own action to become more effective in bringing about the consequences he wants. The rituals, customs, ceremonies, and laws of the culture all insure a greater repeatability in social affairs by providing more predictable directions, enabling more people to chart their courses of action and thereby obtain greater satisfaction for participants.

5. *Assumptions concerning temporal and spatial significances.* Permeating the learning of all varieties of assumptions are their temporal and spatial aspects. These are such an integral part of all the processes of mind that a person is seldom aware of the variety of assumptions concerning both time and space he is taking into account. Social psychologists and cultural anthropologists have often pointed out the different meanings and significances of time and space measures, the different values placed on units of time or space, and the effects of technology on the temporal and spatial standards of different groups in their operational definition of, for example, "promptness." But the assumptions built up concerning subjective time and space become much more complex and subtle when considered from the first-person viewpoint. For example, the "here and now" of an individual, as so often pointed out, is likely to be a span of time or space more or less unique to the context of his own life, his age, his circumstances.

6. *Assumptions concerning the significance of value standards.* In almost any concrete situation in which an individual participates, he is faced with alternative choices of action. Whether he is aware of the process or not, he weighs alternative courses of action in terms of the value significances they are likely to have for him: the relative value satisfactions he will obtain if he does this or that, or if he does nothing at all. Evaluation among various alternatives is made on the basis of the relative probability that each possible course of action will lead to the desired consequences, will produce the desired results.

The process of guessing at the possible value satisfaction particular behavior will bring is enormously complicated, since an almost infinite number of probabilities relating to each of the above classes of significances must be taken into account. The process involves feelings or overtones sometimes only vaguely sensed and often not bounded by space and time, which only become real and meaningful as they operate in determining what to do in the here and now. In this process, a person may consciously or unconsciously refer to certain abstractions embodied in some code of ethics, some political ideology, some religion, and which he has learned to accept as possible guides that may be put to use as tests for appropriate occasions. While not "real" in their own right, these abstractions can become real if they operate effectively in concrete situations. And in this context, they are often indispensible realities. Man has devised these abstractions and symbols in his perpetual attempt to bring order into disorder, to explain to himself various phenomena, or to find universal principles and guides for more ordered living, no matter what the unique purposes or circumstances of any one individual may be at the moment. It is man's capacity to create and to utilize relevant abstractions that makes it possible to share beliefs and ideologies and faiths with people in all ages and places and to communicate them to others.

These are only examples of the types of learned significances. Some of them are fleeting, others endure for a lifetime. And it should be emphasized that by and large the types of significances differentiated here are interdependent in terms of their actual operation in a specific occasion of living. The data acquired in the research reported here provide ample confirmation of this.

All of this obviously functions in and is made possible by the human brain and nervous system. The working hypothesis that all significances have to be learned in the course of development seems to be confirmed by recent research of teams of investigators composed of psychologists, neurophysiologists, pharmacologists, anesthesiologists, and computer specialists who have developed increasingly sophisticated techniques for studying the activity of the brain through the use of freely implanted electrodes.[11] Without going into the experimental evidence here, it may be said that recent observations concerning the functioning of the brain and the nervous system are giving us a new picture: instead of having only the classical sensory and motor systems to control adjustments to the outside world, the nervous system seems to have two control mechanisms. The second one is centered in the recticular formation, and is now known to exert a constant modulating influence on all sensory input as well as on all motor output.

This less discrete and more generalized control of sensory input is of particular importance to the psychologist because the evidence indicates the ability of the brain to "police" its own sensory input as conditioned by past experience and to determine for an individual at any particular time the "significance" of all he may be aware of. And what the individual learns from past experience includes the specific purpose or aspirations acquired in the course of development.

Once assumptions are formed and give significance to certain happenings around us, once they have proved more or less effective in purposive behavior, then they serve as filters for both focusing attention and screening out what is apparently irrelevant. They also serve as reinforcing agents, intensifying other aspects of the environment which seem to have a direct bearing on purposes and aspirations. Thus people do not react *to* their environments in any mechanistic way but transact *with* an environment in which they themselves are active agents.

In large measure, we are what our loyalties are: loyalties to a family, to a tribe, a caste, a class, a neighborhood, a religion, a nation or an ideology, or, more realistically, a combination of many of these. These identifications form an important part of our reality worlds, the worlds we create for ourselves in the course of our transactions of living, the worlds in which we have our being, the only worlds we know.

A person's concept of self develops as a function of his transactions with others and is maintained or altered only by these transactions, since there is the completely interdependent relationship between a person and his society so often noted. In this sense, Marx and Engels were quite correct when they wrote over a hundred years ago that "Our desires and pleasures spring from society; we measure them therefore by society and not by the objects which serve for their satisfaction. Because they are of a social nature they are of a relative nature."

The "self-constancy" so crucial in providing a sense of continuing identity might be roughly defined as the sum total of the estimates one has, based on past experience, of one's own capacity to deal with particular sets of impingements from the environment one is exposed to. Since self-constancy consists of a class of probable or estimated capacities in relation to particular social situations or groups of people at hand, it cannot be referred solely to the individual but must include the individual and his dealing with others. Daniel Lerner has provided useful insights on this problem of self-constancy in his studies of "traditional personalities" who find it so difficult to conceive of being anyone else or living outside their own village, hence having a wide area of "no-commitment" to anything beyond the little world they know.[12]

Since experience is so much a matter of probability—of the bets constantly being made in a changing world as to the significances of things, of people, and of events—a person must do something to put order and repeatability into the world in which he carries on his living. The craving to find some certainty or permanence in the tumult of change around us stems from the need to be able to guess what action will serve our purposes when time for action arrives. We are more comfortable if we think we can predict with a fair degree of accuracy the chain of events that will occur if we undertake a certain action. We crave certainty rather than doubt. We want enough form and pattern in our thoughts and feelings to give direction to flow. Hence we create constancies concerning things, people, and events. We attribute certain characteristics to them, so that we shall be provided with enough interpretation to guess with fair accuracy what the significances and meanings are of the variety of signals that reach our sense organs, without having to make fresh guesses at every turn.

"We are either born with such dissimilitude of temper and inclination, or receive so many of our ideas and opinions from the state of life in which we are engaged, that the griefs and cares of one part of mankind seem to the other hypocrisy, folly, and affectation. Every class of society has its cant of lamentation which is understood or regarded by none but themselves; and every part of life has its uneasinesses which those who do not feel them will not commiserate." So wrote Samuel Johnson in pointing to what I have meant when I say that every individual creates for himself his own reality world with its constancies and that this is the only world he knows.[13] The same concept has been developed by Sir Julian Huxley who uses the phrase "significant worlds" to describe the different ranges and qualities of experience of different forms of animal life.[14]

REALITY WORLDS AS PROCESS

Since the environment in which living occurs, and of which every person is so vital an ingredient, is in a continual state of flux, change and becomingness, ceaseless transitions, are required. And many of them are by no means always smooth. Situations are never exactly alike and many of the situations we face have elements of novelty and diversity for which we sometimes find ourselves unprepared: situations therefore encountered with a particular sense of insecurity, doubt, or apprehension. The consequences of action are by no means always what we have predicted they would be: at times we are disappointed, shocked, frustrated, pleasantly surprised, embittered, or particularly relieved and comforted that our guess turns out to be right. Frequently the reality world brought to an occasion proves inadequate in accounting for the new situations that have been created as the world moves on in an irreversible direction.

The transition from what one is used to, to something new and different has, of course, been enormously accelerated by technological developments, with their unpredictable social and psychological consequences. Sometimes these changes restrict the choice possibilities a person is accustomed to, and, on the other hand, sometimes they open up new areas and opportunities for action. Technological advances bring about the need for more rapid transitions, some of them breathtaking in their social and political implications as they force men to converge more and more on each other.

As Lucian Pye has pointed out, there is great discontinuity, an erratic nature to the changes taking place today, so many of which often occur simultaneously in different areas of life without giving people the chance to accommodate themselves to these changes in any step-by-step fashion.[15] Economic and technological developments may very well stir up more discontent before they alleviate it since they so often require an adaptation or even the complete abandonment of traditional mechanisms of social or economic control.[16]

As the individual faces some of these new situations within which he either must participate or wants to participate, he has few assured guide lines. In some cases he may lack a sense of direction and not know just what value satisfactions he wants to strive for, what his behavior should be anyway, since he has not yet learned exactly what to want amidst the variety of potentialities to which he is being exposed. In other cases his sense of direction may be clear but he may not know how to move ahead. Perhaps more generally, as the research reported here shows, when a person encounters obstacles or difficulties as he meets new and emerging situations, his unsureness as to what he should do involves both a lack of clarity in his directional standards and a lack of confidence about the steps necessary to achieve whatever standards he may finally decide on. Sometimes he may feel completely lost. The reality world of an individual proves inadequate when it fails to provide an accurate interpretation on which purposeful action can be based.

An individual can run into difficulties in any of the areas of significance described above. For example, his assumptions about the nature and property of objects may turn out to be misleading; his experience may show him that people do not react in the way he had thought they would; he may discover that the events he thought would follow as sequences to other events do not proceed as he had expected; the action he takes to reach a particular goal so he can experience some kind of intended value satisfaction may turn out to be inadequate or inappropriate; or the goal he thought was going to bring satisfaction may, when achieved, turn out to be an empty one. Wherever this lack of correspondence occurs, the result is some hitch, some obstacle that frustrates him in the achievements of his purposes. Yet, if he does not despair, these occasions can also provide the opportunity for increasing both the scope and the adequacy of his assumptions through learning.

It is, incidentally, from this point of view that the phrase so often heard, "we must reduce tensions," should be examined. While one may know vaguely what the phrase points to and may applaud the idea, it would perhaps be more accurate psychologically and more effective practically if people could think in terms of directing and controlling tensions rather than reducing them. For tensions in and between social groups and political systems are probably as normal and as inevitable as tensions in and between individuals. Just as there can be no peace of mind for any person plugged into the flow of daily life, there can be no world without tension as long as men and women exhibit what seems to be an inborn characteristic and, as already pointed out, one of the most valuable characteristics human beings have, namely, never to be satisfied, always to be seeking ways and means to assure the repeatability of satisfactions already experienced *and* to extend the range and enrich the quality of new experiences. The achievement of maximum value satisfactions is a constant process of choosing between the alternatives perceived as available. Some tension is an invariable by-product of the process of enriching satisfaction through choices that lead to certain behavior. When man acts as a member of a group, he tries to control and direct his tensions by choices that will protect or enhance values he shares with others.

The process of learning to perceive the world around us, of orienting ourselves so that we can act effectively to carry out our purposes, is a never-ending process of prediction which we make on the basis of faith in the face of uncertainty. Hence we must constantly revise our reality worlds as we experience the inadequacies of the up-to-the-now assumptions we bring to the variety of new and different occasions of living. What we apparently do—sometimes knowingly and sometimes unknowingly—is to create for ourselves reality worlds which will more effectively further our basic purposes as human beings. We do this by using value satisfaction rather than consistency as our guiding standard for revision.

In emphasizing man's apparently ceaseless search for new value satisfactions, I do not by any means underemphasize man's concern to protect and conserve what he has. The bewildering variety of both informal and formal organizations and institutions man has created all appear to be more or less organized social devices to insure greater value satisfactions through their role as protectors of form and habit or as insurance for flow and development, or both. This would include many of the social devices studied by the modern cultural anthropologist which, somewhat like the unseen forces that hold the nucleus of the atom together, keep individuals from splitting off from each other, so that together each can play more of a role on his own: family systems; customs and mores; the use of language and the subtle communications devices provided by many manners and customs; commerce and industry; social, political, military and religious institutions, together with the ideologies behind them.

Like all the constructs of science, the term "reality world" I am using here is arbitrary and man made. But it has proved to be a useful term to describe the complicated and interdependent aspects of experience and behavior as they are found both in the psychological laboratory and in everyday social and political life. The reality world is the matrix within which man's aspirations are imbedded. This term will, however, become worthless if it is regarded as something fixed, static, or real outside the context of on-going situations. Like everything else in nature, it is an irreversible process, constantly changing its form as it operates in here-and-now situations which never exactly repeat themselves. As *process* it is in a continual state of transition focused now on one situation, now on another. It might be thought of as a motion-picture film which gives us a sense of flow and continuity even though it is based on a series of interdependent and discrete exposures. But it is a film taken with a strange camera, a camera that somehow seems self-directed, that maneuvers itself around to select from everything within its purview only those happenings which seem important to it, and focuses itself on those happenings which it regards as significant in terms of adjustments that have worked in the past in similar situations or that seem to be good bets for new situations.

Back in 1874 Paul Blood wrote in his *Anaesthetic Revelation:* "Certainty is the root of despair. The inevitable stales, while doubt and hope are sisters. Not unfortunately, the universe is wild—game-flavored as a hawk's wing."

THE SEARCH FOR SATISFACTIONS THROUGH SOCIAL DEVELOPMENT

In terms of understanding the genesis of aspirations, it can be misleading to think that people only learn or "acquire" the forms of behavior and standards of values of a culture. It is more accurate to say that human beings are so designed genetically that they *require* these cultural forms if they are to function as they are apparently meant to.[17] Not only do people inherit values, they also create them. These values can become instrumental as the individual experiences the consequences of a quality of behavior that makes the values become real through participation in social and political activity.

In the broad perspective of time, the social and political systems people have worked out for themselves can be regarded as experiments— experiments in the organization of social relationships, communications, provision for individual and public welfare, the training of the young, the exchange of goods and services, and the whole host of operations that contribute to social and political cohesion. There is, of course, wide variation in the extent to which these experiments of social and political systems are self-conscious attempts to learn the effects of variables deliberately manipulated. More often than not, people are unaware that the social organization they take for granted is an experiment when viewed in perspective. And the increasing complexity and interdependencies of modern life continually enlarge the demands imposed on these experiments to provide significances and satisfactions for the individual, who can so easily become bewildered and uncertain under all the new pressures and potentialities he confronts. Failure to control a variable or to introduce a new variable as the occasion requires can in turn cause the failure of the whole experimental endeavor of a people.

Experiments in self-government, especially, clearly require a self-conscious extension of the range of significances an individual must learn and act on in his own best interests. Among people who are underdeveloped with respect to any extended or continuous political participation, some order must be imposed before new phases of social and political development can be set in motion. It is for this reason that the political parties established by strong leaders in newly developing countries so often take on the form of social, political, religious, and ideological movements all wrapped into one.[18] In such situations the leader serves to focus a people's consciousness, suggest remedies for the frustrations they feel, and devise means of achieving the aspirations they are learning, thereby giving their strivings an operational setting.

CHAPTER III

Discovering People's Aspirations: The Method Used

The methodological problem faced in this study was essentially that of devising some means to get an overall picture of the reality worlds in which people lived, a picture expressed by individuals *in their own terms;* and to do this in such a way that without sacrificing authenticity or prescribing any boundaries or fixed categories it would still be possible to make meaningful comparisons between different individuals, groups of individuals, and societies. The aim was to uncover the limits and boundaries to aspirations set by internalized social norms, by all the group identifications that people learn in their particular social milieu and that serve as subjective standards for satisfaction or frustration.

The problem is a very basic one for the social scientist. For everyone—whether of high or low status, a Communist or a democrat, a sophisticated Westerner or a caveman—has subjective standards which guide behavior and define satisfactions. These standards can change radically within an individual's lifetime so that what was once regarded as a goal may disappear or be taken for granted as new sights come into play. Furthermore, the quality of any person's relationship to his group or his society is determined by the assumptions he has built up which define for him the degree and nature of his satisfactions or dissatisfactions with that group or society. The problem is to learn what these standards are in a person's own terms and not judge them by our own standards.

Thus, what is needed, of course, is a method that will not obscure the close interdependence between an individual's purposes and his perceptions and one that will differentiate frustrations due to an uncertainty of what goals to strive for from frustrations due to the means of achieving goals that were clearly in mind. Clearly, an accurate appraisal of an individual's reality world can never be obtained if he is forced to make choices or selections between categories, alternatives, symbols, or situations as these are posed in the usual type of question-

21

naire. Yet, without some such preconceived classifications, how can a final research instrument be obtained that allows for quantitative comparisons?

THE SELF-ANCHORING STRIVING SCALE

The solution was to invent what I call the Self-Anchoring Striving Scale, a direct outgrowth of the transactional point of view described in the last chapter.[1] This scale seems to provide a simple, widely applicable, and adaptable technique for tapping the unique reality world of an individual and learning what it has in common with that of others.

Figure III:1
LADDER DEVICE

| 10 |
| 9 |
| 8 |
| 7 |
| 6 |
| 5 |
| 4 |
| 3 |
| 2 |
| 1 |
| 0 |

A person is asked to define on the basis of *his own* assumptions, perceptions, goals, and values the two extremes or anchoring points of the spectrum on which some scale measurement is desired—for example, he may be asked to define the "top" and "bottom," the "good" and "bad," the "best" and the "worst." This self-defined continuum is then used as our measuring device.

While the Self-Anchoring Striving Scale technique can be used on a wide variety of problems, it was utilized in this study as a means of discovering the spectrum of values a person is preoccupied or concerned with and by means of which he evaluates his own life. He describes as the top anchoring point his wishes and hopes as he personally conceives them and the realization of which would constitute for him the best possible life. At the other extreme, he describes the worries and fears, the preoccupations and frustrations, embodied in his conception of the worst possible life he could imagine. Then, utilizing a nonverbal ladder device (see Figure III:1), symbolic of "the ladder of life," he is asked where he thinks he stands on the ladder today, with the top being the best life *as he has defined it,* the bottom the worst life *as he has defined it.* He is also asked where he thinks he stood in the past and where he thinks he will stand in the future. He is then asked similar questions about the best and worst possible situations he can imagine for his country so his aspirations and fears on the national level can be learned. Again, the ladder is used to find out where he thinks his country stands today, where it stood in the past, and where it will stand in the future.

The actual questions, together with the parenthetical instructions to interviewers, are given below:

1. (A) All of us want certain things out of life. When you think about what really matters in your own life, what are your wishes and hopes for the future? In other words, if you imagine your future in the *best* possible light, what would your life look like then, if you are to be happy? Take your time in answering; such things aren't easy to put into words.

   PERMISSIBLE PROBES: What are your hopes for the future? What would your life have to be like for you to be completely happy? What is missing for you to be happy? [Use also, if necessary, the words "dreams" and "desires."]

   OBLIGATORY PROBE: Anything else?

   (B) Now, taking the other side of the picture, what are your fears and worries about the future? In other words, if you imagine your future in the *worst* possible light, what would your life look like then? Again, take your time in answering.

   PERMISSIBLE PROBE: What would make you unhappy? [Stress the words "fears" and "worries."]

   OBLIGATORY PROBE: Anything else?

   Here is a picture of a ladder. Suppose we say that the top of the ladder (POINTING) represents the best possible life for you and the bottom (POINTING) represents the worst possible life for you.

   (C) Where on the ladder (MOVING FINGER RAPIDLY UP AND DOWN LADDER) do you feel you personally stand at the *present* time? Step number _____

   (D) Where on the ladder would you say you stood *five years ago?* Step number _____

   (E) And where do you think you will be on the ladder *five years from now?* Step number _____

2. (A) Now, what are your wishes and hopes for the future of our country? If you picture the future of (name of country) in the *best* possible light, how would things look, let us say, ten years from now?

   OBLIGATORY PROBE: Anything else?

   (B) And what about your fears and worries for the future of our country? If you picture the future of (name of country) in the *worst* possible light, how would things look about ten years from now?

   OBLIGATORY PROBE: Anything else?

    (C) Now, looking at the ladder again, suppose your greatest hopes for (name of country) are at the top (POINTING); your worst fears at the bottom (POINTING). Where would you put (name of country) on the ladder (MOVING FINGER RAPIDLY UP AND DOWN LADDER) *at the present time?* Step number _____

    (D) Where did (name of country) stand *five years ago?* Step number

_____

    (E) Just as your best guess, where do you think (name of country) will be on the ladder *five years from now?* Step number _____

_____

A number of questions were then asked to give details about the individual's background: age, occupation, religion, education, whether or not he owned his own land or was an agricultural worker, marital status, political preference, economic status, and the like. These items, of course, had to be varied in different cultures according to what was and was not relevant, what was and was not possible to obtain, such as political preference in certain countries.

It will be noticed that on the questions dealing with personal aspirations and fears, when a person was asked to imagine his future in the best and worst possible lights, the question was left open without any specification of what was meant by the future; whereas when asked about the future with respect to the nation, the question included the phrase "How would things look, let us say, ten years from now?" But in both the personal and national questions when the ladder ratings were obtained, people estimated where they felt they, or the nation, stood five years before or would stand five years from then. The reason for this was that in careful pretesting it was found unwise and artificial to structure the personal future, but if the future of the nation was left indeterminate, people were bewildered. People could imagine the future of their country as they might like to see it or as they might fear it a decade from the time they were questioned. But when it came to the actual task of making a rating on the ladder, the ten-year interval both for personal and national seemed too far away to be predictable, and so the five-year interval was used.

Interviewers were instructed to take verbatim reports as much as possible. All interviewers were, of course, natives of the country, or, where it was important, of the region of the country in which they interviewed.

In order to organize the study in each country, explain the rationale of the method, and do what training was necessary—in some instances, such as Yugoslavia, where no such survey work had been done before one had to start from scratch—either Lloyd Free or I visited the country, worked out arrangements with the best organization that could be found to do the work, and spent considerable time going over all the details with those who were to cooperate with us.

Some skeptics may continue to say that when people are asked the sort of questions used in this study, they cannot be expected to give honest answers: people will falsify, idealize to their own advantage and glorification, talk in terms of high-sounding abstractions or the like. All of the evidence belies this: the protocols obtained appeared throughout to be plausible, honest, and sincere. Others may say that the survey instrument itself is a crude or slipshod device which taps only superficialities and off-the-cuff reactions. But the instrument of the social survey, like a violin, can be used skillfully or clumsily.

It should be emphasized over and over again that the ratings people assign either themselves or the nation are entirely subjective: hence a rating of, say, 6 given by one person by no means indicates the same thing as a 6 given by another person. This obvious point is mentioned here because experience has shown that some people misunderstand the whole rationale of this technique by assuming that the scale is like an intelligence test where a given rating has a precise and presumably somewhat universal connotation. As will be seen later on in the text, an American who gives himself a rating of 6 for the present may be projecting a standard of living for himself that will include "enough money to own a boat and send my four children to private preparatory school"; the wife of a Havana worker who gives herself the same rating will say that her aspiration is "to have enough food and clothes so we don't have to beg for things"; an Indian sweeper who also rates his present standing on the ladder at 6 will say among other things that "the main thing I want is to have the government give me woolen clothes to wear in the wintertime." Similarly, of course, the shifts in the ladder ratings from past to present and present to future are equally subjective. All ratings are anchored within an individual's own reality world.

It should also be made clear that no claims are made that the Self-Anchoring Striving Scale gets at "everything" it is important to know about an individual. A person is not going to talk about his sexual frustrations, about some misdemeanor or petty theft that may preoccupy him, about many things that are highly personal or socially unacceptable. Furthermore, and most important as noted throughout the later discussion, individuals do not mention aspects of life they take for granted —thus, for example, American college students tend not to mention a high standard of living, which they assume they will have, but on the other hand will talk about the place in society they want to attain or how they measure up to their own standards. Despite such limitations —which would be severe if one were, say, a clinical psychologist—*for the level of accounting* that affords insight into the problems I have set for myself, the Self-Anchoring Striving Scale has proved an enormously rich and useful device. Furthermore, results obtained by this method will, I believe, be meaningful through a long span of time and thus have greater permanence than results based on questions more affected by circumstances and changes of the context within which they are asked.

One of the problems that had to be overcome was translating the original questions from English into the various languages used. In some cases this was by no means an easy task, and considerable time was spent with experts to be sure the translation contained the precise nuances wanted. One of the methods often utilized in this translation process was to have someone who knew the native language, as a native, for example, an Arab, and who also was completely fluent in English translate our questions into Arabic. Then someone whose native language was English but who had a perfect command of Arabic would translate the Arabic back into English so a comparison could be made with the original question and, through discussion and further comparisons, difficulties could be ironed out.

Translations from English had to be made into the following twenty-six other languages which we list here alphabetically: Arabic, Bengali, Cebuano, German, Gujarati, Hausa, Hebrew, Hindi, Ibo, Ilocano, Ilongo, Malayalam, Marathi, Oriya, Polish, Portuguese, Serbo-Croatian, Slovenian, Spanish, Tagalog, Tamil, Telugu, Urdu, Waray, Yiddish, and Yoruba.

THE CODING SCHEME

In order to obtain quantitative comparisons between different individuals, groups, peoples, and cultures, a coding scheme for a content analysis of all material was developed on an empirical basis. In order to get some preliminary feel of the wide variety of comments that I knew would have to be accommodated in such a study, I made a trip around the world, stopping in many countries, and having our questionnaire translated and administered to as many different kinds of people as could be conveniently found. In this way about 3,000 interviews were made entirely on a preliminary basis and without any special regard to careful sampling. These were all translated into English so that I could go over them and, with Lloyd Free, work out our coding scheme. The original code went through several revisions. The code used in classifying the material reported in this book contains 145 different items (34 concerning personal aspirations, 33 for personal fears, 42 for national aspirations, and 36 for national fears). We left in the code all items that received at least 5 percent mention in any country. While these 145 items cover the vast majority of subjects mentioned by people, special categories were added from time to time to take care of unusual preoccupations that loomed uniquely important in particular cultures—for example, the problem of reunification in West Germany, or the problem of the "cheapening of Israel culture" as a national fear in Israel. The complete code used is given in Appendix A.

In dealing with *personal* aspirations and fears, the code moves outward in terms of wider horizons of awareness and concern: from items having to do with self or family (for example, "emotional stability and maturity," "decent standard of living for self or family," "happy family life"); to items involving other people, the community, or the nation ("freedom," "economic stability in general," "equal opportunities irrespective of race or color"); to items dealing with international or world affairs ("peace," "better world").

In the case of *national* aspirations and fears, comments are coded under the following major headings: Political (for example, "honest government," "national unity"); Economic ("improved or decent standard of living in general, greater national prosperity," "employment, jobs for everyone"); Social ("social justice," "eliminate discrimination and prejudice based on race or color"); International Relations, Cold War, Peace ("disarmament, control or banning of nuclear weapons," "maintenance of neutrality"); and Independent Status, and Importance of the Nation ("maintain or attain the position of a world power," "national independence").

Since the coding was of the utmost importance for the validity of our research, either Mr. Free or I usually made a second trip to each country at the time coding was undertaken to explain the coding system and go over a sample of questionnaires that had been translated into English with the individuals who were to work on the coding scheme. It very quickly proved inadvisable, as well as a most expensive and almost insuperable job, to have all questionnaires translated into English for coding by us: it was much better to have the coding done locally or in a neighboring country by highly intelligent and highly trained people so that nuances of meaning in the native language would not be lost. After a week or two of intensive work with the coders, a reliability of around 95 percent between coders with each other or coders with us could be achieved.

In order to make the data more manageable for overall national and personal comparisons, a number of specific code items were later combined into "general categories," which give a broader overview and make it possible to have meaningful comparisons without being swamped with details. These general categories and their use are indicated in Chapter VIII, where the concerns of people in the different countries are compared.

SELECTION OF COUNTRIES, SAMPLES

The thirteen countries in which the Self-Anchoring Striving Scale was administered on sample populations were chosen for a variety of reasons. I wanted some countries that were highly advanced, some that were newly independent, some that were clearly undeveloped, some that appeared to be in a state of political and economic crisis, some that had just gone through major revolutions. Sometimes data were obtained in connection with studies Lloyd Free was making on the political dynamics of a country for other Institute purposes. In all cases, obviously, I had to choose countries where it was possible to work, either from a technical or a political point of view. I tried to get official government permission in certain countries that must be left unmentioned and which I wanted to include in the sample, but unfortunately certain cabinet ministers apparently felt that such inquiries might be a threat to them, even though, as already reported, I offered to transmit all tabulations at once to all people who had cooperated with me in the different countries. I included the Kibbutzim in Israel as a sample of a very special microcosm of highly idealistic people.

The technical details of all the surveys on which the studies are based are given in Appendix B, where the size and composition of the sample are indicated and any weighting procedures are described.

No one knows better than I do that some of the samples leave much to be desired. The Egyptian survey, for example, must clearly be regarded only as preliminary, since it was extremely difficult to get the proper number of rural interviews because of local suspicion of anyone except a government employee who went around asking questions. In the rural areas of the Dominican Republic the interviewers were at times threatened by natives wielding machetes who suspected the interviewers' activity was a subterfuge for locating conscripts for the armed forces, after the precedent set by census takers under the Trujillo dictatorship; in Brazil many of the interviewers had to ride horseback or paddle canoes in order to get to their respondents. In Panama and Nigeria some interviewers were arrested. Comparable difficulties were encountered in a number of other countries. I do feel, however, that in spite of the limitations of some of the samples, in spite of the fact that the quality of the research in the different countries was uneven, the studies were the best that could be done *at the time and under the circumstances,* and I hope academic purists will bear this in mind.[2] I have tried throughout the book to be cautious and conservative in interpretations.

Finally, I should like to emphasize, especially to my fellow social scientists, the very great importance I attach to knowing something about a country firsthand and sharing experiences with its people at all strata of society. Without such a background, one can never really be sure what cold figures refer to. One must immerse oneself in situations that are sometimes extremely unfamiliar and unpleasant: at times visiting Egyptian peasants in their huts with lice and fleas all over the floor; or participating at least symbolically in a meal with an Indian family in a village home which is walled off from other castes and where the faces of sleeping children are covered with flies, knowing full well that one is running a high chance of gastric disorders for the cause of social science.

It has been said that "the study of man is a process of self-education." I felt that I had to educate myself to the level of simplicity or complexity, the lower or higher purposes, the types of value judgments made—in short, the reality worlds—of the people I was studying. For this reason, I visited long enough in a country and traveled extensively enough in that country, meeting all types of people, until I thought I had a feel of the people and their problems. The participating process involves a sort of intuitive, poetic, compassionate attempt to get at the particulars so one can gain an insight into the generalities and universals: to study both persons and People, both men and Man.

Part Two

WHAT PEOPLE ARE CONCERNED ABOUT

CHAPTER IV

Four Westernized Nations

This and the following three chapters contain descriptive reports of the concerns people in each of the countries studied express for themselves and for their nation, together with their estimate of how they and the country stand on the ladder of life and an indication of some of the major variations discernible among different population groups both in the concerns people express and the ratings they give themselves and their countries.

As indicated in Chapter I, it is not the intention of this study to provide up-to-the-minute reports on the state of mind of large groups of people. I was interested, rather, in gathering material as and when I could of people in different countries and necessarily at different times to get a glimpse of the various factors operating on the minds and behavior of people in different social, political, and economic situations.

The order in which the different countries are considered is almost arbitrary. But I shall begin with two of the more advanced nations, the United States and West Germany, and then move on to two nations with quite different social and economic and political systems, Yugoslavia and Poland. This is followed by an addendum on data from Japan. Then, in later chapters, three large and important developing nations—Brazil, Nigeria, and India—are described. The description then moves to the Middle East with a glimpse of Israel, of the Kibbutzim, and of Egypt. The account ends with three small nations in the Caribbean—Cuba, the Dominican Republic, and Panama—and the Philippines.

The few statistics given at the beginning of the account of each country are meant to provide the reader with a reminder of the economic and social context of each country within which our studies occurred. For all countries except the United States, with which most readers will be fully acquainted, a very brief sketch of the country is given for the sole purpose of giving any reader not at all familiar with the country an idea of the economic, social, and political milieu within which our studies took place. Anyone who knows the countries will learn nothing from

33

these sketches, and I have not felt it necessary for my purposes to provide a lengthy discussion of each country since to be adequate any such treatment would have to be a book in itself; an excellent literature on any country can be found by those who are interested. All statistics presented are as close as possible *to the date of the study* in each particular country and are thus not the most recent data available.[1]

THE UNITED STATES

Population	177,800,000
Per capita income	ca. $2,160
Life expectancy	ca. 69
Literacy	98%
Population *outside* agriculture and services	64%
Automobiles per 1,000 persons	343
Religious composition:	
Protestant	36%
Roman Catholic	24%
Jewish	3%
Other	2%
None	35%
Racial background:	
White	88%
Non-white	12%

Not only do people in the United States already enjoy the highest standard of living in the world, but in view of the rapid growth of industrial and agricultural production and its expanding educational, health, and cultural facilities, the country can also be classified as one of the fastest developing nations in the world. The study of the United States was made in August of 1959. It was deliberately designed to include a number of questions that would help give some insight into the factors that lead to happiness and satisfaction in life, questions that were not included in the other countries.[2]

What Americans Were Concerned About

What are the concerns of the American people for themselves and for America?

When all the replies to the first question were coded, the personal hopes and aspirations of Americans fell into the following categories. Only those categories in which 5 percent or more replies were classified are included here.

The meaning of each of these code items with an indication of what they referred to is given in Appendix A. All persons in all countries who did the coding used the same basic lists. All tabulations in the text are based on the number of card units in the sample after any adjustments were made, as described in Appendix B.

Own health	40%
Decent standard of living	33
Children	29
Housing	24
Happy family	18
Family health	16
Leisure time	11
Keep status quo	11
Old age	10
Peace	9
Resolution of religious problems	8
Working conditions	7
Family responsibility	7
To be accepted	6
An improved standard of living	5
Employment	5
Attain emotional maturity	5
Modern conveniences	5

The next question, it will be recalled, asked what a person felt would be the worst possible life. Here is the way the results fall in the classification scheme, again including only those mentioned by 5 percent or more:

Own health	40%
Family health	25
War	21
Inadequate standard of living	18
Children	12
No fears	12
Unemployment	10
Dependency	9
Family responsibilities	5
Unhappy family	5
Loneliness	5
Deterioration in standard of living	5

While these results speak for themselves, a few observations should be noted in passing. In the United States, as in nearly all the countries studied, the major hopes and aspirations are those involved in maintaining and improving a decent, healthy family life. A considerable number of Americans seem to aspire to a resolution of psychological problems such as those concerned with religion, emotional stability, and group acceptance. Only about half as many people are worried about having an inadequate standard of living as aspire to a decent or better standard of living. On the other hand, the fear of war is mentioned twice as frequently as is the hope for peace. It is clear from these results that the two major threats to the aspirations of Americans are health for oneself or family and war.

It is interesting to peruse the list of code items answered by less than 5 percent: these include the desire for success, the desire for personal wealth, a sense of purpose, to do outstanding work, to be of aid to other people. As the analysis proceeds in a comparative fashion from one country to another, it will be seen more clearly which concerns are seldom mentioned because they are so taken for granted, and which are infrequently mentioned simply because they do not exist. In the United States, for example, personal freedom, freedom of speech, and similar categories were mentioned by 1 percent or less of the population, although such categories would obviously jump to very high proportions if Americans felt their freedoms were in jeopardy.

The general categories on the personal hopes of Americans are:

Economic	65%
Health	48
Family	47
Personal values	20
Status quo	11
Job or work situation	10
International situation, world	10
Social values	5
Political	2

On the side of personal fears the general categories are:

Health	56%
Economic	46
Family	25
International situation, world	24
No fears	12
Job or work situation	5
Political	5
Personal values and character	3
Social values	3

It will be noticed here that when the code items are combined in this way, concerns with one's personal economic situation top the list with respect to aspirations, while concern for health tops the list of what people are worried about. It is perhaps noteworthy that a sizable proportion of Americans—well over 10,000,000 adults—want to preserve the status quo or have no fears. The general categories also reflect the sense of threat international events might have to one's personal world, with nearly a quarter of the American people fearful of general world conditions.

The next questions asked about the concerns people had for their country.

Here are the hopes 5 percent or more Americans have for the United States:

Peace	48%
Improved standard of living	14
Employment	13
Economic stability	12
International cooperation	12
No discrimination	9
Improved labor conditions	8
Higher morality	7
Education	7
Maintain status quo	7
Technological advances	6
Medical care	6
Reduction of tensions	5
Good government	5
Tax reduction	5

And, here are the fears Americans have for the United States as given by 5 percent or more of the people:

War	51%
Economic instability	18
Devastation from war	13
Communism	12
Foreign aggression	8
Unemployment	7

It will be noted at once that peace is the overriding hope, and that war, with its devastation, is the overriding fear. It will also be seen that the range of hopes for the country has a much wider spectrum than the fears for the country—the only two basic and widespread fears being war, which implies war with some aggressive Communist power, and economic instability, with consequent unemployment. Again it is interesting to note some of the categories that were mentioned by fewer than 5 percent: social security, 3 percent; national unity, 1 percent; exert ideological or moral leadership, 1 percent; control population rate, less than 1 percent; disarmament, less than 1 percent; help other nations, less than 1 percent.

It will be noticed here at once that, as expected, there is a much wider range of hopes and worries on the personal than on the national side. For example, while only one major issue—war and peace—was mentioned by more than one out of every five Americans among national concerns, there were seven categories in the personal hopes and fears which preoccupied more than 20 percent of the people.

Our general categories with respect to national hopes are filled out as follows by Americans:

International, peace	59%
Economic	45
Social	33
Political	13
Status quo	7
Independent status	4

With respect to national fears:

International, war	57%
Economic	29
Political	23
Social	21
Independent status	11
No fears	4

How Americans Thought They Stood

The average ratings on the ladder could of course range between 0.0 and 10.0. The mean ratings of the American people are as follows:

PERSONAL RATINGS		NATIONAL RATINGS	
Five years ago	5.9	Five years ago	6.5
Present	6.6	Present	6.7
Five years ahead	7.8	Five years ahead	7.4

Clearly the trend for Americans is up, and the differences between the ladder ratings for the various time periods is significant. (The significances of differences between ladder ratings is given by the tables in Appendix C3. When dealing with most of the national samples here, a difference of 0.2 in ladder ratings is significant at the .05 level.) The differences between the past and present and the present and future are, as will be seen, modest in comparison to many other countries. Americans predict a steady, stable progressive development toward their ideals, both personal and national. The shift in personal ladder ratings—a total of 1.9 steps from past to future—is notably greater than the shift assigned the country— a total shift of less than 1 step for the same ten-year period.

The percentage of people who see themselves and the nation going up, down, or remaining stable on the ladder is also revealing:

PERSONAL RATINGS		NATIONAL RATINGS	
Past to present		Past to present	
Present higher	46%	Present higher	37%
No change	29	No change	30
Present lower	23	Present lower	27
No answer	2	No answer	6

PERSONAL RATINGS		NATIONAL RATINGS	
Present to future		Present to future	
Future higher	52%	Future higher	47%
No change	30	No change	28
Future lower	10	Future lower	14
No answer	8	No answer	11

Considerably fewer people predict both that they and the country will go down in the next five years as compared to the number who felt that both they and the nation had gone down in the past few years.

The distributions of the ladder ratings shown in Figures IV:1 and IV:2 indicate that while there are a number of optimists who rate themselves or the nation at the top of the ladder, most people tend to hover around the mean rating with comparatively little bunching of replies at the lower rungs. The actual distributions, rather than standard deviations, are given so interested readers, especially those unfamiliar with statistical notation, can see at a glance how ratings are bunched.

In order to get some idea of the relationship between the rating the same people give themselves and the nation, a correlation of the two ratings each person gave for the period five years ago, for the present, and for the future was made, with the following results for the United States:

Past	0.10
Present	0.08
Future	0.18

It appears that there is considerable psychological distance between the rating a person gives himself and the rating he gives the nation: a correlation between present ratings is almost completely nonexistent, for the past it is insignificant, and for the future it is only slightly higher and by no means implies that as the nation goes the individual will go, or vice versa.

Variations Within the Population

In this and the next three descriptive chapters I am mentioning only a few of the variations within the population that seem especially important. A recital of all the differences to be found would be tedious for the reader and would sidetrack us from our main story. Those interested in further details will find the variations of concerns and ladder ratings by demographic groups in Appendices D and E; the variations of concerns by ladder ratings are given in Appendix D3. I have deliberately not included secondary breakdowns of background data in order not to get bogged down in too much detail.

With respect to personal concerns, the data provide a wealth of information concerning the types and situations of people who express concerns listed under these various general categories. Here, only some of the

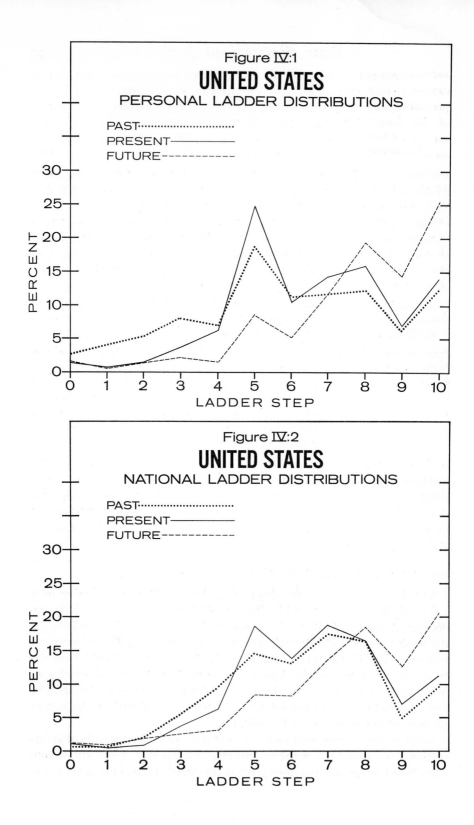

Figure IV:1

UNITED STATES

PERSONAL LADDER DISTRIBUTIONS

PAST⋯⋯⋯⋯⋯
PRESENT———
FUTURE----------

Figure IV:2

UNITED STATES

NATIONAL LADDER DISTRIBUTIONS

PAST⋯⋯⋯⋯⋯
PRESENT———
FUTURE----------

variations can be highlighted. With respect to the *personal economic* category as an aspiration, it is first of all significant that there is no appreciable variation here among people in different economic brackets of the population: 63 percent of those in the upper bracket express such concerns and 66 percent of those in the lower bracket do so. If anything, it is people in the middle class who are most concerned about personal economic matters—51 percent of them are worried or fearful about their economic situation, whereas this percentage drops to 44 percent and 43 percent respectively for the upper and lower economic groups.[6] The greatest single difference found is that between whites and Negroes, with percentage of Negroes concerned with economic matters rising to 76 percent. (The significance of differences between percents of various size samples either within the same sample or between different samples is indicated in Appendices C1 and C2.)

The concern for *children* mentioned by approximately one third of all Americans reveals two rather clear-cut and distinctive meanings found in different segments of the population. The concern for children as an aspiration is, on the one hand, for their personal development and for their education—education, not so much for itself, but because a better education provides a better chance for improving one's lot. The concern for children as a fear or worry, on the other hand, is that children may get into trouble and be a nuisance either to the family or to society. It is the unskilled workers, less educated and less well-off people, who tend to share these worries.

As far as the *job or work* situation is concerned, it is not people in the so-called inferior occupations who are most concerned here, but rather people with a college education, and especially young men. Less than 2 percent of all people in the lowest income bracket are apparently worried about improving their jobs, and, as might be expected, less than 1 percent of people over fifty have any such worries.

With respect to any concern about the *international situation* and the world in general—about which twice as many people are fearful as are hopeful—it is, of course, the more sophisticated who are most involved here: college graduates, better-informed members of the population, as well as Jews and people under thirty.

The thread running through all of the general categories for national concerns in differentiating people is that of political sophistication, as indicated by general education, general information, and awareness. In the United States study a series of "information" questions was included (see Appendix F1) which enabled us to separate respondents into three groups according to how well informed they were.

With respect to the category *international, war and peace,* unlike the inhabitants of other countries studied, the American people express their hopes for peace with about the same frequency as they do their fear of war. (In most of the other countries the fear of war is stronger.) People's replies show that this reflects the sense of responsibility Americans feel in keeping the peace, together with the fact that they have not experienced the ravages of war on their own soil and feel that another war would bring devastation beyond repair. Less concerned are those with grade school education or less, those in the lower income and information groups, and Negroes.

National economic concerns again reflect educational status and information. And American farmers can be added to the less-concerned people.

The concern for *political* matters is very definitely shown to be one where the college graduate, the better informed, the professional and business person, is most alert; the least educated, the lower income groups, and the least informed have relatively little regard for political affairs.

Variations in Ladder Ratings. The ladder ratings given by different groups of the population together with the shift in the ladder rating from past to present to future are reported in full in Appendix D1. Again, only some of the differences that seem significant and give us the feeling of the differential movement of various population groups can be highlighted.

In the United States survey, and in one other national study (Israel), people were asked to tell us what *social* class they felt they belonged in: lower, lower middle, working, middle, upper middle, or upper. Those who identified themselves with the upper class are significantly higher both in their ladder ratings for themselves and for the nation for the past, the present, and the future. A significantly higher shift in the upward direction from past to the future occurs among young people, college graduates, those who are best informed, and white collar workers.

Among those who feel themselves lower than average on the ladder of life are Negro Americans, who rate both their present and future significantly lower than do whites, and who saw little shift upward in August, 1959. Our survey included 160 Negro respondents, a small number in itself, but sufficient to give us reliable comparisons. Americans have now become quite familiar with the low status assigned the Negro American in the mid-twentieth century: more than half of them, for example, are classified in nonskilled service or household work as compared to less than 20 percent of white people, and less than 20 percent of Negroes are involved in business, professional, or white collar occupations, while nearly half of the white population is so involved. In this survey, only 6 percent of the Negro respondents fell into the highest economic level, whereas 33 percent of our white respondents were in this category. Classified in the lowest income group were 67 percent of the Negroes, but only 27 percent of the whites. The Negro's chief economic concern was for better housing—a desire expressed by 45 percent of all Negroes, over twice the percentage of whites concerned with better housing. Since the Negro is so weighed down with economic problems and the other problems he faces as an object of discrimination, it is no wonder he is less concerned than other Americans with the education of his children, the health of himself and his family, or such luxuries as "emotional maturity," let alone with such relatively remote topics as international tensions, cold war, or threat of a hot war.

It is significant, however, that when the ladder rating was repeated on another national sample in January, 1963, at the time racial demonstrations were being launched, the Negro *did* feel that he had made progress in the past five years. There was a considerable overall shift upward as Table IV:1 shows, in spite of a more tempered optimism about the personal future. It will also be noted that in 1963 when the Negro looked back on his situation in 1958 he rated himself lower than he did when he looked back in the year 1959.

TABLE IV:1

Comparison of Negro-White Ratings, 1959–1963

Ratings	Past		Present		Future		Overall shift	
	1959	1963	1959	1963	1959	1963	1959	1963
PERSONAL								
Total sample	5.9	5.6	6.6	6.2	7.8	7.4	1.9	1.8
Whites	6.0	5.7	6.7	6.3	7.9	7.5	1.9	1.8
Negroes	5.9	4.6	5.3	5.2	7.3	6.6	1.4	2.0
NATIONAL								
Total sample	6.5	6.1	6.7	6.6	7.4	7.4	1.0	1.3
Whites	6.4	6.3	6.7	6.7	7.6	7.3	1.2	1.0
Negroes	6.6	5.3	6.3	6.6	7.2	7.7	0.6	2.4

Percentage change (personal ratings)	Total sample		Whites		Negroes	
	1959	1963	1959	1963	1959	1963
Present higher than past	46	45	48	45	33	48
Present same as past	23	30	21	32	44	20
Present lower than past	29	18	30	17	23	23
No answer	2	6	1	6	0	9

Except for variations in the national ratings already mentioned, there were no significant differences among America's population groups, indicating a rather uniform optimism about the nation's development and reflecting the low correlations noted between personal and national ladder ratings.

Some insight into the reasons for the ladder ratings given is also shown when ladder ratings are tabulated by the concerns people express. On the personal side, for example, a significantly higher ladder rating is given by those concerned with maintaining the status quo, and significantly lower ratings are given by those who want an improved standard of living, want to own their own house, or want to have modern conveniences.

Relatively few differences in the concerns people express for the nation are related to the ladder ratings given the nation. Again, those who want to maintain the status quo assign the nation a higher ladder rating, while the concern of the Negroes also shows up again in the lower ladder rating given the nation at present by those who want an end to discrimination.

Summary

Although Americans enjoy the highest standard of living in the world, people in all socioeconomic groups still feel that both they and the country have considerable distance to go in reaching the top of the ladder of life, which is perceived in terms of a healthy, happy family life with increasing opportunities for their children. Among all the population groups, it is the Negroes who feel most frustrated, but there were clear indications that they sensed progress was being made toward their goal of equality.

Aside from the overriding hope that peace can be maintained and made secure, only a small minority of Americans are concerned about other national goals.

WEST GERMANY

Population	50,963,500
Per capita income	ca. $1,113
Life expectancy	ca. 68
Population *outside* agriculture and services	71%
Automobiles per 1,000 persons	40
Religious composition:	
Protestant	51%
Roman Catholic	45%
Other	4%

As everyone knows, World War II brought terrific devastation to Germany in terms of the lives and property destroyed and the millions of people uprooted from their homes. All of this, plus surrender, occupation, and the partition of the country, obviously had a variety of consequences on the thoughts and feelings of the people.

West Germany became a federal republic on May 23, 1949. A constitution was drawn up by the eleven states under French, British, and American administration. Soviet intransigence has prevented the free election agreed upon in Geneva to determine the future of German re-unification.

The West German economy has more than tripled itself since the serious devastation of World War II: the GNP has tripled since the republic was proclaimed and industrial production generally is about three times that of the prewar level. Oil and steel are advanced industries and a major part of the economy. As the few figures listed above show, the people in West Germany enjoy a relatively high standard of living and of health.

West Germany was the first country in which our Self-Anchoring Scale was used on a national sample. The study was made in September of 1957, as the country was well into its phenomenal postwar economic development, was finding its political orientation, and was searching for its proper role in international affairs.

What West Germans Were Concerned About

Here are the personal aspirations mentioned by at least 5 percent of the German people:

Health for self	38%
Have own house	33
Decent standard of living	31
Health of family	20
Peace	15
Recreation	14
Employment	12
Old age	12
Improved standard of living	11
Modern conveniences	11
Congenial family life	11
Social security	10
Children	10
Congenial work for self	8
Have own business	8
Preserve standard of living	5
Be normal, decent person	5
Congenial work for family	5

Among the items mentioned by less than 5 percent are: maintain status quo, 4 percent; higher standard of living, 1 percent; a sense of purpose, less than 1 percent; to be accepted by others, less than 1 percent; personal freedom, less than 1 percent.

The personal worries and fears of the German people are:

War	47%
Ill health for self	38
Ill health for family	22
Inadequate standard of living	18
Unemployment	15
Deterioration of present standard of living for nation	11
Deterioration of present standard of living for self	9
No social security	6
Unemployment (nationwide)	6
Not own a house	5

Among the items mentioned by less than 5 percent are: worries about children, 4 percent; totalitarian aggression, 4 percent; no personal freedom, 2 percent; bad government, 1 percent; no sense of personal worth, less than 1 percent.

It will be noticed in both of these listings that a concern for health of one's self and family comes very high both as an aspiration and a worry. The concern for children is extremely low in both columns, and except for the 5 percent who express a desire to be a normal, decent person there is little mention of other personal matters than those concerned with health, standard of living, peace, and more comforts. The fear of war expressed by half the population as a personal fear clearly reflects the precarious position the Germans feel themselves in, as well as the memories of recent devastation.

When the personal aspirations of the German people are grouped together into our general categories, the results are:

Economic	85%
Health	46
Family	27
International situation, world	15
Personal values and character	11
Job or work situation	10
Status quo	4
Social values	3
Political	1

The grouping of the separate categories of personal fears gives the following:

Economic	51%
Health	51
International situation, world	50
Family	14

Political	8
Personal values and character	3
Job or work situation	2
No fears	2
Social values	2

The hopes the German people have for their country are as follows:

Reunification	44%
Peace	37
Economic stability	24
Decent standard of living	15
Employment	13
Improved standard of living	13
Housing	11
Technological advances	6
National independence	6
Social security	5
A better world	5

Among those aspirations listed by less than 5 percent, it is particularly noteworthy that the aspiration to become a world power is only 3 percent; to be militarily strong, only 1 percent; to exert ideological and moral leadership, 1 percent; to assume regional leadership, less than 1 percent. While 5 percent of the people do mention the national hope that there will be "a better world," only 3 percent are concerned with more social justice, 3 percent with personal freedom, 2 percent with greater sense of social and political responsibility, only 1 percent with eliminating discrimination, and 1 percent with improved education.

What the German people at the time feared for their nation were:

War	66%
Devastation from war's consequences	33
Economic instability	18
Totalitarian aggression	15
Communism	11
Inadequate standard of living	8
Unemployment	8
Lack of personal freedom	6
Disunity among the people	5
No reunification	5

Less than 1 percent of the people expressed a fear that Germany would be militarily weak, would not become a world power, or would not exert ideological or moral leadership. Only 1 percent were concerned that there would be too little social or political responsibility or that Germany would not achieve real democracy.

It should be noted that while the reunification of Germany is at the top of the list of aspirations for the nation and mentioned by nearly half the people, only 5 percent of the population expressed lack of re-unification as a fear. Since there was no evidence that the German people were confident that reunification would occur, this wide discrepancy would seem to indicate that reunification—in spite of the fact that people want it—was *not* a central and highly important issue for most West Germans. It is also significant that European integration was mentioned as a hope by only 3 percent of the people and lack of European integra-tion was mentioned as a fear by less than 1 percent.

When the separate code items for national hopes are brought together under the general categories, the following percentages result:

Economic	69%
Political	49
International, peace	42
Social	16
Independent status	11
Status quo	2

And with respect to national fears:

International, war	70%
Economic	44
Political	27
Independent status	19
Social	15
No worries	1

Clearly the major overriding concerns of the German people are their personal economic situations and their health, along with fear of war and its devastation. Except for the rather modest references to family concerns, the other general categories are mentioned rather infrequently.

How West Germans Thought They Stood

The mean ladder ratings for self and nation follow. Unfortunately, due to a misunderstanding, the ladder rating on the nation five years hence was not obtained in the West German survey. Instead of the standard question, the following was asked: "Do you believe that in the next five years Germany will go forward, backward, or remain about the same?" Fortunately, this was the only slip made in all the surveys.

PERSONAL RATINGS		NATIONAL RATINGS	
Past	4.1	Past	4.1
Present	5.3	Present	6.2
Future	6.2	Future	—

Percentage of changes in ratings for different periods are:

PERSONAL RATINGS		NATIONAL RATINGS	
Past to present		Past to present	
Present higher	50%	Present higher	71%
No change	18	No change	14
Present lower	28	Present lower	4
No answer	4	No answer	11
Present to future		Present to future	
Future higher	42%	Future higher	50%
No change	31	No change	28
Future lower	7	Future lower	18
No answer	20	No answer	4

Figures IV:3 and IV:4 show that the distributions of the ladder ratings on both the personal and national side group around the mean with very little scatter in the bottom or top rungs.

Again a modest and steady rise reflects the confidence in the stability of the social structure in desired directions. It is noteworthy that the rating for the nation on the present was significantly higher than the rating for the self, indicating that people thought their country was making more progress toward the goals assigned it than they were toward the goals set out for themselves.

The correlations between the personal and national ratings were relatively high: for the past, 0.31, and for the present, 0.30. This would indicate that there is a considerable degree of interdependence seen by the people between their own progress and the progress of the nation, reflecting a sense of working together for the reconstruction of the country after the war and tooling up together for the general welfare.

Variations Within the Population

As can be seen from the detailed tables in Appendix E, variations in the population groups with respect to personal concerns are by and large not particularly marked. Without getting lost in details, some of these differences with respect to the general categories listed can be noted. *Personal economic* matters as aspirations are of more concern to men than to women and, as fears and worries, of more concern to people living in larger cities and to younger people. *Health,* as would be expected, is more of a concern for older people, for women, and for the better educated. The *international and world situation* is of much more concern to the better educated and the upper income brackets. With respect to general *political* interests, again the upper-income and better-educated people are more alert.

Variations in Ladder Ratings. On the *personal* ladder ratings, there is a definite shift in the upward direction among all demographic groups,

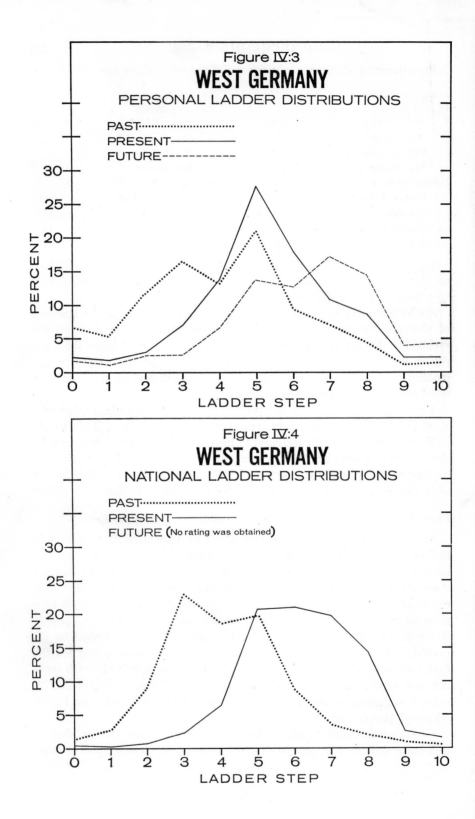

Figure IV:3
WEST GERMANY
PERSONAL LADDER DISTRIBUTIONS

PAST················
PRESENT————
FUTURE——————

Figure IV:4
WEST GERMANY
NATIONAL LADDER DISTRIBUTIONS

PAST················
PRESENT————
FUTURE (No rating was obtained)

with the shift being higher than average among young people and the better educated and lower than average among older people and those in the low income groups. On the *national* ladder ratings there is great uniformity among all groups, the only appreciable difference being that the upper income brackets feel the nation has made more progress in the past five years.

The ladder ratings for the nation are higher than average among those whose hopes for the nation include hope for a better world and for a better standard of living—both of which, presumably, these people feel stand a good chance of realization. The only people who reveal significantly less shift upward from the past to the present are those who mention national independence as an aspiration.

Summary

The West German people reveal rather self-centered aspirations, including concern about their own health, better housing, and a higher standard of living. Concerns for family life and greater opportunities for children are expressed by one out of ten, and only a small minority mention social values of any kind in defining what would be the best way of life either for themselves or for the nation. A fear of war and its devastation quite naturally pervaded their lives.

While the reunification of Germany was the most frequently expressed desideratum with respect to national goals, only a few people were worried that reunification would not be achieved and the indication is that this was not a goal about which most West Germans felt intensely or for which they would care to sacrifice. The nation's total defeat in World War II seemed in 1957 to have dispelled any notions that West Germany should try to achieve great power status or assume the responsibility of exerting any influence of an ideological sort. People thought that West Germany as a whole was doing somewhat better than they were personally.

YUGOSLAVIA

Population	18,538,000
Per capita income	ca. $305
Life expectancy	ca. 57
Literacy	73%
Population *outside* agriculture and services	18%
Automobiles per 1,000 persons	3
Religious composition:	
Orthodox	41%
Roman Catholic	32%
Moslem	12%
Other	15%

Yugoslavia is a federation of six republics—Serbia, Croatia, Slovenia, Montenegro, Bosnia-Herzegovina, and Macedonia. It is a generally mountainous country, heavily covered with forests. Over half of the land is used for agriculture. Industry is socially owned and controlled by Workers Councils and there is a good deal of independence in economic enterprises. Investment and the overall economic plan are centrally controlled. The country has successfully accomplished a massive reconstruction after the severe damages inflicted by the Germans during the war.

World War II left Yugoslavia in social and economic despair. Eleven percent of its total population had been killed, the majority of whom were the backbone of the productive labor force. Twenty-five percent of the total population was homeless and in Belgrade alone, 40 percent of the housing was destroyed. Industry was crippled to one half or one third of prewar capacity.

Yugoslavia proclaimed itself a republic in 1945 after Josip Broz (Tito) and his Partisans defeated invaders from outside and dissenters from within. A year later, Yugoslavia became a federated republic. Tito's independence of Stalin led to the famous 1948 Cominform resolution expelling Yugoslavia as "revisionist." Rapprochement was attempted by Bulganin in 1955 and by Khrushchev more recently. The Yugoslav brand of Communism, "Titoism," has been a major item of dispute between the Soviet Union and the Chinese People's Republic, the latter claiming that Yugoslavia has "lost revolutionary gains" and has sold out to capitalism and is now an "agent" of Western imperialism.

The government is run by the President, a Federal Executive Council, and a bicameral parliament. Each of the six republics is represented and is similarly organized. Political power rests with the League of Communists which dominates the Socialist Alliance, a more broadly based political organization and the only one of any significance in the country.

The study was done in the spring of 1962 before the new constitution was promulgated and before Tito was elected President for life. Three languages were used in the interviewing: Serbo-Croatian, Slovenian, and Macedonian.

What Yugoslavs Were Concerned About

Here are the personal aspirations mentioned by 5 percent or more of the Yugoslav people:

Children	40%
Own house	33
Own health	33
Happy family life	25
Modern conveniences	24

Improved or decent standard of living	21
Health of family	17
Employment	9
Recreation and leisure time	8
Have more money	8
Peace	7
Decrease taxes	7
Social security	7
Concern for studies	6
Concern for relatives	5
Move to town	5
Remain a farmer	5

Five of the items on this list, namely, those involving the desire to have more money, decrease taxes, pursue one's studies, move to town, and remaining a farmer, are new code items introduced in Yugoslavia since they were specifically mentioned by a sizable number of people.

On the side of worries and fears, the items mentioned by 5 percent or more are:

Ill health of self	43%
Ill health in family	31
War	27
Children	14
Unhappy family life	11
Unemployment	8
Deterioration of or inadequate standard of living	8
Poor crop	5
Failure to get an apartment	5

Two of these items were especially added to accommodate the Yugoslav replies—those concerning a poor crop and failure to get an apartment.

It will be noted at once that the list of hopes mentioned by at least 5 percent of the people is almost twice as long as the list of fears. The complex of hope involving children and the family, having one's own house with modern conveniences, together with good health, constitute the overwhelming aspirations of the Yugoslav people. It will be noticed that only about one fifth of the Yugoslavs mention anything concerned with an improved or decent standard of living as a personal goal, although a few more do express simply a desire to have more money. Less than 1 percent of the population mention more freedom as something they aspire to or lack. The mention of fear of war by over one quarter of the population as a personal fear clearly reflects the horrors of war and German atrocities remembered by so many Yugoslavs today.

When the separate code items are grouped together into general categories the results for personal aspirations are as follows. (In this and the following chapters, a blank in a percentage column means that less than 1 percent of the people fall into this category.)

Economic	83%
Family	60
Health	41
Job or work situation	20
Personal values and character	18
International situation, world	8
Social values	4
Status quo	2
Political	——

The general categories for personal worries and fears are:

Health	60%
Economic	33
International situation, world	27
Family	26
Personal values and character	5
No fears	3
Job or work situation	2
Social values	2
Political	——

The aspirations people have for their country are:

Improved or decent standard of living	40%
Maintenance of socialism	27
Peace	25
Reference to industry (more factories, greater industrial production)	24
Tito maintaining health and position	23
Development of agriculture	16
Concern for means of transportation	14
Housing	13
Economic stability	13
Technological advances	9
Employment	8
General development of the country	7
Electrification of villages	6
Decrease taxes for farmers	6
Equalize salaries	5
Education	5
Improved housing conditions	5
National unity	5
Public health	5

In this list the new items added for Yugoslavia are: maintenance of socialism, references to industry, Tito maintaining health and position, development of agriculture, concern for means of transportation, general development of the country, electrification of villages, decrease taxes for farmers, equalization of salaries, and improved housing conditions. It will be seen that many of these new categories deal with very specific improvements within the country about which a large number of people are very self-conscious and eager.

The fears people have for their country are:

War	76%
Natural disasters	19
Change of socialist system	7
Death of Marshal Tito	6
Disunity among the people of the nation	5
Occupation by another country	5
No fears expressed	6

Again, as with the personal concerns, less than 1 percent of the people mention freedom as an aspiration or lack of freedom as a fear.

National concerns for the Yugoslav people seem quite clear: because of their experience with war and their previous occupation by an enemy country, the fear of war—expressed by three quarters of the population—is the predominating national concern. Next to the desire for an improved standard of living in the nation as a whole comes the definite interest in maintaining their socialist system and within it making specific improvements throughout the nation which will help the individual. The Yugoslav people believe they have a good government now: there seems to be almost complete satisfaction with it; the only concern is how to improve the situation, not change it. Less than 1 percent of them express as an aspiration having a more honest government, a more efficient government, a more balanced government, a more representative government, or greater political stability. And it is noteworthy that there is apparently no concern among the Yugoslav people to spread their ideology—less than 1 percent mention as national aspirations ideological leadership, spreading of socialism in the world, or achieving better relations with the communist bloc. The Yugoslav people seem to know what they want and are confident in their country and its development.

With respect to aspirations people had for the nation, our general categories turn out to be:

Economic	81%
Political	47
Social	31

International, peace	31
Independent status	6
Status quo	—

The general categories of fears and worries held by Yugoslavs are:

International, war	79%
Political	19
Economic	12
No fears	6
Independent status	5
Social	2

How Yugoslavs Thought They Stood

The mean ladder ratings for Yugoslavia are:

PERSONAL RATINGS		NATIONAL RATINGS	
Past	4.3	Past	4.9
Present	5.0	Present	6.8
Future	6.7	Future	8.6

The percentage shifts on the three ratings are:

PERSONAL RATINGS		NATIONAL RATINGS	
Past to present		Past to present	
Present higher	57%	Present higher	77%
No change	18	No change	6
Present lower	24	Present lower	16
No answer	1	No answer	1
Present to future		Present to future	
Future higher	76%	Future higher	88%
No change	12	No change	8
Future lower	10	Future lower	2
No answer	2	No answer	2

Figures IV:5 and IV:6 show that distributions tend to cluster around the means with very few people using lower rungs of the ladder to indicate their position or that of the nation. People are clearly optimistic both about themselves and the nation: 43 percent put themselves at step 8 or above on the ladder and 79 percent believe the nation will be at step 8 or above in the next five years.

In addition to the optimism these figures reveal both for the individual and for the nation, it is especially significant to notice how much higher the present and future ratings are for the nation than for the individual. There is no doubt of the confidence people have in the development of their country even though they apparently do not feel that all of this national development will spill over to help them in the immediate future. The correlations between the personal and national ratings are: for the past, 0.26; for the present, 0.21; and for the future,

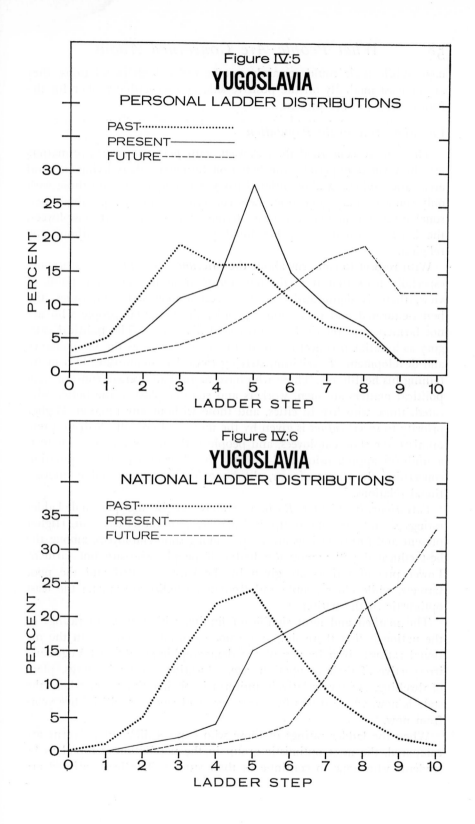

Figure Ⅳ:5
YUGOSLAVIA
PERSONAL LADDER DISTRIBUTIONS

PAST······················
PRESENT————
FUTURE————————

Figure Ⅳ:6
YUGOSLAVIA
NATIONAL LADDER DISTRIBUTIONS

PAST······················
PRESENT————
FUTURE————————

o.go. While these could certainly not be called high correlations, they are at least modestly on the positive side and somewhat higher for the future than for the present.

Variations Within the Population

Those more concerned than average with *personal economic* matters are the farmers (especially the better-off farmers), others living in rural areas, the workers as differentiated from state employees, and those with only some primary education. Less concerned than average about personal economic matters are those living in the cities, state employees, the better-educated and professional people, and those without any religion.

With respect to concerns about the *international and world situation,* especially fears that it might deteriorate from the Yugoslav point of view, there is significantly more interest among state employees, the better-educated and professional people, the better-off people who are not farmers, and relatively sophisticated Slovenians. The political category as a national concern here includes such items as the maintenance and development of socialism, striving toward Communism, Tito maintaining his health, etc. Those who have more than average concern with political matters are men, workers and state employees, the better educated, those who live in cities, and those without any religion. Higher priority to *social values* is given by the more zealous and idealistic Communists, the state employees, and people without any religion. There is a uniform apprehension and anxiety in all groups of the population concerning the threat of war, the hope for peace, and stable international relations.

Variations in Ladder Ratings. Differences in the personal ladder ratings given by various groups in Yugoslavia are rather clear-cut. Higher present and future ratings are found among state employees, among the best educated and among the better-off people who are not farmers. Lower present ratings are given by the least educated and the poor farmers, while older people and Roman Catholics are among the least optimistic in the nation.

The marked and most significant finding with respect to ratings of the nation is that there simply are no significant differences in the national ratings given by any of the demographic groups. All Yugoslavs, irrespective of their occupation, age, education, economic status, place of dwelling, etc., are relatively uniform in their estimates of where the state is now, where it was five years ago, and where it will be five years from now.

When the ladder ratings of those who express different concerns are compared, the most optimistic group in the population is found to be students who hope to continue in their studies. The least satisfied are people still concerned with economic problems such as those worried about social security, high taxes, or an improved standard of living. It is also significant that both the people who express peace as an aspiration and war as a fear give higher present ladder ratings for themselves than do those who express no such personal worries. Presumably those who are concerned about peace and war in their personal lives are not sufficiently apprehensive about the probability of war to allow it to lower their personal ladder ratings.

With respect to different ladder ratings according to different aspirations or fears expressed for the country, there is again almost complete uniformity throughout the population with a homogeneous optimism marred only by the somewhat lower ladder ratings given the nation by farmers who are worried about their taxes.

Summary

The picture in Yugoslavia is one of a confident people who have a wide range of aspirations and who have set specific economic and social goals for the nation to achieve. Yugoslavs feel that the nation has made somewhat more progress than they have personally and that it will continue to do so in the next five years. But since they are living in a socialist economy which, although centrally controlled, provides for the free working of economic incentives, an economy with which they are rather uniformly satisfied and to which they seem dedicated as a system, they are most optimistic about the position they, too, will achieve in life as individuals five years from now. The overwhelming majority, of course, are fearful of another war which would again bring devastation to their land.

In many ways, Tito is the George Washington of Yugoslavia: a leader who has demonstrated his independence of thought in international affairs, and who is respected on almost every side by almost all elements of the population as a person who has skillfully led the country he united through a massive reconstruction effort after the severe damages inflicted by the Germans during the war.

POLAND

Population	29,731,000
Per capita income	ca. $468
Life expectancy	ca. 65
Literacy	94%
Population *outside* agriculture and services	47%
Automobiles per 1,000 persons	4

Polish nationalism has deep roots in the past. In many ways, Poland is the oldest nation-state in our sample, tracing its national development back to the tenth century. For several centuries before the partitioning processes began under the hands of various conquerors, Poland was one of the great powers.

As everyone knows, World War II began with the Nazi invasion of Poland in September 1939, quickly followed by the invasion of Soviet troops. Polish suffering during the war was intense and prolonged. Her prewar population of thirty-five million was reduced by nearly 25 percent, with over three million Jews murdered by the Nazis and other millions of Poles deported to Germany or to the Soviet Union. After an abortive uprising led by the Polish underground in 1944, which had expected assistance that never came from Soviet troops that had reached the Vistula, the Germans intensified their systematic destruction of property, liquidated members of the underground, and left Poland a shambles. There is scarcely a family in Poland today that did not lose at least one member during World War II.

After the war, Communism was imposed on Poland by Soviet power. Landowners were dispossessed, farms collectivized, and the Church suppressed. The harsh conditions were protested by an uprising of workers in Poznan in 1956, after which the Soviets allowed Wladyslaw Gomulka to leave jail and assume leadership of the Communists (United Workers) Party. Gomulka dissolved most of the collective farms under which agricultural production had severely suffered, purged Stalinist extremists, intensified the rebuilding of the shattered country, and made a truce with the Church, which, among other things, allowed religious instruction in state schools. Church attendance in Poland is extremely high since religion is as much an expression of nationalism as of piety. Most industries remain nationalized, with the state the only major employer and workers councils under party control.

Just as Communism was imposed by Soviet power, it is still maintained by Soviet power. All Poles know that Soviet troops are never far away. With this shadow of the Soviet army everywhere, personal liberty and freedom are rationed according to what is currently politically acceptable, as illustrated by the opportunity to conduct this study utilizing the questions concerned with personal hopes and fears but *not* the questions dealing with aspirations and fears for the nation. The interviewing in Poland took place in the spring of 1962.

I visited Poland in the summer of 1962 to work on the coding, all interviewing having been completed by that time. Since it turned out to be impossible to have either the questionnaires or the punch cards sent out of the country, I later sent a list of the tabulations I wanted and had hoped these would be in my hands at least by January of 1963. But the tabulations did not arrive until the late spring of 1964 after the manuscript of the book had been completed. For these reasons I was unable to include the Polish data in most of the tabulations reported in this volume, although a few of the marginal totals and the mean ladder ratings are inserted from time to time for comparative purposes.

What Poles Were Concerned About

The personal aspirations expressed by at least 5 percent of the Polish population are:

To have one's own house or apartment; to have a better house or apartment	40%
Improved standard of living for self or family	39
Children's welfare	38
Happy family life	31
Modern conveniences	29
Good job, congenial work	22
Recreation and leisure time	21
Peace	20
Own health	19
Secure old age	16
Self-development or improvement	15
To have own land; expand farm	13
Health of family members	11
Concern for welfare of relatives	7
Be normal or decent person	6
Live in town; live in a larger town	5

The code item "to live in town or in a larger town" is a new one added for Poland. Another new category, expressed by 4 percent, is the wish that one's wife did not have to work outside the home.

The fears and worries expressed by at least 5 percent of the Poles are:

War	62%
Ill health of oneself	39
Ill health of family members	17
Unhappy family life	16
Inadequate standard of living for self or family	16
Children's welfare	13
Fear of collectivization of farms	6
Be dependent on others	6
Be alone	6

Here the concern that farms might be collectivized is a new category added especially for Poland.

Particularly outstanding in these lists is the high percentage of Poles who express a fear of war in the context of a *personal* fear, a higher figure than those found for any other people. Anyone who knows Poland or who has traveled about the country is aware of how the people are still recovering from the experiences suffered in the last war, how the ravages of that war remain highly visible, and how the destruction of so much property contributes to the aspirations so many Polish people have for improved living conditions which would replace the apartments and homes lost during the war, accommodate the increasing population, and provide the conveniences people have learned to expect from modern housing.

How Poles Thought They Stood

The mean personal ladder ratings for Poland are:

Past	4.0
Present	4.4
Future	5.5

The percentage shifts on the ratings are:

Past to present	
Present higher	54%
No change	18
Present lower	27
No answer	1
Present to future	
Future higher	66%
No change	19
Future lower	14
No answer	1

While distributions cluster around the mean on past and present ratings, there is considerable spread on the ratings regarding the future. Most Poles felt they were better off when the study was made than they were five years previously and even more felt the future would be brighter than the present.

Variations Within the Population

As already indicated, the IBM cards for Poland were not available, so I was unable to make my own tabulations on general categories. Hence, data on Poland are omitted in Appendix E but are included in Appendix D covering the ladder ratings by various demographic groups. Inspection of the separate code items tabulated by the various demographic groups reveals some significant tendencies: for example, younger people are more concerned than others with a happy family life, obtaining congenial work, and with self-development; the better educated also mention the importance of congenial work and self-development much more frequently than those with less than higher education. Collectivization of farms is a fear for 13 percent of farmers but only 1 percent of urban dwellers. The importance of having an apartment or house of one's own or better living accommodations in general is found rather uniformly in all groups, and the fear of war uniformly leads the list by far in all the subpopulations.

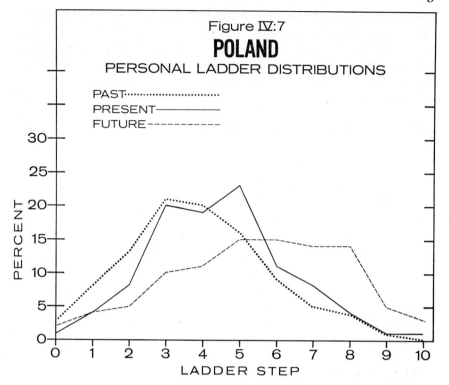

Figure IV:7
POLAND
PERSONAL LADDER DISTRIBUTIONS

PAST..........................
PRESENT————————
FUTURE—————————

Variations in Ladder Ratings. The most outstanding difference in ladder ratings appears among those with different degrees of education, the better-educated people giving significantly higher ratings for the past, the present, and the future. The highest mean ladder ratings of all for the future are given by students (6.6), by younger people (6.1), and by those in the upper income bracket (6.1).

Summary

The hopes of the Polish people center around their aspirations for better living accommodations along with a better standard of living and a good family life. Poles are still haunted by the memory of war and in their exposed position are fearful of another war. They feel they have made some progress in the past five years and will make even more in the five years ahead, but they realize they have a long way to go to achieve the kind of life they want.

AN ADDENDUM ON JAPAN

As previously indicated, the Central Research Agency of Japan used the Self-Anchoring Striving Scale in a survey made in the fall of 1962.

By the time I learned about it, the original material had been destroyed, and since those who conducted the study were unaware of our own coding scheme, I have no reliable comparisons about the concerns of the Japanese people. However, because the Central Research Agency kindly made a copy of their data available, at least a report on the ladder ratings can be made, thus adding a bit of information about this important country.

The mean ladder ratings for Japan are:

PERSONAL RATINGS		NATIONAL RATINGS	
Past	4.6	Past	4.2
Present	5.2	Present	5.3
Future	6.2	Future	6.4

The percentage changes in ratings are:

PERSONAL RATINGS		NATIONAL RATINGS	
Past to present		Past to present	
Present higher	42%	Present higher	48%
No change	30	No change	13
Present lower	13	Present lower	7
No answer	15	No answer	32
Present to future		Present to future	
Future higher	44%	Future higher	43%
No change	18	No change	9
Future lower	4	Future lower	4
No answer	34	No answer	44

The distribution curves in Figures IV:8 and IV:9 show a definite clustering around the mean with very few people rating themselves extremely high or low. An exceptionally high proportion of people were unable to give any ladder rating, especially with respect to the nation in all categories and to themselves for the future.

There is a clear and steady trend upward on all ladder ratings with a very small number of people indeed feeling either that they or the country will be worse in the future. Personal and national ratings parallel each other closely, although slightly more progress is seen for the nation than for the individual during the ten-year span covered from past to future ratings. Correlations between personal and national ratings are moderately high, indicating a sense of interdependence between individual and national progress. The correlation on ratings for five years ago was 0.23; for the present, 0.31; and for the future, 0.33.

Variations in ladder ratings by different demographic groups are few but clear: higher personal ratings for the present and future are given by the better educated and the better-off, lower ratings by the lower income group. The oldest members of the population, those over sixty-five, see least trend upward in their ratings. Insofar as national ratings

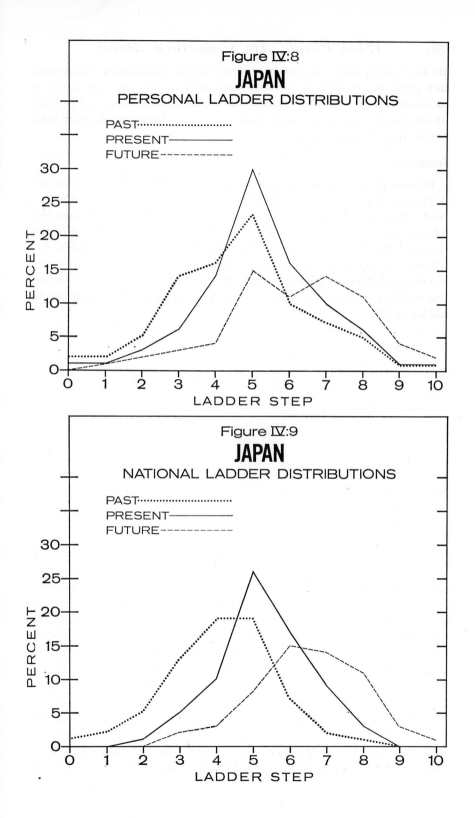

Figure Ⅳ:8
JAPAN
PERSONAL LADDER DISTRIBUTIONS

PAST············
PRESENT———
FUTURE----------

PERCENT

LADDER STEP

Figure Ⅳ:9
JAPAN
NATIONAL LADDER DISTRIBUTIONS

PAST············
PRESENT———
FUTURE----------

PERCENT

LADDER STEP

are concerned, there are simply no appreciable variations in the evaluation given the country by persons who differ in sex, age, education, or socioeconomic status. The "nation" for the Japanese is perceived in quite uniform fashion as far as its progress is concerned toward whatever goals people have in mind for it.

Summary

Because all interviewing schedules had been destroyed by the research organization in Japan that used the Self-Anchoring Striving Scale in a study of its own before I could code replies according to the standard scheme, no comparable data revealing the way in which the Japanese people define their own goals or those for the nation were available. But whatever these goals are, the Japanese people feel that both they and the nation have come about halfway in achieving them, and they are optimistic that the next five years will carry them up another rung on the ladder of life.

CHAPTER V

Three Underdeveloped Giants

This chapter reviews the findings in three large, important, and relatively underdeveloped countries in the world today: Brazil, Nigeria, and India.

BRAZIL

Population		70,799,350
Per capita income	ca.	$268
Life expectancy	ca.	42
Literacy		49%
Population *outside* agriculture and services		36%
Automobiles per 1,000 persons		8
Religious composition:		
Roman Catholic		94%
Protestant		3%
Other		3%

Brazil, the largest country in Latin America both in area and population, is a land of vast, undeveloped resources. Mineral wealth includes rich deposits of iron, thorium, and gold. Brazil is the world's greatest coffee exporter and, in addition, she exports large quantities of fruits, rice, and cocoa.

Three main racial strains are present in modern Brazil: Indian, African Negro, and Portuguese. When the Portuguese arrived on the shores of Brazil in the sixteenth century they brought with them diseases and a way of life that either killed or drove away most of the native Indians. In time, a labor shortage developed and the Europeans turned to Africa for labor. There was little race prejudice and the Portuguese mixed freely with the non-white population. This racial equality has become a major part of the Brazilian national heritage. The traditions brought by the Portuguese, especially Roman Catholicism, have blended with those of the African Negroes.

Regional differences within the country are created by the variety of environments varying from ranch country to farmland to semidesert to dense tropical forests of the Amazon valley. As the figures above indicate, most Brazilians are agricultural workers with a very low standard of living. Half of the total population remains illiterate.

The United States of Brazil was established in 1889. A military junta took over in 1930, and in 1933, under a new constitution, Vargas was elected President. His stormy career, being for a time out of office, re-elected in 1950, forced out by the military and committing suicide in 1954, reflects the state of Brazilian politics and a continuing unstable situation in which inflation and economic crises have characterized Brazilian affairs since 1930.

This study was done in late 1960 and early 1961 after Janio Quadros was elected President in 1960 and just prior to his dramatic resignation from office. His government was characterized by domestic stabilization and the attempt to check the raging insolvency of the previous Kubitschek regime. Quadros was expressly anti-Communist and a critic of pseudo-nationalism, leading Brazil on a neutral path which disrupted the previously solid inter-American front against the Soviet bloc.

As far as I am aware, this survey was the first one in Brazil to include a sample of the scattered, relatively inaccessible rural areas.[1]

What Brazilians Were Concerned About

Here are the personal aspirations of Brazilians as mentioned by at least 5 percent of the population:

Health for self	34%
Decent standard of living	28
Have own house	18
Children	17
Improved standard of living	15
Own land	12
Happy family life	10
Health of family	9
Employment	7
Own business	7
Wealth	6
Modern conveniences	6
Congenial work	5

Among the items listed by 2 percent or less of the population are such concerns as: self-development or improvement; achieving a sense of personal worth; being a normal, decent person; acceptance by others; useful to others; lead a disciplined life; freedom of religion or speech; equal opportunities irrespective of race or color; concern for future generations; social security.

The personal fears and worries of Brazilians are:

Ill health for self	30%
Ill health for family	20
Inadequate standard of living	15
Children	9
Inability to work; sickness or old age	7
Deterioration of present standard of living	5
Unhappy family life	5
Unemployment	5

Among the items mentioned by 2 percent or less of the people are: not being accepted by others; disintegration of social values; no self-development or improvement; becoming dependent on others; political instability; no social security; lack of freedom of speech and religion; no improvement in present government; inequality of opportunity by race or color; totalitarian aggression.

It will be seen that all personal concerns mentioned by at least 5 percent both as hopes and as fears deal with the complex of interests revolving around health, family, and standard of living.

When all code items are grouped into our general categories with respect to the personal aspirations of the Brazilian people, results are:

Economic	68%
Health	34
Family	28
Personal values and character	14
Job or work situation	8
Status quo	1
Social values	1
International situation, world	1
Political	——

The general categories regarding personal fears are:

Health	42%
Economic	30
Family	17
Personal values and character	7
No fears	4
International situation, world	3
Job or work situation	2
Social values	2
Political	1

It will be noticed immediately here that items concerned with the standard of living are expressed by two thirds of the people as a hope, while such items are mentioned as worries or fears by less than one third of the population. Health either for themselves or their families is the most frequently mentioned worry.

The concerns expressed for the nation in terms of the people's hopes for Brazil are:

Economic stability	28%
Decent standard of living	20
Technological advances	15
Efficient government	8
Education	6
Social justice	6
Public health	5
Honest government	5

It is noteworthy that the category of "political stability" was referred to by only 4 percent, as was the category of "peace." Concerns expressed by 2 percent or less of the population include: maintaining or attaining the situation of a world power; agrarian reform; social security; the social, political responsibility of the people; democratic representative government; national unity; elimination of discrimination; controlling the population; better relations with Communist bloc; friendly relations with all countries; maintaining neutrality; enhancing international status; exerting ideological or moral leadership.

The fears and worries expressed for the nation by 5 percent or more are:

Economic instability	19%
War	19
Political instability	14
Failure to preserve present standard of living	9
Communism	7
Inadequate standard of living	5

Only 3 percent express as a worry for the nation that there would be no improvement in the standard of living through technological advances and no higher productivity; only 3 percent mention inefficient government, social injustice. Two percent or less mention dishonest government, foreign aggression or threat of domination, national disunity, lack of freedom of speech or religion, inadequate educational facilities, the population problem, lack of sense of social and political responsibility, inability to maintain neutrality; failure to exert moral or ideological leadership, and not attaining the position of a world power.

As for national concerns, the most widely expressed interest is to achieve economic stability, and a sizable percentage of people believe this cannot be done in the present state of political instability. While war is mentioned as a fear by nearly one fifth of the population, peace is mentioned as a hope by only 4 percent. It is noteworthy that only 1 percent of all Brazilians are concerned about democracy, representative government, or national unity either as a hope or a fear, and only 7 percent are sensitive to the threat of Communism.

The general categories for national hopes are:

Economic	58%
Social	19
Political	16
International, peace	5
Independent status	4
Status quo	1

And the general categories for national fears are:

Economic	34%
Political	24
International, war	19
Social	8
Independent status	3
No fears	2

How Brazilians Thought They Stood

Mean ladder ratings given by the representative sample of Brazilians are:

PERSONAL RATINGS		NATIONAL RATINGS	
Past	4.1	Past	4.9
Present	4.6	Present	5.1
Future	7.3	Future	7.6

The percentage of people who shifted their positions on the various ratings are:

PERSONAL RATINGS		NATIONAL RATINGS	
Past to present		Past to present	
Present higher	41%	Present higher	32%
No change	15	No change	7
Present lower	23	Present lower	27
No answer	21	No answer	34
Present to future		Present to future	
Future higher	47%	Future higher	43%
No change	6	No change	4
Future lower	3	Future lower	6
No answer	44	No answer	47

Figures V:1 and V:2 show that the distributions of the ratings show a relatively wide spread with 17 percent of the people rating themselves at step 0 or step 1 for the past while 15 percent put themselves at the top of the ladder with respect to the future.

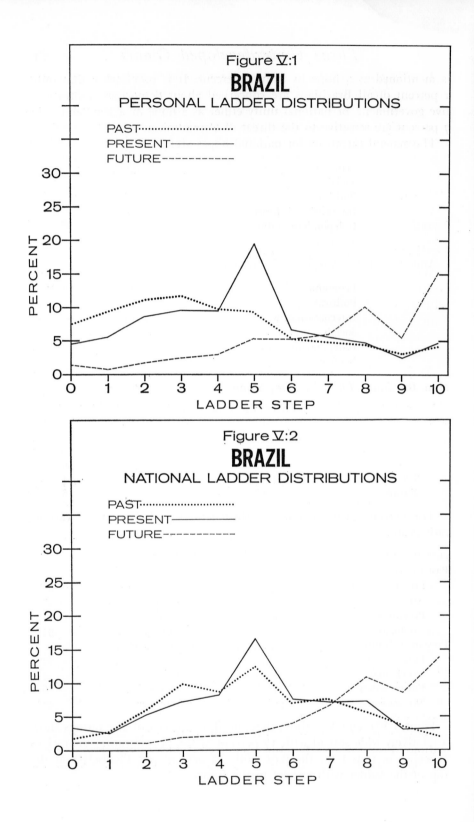

Figure V:1
BRAZIL
PERSONAL LADDER DISTRIBUTIONS

PAST··················
PRESENT————
FUTURE----------

Figure V:2
BRAZIL
NATIONAL LADDER DISTRIBUTIONS

PAST··················
PRESENT————
FUTURE----------

It will be noticed that a sizable proportion of Brazilians were unable to assign themselves positions on the ladder, especially with respect to the ratings for the country. But those who could rate themselves or the nation felt there was no appreciable improvement in the national situation during the past five years, although their ratings for their personal lives did go up by half a step. And while Brazilians felt that little progress toward the ideal had been made during the past five years, they were optimistic about the future both for themselves and the country. Correlations between the personal and national ratings, though positive, were low: for the past, 0.22; the present, 0.15; and the future, 0.26.

Variations Within the Population

With respect to variations among the population dealing with personal concerns, while over half of all demographic groups are concerned with *personal economic* problems, there is significantly less involvement with such matters as aspirations among those who are better-off. The illiterates and people who live in the northeast section of the country are also less worried about economic affairs.

As for the hopes and aspirations, the worries and fears, for the nation, the Brazilian population can be divided into two separate groups: the sophisticated elite represented by the better-educated, the better-off, and the nonrural members of the population, as distinguished from the poorly educated, the lower income groups, and the rural population. It is the elite who are more worried about the nation's *economic, social,* and *political* future and about its *independent status* as a nation. In general, the percentage difference between these two groups is large: for example, political matters are mentioned as aspirations by 53 percent of those with higher education and by only 10 percent of those who are illiterate; the economic future of the country is a concern to nearly three quarters of the top income group but to less than one half of the lowest income group.

Variations in Ladder Ratings. This differentiation between the elite and the depressed groups of the population also shows itself with respect to the personal ladder ratings on the past, present, and future and the shift in these ratings: by and large, the upper income groups, the better educated, and the nonrural give themselves higher ratings and are more optimistic about the future, while those who are illiterate, those in the lower income group, and those in rural areas and the northeast section of the country give either lower ladder ratings for themselves or reveal less of a shift upward.

While it is the elite who express most concern for various aspects of national life, it is also the elite who give the nation higher ratings and are most optimistic about its future. Their general concern for the nation is apparently tinged with confidence that national affairs will work out satisfactorily.

When the ladder ratings by the types of personal concerns expressed are examined, on the lower rungs of the ladder are found those who aspire to a decent standard of living or fear an inadequate standard of living, those who want wealth for its own sake, and, more than any other group, those who want to own their own land.

Summary

The political and economic instability of Brazil shows through in the concerns Brazilians have for their country and further reflects itself in the aspiration of many Brazilians for a decent standard of living including better health. Only a relatively small minority of Brazilians are worried about war and still fewer about Communism.

The fluid and relatively chaotic state of affairs is indicated by the fact that when Brazilians try to rate themselves on how far they have come in life in achieving the goals they have defined, a sizable minority are unable to place themselves as far as their personal lives are concerned, and nearly half are unable to rate the nation. Those who do rate themselves feel they have made little headway during the past five years and see Brazil as a nation about at a standstill compared to five years ago. However, people are optimistic about the future both for themselves and the nation, with optimism especially high among those more favored by higher incomes and better educational backgrounds. Apparently the elite groups, who are most aware of Brazil's problems, are also those who feel more than others that these problems will be resolved. But the picture is one of a people potentially ripe for political rebellion if they should lose confidence that existing governments will find remedies for their unstable and depressed conditions.

NIGERIA

Population	31,834,000
Per capita income	ca. $84
Life expectancy	not available
Literacy	11%
Population *outside* agriculture and services	8%
Automobiles per 1,000 persons	1

The Federation of Nigeria under British rule was proclaimed in 1954. It consisted of three regions: the North, East, and West. Regional autonomy, each state with its own administration, was preserved when independence for Nigeria within the British Commonwealth was achieved on October 1, 1960, establishing a constitutional, parliamentary political system with a bicameral legislature.

Tribal divisions with strong tribal loyalties are along regional lines and while there are over 250 tribal and linguistic groups in the country, the most important tribes are the Hausa and Fulani in the North, the Yoruba in the West, and the Ibo in the East. Differentiations between the Nigerian people are not so much by racial and cultural variation as by language ties.

Nigeria is the most populated country in Africa, predominately rural with land holdings of two or three acres. The largest employer is the civil service. Major industries are tin, lead, fishing, flour-milling, and sugar.

The research in Nigeria was done between September and November of 1962 and in the spring of 1963. The three main languages were used in interviewing: Yoruba, Ibo, and Hausa.[2]

What Nigerians Were Concerned About

The personal aspirations mentioned by at least 5 percent of the Nigerian people are:

Improved or decent standard of living	69%
Children	61
Health for self	44
Happy family	41
House	37
Own business	22
Self development	22
Resolution of religious problems	19
Happy old age	18
Congenial work	14
Be useful to others	14
Relatives	13
Modern conveniences	10
Agricultural bounty	7
Own land	6
Success	5
Wealth	5

Agricultural bounty was introduced as a new category in the Nigerian code and refers to a good harvest and good prices.

The personal fears and worries of the Nigerians are:

Inadequate standard of living	60%
Ill health for self	59
Children	17
Ill health in family	14
Failure to achieve religious goals	8
Unhappy family life	8
No fears or worries	8
Unemployment	7

No self-development or improvement	7
Separation from relatives	6
Fear of litigation	5
Insecurity of or threat to property	5
Agricultural dearth	5

Four of these categories were especially added to accommodate properly and without distortion the fears and worries expressed by Nigerians: failure to achieve one's own religious or spiritual satisfactions; agricultural dearth, meaning bad harvests, crop failures, or poor prices for agricultural products; insecurity of or threat to property, including an increase in petty crime and burglary; and fear of litigation, including false allegation by enemies or involvement in court cases.

It is apparent at first glance that a very large number of items indeed are mentioned as hopes and aspirations by at least 5 percent of Nigerians, and while the complex of categories involving a standard of living, children, health, family, etc., is very high, some of the other items mentioned by a sizable proportion of people fall in the general area of self-realization: for example, the desire for self-development, for resolution of religious problems, for being useful to others, for having congenial work. Some of these items also turn up as fears expressed by at least 5 percent. It is noteworthy that the code item of social injustice had to be used in classifying only 4 percent of the replies while the category of political instability as a fear was referred to by only 3 percent of the people.

When the separate code items are classified into general categories, the results on personal aspirations are:

Economic	90%
Family	76
Health	45
Personal values and character	42
Job or work situation	19
Social values	14
International situation, world	——
Status quo	——
Political	——

The general categories with respect to personal fears and worries are:

Economic	65%
Health	64
Family	27
Personal values and character	17
Social values	20
No fears	8
Political	5
Job or work situation	2
International situation, world	1

The aspirations the Nigerians have for their country are:

Technological advances	63%
Education	47
Public health	39
Agrarian reform	32
Employment	31
Modern amenities	31
Political stability	31
National unity	24
Improved or decent standard of living	18
Improved internal trade	11
Honest government and honest leaders	10
Obtain status of a republic	9
Moral, ethical, or religious standards	9
Agricultural bounty	7
Increase foreign trade	6
National independence and status	6
Law and order	5

Again several new categories had to be added to cover the expressed aspirations of Nigerians without distortion: the category of modern amenities refers to such things as better buildings, good roads, street lights, etc.; agricultural bounty and the improvement of internal trade are new items, as is the aspiration to achieve the status of a republic. In coding Nigerian replies the category of honest government or leaders was extended to mean fair and just; morality, honesty on part of government leaders or of leaders (whether strictly governmental or traditional); no bribery, corruption, or nepotism.

The fears and worries expressed by Nigerians for their nation are:

Political instability	51%
Failure to preserve the present standard of living	25
National disunity	23
Unemployment	19
Dishonest government	16
Lack law and order	16
Social injustice	14
Public health	13
War	10
Continued class discrimination	9
Higher taxes	9
Inadequate educational facilities	8
Lack of moral and ethical standards	7
No agrarian reform	6
Disunity among government and other leaders	6

| Crisis in western region | 6 |
| No improvement or inadequate standard of living | 6 |

Certain new categories also had to be added here for Nigeria: public health, which was on the regular code only as an aspiration, turned out to be something 13 percent of the Nigerians fear they will not achieve; no agrarian reform is another new item, as are the political items mentioning disunity among the government and other leaders and the crisis in the western region of the country. Again the category of dishonest government or leaders was extended to include dishonesty on the part of any leaders, whether strictly governmental or whether traditional leaders.

As was the case with personal aspirations in Nigeria, the people also have a large number and wide range of aspirations for their country, with education, technological advances, public health, and agrarian reform leading the list. The Nigerians seem highly conscious of the political and governmental troubles their country was going through at the time, with political instability the most frequently mentioned fear for the country and with the attainment of political stability through an honest government, the enforcement of law and order, and unity among leaders mentioned by a very sizable proportion of the population.

The general categories concerning national hopes are:

Economic	81%
Social	66
Political	50
Independent status	24
International, peace	12
Status quo	——

The general categories concerned with fears for the nation are:

Political	69%
Economic	43
Social	37
International, war	11
Independent status	7
No fears	4

How Nigerians Thought They Stood

The mean ladder ratings of Nigerians are:

PERSONAL RATINGS		NATIONAL RATINGS	
Past	2.8	Past	4.0
Present	4.8	Present	6.2
Future	7.4	Future	8.2

The percentage shifts on the three ratings are:

PERSONAL RATINGS		NATIONAL RATINGS	
Past to present		Past to present	
Present higher	83%	Present higher	76%
No change	6	No change	2
Present lower	5	Present lower	6
No answer	6	No answer	16
Present to future		Present to future	
Future higher	67%	Future higher	66%
No change	5	No change	3
Future lower	1	Future lower	2
No answer	27	No answer	29

Figures V:3 and V:4 show that, while distributions tend to cluster around the mean, there is a noticeable percentage of people who put both themselves and the nation on the top rung of the ladder as far as the future is concerned.

Several aspects concerning the Nigerian ratings will be noticed. In the first place, there is great movement and shift upwards from the low past through the present and on to a high future. This shift upwards occurs both in the personal ratings and the ratings for the nation. It will also be seen that the national ratings are considerably higher than those given by people for themselves. Even though the majority are very optimistic about the future, over a fourth of the Nigerian people were unable to estimate where either they or the country will be on the ladder in the next five years.

The correlations roughly indicating the degree of interdependence between personal and national ratings are quite high: for the past, 0.38; for the present, 0.40; and for the future, 0.44.

Variations Within the Population

Before discussing the variations within the population, a word should be said about two of the demographic background items used in the analysis. The socioeconomic class of Nigerians is differentiated into only two groups: those who are not poor and those who are poor, the latter category constituting 96 percent of the sample. The educational background includes the differentiation between those who are illiterate and those who have no education but still can read and write to some extent.

The category of *personal economic* concerns includes, as would be expected, fewer replies proportionately from the tiny percentage of people who were in the "nonpoor" group. Concern for the *job or work situation* is greater among those with some education and especially those who are the best educated, with nearly half of them expressing an aspiration

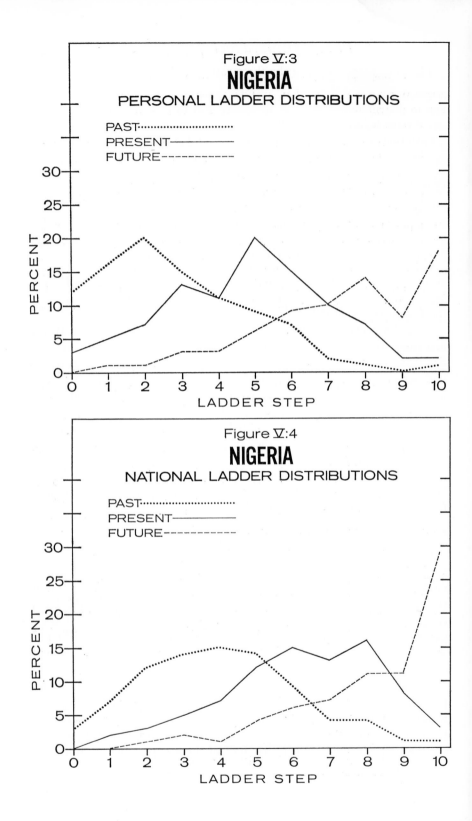

Figure Ⅴ:3
NIGERIA
PERSONAL LADDER DISTRIBUTIONS

PAST·············
PRESENT————
FUTURE— — — —

Figure Ⅴ:4
NIGERIA
NATIONAL LADDER DISTRIBUTIONS

PAST·············
PRESENT————
FUTURE— — — —

to get a congenial position for themselves. A higher concern for *social values* is expressed more than average again among those who are better educated and better-off, among Christians, and among those in large urban centers.

Variations in Ladder Ratings. As far as the personal ladder ratings are concerned, higher ratings are given throughout and a greater shift upward appears among the tiny minority who are not poor and among members of the Hausa and Fulani tribes. When the concerns expressed for the nation are compared to the ladder ratings given the nation, a lower present rating is assigned the nation among those who are worried about dishonest government and disunity in the nation's leadership. People more concerned about social injustices assign the nation a lower rating on both the past and the present. Lower present ratings are also given more than average, as might be expected, by people who fear that there will be no improvement in their standard of living and are worried about unemployment.

Summary

The study reveals the Nigerians as a people bubbling with aspirations both for themselves and for the country as a whole. In spite of the fact that "objective" indices reflect Nigeria as being at a low stage of development, the people are quite sophisticated with respect to their desire for cultural as well as economic development. They are self-consciously concerned with this development which they see possible if, above all else, they can attain greater unity among the regional and tribal factions now dividing the country and then raise their standard of living through technological development and provide themselves with better educational and health facilities. They feel that they would thus have more chance for self-development and more of the amenities of life which they know people in other countries enjoy.

Comparatively few Nigerians are burdened with a fear of war and most are buoyantly optimistic about the future. Nigerians feel that they as individuals and that Nigeria as a nation have made great progress in attaining their goals during the past five years, with the nation itself closer to achieving goals the people set for it than they are in realizing what they want for themselves.

INDIA

Population	440,316,000
Per capita income	ca. $70
Life expectancy	ca. 32
Literacy	17%
Population *outside* agriculture and services	17%
Automobiles per 1,000 persons	1

Religious composition:

Hindu   85%
Moslem   10%
Other   5%

Throughout its history India has been characterized by cultural diversity: various racial and ethnic stocks successively invaded or migrated to South Asia, the vast majority retaining their early traditions and identities. India was first unified by the British East India Company for its profit-seeking purposes. The protests against Western intrusion led to the Sepoy Mutiny of 1857, after which the British government directly took over Indian affairs and began to introduce sound administrative practices and Indian civil service. While colonial impacts continued during the nineteenth and early twentieth centuries, an administrative and legal system was established which provided certain civil liberties and a framework for economic and social development for the emerging Indian society as a whole.

The Indian National Congress was first organized as a nationalist movement in 1885. In 1919 Gandhi began his appeal for the economic and political independence of India, gaining mass support through his technique of nonviolent noncooperation for reforms, including the removal of untouchability.

India became a sovereign democratic republic on January 26, 1950, and immediately faced a number of major problems. Its independence had been won at the expense of partition and the creation of Pakistan, while a continuation of religious strife remained involving the loss of thousands of lives and no solution of the Kashmir problem. Over five hundred princely states had to be integrated into the body politic; linguistic cleavages permeated the new society with fourteen languages declared "official" by the Constitution, but these represented only a tiny fraction of the more than two hundred languages used in India today. Above all, India faced the problem of somehow managing its traditional communalism with the vast majority of its people illiterate and living in both geographical and psychological village isolation.

Politically, socially, and economically, India is heaving with change and contradictions: it is a federation, yet economic planning is centrally controlled; it is a parliamentary democracy which has so far held three elections, yet extraordinary powers are granted to the Prime Minister and the central government. The central government has instituted various economic and social reforms through its three Five-Year Plans. And though technical and economic advances have been made—for example, the first Five-Year Plan increased the national income by 18 percent— these gains have been largely absorbed by an increasing population due to improved sanitation and public health facilities. Migration to the cities by villagers seeking to improve their lot has created a population density which may reach 80,000 persons per square mile (as in Calcutta), without multistory buildings to alleviate crowding and without the facilities necessary to alter the traditional image of India as a land of poverty and people so clearly revealed by the few statistics cited above.

The data reported here were drawn from a survey completed in the late summer of 1962, a few months before the Sino-Indian Border skirmishes which began on October 22, 1962. A second and entirely comparable survey of India was conducted shortly after the border incident in order to study its effects. The results of this survey are reported at the end of this section. In both surveys twelve different languages were used. In addition to English the languages were Hindi, Urdu, Oriya, Tamil, Bengali, Kannada, Gujarati, Malayalam, Punjabi, Telugu, and Marathi.

What Indians Were Concerned About

The personal aspirations expressed by 5 percent or more of the Indian people are:

Improved or decent standard of living	40%
Concern for children	33
Own land or farm	25
Good job, congenial work	22
Own house	20
Own business	11
Being useful to others	7
Self-development or self-improvement	6

Among the categories used to bracket less than 5 percent of the comments made are: happy family life and lonesome for relatives, 4 percent; resolution of own religious, spiritual, or ethical problems, 2 percent; have modern conveniences, 3 percent; health for oneself, 2 percent; health of family, 2 percent; social justice, 1 percent; lead disciplined life, less than 1 percent.

The personal worries mentioned by more than 5 percent are:

Deterioration or inadequate standard of living	39%
Concern for children	14
Ill health of self	14
Ill health in family	10
No fears or worries	8
Not own land or farm	7
Poor job or uncongenial work	5

Among the items mentioned by less than 5 percent are: fear that person would not have sufficient dowry to marry off a daughter, 4 percent; unemployment, 4 percent; unhappy family life, 2 percent; being dependent on others, 2 percent; resigned to fate or to God's will, 1 percent.

Among the items mentioned by less than 1 percent of the population are: unable to care for expanding family; spiritual, ethical, moral or religious disintegration; threat of Communist aggression; war.

Again the complex of interests revolving around a decent standard of living, a decent job, a house or farm of one's own, and opportunities for children are the most widespread concerns of the Indian people. In spite of the "objective" conditions obtaining in India at the time of the survey, even the percentages of people concerned with these items seem low indeed: it is noteworthy that in view of the sickness, disease, and malnutrition in India only a tiny proportion of people mentioned better health for themselves or their families as an aspiration and only a relatively small minority mentioned ill health as a worry for themselves or their families. For the vast majority of Indians, health is accepted as it comes and few people seem to realize that one can have better health if certain preventive measures are taken. In spite of the characterization so often used both by Indians themselves and some observers of the Indian scene that the people are dedicated to "spiritual" rather than to "material" concerns, the data indicate that such a characterization, if true at all, obtains for only a very small minority.

When the personal aspirations of the Indian people are combined in the general categories, the results are as follows. It should be remembered that in India, as in Nigeria, "family" references have a much broader base than they do in the other countries studied because of the joint family system.

Economic	70%
Family	39
Job or work situation	22
Personal values and character	14
Social values	8
Health	4
Status quo	2
Political	——
International situation, world	——

General categories encompassing personal fears are:

Economic	51%
Health	23
Family	19
No fears	8
Job or work situation	6
Personal values and character	5
Social values	2
Political	——
International situation, world	——

The aspirations the Indian people express for their nation are:

Improved or decent standard of living	33%
Technological advances	22
Employment	12
Education	11
Agrarian reform	11
Prosperity through planning	6

The code item of prosperity through planning is a new one especially added for India, while within the regular code items used in classifying Indian responses the range of meaning was slightly extended to include certain replies that frequently occurred: under the code item improved standard of living the replies of those who simply wanted sufficient food to eat were classified; under agrarian reform those who mentioned cooperative farming and planned rural development were included; under enhancement of status and importance of the nation were included those who wanted India to be on a par with advanced and developed countries; and under national independence were included those who hoped India could become free from excessive foreign debt.

Among the items mentioned by less than 5 percent of the people are: enhanced status of nation, 4 percent; elimination of discrimination based on color or race, 1 percent; housing, 2 percent; public health, 2 percent; improved morality, ethical or religious standards, 1 percent; elimination of discrimination based on class or economic group, 1 percent; be militarily strong, 1 percent; have greater sense of social and political responsibility, 1 percent; have better relations with the Communist bloc, less than 1 percent; exert ideological or moral leadership, less than 1 percent; limit or control population growth, less than 1 percent; improved public health facilities, 2 percent; and peace, 1 percent.

The fears and worries the people have for India are:

Chinese aggression	22%
Pakistan-Kashmir problem	8
Disunity	7
No improvement or inadequate standard of living	7
Dishonest government	7
No fears or worries	7
Economic instability	6
Population growth	5
Lack of or loss of national independence	5

Under the code item dishonest government comments concerning selfish leadership mentioned by a number of people were included; the item disunity among people of the nation included rivalry among political leaders and what the Indians called "dissidentialism"; under the item inadequate standard of living was included the reference that India had insufficient food for its people. Mentioned by less than 5 percent of the people are: lack of morality and standards, 4 percent; unemployment, 4 percent; planning may fail, 3 percent; war, 3 percent; Communism, 2 percent; no technological advances, 2 percent; social injustice, 2 percent; inadequate educational facilities or schooling, 1 percent; no sense of social or political responsibility, 1 percent. National worries expressed by less than 1 percent of the people are: lack of or loss of freedom, poor or unfair working conditions, inability to maintain neutrality, and failure to exert ideological or moral leadership.

It can be noticed, especially from the list concerning the aspirations for the nation, that by and large the people of India are still both unaware of their problems and even to a greater extent unaware of or lacking confidence in the capacity of the government to assist them in resolving these problems. Aside from the fact that one quarter of the Indian people mention Chinese aggression as a fear for the nation, other concerns were shared by only a small minority of the Indian people. Thus we see that again in spite of the "objective" conditions obtaining in India, only 7 percent feel that a lack of improvement or inadequate standard of living is a national problem, and only 5 percent are concerned about India's population growth which has become a nightmare to well-informed people both in India and in the rest of the world. "Idealistic" concerns about the role India as a nation might play in the world are few and far between.

There appears to be a sort of fatalistic confidence that things will go on and that there will be slight improvement, and a reflection that the admonitions and exhortations of Nehru and the government were largely abstractions to most Indians.

The general categories with respect to the aspirations for the nation are:

Economic	70%
Social	19
Political	9
Independent status	9
International, peace	3
Status quo	——

In the general category of fears for the nation are:

International, war	25%
Economic	24
Political	20
Social	14
Independent status	8
No fears	7

How Indians Thought They Stood

The mean ladder ratings for Indians are:

PERSONAL RATINGS		NATIONAL RATINGS	
Past	3.4	Past	3.5
Present	3.7	Present	4.9
Future	5.1	Future	6.7

The percentage shifts in the three ratings are:

PERSONAL RATINGS		NATIONAL RATINGS	
Past to present		Past to present	
Present higher	43%	Present higher	63%
No change	21	No change	3
Present lower	16	Present lower	5
No answer	20	No answer	29
Present to future		Present to future	
Future higher	59%	Future higher	65%
No change	13	No change	4
Future lower	4	Future lower	2
No answer	24	No answer	29

The distributions of the ratings given by Indians both for themselves and for the nation very definitely tend to hover around the means (see Figures V:5 and V:6).

It will be noticed at once that the low mean ratings Indians assign themselves for the present are not appreciably higher than the ratings they give themselves for the past, although the present rating for the country is noticeably higher than for the past. The future, however, appears relatively bright to Indians both for themselves and for the nation—only 17 percent feel their own station in life will either not change or will decline, and only 6 percent feel this way about the country as a whole. While only 2 percent rated themselves at step 8 or above at the present time and only 4 percent rated the nation at present as being at step 8 or above, 9 percent saw themselves at such heights in the future and 24 percent foresaw the nation advancing to the top three rungs in the next five years.

The correlations between the personal and national ratings are moderately significant: past, 0.30; present, 0.30; and future 0.29, indicating some sense of personal involvement with the fate of the country as a whole.

Variations Within the Population

The differences in the frequency with which *personal economic* references occur in the general personal category is clear cut: it is the illiter-

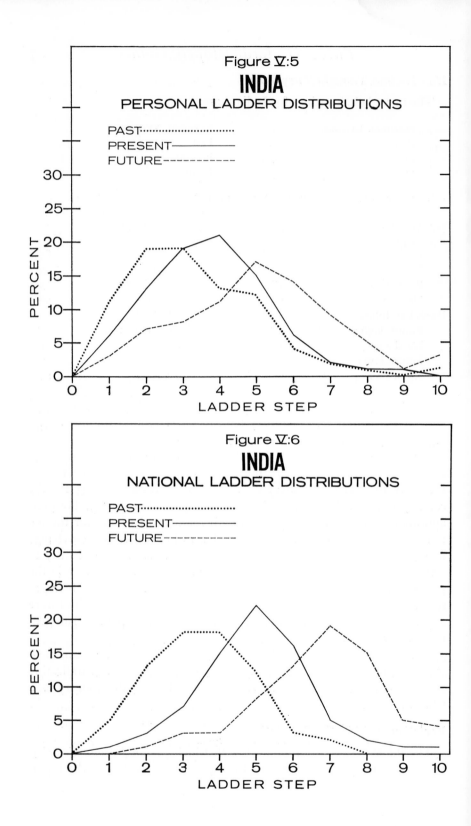

Figure Ⅴ:5
INDIA
PERSONAL LADDER DISTRIBUTIONS

PAST············
PRESENT———
FUTURE-------

Figure Ⅴ:6
INDIA
NATIONAL LADDER DISTRIBUTIONS

PAST············
PRESENT———
FUTURE-------

ates, the unskilled workers, those earning less than 75 rupees ($15) per mensem (approximately one month), agricultural owners and workers who are more concerned than average about economic matters both as aspirations and as worries. Sixty percent of the Harijans (the untouchables) express economic worries.

The *job or work situation* is referred to more frequently by the better educated and professional people, white collar or skilled workers, and younger people, the group apparently with greatest aspirations for a more congenial and worthwhile work situation; while the illiterates, agricultural owners and workers, and persons over forty years of age express less than normal aspirations about their work. *Personal values and character* as well as *social values* were more frequently referred to again by the elite of the population. While *health* as something aspired to is mentioned by only 4 percent of all the people in India, one out of every five persons makes some mention of health as something to worry about. This lack of of awareness that health is something that can be improved by taking certain precautions is almost uniform throughout all population groups.

Within the general categories grouping the concerns for the nation, it is the better educated, the professional and white collar groups, those above average in income, who express both greater hopes and greater fears for the nation almost all along the line. On the other hand, the illiterates, agricultural workers, the untouchables, the unskilled workers, and those in the lowest income group are appreciably less involved with national problems.

Variations in Ladder Ratings. As would be expected, significantly lower ladder ratings for the present, the past, and the future are given by the untouchables, the illiterates, those earning less than 75 rupees per mensem, and unskilled and agricultural workers. As far as the ratings given the nation are concerned, no significant differences or shifts appear among any of the demographic groups studied. There is apparently a rather uniform evaluation and an optimism among all groups of the population.

When the personal ladder ratings are related to the personal concerns people express, greatest pessimism is found among those who want to own their own land or farm and those who want to own their own house. Lower present and future ratings are also given by those who are worried about the deterioration of or an inadequate standard of living.

When the ratings given the country are compared to the concerns for the country, no significant differences show up anywhere with respect to the aspirations people have for India—apparently no matter what their hopes may be for the country, they rate it quite uniformly with respect to the past, present, and future. But as far as fears for the country are concerned, a somewhat lower rating is given India by those who are worried about the lack of moral and ethical standards in the nation and about the divisive forces making for internal disunity.

The Impact of the Chinese Border Skirmish in 1962

In order to study the impact of a major event on the cohesion of the people in a nation and their perception of the event itself, I launched another survey in India after the Chinese border fighting broke out on October 22, 1962.[3] When the personal hopes and fears expressed by the Indian people in the two surveys are compared, it appears that the whole Sino-Indian conflict was indeed rather remote to the vast majority of the people.

Comparisons between the two studies are:

	India I	*India II*	*Difference*
PERSONAL HOPES			
Improved standard of living	40%	34%	−6
Opportunities for children	33	36	+3
Own land or farm	25	28	+3
Good job; congenial work	22	19	−3
Own house	20	18	−2
Own business	11	13	+2
Be useful to others	7	8	+1
Self-development and improvement	6	4	−2
PERSONAL FEARS			
Deterioration in standard of living	39%	36%	−3
Lack of opportunities for children	14	20	+6
Ill health for self	14	7	−7
Ill health for family	10	5	−5
No fears or worries	8	14	+6
Not own land or farm	7	9	+2
Poor job; uncongenial work	5	6	+1
Not own business	3	5	+2

It was, of course, unlikely that the border conflict would have as much effect on personal concerns as on concerns for the nation. However, the absence of any noticeable changes throughout the list is still somewhat surprising, reflecting the apparent fact that for most Indians a personal involvement in the government's problems and the confidence in the help government can provide them in their personal lives is quite remote in spite of the glowing abstractions they have become used to from government leadership.

The effect of the border conflict on the aspirations for the country is shown in the following comparison:

	India I	India II	Difference
NATIONAL HOPES			
Improved standard of living	33%	29%	−4
Technological advances	22	31	+9
Full employment	12	17	+5
Educational facilities and opportunities	11	17	+6
Agrarian reform	11	13	+2
Prosperity through planning	6	6	0
To enhance status as a nation	4	2	−2
To preserve national independence	3	7	+4
To be militarily strong	1	8	+7

It will be noticed that while there is a slightly greater mention of technical advances, military strength, and the preservation of national independence, even these changes are scarcely of statistical significance. (A difference of 4 percent between percentages is required for significance at the .05 level.) Even after the excitement of the Chinese advance into India, still less than 10 percent of the people expressed a desire that India be militarily strong or a self-conscious concern that independence was something to be cherished.

The impact on national fears is shown by the following figures:

	India I	India II	Difference
NATIONAL FEARS			
Chinese aggression	22%	45%	+23
Pakistan/Kashmir	8	5	−3
National disunity	7	4	−3
Deterioration of standard of living	7	8	+1
Dishonest government	7	9	+2
No fears or worries	7	10	+3
Economic instability	6	5	−1
Lack or loss of national independence	5	2	−3
Population growth	5	4	−1
Lack of moral, ethical, or religious standards	4	2	−2
Unemployment	4	4	0
Planning	3	4	+1

While the fear of Chinese aggression was the most wide-spread fear in both studies and doubled in the second study, still less than half of the Indian population mentioned this as a national concern even after the outbreak of fighting. And code categories one would tend to associate with a threat of an aggression which was rapid and successful seemed little affected: national disunity, economic instability, and loss of national independence. It is also noteworthy that 10 percent of the people expressed no fears for their country or were unwilling to face up to any national worries, and that this percentage is higher in frequency than comments dealing with the lack of independence, national disunity, or economic instability.

On both the studies in India a number of additions were designed by Lloyd Free to help him get further information on the dynamics of Indian political behavior.[4] One of these questions was "Which of the problems facing India at the present time are you personally most concerned about?" The replies to this question which have some bearing on the impact of the border incident are:

	India I	*India II*	*Difference*
Chinese aggression	24%	41%	+17
Economic instability	20	14	−6
Defense of the country	3	5	+2
Loss of national independence	3	——	−3
Communism is a danger	1	——	−1
Nuclear war	——	——	0
Maintaining neutrality	——	——	0
Loss of democracy	——	——	0

Again, less than half the population mention Chinese aggression as a problem they are concerned about for India, and the Chinese advance is not seen as a threat to the economy, to national independence, to neutrality, to democracy, or apparently to the individual personally. Furthermore, the threat seems to be China and not Communism. The border incident was apparently perceived only as an "incident" and after the initial excitement any wider repercussions on the nation evaporated if they ever existed.

Comparisons of the ladder ratings from the two studies are:

	India I	*India II*	*Difference*
PERSONAL			
Past	3.4	2.8	−0.6
Present	3.7	3.4	−0.3
Future	5.1	4.6	−0.5
NATIONAL			
Past	3.5	3.1	−0.4
Present	4.9	4.6	−0.3
Future	6.7	6.5	−0.2

It will be noticed that all the ladder ratings given in the second study are lower than those in the first (a difference of 0.2 in ladder ratings between the two studies is significant up to the .05 level). The slight drop throughout all ratings would seem to indicate, as comments revealed, that most people felt things were not as good with India as they thought they were, a feeling that their national pride had been hurt and that the government's preparation and handling of the border situation left much to be desired.

A further set of questions helps us understand what is often referred to as India's "pro-Western neutralism" or, more accurately expressed, her pro-Western nonalignment. One question asked was, "In your opinion, with which country should India cooperate very closely under present conditions?" The results were:

	India I		India II		Difference
United States	49%		58%		
United Kingdom	26	}75	36	}94	+19
U.S.S.R.	43		16		
China	3	}46	——	}16	−30
Other	43		19		
Don't know	38	}81	32	}51	−30

Compared to the small changes we noticed in both personal and national concerns, these shifts of opinion are somewhat dramatic. It will be seen that more people express opinions after the border conflict than before; that considerably fewer people mentioned countries other than the United States, United Kingdom, U.S.S.R., or China and that there was a shift in the direction of favoring cooperation with the United States and United Kingdom and away from cooperation with the Soviet Union and, of course, China.

Another question asked was, "In the present world situation, do you personally think that, on the whole India should _____?"

	India II
Side with the United States, United Kingdom, and their allies	36%
Side with the U.S.S.R.	1
Side with neither	30
Don't know	33

The traditional Indian nonalignment again shows up here with two thirds of the people saying that India should side with neither of the power blocs or giving no answer at all. For the rest, nonalignment appears useless, and nearly all prefer to side with the countries they know best and that have done most for them.

The final question which gives us some insight into Indian nonalignment was: "Now, I'd like you to show me on the ladder whether you have a good or bad opinion of several countries. This time the top of the ladder means the very best opinion you could possibly have; the bottom means the very worst opinion you could possibly have. Please show me on the ladder your opinion of (country)."

	India I	*India II*	*Difference*
United States			
Mean ladder rating	7.5	8.4	0.9
No opinion	40%	27%	−13%
United Kingdom			
Mean ladder rating	5.9	7.3	1.4
No opinion	42%	29%	−13%
U.S.S.R			
Mean ladder rating	6.9	5.9	−1.0
No opinion	40%	31%	−9%
China			
Mean ladder rating	2.6	0.9	−1.7
No opinion	45%	28%	−17%

It will be seen that there is a clear-cut shift here in favor of the United States and the United Kingdom, a decrease in the mean ladder rating given both the Soviet Union and China, but that the rating given the Soviet Union is relatively high and, on the first survey, was higher than the mean rating given the United Kingdom. Throughout, there is a decrease in the size of the "no opinion," uncommitted replies.

Indian nonalignment seems to be an aspect of the transitional phase the country is going through from its status as a subject to a participant nation. After talking with dozens of Indians of all social classes, including many government officials, I tried one time to project myself into Indian "mentality" to see what this nonalignment meant. When an Indian says "I favor non-alignment" I think he means approximately: "Some people think that because we call ourselves neutral and profess a foreign policy of nonalignment that we have no clear-cut policy; others say our policy is one of 'positive neutrality,' that while we remain neutral we favor one side over another. What do *we* mean in our own terms? We do *not* mean that we don't care whether A or B wins the power struggle; we do *not* mean there is no priority in our minds concerning the values represented in democracy vis-à-vis totalitarianism. We do not like totalitarianism of the Soviet or Chinese brand. Nor do we like or want Communism as practiced in those countries. We believe in individual rights and in providing as fast as possible the standards of living and the freedoms of action that are requirements for greater dignity and well-being of the individual. For us, a socialist system can be the only answer. We have no source of private capital to develop our country or ourselves.

"We depend on others to help us develop. We look for this aid from any likely source. We believe we deserve this aid from the more advanced countries, especially from the United States. Obviously, the good things of life are now unjustly distributed among nations as they are within

nations in many lands. The more advanced nations can well afford
to give us aid. We deserve medical, educational, scientific, and economic
aid to help us develop; we deserve military aid to protect us from any
nation or neighbor that would try to take advantage of our present
weakness for its own expansion. Such aid is among our rights as a new
and retarded nation, just as provision for a better life is the right of any
individual whose development is thwarted because of the circumstances
of his birth. We take this aid for granted. We are annoyed if it is too
little or too late. Why should we be grateful for receiving only what we
deserve anyway? And why should we publicly pledge loyalty and alle-
giance to any nation or any ideology which does for us only what it
should?

"We'll put our own house in order and work out our own political
system and our own philosophy. That is what the more advanced nations have done and what we intend to do. We resent any nation or
group of nations thinking they can buy us. We are not for sale. We are
proud. To those who say we lack courage or gratitude, we say, 'Put
yourselves in our position for ten years and see how courageous or grateful *you* are.' "

On the second survey we also asked a question that attempted to ascertain the degree of identification with various groups: "How important
to you personally is your _____?" People were again asked to rate
importance on the ten-step ladder. The results were:

	Mean ladder ratings	Don't know
India	9.2	14%
Family	7.9	15
State	7.8	19
Language group	6.9	22
United Nations	6.4	61
Commonwealth	5.2	66
Caste	4.2	19

It is clear that "India" was a meaningful concept with which people
strongly identified themselves after the border conflict, and possibly
before it. The rank order assigned other identifications is revealing.
The percentages of people who could not make any ladder rating with
respect to the United Nations and the Commonwealth show how remote
these concepts still are to the majority of Indians. The low rating given
caste, while interesting in itself, may in part reflect the hesitancy many
people in India have to discuss such a thing with anyone outside the intimate group.

The Institute's special report on this subject ends with the following conclusion: China's challenge to India only remotely impinged upon the restricted concerns that direct Indian aspiration and anxiety. The invasion was perceived as Chinese, not Communist. It brought the call for a military buildup but did not threaten national independence. It stimulated a marked trend of opinion favorable to the United States but did not change the position of Indians on their nonalignment policy.

It has been said that it may be only Mao who will be able to unite the Indian people. Yet on the basis of the data here it appears that a greater awareness of national interests or any consolidation of opinion in other than the most general form is a prospect distant to a nation still so bound by circumstance and the immediate considerations of subsistence.

Summary

India is a vast land with nearly a half billion people, a people whose life expectancy is low, who are largely illiterate, and whose per capita income is around $70 a year. Within this context one would expect the most frequently expressed aspiration to be that for a higher standard of living and the most widespread worry to be that involving an inadequate standard of living or one that might even further deteriorate. Such is the case. But much more noteworthy is the fact that nearly two thirds of all Indians do not express such concerns. Also, only a minority mention either hopes or fears for their children while only about one in ten indicates any worry about ill health. The picture, then, is of a people too depressed to have many ambitions for themselves, resigned to their situations and to what their religion tells them is their lot in this particular round of life.

Aspirations for the nation are also at a relatively low pitch, with less than a third of the people worried about the nation's economic plight and only a quarter of them expressing concern about Chinese aggression only a few weeks before it became a reality. While Indians felt the nation had made some progress during the past five years, they saw little improvement in their own lot but remained sanguine about their own as well as the nation's future.

A repeat study after the Sino-Indian border clash in the fall of 1962 showed that while this event did increase the fear of Chinese aggression until nearly half the population became concerned about it, it did not appreciably alter the affirmation of a nonalignment policy, even though opinions toward the United States and the United Kingdom improved while those toward the U.S.S.R. deteriorated. There was no evidence that the event created any significantly greater awareness or sense of urgency about the threat to national independence, about the need for national unity, or the desirability of increasing the military strength of India.

The fact that Indians gave themselves and the nation lower ratings after the border incident than they had before it occurred indicates a feeling that things were even worse than people had thought they were, together with a sense of hurt pride. At the same time, both the charisma of the late Nehru's leadership and confidence in the government would seem to have been somewhat tarnished in the process.

CHAPTER VI

Samples from the Middle East

This chapter considers two nations in the Middle East—Israel and Egypt—that have been and still are in conflict with each other and includes a description of the Kibbutzim microcosm situated within the larger macrocosm of Israel.

ISRAEL

Population		2,144,000
Life expectancy	ca.	72
Per capita income	ca.	$735
Literacy		94%
Population *outside* agriculture and services		76%
Automobile: per 1,000 persons		14
Religious compositions		
Jewish		89%
Moslem		7%
Christian		2%
Other		2%

Israel was created largely by armistices. In 1947 the United Nations General Assembly voted to divide Palestine into two sovereign states: Western Galilee and a narrow corridor to Jerusalem were to become part of the new state of Israel; Jerusalem was divided, Israel taking over the New City, Jordan the Old City. In mid-1949 the armistice with Syria (the last to be signed) demilitarized the eastern side of Lake Huleh and the southeastern side of Galilee. But ever since the armistices were signed, tensions have remained high. Israel has been invaded variously by Syria, Egypt, Jordan, Iraq, Lebanon, and Saudi-Arabia. Border skirmishes are frequent, Israeli goods are boycotted throughout the Arab world, and Israeli commerce is hindered by the inaccessibility of the Suez Canal.

With independent status as a parliamentary democracy proclaimed on May 14–15, 1948, immigration restrictions were lifted and since then about 70,000 persons have arrived each year from all over the world.

The Israeli economy is unique to the Middle East: per capita income is high and foreign investments are secure. German reparations payments augment rising foreign investments. Industrial expansion leads to regular growth of the GNP (about 9 percent per year) with accompanying increases in per capita income (about 5 percent per year in real terms). Agriculturally, citrus fruits and grains are expanding as exports as increasingly large portions of the land become arable through irrigation.

Interviewing on the study in Israel was done during the last two months of 1961 and in the first six months of 1962. Hebrew, Yiddish, and German were used.

What Israelis Were Concerned About

The personal aspirations of Israelis are:

Children	50%
Decent standard of living	35
Have a house	34
Health for self	33
Health for family	29
Concern for relatives	28
Happy family life	26
Recreation and leisure	24
Modern conveniences	22
Congenial work	22
Employment	16
Self-development and improvement	14
Peace	12
Improved standard of living	12
Own business	10
Freedom from debt	8
Job or work situation	8
Job providing for self-development	6
Be normal, decent person	6
Be useful to others	5

Two of the categories were added especially to accommodate the answers given in Israel: freedom from debt and job providing for self-development, which includes opportunities for one's self, one's spouse, or other family members. The standard category of concern for relatives was extended to mean to keep them together or get them together again, live up to their expectations, keep children well and out of mischief. The category of recreation and leisure time in Israel included a

number of replies indicating the desire to live close to nature. Among
the new categories answered by less than 5 percent was one labeled "To
have roots, sense of community, attachment to nonfamily primary group"
used to classify some of the answers of 4 percent of the people.

The personal fears and worries of Israelis are:

Ill health for self	41%
Ill health in family	30
Inadequate standard of living	29
War	26
Unemployment	19
Children	18
Relatives	15
Unhappy family life	13
Deterioration in present standard of living	9
Be dependent	8
Poor job or uncongenial work	6
No fears or worries	6
Old-age problems	6
Be alone	5

Here the only new category added to take care of the comments of 6
percent of the people is that of old-age problems, involving chiefly economic dependence.

It will be seen at once from both the aspirations and the fears that a
large number of concerns are expressed by over 10 percent of the Israel
population. It will also be noted that the concern for children—as children—tops the list of aspirations, while the concerns for health, for
relatives, and for a happy family life are also extremely high. The same
general pattern is revealed by the expression of fears or worries, but
with the possibility of war added as a personal concern by a quarter of
the population. It is also noteworthy that the category of self-development and self-improvement is used to classify replies of 14 percent of the
people and that self-development is expressed as the criterion for a good
job by 6 percent.

The general categories that bring together all personal aspirations are:

Economic	80%
Family	76
Health	47
Job or work situation	35
Personal values and character	29
International situation, world	12
Social values	10
Status quo	4
Political	2

The general categories with respect to personal worries and fears are:

Health	58%
Economic	55
Family	44
International situation, world	27
Job or work situation	10
Personal values and character	10
No fears	6
Social values	4
Political	2

It will be noticed at once that the percentages here are quite high: the people in Israel are concerned, are aware, are self-conscious. Over three quarters of the population mention some sort of personal economic or family concern, over one half of them express a worry about their health or the health of their family, about one third of them aspire to more congenial jobs, and about the same number mention aspirations that refer to personal values and character.

The range and frequency of aspirations expressed for the nation are:

Peace with the Arabs	55%
Technological advances	47
Increase in population	36
Improved or decent standard of living	34
National independence	18
Economic stability	18
Increased foreign trade and exports	16
Peace	16
Be militarily strong	14
Employment	13
Education	13
Change the election system	11
Eliminate discrimination	11
Improve cultural standards	10
Free secondary education	9
Housing	9
Improve moral, ethical, and religious standards	9
National unity	8
Political stability	7
Sense of social and political responsibility	7
Public health	6
Friendly relations with all countries	6
Social justice	5
Social security	5
Enhance status	5

Among these categories mentioned by at least 5 percent, several new ones were especially added for Israel: peace with the Arabs, change the election system, improve cultural standards, and free secondary education.

Among other new categories added to accommodate Israeli replies are: proper ideals for youth, hope for Torah (religion)-guided society, hopes concerning Diaspora Jewry. These categories were used in classifying 3 or 4 percent of the replies.

The fears and worries expressed for the nation are:

War with the Arabs	49%
War in general, any kind	30
Economic instability	12
No improvement or inadequate standard of living	12
Population problem	10
Higher taxes	9
No technological advances	9
Lack national independence	9
Unemployment	8
Failure to preserve present standard of living	7
Political instability	7
No fears or worries	6
National disunity	6
Be militarily weak	5

War with the Arabs was among the new items added for Israel to express fears for the nation. Certain new items mentioned by less than 5 percent of the people, which have considerable significance in reflecting the ethos of the society, are: lack of ideal for youth, 4 percent; cheapening or decline of cultural standards, 3 percent; orthodox religious domination of the society, 1 percent.

It is apparent first of all that Israel is a nation of wide-ranging hopes, with fourteen different categories expressed by at least 10 percent of the people. On the other hand, except for fear of war with the Arabs or the fear of war in general, there are relatively few fears for the nation expressed by 10 percent or more. It is also significant that aspirations dealing with technological advances within the nation are mentioned by nearly half the population, whereas fears that there may be no technological advances are mentioned by only 9 percent, indicating considerable confidence that such advances will be made. Attention should also be drawn to the new category of aspirations we labeled "Maintaining or improving cultural standards" to accommodate answers given by 10 percent of the people, with the counterpart on the side of national worries that cultural standards would be cheapened mentioned by 3 percent. Also noteworthy is the desire of Israelis that their population should be larger.

The general categories of aspirations for the nation are:

Economic	79%
Social	70
International, peace	69
Independent status	37
Political	35
Status quo	1

The general categories of fears and worries for the nation are:

International, war	72%
Economic	44
Social	30
Political	23
Independent status	16
No fears	6

How Israelis Thought They Stood

The mean ladder ratings for Israel are:

PERSONAL RATINGS		NATIONAL RATINGS	
Past	4.7	Past	4.0
Present	5.3	Present	5.5
Future	6.9	Future	7.5

The percentage shifts on the various ratings are:

PERSONAL RATINGS		NATIONAL RATINGS	
Past to present		Past to present	
Present higher	52%	Present higher	75%
No change	23	No change	7
Present lower	23	Present lower	12
No answer	2	No answer	6
Present to future		Present to future	
Future higher	62%	Future higher	79%
No change	21	No change	8
Future lower	6	Future lower	3
No answer	11	No answer	10

The distributions of both personal and ladder ratings are bunched around the mean for the past and present but tend to spread out more with respect to the future (see Figures VI:1 and VI:2).

It is significant that the mean ladder ratings given for the nation show a greater spread from past through the present and on to the future than do the personal ratings: the nation is rated lower for the past and higher for the future. This is also shown by the percentage shifts where an appreciably larger number of people rate both the present higher than the past and the future higher than the present when they assign a position to the nation than when they rate their own progress. Thus

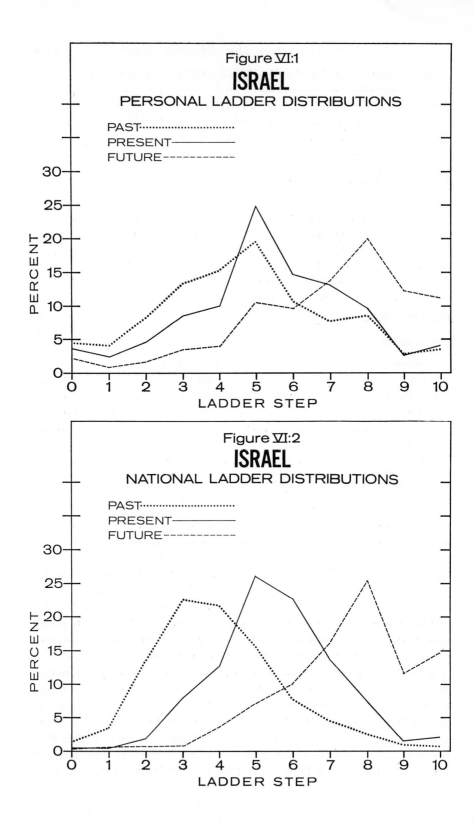

Figure Ⅵ:1
ISRAEL
PERSONAL LADDER DISTRIBUTIONS

PAST·····················
PRESENT————
FUTURE————————

Figure Ⅵ:2
ISRAEL
NATIONAL LADDER DISTRIBUTIONS

PAST·····················
PRESENT————
FUTURE————————

while there is optimism in both the personal and national spheres, optimism and confidence in national progress is greater. This discrepancy is reflected in the relatively low correlations between personal and national ratings: for the past, 0.23; the present, 0.12; and the future, 0.14. Israelis apparently see somewhat less interdependence between themselves and the nation for the present and the future than they did for the past.

Variations Within the Population

Concerns about *personal economic* matters are found with somewhat greater frequency among the skilled and unskilled workers, farmers, the less educated, the less well-off, and those who have come from the Middle East or Asia. It is the business and professional people, those in the upper income brackets, and those born in Palestine who tend to have less than average involvement with personal economic concerns. A good *job or work situation* is mentioned somewhat more frequently by two rather different varieties of people: on the one hand, farmers and unskilled workers, and, on the other hand, university graduates and those who identify themselves with the upper or upper middle classes as well as natives of Palestine and young people. The *international and world situation,* mentioned as a worry or fear by over a quarter of the population, was more of a concern to the elite: professional and business people, university graduates, upper income and upper class people, and those who came from Western Europe or the United States. With respect to *social values,* mentioned as an aspiration by 10 percent of the population, it is noteworthy that one quarter of the Israeli farmers, who number among themselves a high proportion of Israel's idealists, expressed the aspiration that Israel have higher social and cultural standards.

By and large it is the elite who express more than average concern for the nation on the various categories. With regard to worries about the *economic* problems facing the nation, it is interesting to notice that there are more worries among professional people whom we have noted were *less* than average concerned about their personal economic problems; similarly those in the low income and low educational brackets are less worried about national economic problems although they are *more* than average concerned about their own economic affairs. It is also noteworthy that in the general category of *international, war and peace,* mentioned by two thirds of the Israeli people, in addition to the elite, emigrants who arrived in Israel during the tumultuous and tortuous years of 1939 to 1948 were more concerned than average while those who arrived after 1948 were less concerned than others.

Variations in Ladder Ratings. Comparisons of the ladder ratings various demographic groups assign themselves show that the elite of Israel rate themselves higher on the past, the present, and the future. Those who are natives of Palestine or who came to Palestine before 1939 also assign themselves a higher rating on the present and the past. With respect to the ratings given the nation, it is significant that while professional people and university graduates rate themselves higher than average on the personal side, they see less shift upward for the nation than do the majority of the people. On the other hand, unskilled workers, the least educated, and those with Middle East or Asian origins, who assign themselves lower ratings on the personal ladder, see the nation moving upward more than do other people.

When the ladder ratings for the nation are compared to the concerns expressed for the nation, it turns out that people with all varieties of concern are uniformly optimistic about Israel with similar ratings given throughout.

Summary

The people in the new and independent nation of Israel are seething with aspirations for themselves, many people expressing a wide variety of hopes to be realized in the home the Jews now have for themselves. Topping the list of their personal hopes is that their children will have opportunities; topping the list of hopes for the nation is the desire for peace with the Arabs. In addition to the more usual concerns for a better standard of living and for health, many people in Israel seem self-consciously dedicated to improving the quality of the people and opportunities for their self-development.

Israel is a nation of people who feel uniformly confident that if war can be avoided, they and the nation will continue to move forward, advancing technologically, solving economic and agricultural problems, and controlling population growth.

THE KIBBUTZIM

As previously indicated, the sample of different areas of the world included the microcosm represented by the Kibbutzim of Israel—those small Utopian collective communities deliberately and painstakingly established to create societies for mutual aid without class distinction and with complete equality practiced. Everything in a Kibbutz is democratically decided, assemblies of all adults taking place in the dining hall or some other large room where all communal problems are discussed and the majority vote carries. People who do not conform to the majority vote must leave the Kibbutz. Frictions between individuals or groups within the Kibbutz are taken to special committees for resolution and very few of them ever have to go to courts for settlements. There is a collective ethic which changes with the revisions new conditions may seem to warrant.

In most of the Kibbutzim in Israel, children live in nearby communal centers rather than with their parents. But even though children do live in their own "home," they visit their parents frequently. This communal care of children allows mothers to be free for work in the community and to have some personal independence. Children are cared for and educated by a few trained people.

Everyone is assigned a job within the community and if his work within the community is not a full-time job and he works outside of the Kibbutz, then he puts all of his wages into the common Kibbutz pool.

The first Kibbutz was established in Palestine in 1909 and there are now over two hundred of them. A number of these were established in the mid-twenties and up to 1939, mostly by people of Eastern European origin who had come to escape the harsh and unjust treatment suffered in the countries of their origin, where many had been forced to live in ghettos. While the migration to Palestine was uprooting, these people were lured by the hope of ridding themselves of all the discrimination suffered as Jews and establishing themselves in a social environment where the individual could develop himself as a human being, where he could have economic and personal security within a collective, and where children would have opportunities and learn to respect the values cherished by their parents.

Up to the formation of the State of Israel in 1948 the life of a Kibbutz represented essentially the ideal norm for Palestinian Jewish youth. At the same time they took a most active part in the creation and maintenance of the State of Israel and provided many of its members of Parliament and its military officers. As would be expected, since the State was established there has been a decline in the role of the Kibbutz movement. The growth of the Kibbutzim population has lagged far behind the growth of the population of Israel as a whole. Since that time most new Kibbutz members are people who were born in the Kibbutzim.

At the end of 1960 there were slightly over 75,000 members in the total Kibbutzim population. The sample of 300 Kibbutz members interviewed between July and October of 1962 represents as faithfully as possible the original date of settlement of the Kibbutz and their religious and political affiliations.

What Kibbutzim Members Were Concerned About

The personal aspirations expressed by Kibbutzim members are:

Happy family life	44%
Good job, congenial work	41
Self-development or improvement	38
Children	37
Recreation and leisure; live close to nature	24
Peace	22

Relatives	20
Younger generation remaining in Kibbutz or maintaining Kibbutz values	20
Roots, sense of community attachment	19
Remain in Kibbutz	19
Maintain or improve social-personal relations in Kibbutz	18
Health of self	16
Being useful to others	16
Health of family	14
Economic success of Kibbutz	12
No change in traditional Kibbutz values	11
Achieve sense of own personal worth	10
Decent standard of living	10
Success	9
Kibbutz relations to broader society	9
Acceptance by others	7
Have own house	6
Job providing self-development opportunity	6
Maintain status quo in general	6
Improved standard of living	6
Have modern conveniences	5
Employment	5

It will be noticed that a considerable number of personal aspirations were added here to accommodate the hopes and ideals of members of the Kibbutzim: the desire that people remain in the Kibbutz and retain Kibbutz values, a sense of community attachment, the improvement of social and personal relations in the Kibbutz, the economic success of the Kibbutz, the maintenance of Kibbutz values, and the relation of the Kibbutz to the larger society of Israel and the world.

It will also be noticed that a very long list of aspirations is mentioned by at least 10 percent of the people in the Kibbutzim, and it will be seen that many of these are value laden, concerned not only with a happy family life and children's welfare, but with self-development or improvement, with attaining a sense of community, and with personal relations within the community.

The fears and worries expressed by Kibbutzim members are:

War	43%
Ill health of self	36
Ill health of family	32
Leave Kibbutz, disintegration of Kibbutz	31
Unhappy family life	24

Alienation or rootlessness	22
Relatives	16
Poor job, uncongenial work	15
Children	14
No self-development or improvement	11
Being dependent on others	10
Not being accepted by others	10
Unemployment	9
Problems of old age and economic dependence	9
Emotional instability and immaturity	8
No sense of personal worth	8
Not having good relations with broader society	8
The younger generation leave the Kibbutz or reject its values	8
Inadequate standard of living	7
Specific impact of war on Kibbutz	7
Economic failure of Kibbutz	6
Deterioration of present standard of living	6
Failure in work	6
Change in traditional Kibbutz values	5

Worry about the possibility of war, which tops the list of worries, reflects not only the microcosm of Israel but also the exposed border positions of many of the Kibbutzim. In the list of personal fears, again a number of new categories had to be added to accommodate the fears and worries of the members.

It will be noted in both the list of personal hopes and personal fears that economic concerns are relatively and frequently expressed, and that running throughout both types of concerns are those related to the perpetuation and success of the Kibbutzim idea itself.

For the sake of comparison with the larger macrocosm of Israel, the Israel percentages for the general categories along with those found for the Kibbutzim are repeated.

The following are the general categories for personal hopes:

	Kibbutzim	Israel
Family	74%	76%
Social values	63	10
Personal values and character	59	29
Job or work situation	51	35
Economic	41	80
Health	24	47
International situation, world	23	12
Status quo	6	4
Political	3	2

The general categories for personal fears and worries are:

	Kibbutzim	Israel
Health	52%	58%
Social values	51	4
Family	48	44
International situation, world	48	27
Personal values and character	45	10
Economic	33	55
Job or work situation	20	10
Political	4	2
No fears	2	6

It will be noticed at once how much more concerned Kibbutzim members are than the Israel population as a whole with the general items of social values, personal values and character, job or work situation, and the impact of the international or world situation on their personal lives; only about half of them are as much concerned about their personal economic situation either as an aspiration or a fear.

The aspirations the members of the Kibbutzim have for the State of Israel are:

Peace with Arabs	73%
Improved standard of living through technological advances	59
Population	52
Improved or decent standard of living	40
National independence	33
Social justice	31
Socialistic government, unity of workers' parties	31
Maintain cultural standards, and develop an indigenous cultural life	22
National unity	22
Eliminate discrimination	20
Peace	19
Education	18
Increase foreign trade or exports	17
Moral, ethical, and religious standards	16
Free secondary education	15
Employment	13
Hopes for Diaspora Jewry	13
Sense of social and political responsibility	11
Ideals for youth	11
Freedom of speech and religion	10
Economic stability	10
Enhance the status and importance of Israel	9

Democratic representative government	8
Be militarily strong	8
Use of military and security expenditures for production	8
Housing	7
Maintain neutrality	7
Change election system	7
Friendly relations with all countries	6
Honest government	6
Social security	6

As was true with Israel as a whole, the range of aspirations for the nation is wide. But when the list of aspirations for Israel mentioned by people in the Kibbutzim is compared to the list given by a sample of the total Israel population (page 101) a number of significant differences appear. For example: peace with the Arabs is mentioned by 73 percent in the Kibbutzim, by 55 percent of the total Israel sample; technological advances to improve the standard of living are self-consciously aspired to by 59 percent in the Kibbutz, by 47 percent in Israel as a whole; an increase in population is mentioned by over half of those in the Kibbutz, but by only about a third of those in Israel; social justice as an aspiration was mentioned by 31 percent of the Kibbutz, by 5 percent of Israel as a whole; improving cultural standards and developing an indigenous cultural life, something 22 percent of the Kibbutz members want, was mentioned by only 10 percent in Israel; the elimination of discrimination was mentioned by 20 percent in the Kibbutz and about half that number in Israel; references to moral, ethical, and religious standards occurred in 16 percent of the Kibbutzim interviews and in only 9 percent of those in Israel in general.

The fears people in the Kibbutz express for Israel as a nation are:

War with the Arabs	56%
War of any kind	37
Lack national independence	23
Population problem	20
No democratic or representative government	19
No technological advances	17
Disunity among people of the nation	16
No improved or an inadequate standard of living	15
Social injustice	14
Lack moral, ethical or religious standards	13
Cheapening or decline of cultural standards	12
Economic instability	11

No sense of social or political responsibility	10
Lack of ideals for youth	10
Political instability	9
Continued discrimination	9
Fear of orthodox religious domination of society	9
Failure to preserve present standard of living	9
Fears for Diaspora Jewry	9
To be isolated	8
Inadequate educational facilities	8
Too much mechanization and standardization	8
Lack of freedom of speech or religion	7
Unemployment	7
Be militarily weak	6
Dishonest government	5

Again, while these fears for the nation resemble those expressed by the Israel population as a whole, certain differences stand out: the fear that there would be no democratic or representative government, mentioned by 19 percent in the Kibbutz, was mentioned by only 3 percent in Israel; the concern that there would be no technological advances was mentioned by 17 percent in the Kibbutz and by only 9 percent in Israel; disunity in the nation was feared by 16 percent in the Kibbutz and by only 6 percent in Israel; the lack of moral, ethical, or religious standards was mentioned by 13 percent in the Kibbutz, by 3 percent in Israel; the new item introduced for Israel as a whole and concerned with the cheapening or decline of cultural standards was something 12 percent in the Kibbutz were concerned about, but only 3 percent in Israel; the lack of a sense of social responsibility was a concern to 10 percent in the Kibbutz, to 3 percent in Israel; the lack of ideals for youth again concerned 10 percent in the Kibbutz and 4 percent in Israel; the fear of the Orthodox religious domination of society worried 9 percent of Kibbutzim members but only 1 percent in Israel as a whole; and fears for the Diaspora Jewry were mentioned by 9 percent in the Kibbutz and only 2 percent in Israel as a whole.

The general categories for national hopes are:

	Kibbutzim	Israel
International, peace	94%	69%
Social	89	70
Economic	83	79
Political	62	35
Independent status	46	37
Status quo	1	1

The general categories for national fears and worries are:

	Kibbutzim	Israel
International, war	87%	72%
Social	65	30
Economic	50	44
Political	49	23
Independent status	30	16
No fears	——	6

It will be noticed at once that on all general categories for all national hopes and fears, the members of the Kibbutzim appear more self-consciously aware of the whole range of national goals and problems. This is especially noticeable in the list of fears and worries for the nation, where approximately twice as many people in the Kibbutz as in Israel as a whole express a concern for social values, for the political problems facing the nation, and for the maintenance of Israel's independent status.

How Kibbutzim Members Thought They Stood

The mean ladder ratings assigned by Kibbutzim members are given here along with those of Israel as a whole for comparison:

	Kibbutzim	Israel
PERSONAL RATINGS		
Past	6.3	4.7
Present	7.0	5.3
Future	7.9	6.9
NATIONAL RATINGS		
Past	4.5	4.0
Present	5.3	5.5
Future	6.5	7.5

The percentage shifts in the ratings for the Kibbutzim are:

	Kibbutzim	Israel		Kibbutzim	Israel
PERSONAL RATINGS			NATIONAL RATINGS		
Past to present			Past to present		
Present higher	50%	52%	Present higher	60%	75%
No change	27	23	No change	16	7
Present lower	20	23	Present lower	22	12
No answer	3	2	No answer	2	6
Present to future			Present to future		
Future higher	53%	62%	Future higher	72%	79%
No change	32	21	No change	13	8
Future lower	8	6	Future lower	8	3
No answer	7	11	No answer	7	10

There is some spread of the ladder ratings around the mean. The correlations between personal and national ladder ratings for the Kibbutzim are: past, 0.08, present, 0.16, and future, 0.14; and for Israel as a whole correlations are 0.23, 0.12, and 0.14 respectively. While all these correlations are low, the considerably lower apparent relationship between the personal and national ratings for the past among Kibbutzim members seems to reflect the sense of independence from the State they felt they had five years prior to the study.

Several variations appear between the ladder ratings given by those in the Kibbutzim microcosm and those given by Israelis living in the larger macrocosm. It will be noticed that all ratings assigned by Kibbutzim members for themselves are significantly higher than those assigned by Israelis in general. On all three ratings, the estimates Kibbutzim members make for themselves are higher by a sizable margin than those assigned the nation as a whole. And Kibbutzim members are definitely not as optimistic about the future of Israel as are other Israelis, even though they do see a trend upwards for the nation.

Variations Within the Population

Since our Kibbutzim sample had only 300 cases, the only comparison we tried to make between different members of the population was that generally regarded as the most crucial for the fate of the Kibbutzim— differences between age or generation. No significant differences on the ladder ratings occur, although there is a tendency for the younger Kibbutz members to rate their own future status higher than do members of the population over thirty years of age. (With such small samples in the two age groups, a difference of 0.7 in ladder ratings is required for significance at the .05 level.) However, there is a statistically significant difference in the overall shift between the past through the present onto the future between the two age groups: among those under thirty the total shift in the ladder ratings is 2.2, among those over thirty it is 1.2. No significant differences appear in the ladder ratings given the nation by the two age groups.

Summary

The whole Kibbutzim picture is one of a highly self-conscious microcosm whose members are intent upon preserving the values around which their society was created: a devotion to social justice and to egalitarianism, along with a high sense of national identity and national dedication. Among both the older and younger generations, there is an eagerness to protect and to develop the Kibbutzim microcosm within the larger state and the larger world, which are increasingly involved with material values and status strivings, although many in the Kibbutzim seem to suspect they may be fighting a losing battle.

EGYPT

Population	24,026,000
Per capita income	ca. $150
Life expectancy	51
Literacy	23%
Population *outside* agriculture and services	36%
Automobiles per 1,000 persons	3
Religious composition:	
Moslem	91%
Christian	9%

Egypt, a Moslem country, was granted independent status by Great Britain in 1922, although British occupation did not end at that time. A nationalist uprising, led by Gamal Abdel Nasser and the Society of Free Officers, forced the abdication of the profligate King Farouk on July 23, 1952, sending him on his way to Italy with a twenty-one gun salute. A transitional government under Major General Mohammed Naguib was then instituted. A year later Nasser ousted Naguib as Premier and in 1956 Nasser was elected President, the only candidate to appear on the ballot.

When the United States, Britain, and the International Bank withdrew support for the Aswan Dam Project, Nasser nationalized the Suez Canal and seized the assets of the Canal Company. At the same time tensions with Israel renewed earlier fighting. Israeli forces invaded the Sinai Peninsula and the Gaza Strip. When Egypt rejected a British and French cease-fire proposal, the British and French bombed Egypt and landed forces in the Port Said area, amid protests from the United States and the United Nations. A cease-fire was achieved on November 7, 1956.

Agrarian reform limiting the amount of land any one person could own began in 1952, and measures were also taken to increase the variety of agricultural products, to institute cooperatives and teach the *Fellahin* how to use insecticides, how to improve the breed of their stock, etc. Only about 5 percent of Egyptian land is available to cultivation, the rest being desert. The vast majority of industry and agriculture has been nationalized. A Five-Year Plan instituted in 1960 was primarily industrial in its scope. Over 90 percent of the working force is unskilled labor.

Population increase is one of Egypt's major problems: the average family has 7.9 children, and one person is added to the population every minute. Children, especially boys, are economic assets to the *Fellahin* and symbols of status to Moslem women. What gains are made in increasing Egypt's gross national product are just about absorbed by its growing numbers of people. The per capita income of $150 noted above reflects the low standard of living, especially if we remember that the vast majority of Egyptians do not achieve this average because of the way income is distributed.

As already noted, this study in Egypt should be regarded as a preliminary pilot survey. Although permission to conduct the survey was given at the ministerial level, this in no way affected the difficulties encountered by nongovernment interviewers who went around the country asking questions. Local police and other officials, particularly in the villages, were suspicious at the time our survey was conducted in the fall of 1960 and for various other reasons a true cross-section of the population could not be obtained at the time. While five hundred people were interviewed, these greatly overrepresent the better-educated and urban segments of the population, whereas the rural areas where two thirds of Egyptians live are greatly underrepresented. We tried to even up the discrepancy between urban and rural proportions by weighting rural interviews so that our overall figures would be likely to have somewhat greater reliability. (See Appendix B1.)

What Egyptians Were Concerned About

The personal aspirations mentioned by at least 5 percent in our pilot study are:

Family life	35%
Decent standard of living	26
Success	24
Health of self	22
Congenial work	22
Success for children	20
Acceptance by others	13
Wealth	11
Recreation and leisure	10
Sense of personal worth, self-satisfaction	10
Be useful to others	9
Emotional stability	9
Have own house	9
Have own land	9
Concern for relatives	6

Among the items mentioned by less than 5 percent are: to have modern conveniences, 3 percent; health of family, 2 percent; freedom of speech, 2 percent; peace, less than 1 percent.

The personal worries and fears are:

Ill health of self	35%
Inadequate standard of living	27
Unhappy family life	14

Failure in work	14
Unemployment	11
Ill health in family	9
No fears or worries	9
Not be accepted	8
Be alone	8
Concern for relatives	7
No sense of personal worth	7
Uncongenial work	7
Emotional instability	5

Some of the personal worries and fears mentioned by less than 5 percent are: war, 4 percent; deterioration of present standard of living for self or family, 3 percent; lack of freedom of speech, 2 percent; economic instability, 1 percent; inequality of opportunity because of race, less than 1 percent.

It will be noticed that the complex of factors concerned with standard of living, happy family life, and health for oneself are high in Egypt just as we have found them in many other countries so far. The widespread concern for success in one's job and for congenial work at least in part reflects the consequences of the huge migrations into the cities by agricultural workers who had left the land, as well as the frustrations of better-educated people who were finding it difficult to obtain congenial and challenging work outside the bureaucracy.

The combined general categories for all personal aspirations are:

Economic	70%
Family	53
Job or work situation	42
Personal values and character	39
Health	24
Social values	9
Political	4
International situation, world	2
Status quo	——

The general categories combining all personal fears and worries are:

Economic	46%
Health	42
Family	30
Personal values and character	23
Job or work situation	20
No fears	11
Political	4
International situation, world	4
Social values	2

The aspirations Egyptians had for the country as a whole are:

Decent standard of living	30%
Technological advances	26
National independence	15
Better education	14
Become a world power	12
Social justice	10
Peace	9
National unity	8
Public health	7
Be militarily strong	7
Democratic government	6
Freedom	6
Enhance international status	6
Employment	5
High moral, ethical, and religious standards	5

Among the categories mentioned by less than 5 percent of the people as hopes for the nation are: exert ideological or moral leadership, 4 percent; control size of population, 2 percent; maintain neutrality, 2 percent; honest government, 1 percent; and efficient government, 1 percent.

The fears and worries expressed for the nation are:

Foreign aggression	31%
War	22
Inadequate standard of living	18
Communism	8
Inadequate educational facilities	6
Political instability	6
No technological advances	5
Dishonest government	5
National disunity	5
Lack national independence	5

Among the items mentioned by less than 5 percent are: concern with the population problem, 4 percent; lack of freedom of speech, 3 percent; lose or attain no international status, 1 percent; and failure to exert ideological or moral leadership, 1 percent.

It will be seen from the list of aspirations for the nation that in addition to a concern for a better standard of living through technological advances, there is clearly a concern that Egypt's nationalism be respected and enhanced—the fear of foreign aggression is understandably high after the troubles with Israel and the Suez crisis; and a sizable proportion of Egyptians are concerned with national independence, becoming a world power, and being militarily strong. It is noteworthy that in a country where the population explosion presents such a problem to those who observe the Egyptian scene as well as to its government leaders, relatively few of the people themselves are bothered about it. It is also significant that few people mention freedom of speech as a desideratum in a country where there are so many limitations on this freedom.

The general categories concerning aspirations for the nation are:

Economic	58%
Independent status	44
Social	36
International, peace	29
Political	26
Status quo	1

And the fears and worries for the nation when combined into general categories are:

Independent status	37%
International, war	35
Economic	29
Political	26
Social	19
No fears	4

How Egyptians Thought They Stood

The mean ladder ratings assigned by those interviewed in this pilot study are:

PERSONAL RATINGS		NATIONAL RATINGS	
Past	4.6	Past	3.5
Present	5.5	Present	5.9
Future	8.0	Future	7.5

The percentage shifts in the ladder ratings are:

PERSONAL RATINGS		NATIONAL RATINGS	
Past to present		Past to present	
Present higher	67%	Present higher	85%
No change	12	No change	5
Present lower	20	Present lower	8
No answer	1	No answer	2
Present to future		Present to future	
Future higher	86%	Future higher	81%
No change	9	No change	5
Future lower	4	Future lower	10
No answer	1	No answer	4

The distributions of the ratings show somewhat more of a spread when they are concerned for the past and present than when they are assigned for the future (see Figures VI:3 and VI:4).

It will be noticed at once that there is a great change upwards in the

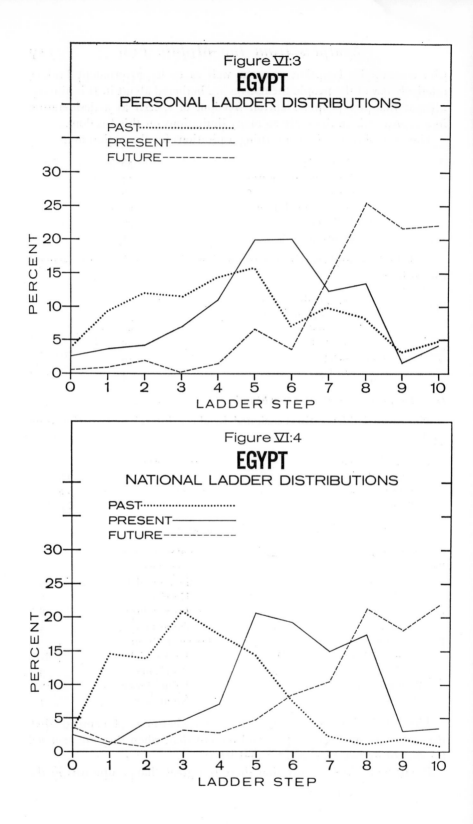

ladder ratings both from the past to the present and the present to the future. Clearly the people in our sample feel that both they and the nation have made progress during the past five years in achieving what they regard both as personal and national goals. They are also extremely optimistic about their own and the nation's future, nearly 70 percent placing themselves at step 8 or above on the ladder in their own ratings for the future and over 60 percent placing the nation this high in the future.

In spite of this parallel optimism for self and nation, the correlations between the personal and national ratings are of a low order: for the past, 0.24; the present, 0.14; and the future, 0.27.

Variations Within the Population

While I must again enter a word of caution concerning the Egyptian data because of the sample obtained in this preliminary study, certain differences worth noting do appear. Above average *personal economic* concerns are expressed by the *Fellahin,* skilled workers, and the older people as aspirations but, as fears, more than average by the farm owners worried about further land confiscation. Congenial *job or work situation* is more of a concern for people living in the city, for young people, for the better educated and for government officials, and less of a concern for older people and those living in rural areas.

With respect to the concerns different demographic groups expressed for the nation, it is interesting to notice that the *Fellahin* who express more concern for themselves personally about economic matters, are less concerned than others about the *economy of the nation* as a whole. As would be expected, again the farm owners are more worried than most people about the state of the national economy.

Variations in Ladder Ratings. On the personal ladder ratings, while professional people and farm owners give themselves higher present ladder ratings but not significantly higher future ladder ratings, the agricultural workers (*Fellahin*) rate themselves lower than average on the past and present but show a greater shift upward than any other population group in their ladder ratings from the past through the present and into the future. Egypt's progress in land distribution is clearly reflected here. As far as the ratings for the nation are concerned, again the *Fellahin* reveal the greatest shift upward in their ladder ratings while businessmen, suffering from Nasser's program of nationalizing industries and business, assign the nation a lower than average rating for all three periods of time.

When the personal ladder ratings and shifts in ratings are related to the personal concerns expressed by the Egyptians sampled, by far the greatest shift in the upward direction and the highest future rating is given by those who say they want to own land. Furthermore, those who aspire to a sense of their own personal worth—that is "achieve sense of my own personal worth; self-satisfaction; feeling of accomplishment; life of content"—assign themselves a higher than average rating for the future and show a significantly greater trend in their overall shift upward. These relationships assume particular importance in Egypt for they would appear to be two of the most essential ingredients for stabilizing a revolution in an agrarian culture: owning one's own land and achieving a sense of personal dignity in the process.

Summary

This pilot study of Egyptians reveals a people predominately concerned with their economic problems but with high confidence in the ability of Nasser's regime to move them a considerable distance ahead in the future, as they feel it has in the past, toward the goals they have set for themselves and for the nation. However, very few Egyptians indeed appear to be aware of the country's alarming population increase. As would be expected subsequent to Nasser's land reform program and conscription of much of Egypt's industry and business, the *Fellahin* are the most optimistic about the future, the businessmen least sanguine. The major threat to the further development of Egyptian nationalism and the consolidation of her rather recently attained independent status is, of course, that from foreign aggression.

CHAPTER VII

Three Caribbean Nations and the Philippines

The description of the aspirations of people in different nations is concluded with a report on three Caribbean countries and the Philippines, each of which represented a special set of social and political circumstances at the time our studies were made. Cuba had recently been through a revolution; the Dominican Republic had ousted a dictator and was trying to work out a more representative form of government; Panama was controlled by a few wealthy families and had no strong democratic leadership to deal with its problems; the Philippines provided an example of an Asian country which exhibited a reasonably viable form of Western democracy.

CUBA

Population	6,131,000
Per capita income	ca. $413
Literacy	78%
Population *outside* agriculture and services	57%
Automobiles per 1,000 persons	23

The corrupt regime of Major General Fulgencio Batista established in 1952 was overthrown with Batista's resignation on January 1, 1959. Fidel Castro, who had led guerrilla opposition to the Batista regime, proclaimed Dr. Manuel Urrutia Lleo Provisional President the following day. Within a few weeks Castro had become Premier.

The economy was patterned along leftist lines, affecting the sugar industry which accounts for about one fourth of the national product and well over half of Cuban exports. The Agrarian Reform Law (May 18, 1959) became the keynote of the new economic and social changes. Resistance to changes was stifled as dissidents were executed and moderates ousted from positions of responsibility. Private enterprise was brought under the Central Planning Board and the banks and industry generally had been nationalized by 1960.

The survey in Cuba was carried out in April and May of 1960—approximately fifteen months after Castro attained power, a year before the abortive American invasion of Cuba in April of 1961, and considerably prior to the Soviet attempt to establish missile bases on the island.[1]

In spite of the difficulties anticipated in conducting this survey, Lloyd Free and I were eager to obtain a sample of data from a country that had just experienced successful revolution. Because the revolutionary fervor had so penetrated rural areas that people living in them were excessively suspicious, the sample of 1,000 cases was limited to a cross-section of the people of Havana, together with those living in other urban centers and people in semi-urban areas outside Havana. Nearly all respondents seemed quite willing to answer the questions and to talk frankly.

What Cubans Were Concerned About

The personal aspirations of the Cuban people at the time were:

Health for self	37%
Decent standard of living	34
Family life	28
Children	24
Employment	23
Own house or land	19
Health of family	17
Self-improvement	12
Concern for relatives	12
Congenial work	11
Emotional stability	10
More leisure time	10
Improved standard of living	9
Domestic tranquility	7
Have modern conveniences	7
Acceptance by others	6
Success of revolution	6
Wealth	5

Two of these categories were especially added to accommodate the replies given in Cuba: domestic tranquility and success of the revolution. The desire for personal freedom of speech was mentioned by only 2 percent of the people.

On the side of personal fears and worries, the replies were:

Ill health for self	28%
Unemployment	22

Ill health for family	21
Inadequate standard of living	19
Success of children	10
No fears or worries	9
Emotional stability	9
Concern for relatives	6
Family life	6
No self-improvement	5
Be alone	5
No acceptance by others	5
Failure of the revolution	5
No sense of personal worth	5

Among this list the item of failure of revolution was added for Cuba, as were two other items mentioned by less than 5 percent: return to past conditions, 4 percent; disunity among the people, hatred and antagonism, civil war, mentioned by 2 percent. Our category of no personal freedom was mentioned by only 1 percent of the population. It will be seen from these listings that the emphases were on health, the family, children, and various aspirations that concern economic problems, including a widespread concern about unemployment.

Grouping the code items into general categories produced the following results:

Economic	73%
Family	52
Health	47
Personal values and character	30
Political	15
Job or work situation	14
Social values	4
International situation, world	3
Status quo	1

The general categories for personal fears are:

Economic	47%
Health	42
Family	24
Personal values and character	23
Political	15
No fears	9
International situation, world	5
Work or job situation	4
Social values	3

The hopes the Cuban people had for the nation at the time were:

Employment	31%
Domestic tranquility	25

Improved standard of technology	23
Improved standard of living	23
Success of revolution	21
Decent standard of living	13
Education	9
National independence	9
Agrarian reform	8
Social justice	6
Individual freedom	5
Honest government	5
Democratic government	5

Again the categories of domestic tranquility and success of the revolution were added to our standard items. Mentioned by fewer than 5 percent of the people were friendly international relations, 4 percent; respect from all countries, 1 percent; and representative government, 3 percent.

The national fears expressed for the country were:

Return to past conditions	30%
No fears or worries	14
Failure of the revolution	13
Internal disunity	11
Unemployment	8
Inadequate standard of living	7
Fear of Communism	7
Aggression by the United States	6
Aggression by any power	6

New code items in this listing were: return to past conditions, failure of the revolution, internal disunity, fear of Communism, and aggression by the United States. Among the items mentioned by less than 5 percent of the people were: lack of freedom, 4 percent; no democracy, 3 percent; excessive government intervention, 1 percent; and social injustice, 1 percent.

It will be seen at once from these lists how hopeful the people were that the revolution would be consolidated, how apparently little concerned they were that the Castro dictatorship would cut down personal freedom, and how paramount problems involving an improved standard of living and employment were at the time.

The general categories of hopes for the nation are:

Economic	75%
Social	21
Political	18
Independent status	13
International, peace	7
Status quo	2

The general categories of fears for the nation are:

Political	59%
Economic	24
No fears	14
Independent status	11
International, war	10
Social	8

How Cubans Thought They Stood

The mean ladder ratings given by the Cuban people in the spring of 1960 are:

PERSONAL RATINGS		NATIONAL RATINGS	
Past	4.1	Past	2.2
Present	6.4	Present	7.0
Future	8.4	Future	8.8

The percentage shifts on the ratings given for different periods of time are:

PERSONAL RATINGS		NATIONAL RATINGS	
Past to present		Past to present	
Present higher	65%	Present higher	86%
No change	17	No change	3
Present lower	17	Future lower	8
No answer	1	No answer	3
Present to future		Present to future	
Future higher	74%	Future higher	73%
No change	17	No change	19
Future lower	6	Future lower	5
No answer	3	No answer	3

While the distributions of both the personal and national ratings were somewhat scattered with respect to the present and the past, there is a clear tendency for people to bunch their ratings for the future into the top three steps: 75 percent did so on their personal future ratings and 82 percent put the nation on step 8 or above for the future. (See Figures VII:1 and VII:2.)

The comparison of the past, present, and future ladder ratings assigned by Cubans both for themselves and the nation is dramatic indeed: they felt that both they and especially the nation had made enormous strides during the past five years as a result of the revolutionary take-over, and they foresaw an extremely bright future both for themselves as individuals and for the nation as a whole. The interdependence Cubans felt between their own welfare and the state of the nation is reflected in the relatively high correlations between personal and national ratings: for the past, 0.35; the present, 0.38; and the future, 0.41.

Variations Within the Population

The differences in the complex of replies given by people in various demographic groups of the population and classified into general categories show, as would be expected, that people who are better-off economically have fewer *personal economic* concerns either as aspirations or worries. With respect to general categories concerned with the hopes and fears of the nation, there is clear indication that the more sophisticated elite, as judged by education and income, are more concerned than others about the state of the nation which they still see as somewhat critical: those who have graduated from secondary school or college are more worried about Cuba's political future than others, and it is

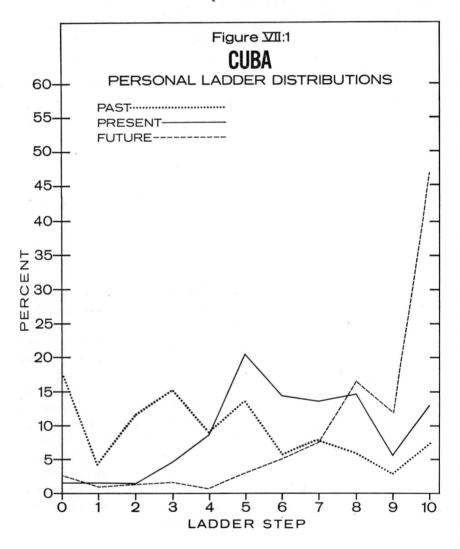

Figure VII:1

CUBA

PERSONAL LADDER DISTRIBUTIONS

PAST ····················
PRESENT ————
FUTURE ----------

this same group, along with those who enjoy economic advantages, who express more than average concern for Cuba's independent status and the achievement of social values.

Variations in Ladder Ratings. With respect to the ladder rating and the shifts in ladder rating referring both to the people and the nation, the picture is relatively clear-cut: greater than average shifts upward are found in the ladder rating among low income people, among the least educated, and among young people. When the personal ladder ratings are related to the concerns people express for their own lives, those who are significantly higher on the ladder are those for whom the revolution apparently meant most; the higher ladder ratings they give themselves indicate that their hopes for the future outweigh the

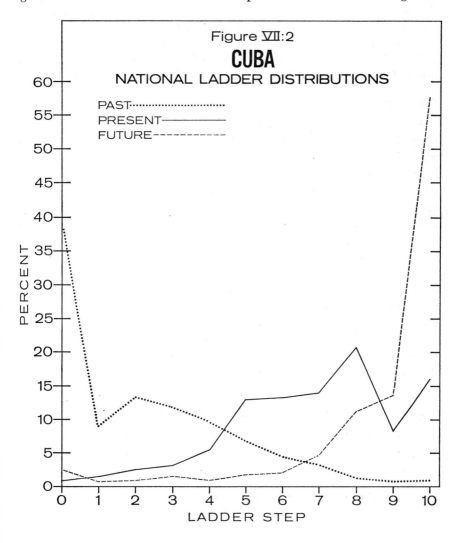

Figure VII:2

CUBA
NATIONAL LADDER DISTRIBUTIONS

PAST·················
PRESENT———
FUTURE----------

anxieties they also have that the revolution may fail. Significantly higher ladder ratings were given by those who, in their discussions of personal aspirations and worries, mentioned more frequently than others the success of the revolution, the achievement of domestic tranquility, together with the fear that the revolution might fail.

The relationship between the ratings assigned the nation and concerns expressed for the nation is also clear-cut: higher ratings and significantly greater shifts up are found among those who aspire to the success of the revolution and who worry about its possible failure and that they may return to past conditions or be subject to attack by the United States or some other power. But here, again, the higher ladder ratings assigned the nation seem to indicate a confidence that, come what may, the revolution will succeed. It is also noteworthy that lower than average ratings for the nation were given by those who mentioned individual freedom and social justice as aspirations for Cuba and by those who mentioned as fears for Cuba that it might become Communistic or be subject to internal disunity, unemployment, or an inadequate standard of living.

Summary

At the time of the survey, the spring of 1960, about fifteen months after Castro led his successful revolution, the Cuban people were overwhelmingly enthusiastic about his regime and what it promised, believing that in the near future they would be 100 percent closer to their goals than they were five years ago and feeling the nation had already jumped up 300 percent and would go up another 100 percent over ratings given it for the past. All segments of the population expressed as a major desire that tranquility be restored and the revolution be consolidated. They were fearful of a return to anything like the Batista rule which at the time seemed to be regarded as the only alternative to the stabilization of the gains made. Less than one out of ten persons in 1960 expressed any fear of Communism. There was little concern with freedom of speech, although there was a clear indication that the elite of the population were somewhat more worried about the long-range effects of Castro's dictatorship than were the very enthusiastic masses of people in the lower income and poorly educated brackets.

THE DOMINICAN REPUBLIC

Population	3,013,500
Per capita income	ca. $251
Literacy	66%
Population *outside* agriculture and services	31%
Automobiles per 1,000 persons	4

Religious composition:

Roman Catholic	98%
Protestant	1%
Other	1%

Racially, the Dominican Republic is mulatto, white, and Negro, most traces of Indian ethnic strains having been absorbed through Spanish occupation and the introduction of a sizable African Negro population. Although there is no state religion and all religions are tolerated, virtually the entire population is Roman Catholic.

Recent history of the Dominican Republic has been dominated by the regime of General Rafael L. Trujillo. Elected President of the Republic in 1930, Trujillo ruled relentlessly until his assassination on May 27, 1961. His control of the country was complete: through the army, the dominating Dominican Party, and the government-dominated labor organizations Trujillo was able to direct the entire course of national affairs. Although he stepped aside occasionally to let a friend or member of his family become President, he always held the reins himself. Political opposition to the Trujillo regime was dealt with ruthlessly.

In 1960 the Organization of American States, upon a request from Venezuela, investigated mass arrests made by the Trujillo regime. Trujillo was denounced by the OAS for plotting to assassinate President Betancourt of Venezuela and diplomatic relations between OAS members and the Dominican Republic were severed. Trujillo was assassinated in May 1961 and in January 1962 Joaquin Balaguer was elected President. Then in September 1963, the constitutional government, with Juan Bosch as President, was overthrown by a combination of military leaders and ultraconservatives.

The majority of the population are subsistence farmers. Sugar and cacao are major products. Land ownership has tended to be highly concentrated, especially under Trujillo. Trade ties with the United States have been strong, with the United States accounting for over half of the Dominican Republic's imports.

This study of the Dominican Republic gives another glimpse into the state of mind of a people who have recently gone through political turmoil. The survey was made in April of 1962, approximately one year after Trujillo's assasination by his political enemies, while the country was governed by a seven-member council striving to consolidate its new democracy.

What Dominicans Were Concerned About

Here are the personal hopes of people in the Dominican Republic as expressed by 5 percent or more of them:

Have own house	54%
Improved standard of living	36
Decent standard of living	36
Own land or farm	27
Employment	25
Concern for children	24
Congenial work	23
Health of self	16
Happy family life	13
Modern conveniences	10
Be normal, decent person	9
Own business	8
Relatives	5

The fears and worries the people expressed for themselves are:

Inadequate standard of living	53%
Unemployment	24
Deterioration in present standard of living	23
Ill health of self	20
Children	16
Ill health in family	12
Uncongenial work	9
Relatives	6
Political instability	6

The list of personal aspirations shows that all those mentioned by over 20 percent of the people deal with the complex of standard of living —employment and opportunities for one's children. The same concern is reflected in the list of personal worries and fears, with the addition of ill health as a widespread concern. People apparently felt they had gotten rid of dictatorship once and for all, only 1 percent of them mentioning "another dictatorship" among their personal fears.

When the complete list of items used to classify personal hopes is put together into general categories, the results are:

Economic	95%
Family	39
Job or work situation	25
Health	17
Personal values and character	15
Political	9
Social values	2
International situation, world	——
Status quo	——

When all fears and worries expressed by the people for themselves personally are combined into the general categories, the results are:

Economic	82%
Health	29
Family	25
Job or work situation	10
Political	9
Personal values and character	4
Social values	1
International situation, world	1
No fears or worries	——

The hopes expressed for the country are:

Political stability	58%
Improved or decent standard of living	47
Employment	42
Efficient government	26
Technological advances	20
Democratic representative government	10
Freedom	9
National unity	7
Agrarian reform	7
Sense of social and political responsibility	6
Economic stability	5

The fears expressed for the nation are:

Political instability	49%
No improvement or inadequate standard of living	26
Communism	22
Unemployment	16
No democratic or representative government	12
Inefficient government	10
War	9
Economic instability	7
Foreign aggression	5

The concerns for the nation show two rather interdependent complexes: a desire for political stability with efficient government and the widespread concern for a decent standard of living and employment. A similar pattern is reflected in fears for the nation, with the addition of a fear of communism which was at the time not a menace but which many people feared might rapidly spread in conditions so ripe for Communist appeals and leadership.

The general categories combining hopes for the nation are:

Economic	84%
Political	78

Social	14
International, peace	2
Independent status	1
Status quo	——

General categories combining fears for the nation are:

Political	74%
Economic	42
International, war	9
Independent status	8
Social	4
No fears or worries	2

How Dominicans Thought They Stood

The mean ladder ratings given by people in the Dominican Republic are:

PERSONAL RATINGS		NATIONAL RATINGS	
Past	1.6	Past	1.7
Present	1.6	Present	2.7
Future	5.8	Future	7.0

The percentage shifts on the three ratings are:

PERSONAL RATINGS		NATIONAL RATINGS	
Past to present		Past to present	
Present higher	34%	Present higher	56%
No change	40	No change	22
Present lower	24	Present lower	18
No answer	2	No answer	4
Present to future		Present to future	
Future higher	94%	Future higher	90%
No change	2	No change	3
Future lower	1	Future lower	2
No answer	3	No answer	5

The distributions of the ladder ratings dramatically illustrate the state of affairs at the time: 43 percent of the total population places itself and the nation on the bottom rung of 0 for the past and nearly three quarters of the population rates itself no higher than step 2 for the present. While the ratings given are appallingly low both for the past and the present in terms of the goals people see for themselves and the nation, there is widespread optimism about the future. (See Figures VII:3 and VII:4.)

That the people see their own fate tied to that of the country is reflected in the moderately high correlations between personal and national ratings: the past, 0.32; the present, 0.28; and the future, 0.33.

Variations Within the Population

Two facts should be borne in mind as the differences found in the population of the Dominican Republic are reviewed. First, the socio-economic class of the population was divided into only two groups, with those classified in the low socioeconomic bracket constituting 91 percent of the people. Second, the highest educational category it was feasible to use was the one bracketing people who had some secondary education and constituting only 7 percent of the population. Over three quarters of the people lived in rural areas and only 3 percent of these were not in the low income category.

As already seen, aspirations having to do with *personal economic* matters are mentioned by 95 percent of the people. This includes 88 percent of those who are the best educated and 81 percent of those who are in the upper socioeconomic bracket. It is generally the elite who are most

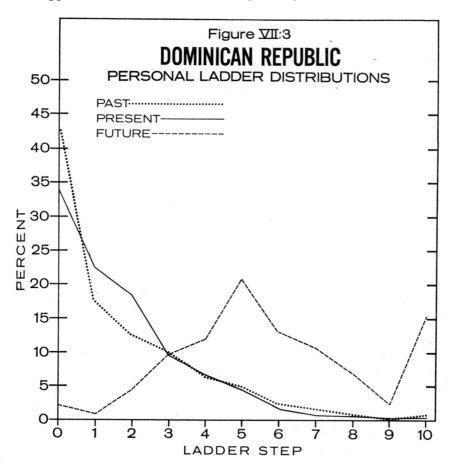

Figure VII:3

DOMINICAN REPUBLIC

PERSONAL LADDER DISTRIBUTIONS

PAST················
PRESENT————
FUTURE----------

concerned about politics and social values and who can afford to be concerned about congenial jobs, their families, and personal values.

Variations in Ladder Ratings. Higher than average personal ladder ratings for present and future are found among the better educated and the top income group. It is also the better educated and the tiny minority in the upper income groups who rate the nation higher. When the ratings for the nation are compared to the different concerns expressed for the country, it is found, significantly, that the only outstanding difference is that people who aspire to land reform rate the nation lower, both on the past and the present, but higher on the future. They thus show a significantly greater shift in the upward direction, revealing this as possibly the most important expectation to be realized after the overthrow of a corrupt and dictatorial government in agrarian society.

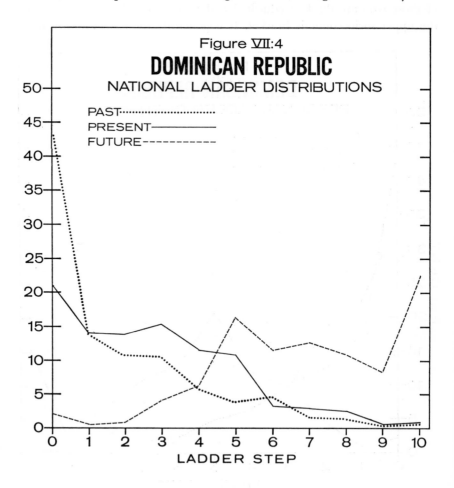

Figure VII:4
DOMINICAN REPUBLIC
NATIONAL LADDER DISTRIBUTIONS

PAST ············
PRESENT ———
FUTURE - - - - - -

LADDER STEP

Summary

In the study of the people of the Dominican Republic, we get an insight into the state of mind that breeds revolution and impels people to follow a strong leader unless the aspirations felt so intensely are rather immediately met by a more democratic government. Former President Juan Bosch has said, "My country is one of hope and hunger." But while it was shown that everyone tended to be optimistic about themselves and the country, still the concerns people express were clearly those revolving around their own distress, and it was those already at the top who were most optimistic.

PANAMA

Population	1,075,500
Per capita income	ca. $283
Life expectancy	ca. 61
Literacy	70%
Population *outside* agriculture and services	36%
Automobiles per 1,000 persons	15
Religious composition:	
predominately Roman Catholic	

Panama declared independence from Colombia in 1903 with United States recognition. On November 18, 1903, the Panamanian government granted the Canal Zone to the United States for $10 million compensation and assurances of continued Panamanian independence.

Panama is predominately an agricultural country with half of its arable land cultivated. Trade is chiefly with the United States and includes bananas, other fruits, coffee, and sugar. In recent years imports have far exceeded the value of exports. Income within the country is very unevenly distributed and the cost of living is high since the Panamanian economy is geared to that of the United States and the Canal Zone.

Panama was chosen as one of the countries for the sample since within its tiny microcosm the difficulties faced by many Latin American countries are represented: Panama is dominated by a few wealthy families who have demonstrated little inclination to use their positions to improve the lot of the people; it is dependent on the United States; it has active groups of Communists exploiting the needs of the people and directing propaganda against America; and it suffers from the lack of strong, dedicated democratic leadership. The study was done in January and March of 1962.

What Panamanians Were Concerned About

The personal aspirations of Panamanians are:

Improved standard of living	50%
Health of self	39

Concern for children	36
Own house	31
Decent standard of living	25
Congenial work	23
Employment	22
Happy family life	19
Own land	14
Be a normal, decent person	13
Own business	13
Health of family	12
Concern for relatives	9
Modern conveniences	8
Self-development or improvement	7
Emotional stability	6

Among the items mentioned by less than 5 percent are: achieve sense of personal worth, 1 percent; concern for freedom, less than 1 percent.

The personal worries and fears of the Panamanian people are:

Ill health of self	42%
Ill health in family	40
Inadequate standard of living	27
Unemployment	22
Deterioration in present standard of living	18
Children	18
Relatives	10
Unhappy family life	6
To be alone	5

Among the items mentioned by less than 5 percent of the people are: poor or uncongenial job, 3 percent; war, 2 percent; lack of freedom, 1 percent; inequality of opportunity, less than 1 percent.

Again these lists show that the complex of interests revolving around the standard of living, a good family life, good health, and having one's own house are people's primary concern in Panama.

When the personal aspirations are combined into the general categories, the results are:

Economic	90%
Family	53
Health	43
Job or work situation	26
Personal values and character	26
Social values	3
Political	1
Status quo	1
International situation, world	——

And when the personal fears and worries are combined into general categories we have:

Health	64%
Economic	57
Family	37
Personal values and character	7
Job or work situation	6
International situation, world	3
Political	1
No fears or worries	1

The aspirations people had for their country are:

Employment	36%
Technological advances	27
Housing	17
Education	15
Efficient government	15
Improved or decent standard of living	14
Economic stability	12
Agrarian reform	11
Improved system of highways and roads	6
Public health	5

New categories added here to accommodate the replies given by Panamanians are the two dealing with agrarian reform and an improved highway system. Other new categories were introduced, but fewer than 5 percent of replies fell into them. For example: concern for both law and order was mentioned by only 3 percent; the elimination of discrimination by class or income was mentioned by only 2 percent; the elimination of discrimination because of race or color was mentioned by less than 1 percent. Only 1 percent of the Panamanians expressed any concern for the population problem and only 1 percent mentioned peace as an aspiration.

The fears expressed for the nation are:

War	20%
Communism	19
Unemployment	14
Economic instability	12
Inefficient government	10
Political instability	7
No improvement or inadequate standard of living	6
Lack of law and order	6

Again the worry about continued discrimination either because of economic class or color or race was mentioned by 2 percent or less of the people; the population problem was mentioned by less than 1 percent; and lack of freedom was mentioned by only 1 percent.

It will be noticed from the list of aspirations for the country that Panamanians have relatively specific comments to make about what would improve the nation, such as agrarian reform and an improved highway system, with only 14 percent of the population mentioning the general situation involving the standard of living. And it is noteworthy that one out of every five respondents sensed the potential dangers of Communism in the situation that obtained in Panama at the time.

When national aspirations are combined into our general categories, the results are:

Economic	74%
Social	31
Political	22
International, peace	7
Independent status	3
Status quo	—

The general categories combining the fears felt for the nation are:

Political	41%
Economic	33
International, war	23
Social	15
Independent status	6
No fears or worries	2

How Panamanians Thought They Stood

The mean ladder ratings given are:

PERSONAL RATINGS		NATIONAL RATINGS	
Past	4.5	Past	5.0
Present	4.8	Present	6.0
Future	7.0	Future	7.7

The percentage shifts in the various ratings are:

PERSONAL RATINGS		NATIONAL RATINGS	
Past to present		Past to present	
Present higher	46%	Present higher	67%
No change	21	No change	8
Present lower	31	Present lower	20
No answer	2	No answer	5

PERSONAL RATINGS		NATIONAL RATINGS	
Present to future		Present to future	
Future higher	71%	Future higher	74%
No change	9	No change	9
Future lower	9	Future lower	9
No answer	11	No answer	8

The distribution of the ratings tends to scatter around the mean, bunching somewhat more with respect to the ratings given the future of the nation (see Figures VII:5 and VII:6).

It will be seen that the mean ratings assigned the nation are higher throughout than those the people give themselves, especially for the present, where a difference of over one full ladder step appears. While Panamanians are quite optimistic both about their own future and the future of the country, there is a very low order correlation between the personal and national ratings: the past, 0.21; the present, 0.18; and the future, 0.24.

Variations Within the Population

As was the case with the Dominican Republic, the representative sample of Panamanians was divided into only two economic groups, with the lower group including 71 percent of the population and with 84 percent of those living in rural areas classified in this lower group. Education was again classified so that the top educational group, constituting 25 percent of the population, included those who had only had some secondary education. Only 8 percent of people living in rural areas qualify for this top educational category, in contrast to 49 percent of the people living in urban areas.

Some of the different emphases given by various demographic groups can again be seen with reference to our general categories. The general category of involvement with *personal economic* affairs, expressed by 90 percent of the people as an aspiration, is not mentioned with significantly greater frequency by those in the low income bracket but, on the contrary, is mentioned less frequently as a worry by those who are least educated and whose comments reveal either resignation or lack of awareness that things might improve for them.

Variations in the frequency with which different concerns for the nation were expressed tend to show throughout that it is again the elite of the population, in terms of those who are better-off and better educated and those living in urban centers, who are most aware of and involved with problems besetting Panama as a nation. In addition to the concerns about inefficiency and instability in the government, the high percentage of political concerns for the nation (41 percent) reflects worries that there may be a Communist take-over in Panama—a possibility

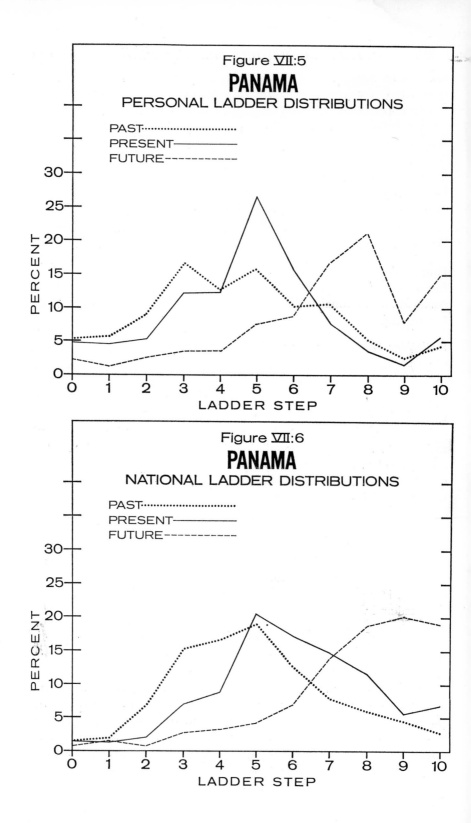

Figure VII:5

PANAMA

PERSONAL LADDER DISTRIBUTIONS

PAST·············
PRESENT————
FUTURE ----------

Figure VII:6

PANAMA

NATIONAL LADDER DISTRIBUTIONS

PAST·············
PRESENT————
FUTURE ----------

mentioned by 33 percent of the better-off people in contrast to only 14 percent of the less well-off, and mentioned also by 33 percent of the better educated in contrast to 7 percent of those with least education.

Variations in Ladder Ratings. The difference assigned in the ladder rating by the various demographic groups shows that it is also the elite— the better educated, the better-off—who tend to rate themselves higher on the ladder, but that the better educated, sensitive to the problems of Panama, give the nation a lower present rating. When it comes to the rating given the nation by the concerns expressed for the nation, a clear-cut pattern emerges: the nation is given a lower rating by those who are worried in general about "bad government," "inefficient government," "political instability," "lack of law and order," and consequently a greater-than-average fear of Communism.

Summary

While Panamanians are not nearly as desperate as people in the Dominican Republic, they still feel they have made little progress during the past few years, and they express a pattern of preoccupations for themselves and the nation that calls for strong leadership and basic reforms if their optimism about the future is to be fulfilled at all. At the same time, Panamanians have a low opinion of Communists and Communism but many are worried about it, especially the elite who are more sensitive to the problems facing the country than are the poor and uneducated masses of the population.

THE PHILIPPINES

Population		27,455,800
Per capita income	ca.	$188
Life expectancy	ca.	50
Literacy		75%
Population *outside* agriculture and services		35%
Automobiles per 1,000 persons		3
Religious composition:		
Christian (Roman Catholic)		93%
Moslem		4%
Other		3%

The Filipino people represent a variety of racial and ethnic strains more or less blended into a broad cultural group conforming to the traditions imparted by Spanish rule and United States occupation. The basic cohesive forces in this predominately rural country are the strong family and kinship loyalties. Language serves as an important identifying feature of the different racial and ethnic strains that have come together in the Filipino blend, and today there are about seventy-five different linguistic groups.

The independent, constitutional republic of the Philippines was proclaimed on July 4, 1946, following the prescription set out in an act passed by the United States Congress in 1934. The introduction of democratic government seemed to provide new opportunities for people to express kinship loyalties in political life and in turn extract what privileges they could from those holding official positions.

The Philippines are rich in resources such as gold, silver, lead, and zinc, while favorable trade relations with the United States account for three fourths of Philippine exports with copra, sugar, lumber, and canned pineapple among the principal export items.

The Filipinos experienced great suffering during World War II under three and a half years of Japanese occupation: about 1,000,000 people were killed, 85 percent of the shipping industry was destroyed as was 70 percent of the transportation network, in addition to the devastation of dwellings throughout the islands and the disruption of the entire economy of Manila.

This study of the Philippines should also be regarded as somewhat provisional since, as in Egypt, the rural areas were somewhat underrepresented in this sample for various reasons and had to be weighted to give an approximate national average. However, the study does represent conversations with five hundred Filipinos in seven different languages. In addition to English, the following languages were used: Tagalog, Ilocano, Cebuano, Ilongo, Bicol, and Waray. The survey was made in the spring of 1959, a low point in Philippine political and social life.

The Philippines were deliberately chosen for investigation at that time because, as Lloyd Free reported: "In the face of a number of other Asian countries where the forms of Western democracy had broken down in recent times, the Philippines democratic system seems to have exhibited a reasonable degree of viability. Yet difficulties are evident. While probably no more extensive than in a good many other countries, especially in Asia, graft and corruption are so rampant, so flagrant, and so systematized, with the 'squeeze' going up all the time, that the Garcia Administration (in power at the time) seems bent upon establishing something of a record for the Philippines. This country, which possesses such an enormous potential for development, is simply inching forward at the present time, if not standing still. The primary cause of this situation of stagnation would appear to be nothing more nor less than a lack of sufficiently able, sufficiently dynamic political leadership." [2] It is important to remember, then, that this survey was made before the reform administration of Macapagal came into power.

What Filipinos Were Concerned About

The aspirations Filipinos had for themselves are:

Children	37%
Decent standard of living	19
Family life	17
Have own house	17
Have own business	13
Have wealth	10
Success	9
Have modern conveniences	8
Improved standard of living	7
Recreation and leisure	6
Congenial work	5
Health for self	5

Among the aspirations expressed by less than 5 percent are: desire for self-improvement, 2 percent; health of family, 2 percent; freedom of speech, less than 1 percent.

It should be mentioned that the majority of references dealing with concern for children were in the basic context of wanting an economic situation that would permit an opportunity for their children's education. Broadly speaking, the economic aspirations of the Philippine people were modest, concerned with obtaining what they would regard as a decent minimum standard of living for themselves and their families. Outside the context of personal aspirations dealing with the family and its standard of living there were few more generalized aspirations: not a single person spoke of improvement in the standard of living of the Philippine people as a whole, and only one person out of all five hundred interviewed mentioned "good government."

The personal fears mentioned by the people are:

War	22%
Inadequate standard of living	22
Concern for children	22
Ill health of self	20
Family life	9
Ill health in family	7
Failure in job	6
Deterioration of present standard of living	6

Among the worries mentioned by fewer than 5 percent are: unemployment, 4 percent; concern for relatives, 1 percent; fear of Communism, 1 percent.

It will be noticed again that the Filipinos' complex of concerns revolves largely around an interest in the family, children, and a decent standard of living. Since the people had experienced the ravages of war, it was not surprising that 22 percent of them are fearful that war might again affect their personal aspirations. It is noteworthy that 10 percent of the total population wants wealth for its own sake and that no items dealing with a sense of personal values—other than those concerned with the family, health, recreation and leisure, or standard of living—occur among more than 5 percent of the people.

The marked preoccupation with the health of one's self and one's family was often seen in the economic context. For example, one person said, "If my health gives out, what will happen to me and my family? I have no savings." Again, apart from the reference to war and the standard of living for the family, few more generalized references appear: only one respondent mentioned "bad government" as a personal worry and none at all spoke of "no improvement in the present government."

When the personal hopes are combined into general categories, the following figures are obtained:

Economic	60%
Family	52
Job or work situation	11
Personal values and character	9
Health	6
Social values	5
Political	——
Status quo	——
International situation, world	——

The general categories for personal fears are:

Economic	38%
Family	30
Health	25
International situation, world	23
Job or work situation	7
No fears	3
Personal values and character	2
Political	1
Social values	1

The aspirations Filipinos had for their nation at the time are:

Good government	34%
Technological advances	24
Improved standard of living	17
Employment	11
Peace	10
Economic stability	8
National independence	6

Mentioned by less than 5 percent of the people were such items as: sense of social and political responsibility, 1 percent; public health, 1 percent; regional leadership, 1 percent; eliminate discrimination, less than 1 percent; control population, less than 1 percent.

The fears expressed for the nation are:

War	44%
Communism	17
Totalitarian aggression	14
Disunity	11
Bad government	11
Economic instability	7
No fears or worries	6
Inadequate standard of living for the people	5

Only 1 percent or less of the people were concerned either about social injustices, an overexpanding population, lack of law and order, lack of morality or religion among the people, or lack of national independence. The fear of Communism expressed by 17 percent of Filipinos is undoubtedly due in large part to lingering memories of the Huk rebellion, a Communist revolt right in their midst.

The most frequently mentioned aspiration for the country—"good government"—clearly reflects the inefficiency and corruption of the Garcia regime, while the fear of war mentioned by nearly half the people reflects the Filipinos' experience during World War II rather than any imminent danger.

The general categoies of hopes expressed for the nation as a whole are:

Economic	52%
Political	37
Social	13
International, peace	10
Independent status	9
Status quo	——

while the general categories of national fears are:

International, war	45%
Political	34
Independent status	17
Economic	14
Social	8
No fears or worries	6

How Filipinos Thought They Stood

The mean ladder ratings given in the spring of 1959 are:

PERSONAL RATINGS		NATIONAL RATINGS	
Past	4.9	Past	6.1
Present	4.9	Present	5.1
Future	6.7	Future	6.1

The percentage shifts on the three ratings are:

PERSONAL RATINGS		NATIONAL RATINGS	
Past to present		Past to present	
Present higher	37%	Present higher	19%
No change	30	No change	23
Present lower	33	Present lower	58
No answer	——	No answer	——
Present to future		Present to future	
Future higher	70%	Future higher	58%
No change	21	No change	20
Future lower	4	Future lower	18
No answer	5	No answer	4

While there is considerable cluster around the means, the distributions of the ladder ratings do show an appreciable number of people rating both their own and the nation's future at Steps 9 or 10 of the ladder (see Figures VII:7 and VII:8).

It will be noticed first of all that Filipinos saw no improvement in their personal lot over the past five years and felt the nation had significantly deteriorated in its position. While people foresaw a relatively bright future both for themselves and the nation, they rated themselves higher. This lower rating for the nation for the present compared to the past and the lesser shift upwards in the future for the nation clearly reflect a differentiation made by Filipinos between their own placement on the ladder and that of the nation as a whole. These trends are shown even more clearly in the percentage shifts indicated in the ladder ratings: well over half the population rated the nation lower at the time than it was five years ago and only a third rated themselves lower. It is no wonder, then, that the correlations between personal and national ratings were insignificant: for the past, 0.15; the present, 0.13; and the future, 0.09.

Variations Within the Population

Those who aspire more than average to a better *personal economic* situation are people in the lower income group, manual workers, both farm owners and farm tenants, and the less well educated, with progressively greater economic concern as educational background diminished.

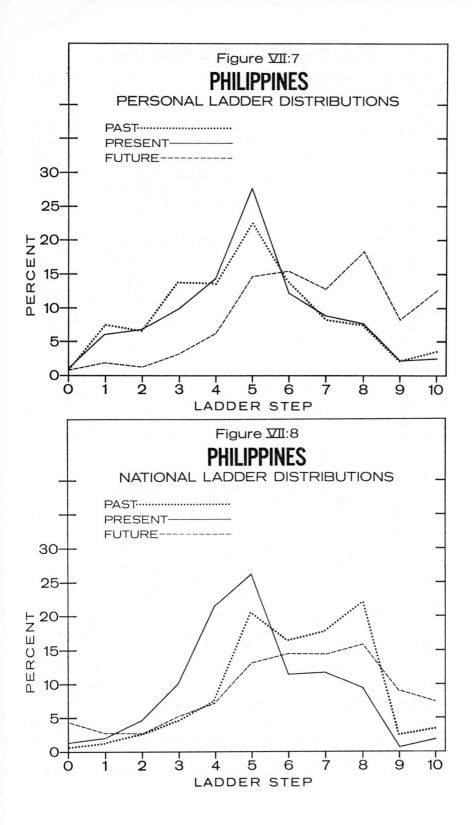

Greater concern about the *job or work situation* is expressed by the elite: the less education a person has, the lower his aspiration for congenial work.

Variations with respect to concerns for the nation by and large show that *economic, political,* and *social* aspirations and fears are mentioned more frequently than average by the better educated, the better-off, and Protestants. The higher economic concern found among the lower income and educational brackets as far as their personal lives are concerned contrasts with their relative lack of concern for economic problems facing the nation.

Variations in Ladder Ratings. Those who judge themselves better-off in terms of their placement on the ladder ratings and who can be regarded as the most optimistic are those in the upper income groups, the better educated professional and business people. When it comes to ratings assigned the nation, it is noteworthy that it is also the elite of the population who give the nation a *lower* ladder rating for the present, even though these same people give themselves personally a higher rating.

With respect to the national ladder ratings of people who expressed different concerns for the nation, the only appreciable differences are that a higher present and future rating, as well as a greater overall shift, are given by those who aspire to an improved standard of living for the nation, indicating that apparently they felt the crisis the nation was in at the time was temporary. On the other hand, those who feared economic instability and disunity for the nation assigned it a lower present and future rating, apparently revealing a lack of confidence that things would improve in the foreseeable future.

Summary

Filipinos are preoccupied with matters that are rather narrow and highly personalized in their scope; their concerns are with those aspects of living that very directly and very immediately affect them and their families.

While Filipinos are by no means satisfied with their lot, they apparently did not feel at the time of the study that they were too badly off and they were optimistic about the future both for themselves and for the nation. As indicated at the very beginning of our report on the Philippines, people on these islands are probably better off than people in any nation in Asia except Japan with respect to per capita income, lack of unemployment, natural resources, education, and other potentialities that give them modest satisfaction with the present and optimism concerning the future.

Furthermore, the Filipinos have demonstrated to themselves and the world that they have maintained political stability since gaining independence and that this stability is rather firmly rooted in a viable democratic system which has suffered no coups. Also, at the time of the study there was no threat of Communism, no widespread Communist infiltration, even though the Chinese minority did represent a potential threat if it should come under the aegis of Red China.

Part Three

CROSS-NATIONAL COMPARISONS

CHAPTER VIII

Concerns Compared

In this chapter our descriptions of the reality worlds of people in different countries is continued, comparing the results obtained across the board.

I have tried not to get lost in details: any reader interested in a specific point or a specific country will find further details in the Appendices. Many of the comparisons in this chapter are based on the general category classifications of personal and national concerns which, as already indicated, were constructed primarily for the purpose of making meaningful comparisons between people in different areas concerning the direction and the nature of their basic strivings.

THE VOLUME, RANGE, AND CONCENTRATION OF CONCERNS

1. *The volume of concerns.* In order to get some index of the total concerns of people in the different nations studied, all the concerns ex-

TABLE VIII:1

TOTAL PERCENTAGE OF ALL CONCERNS MENTIONED

Kibbutzim	1999
Israel	1484
Nigeria	1348
West Germany	1002
Yugoslavia	965
Dominican Republic	944
Cuba	917
Panama	909
Egypt	892
United States	812
Philippines	625
India I	583
Brazil	559

pressed by the people in each country were added together. These are indicated by Table VIII:1 in rank order of volume.

Table VIII:2 shows the volume of concerns, separated into personal hopes and fears and hopes and fears for the nation.

TABLE VIII:2

TOTAL PERCENTAGES OF CONCERNS BY HOPES AND FEARS

Country	Personal Hopes	Personal Fears	National Hopes	National Fears
Kibbutzim	497	397	682	423
Israel	471	281	472	260
Nigeria	421	229	419	279
West Germany	303	241	240	218
Yugoslavia	307	185	322	151
Dominican Republic	319	190	257	178
Cuba	328	205	241	143
Panama	357	220	197	135
Egypt	295	199	230	168
United States	268	207	194	143
Philippines	183	147	160	135
India I	204	132	133	114
Brazil	205	126	125	103

It will be noticed at once how very high the people in the Kibbutzim are in the total volume of their concerns and that they also exceed all other population groups studied in the extent of their concerns in each of the four categories. Kibbutzim members are particularly zealous concerning their hopes and fears for the future of Israel. Israelis rank next to the top in personal hopes and fears and in national hopes. Then follow the Nigerians, enthusiastic about the potentialities of their newly achieved independence and especially high in their hopes both for themselves and for their country. It will be noted again here how self-conscious and confident the Yugoslavs are with enthusiasm about the possibilities of reconstruction of their country. This is shown in their high national hopes which are not diluted by any appreciable proportion of fears or worries either on the personal or national side.

By contrast, the people in certain other nations are lethargic: in spite of the problems facing themselves and their nation, the Brazilians, for example, exhibit few national or personal fears; the Indian people also showed little concern, as did the Filipinos. Americans, too, are more or less satisfied and complacent, relatively high in their personal hopes but relatively low in terms of both their hopes and fears for the nation. The three Caribbean countries, together with Egypt, cluster more or less together in the lower range.

2. *The range of concerns.* In order to get some idea of the range or spread of concerns among people of different nations, the number of concerns expressed by 5 percent or more in the population were simply counted. The total range of concerns is shown in Table VIII:3.

TABLE VIII:3

INDEX OF TOTAL RANGE OF CONCERNS

Kibbutzim	108
Israel	71
Nigeria	63
Cuba	52
Egypt	52
Yugoslavia	51
United States	50
West Germany	48
Panama	43
Dominican Republic	42
Brazil	35
Philippines	34
India I	28

The range of personal hopes, personal fears, national hopes, and national fears is shown in Table VIII:4.

TABLE VIII:4

RANGE OF CONCERNS BY HOPES AND FEARS

Country	Personal Hopes	Personal Fears	National Hopes	National Fears
Kibbutzim	27	24	31	26
Israel	20	13	25	13
Nigeria	17	12	17	17
Cuba	18	13	13	8
Egypt	15	12	15	10
Yugoslavia	17	9	19	6
United States	18	11	15	6
West Germany	17	10	11	10
Panama	16	9	10	8
Dominican Republic	13	9	11	9
Brazil	13	8	8	6
Philippines	12	8	7	7
India I	8	6	6	8

Although the results shown in the tables are self-explanatory, a few points should be noted here: people in the Kibbutzim show by far the widest spectrum of interests, not only on the total but on each of the four subcategories; the Israelis show a wide spread both on personal and national hopes. The Nigerians are high throughout, revealing about the same number of national fears as national hopes. Cuba is high on both personal and national hopes but the ratio of hopes to fears on both personal and national sides is even higher among Yugoslavs. Americans are especially low on the range of their national fears. It is noteworthy that while India is low throughout, the range of national fears is somewhat greater than that of national hopes.

It will also be noticed here that the total range of concerns for the nation is higher among the people in the Kibbutzim, Israel, and Nigeria than the total range of concerns for the individual and that the same number of each are expressed in Yugoslavia. While the relationship of personal to national concerns is discussed more in detail in Chapter XI, a glimpse is provided here of the greater personal-national identification of the people in these sensitized populations.

3. *The concentration of concerns.* The concentration or clustering of concerns can be shown by dividing the total volume of concerns expressed by the number of separate concerns mentioned by 5 percent or more of the people. This clustering or concentration is shown in Table VIII:5.

TABLE VIII:5

INDEX OF CONCENTRATION OF CONCERNS

Dominican Republic	22
Nigeria	21
Panama	21
Israel	21
West Germany	21
India I	21
Yugoslavia	19
Kibbutzim	19
Philippines	18
Cuba	18
Egypt	17
United States	16
Brazil	16

It will be seen here that while there is somewhat less clustering of concerns in Israel, the Dominican Republic, and others at the top of the list than there is among Americans and Brazilians and others at the bottom of the list, the differences are relatively small.

In order to get a somewhat more precise idea of the relationship between the concentration of personal hopes and personal fears, the ratio of the total percent of personal hopes mentioned by at least 5 percent of the people was divided by the number of code items mentioned by at least 5 percent, and these were arranged in rank order of decreasing size of ratio. The same process was used to rank order the concentration of personal fears. When these rank orders are correlated, the correlation is 0.51. This is significant at the 95 percent level of confidence and indicates that the more concentrated the personal hopes in the countries studied, the more concentrated also are the personal fears in those countries. When similar rank order correlations are obtained between the clustering of national hopes and national fears, the correlation, while positive (0.28), is not significant, indicating that there is only a tendency for the concentration of national hopes to be associated with the concentration of national fears in a given country.

COMPARISONS OF CONCERNS

Personal Concerns

Since the comparisons in this section are based entirely on the general categories, it would be well to review the specific code items subsumed under each of the general categories used. Here is the total listing of items constituting the *personal* general categories:

PERSONAL VALUES AND CHARACTER
As hope
    Emotional stability and maturity
    Be a normal, decent person
    Self-development or improvement
    Acceptance by others
    Achieve sense of personal worth
    Resolution of religious, spiritual, etc., problems
    Lead disciplined life
    Miscellaneous hopes—personal values and character
As fear
    Emotional instability and immaturity
    Become antisocial; take to crime
    No self-development or improvement
    Not be accepted by others
    No sense of personal worth
    To be a person without character
    Miscellaneous worries about personal character

PERSONAL ECONOMIC SITUATION
As hope
    Improved or decent standard of living—self or family
    Own business

Own land or farm
Own house
Have modern conveniences
Have wealth
Miscellaneous—personal economic
Employment
Happy old age
Recreation, travel, leisure time
Miscellaneous—self
Social security

As fear

Deterioration/inadequate standard living—self or family
Miscellaneous—economic, personal
Unemployment
Be dependent on others
Miscellaneous—worries, self
No social security

JOB OR WORK SITUATION

As hope

Good job, congenial work
Success in work
Miscellaneous—job/work

As fear

Poor job, uncongenial work
Failure
Miscellaneous—job/work

HEALTH

As hope

Own health
Health of family

As fear

Ill health, accident, death—self
Ill health, accident, death—in family

FAMILY REFERENCES

As hope

Happy family life
Relatives
Children
Miscellaneous aspirations—family

As fear

No or unhappy family life
Relatives
Children
Miscellaneous—family

POLITICAL

As hope

    Freedom

    Miscellaneous—political

As fear

    Lack of freedom

    No improvement in present government

    Political instability

    Miscellaneous—political

SOCIAL VALUES

As hope

    Social justice

    Future generations

    Miscellaneous—social

    Be useful to others

    Miscellaneous—public service, morality in general

As fear

    Social injustice

    Future generations

    Miscellaneous—social

    Not be useful to others

    Spiritual, ethical, moral or religious disintegration

    Miscellaneous—public service

INTERNATIONAL SITUATION AND WORLD

As hope

    Peace

    Better world

    Miscellaneous—international/world

As fear

    War

    Militarism and armaments

    Threat, aggression—Communist

    Miscellaneous—international/world

MAINTAIN STATUS QUO (HOPE)

NO FEARS

Table VIII:6 shows how the volume of concerns expressed in our different categories compare when the people of all countries are pooled together. (For the reasons given in Chapter IV, Poland is not included in any of the tabulations in this chapter.)

The results are self-explanatory: concern with personal economic matters far outweighs all other concerns, with family and health next in line and with ill health as a fear expressed more frequently than good health as a hope. The reverse is true with respect to expressions of fam-

TABLE VIII:6

AVERAGE PERSONAL CONCERNS BY GENERAL CATEGORIES

Concern	Personal overall average	Average of hopes	Average of fears
Personal economic	60%	71%	48%
Family	35	46	24
Health	34	27	41
Values and character	14	20	7
Job or work situation	13	19	6
International-world situation	6	3	9
Social	5	6	4
Political	3	2	4
Maintain status quo or no fears	4	2	6

ily interests, which are almost twice as frequent on the hope side as on the fear side. Concerns with personal value and character and with the job or work situation are also found much more frequently in the hope column, whereas a deterioration of the international situation with its personal consequences is much more frequently expressed as a worry than is its opposite as a hope.

The understanding of people in each country should be improved if the concerns they have on each of these categories are compared with the concerns of people in other countries. These are indicated in tables that follow.

Personal Economic

First of all, it will be noted that where there is a high mention of economic concerns as a hope, there is also a high mention as a fear—the two tending to go together except in the case of Yugoslavia where the aspirations far outweigh the fears. Second, concern for economic matters is high among all people except members of the Kibbutzim, who have few personal economic problems in their communal life. In the Dominican Republic, which was studied while it was undergoing its tortuous period of stabilization, the fears almost equal the hopes.

With regard to some of the specific code items that enter into this general category, there was generally little mention of the desire for wealth for its own sake, being highest among the Egyptians (11 percent) and the Filipinos (10 percent). The aspiration to have a house or one's own land was also much higher than the specific fear that one would not sometime have a house or one's own land.

TABLE VIII:7

PERSONAL ECONOMIC CONCERNS

Country	Average	Hopes	Fears
Dominican Republic	89%	95%	82%
Nigeria	78	90	65
Panama	74	90	57
West Germany	68	85	51
Israel	68	80	55
India I	61	70	51
Cuba	60	73	47
Yugoslavia	58	83	33
Egypt	58	70	46
United States	56	65	46
Brazil	49	68	30
Philippines	49	60	38
Kibbutzim	37	41	33
Average	*62*	*75*	*49*

Family References

Table VIII:8 shows again that hope and anxiety are two sides of the same coin: where there is one there is also the other. Aspirations throughout are much greater than fears, with the lowest ratio of fears to hopes

TABLE VIII:8

FAMILY REFERENCES

Country	Average	Hopes	Fears
Kibbutzim	61%	74%	48%
Israel	60	76	44
Nigeria	52	76	27
Panama	45	53	37
Yugoslavia	43	60	26
Egypt	42	53	30
Philippines	41	52	30
Cuba	38	52	24
United States	36	47	25
Dominican Republic	32	39	25
India I	29	39	19
Brazil	23	28	17
West Germany	21	27	14
Average	*40*	*52*	*28*

found in Yugoslavia and Nigeria. Family references are extremely high in the Kibbutzim, in Israel, and in Nigeria, but are extremely low in West Germany and Brazil.

Health References

Table VIII:9 shows that, with the single exception of Cuba, the fear of ill health is mentioned much more frequently than the aspiration

TABLE VIII:9

HEALTH REFERENCES

Country	Average	Hopes	Fears
Nigeria	55%	45%	64%
Panama	54	43	64
Israel	53	47	58
United States	52	48	56
Yugoslavia	51	41	60
West Germany	49	46	51
Cuba	45	47	42
Brazil	38	34	42
Kibbutzim	38	24	52
Egypt	33	24	42
Dominican Republic	23	17	29
Philippines	16	6	25
India I	14	4	23
Average	*40*	*33*	*47*

for good health—especially in India, the Philippines, and the Dominican Republic. Ill health is obviously viewed as the major threat to personal and to all other development. It will also be noticed how high health is as a concern in the advanced nations of the United States, Israel, and West Germany as well as in the countries of Nigeria, Cuba, and Panama, how low good health is as an aspiration among the Filipinos; while it is lowest of all in India where health conditions are worse than in any of the other countries studied.

Personal Values and Character

Table VIII:10 shows that aspirations are much higher than worries about not achieving the desired personal values and the kind of character aspired to; less than 10 percent of all the people in eight of the countries listed express these concerns as worries. If hope is high there is a tendency for the fear of not attaining that hope to be higher. This is especially true among members of the Kibbutzim where the striving for personal values and character is more of a functional reality. The

TABLE VIII:10

REFERENCES TO PERSONAL VALUES AND CHARACTER

Country	Average	Hopes	Fears
Kibbutzim	52%	59%	45%
Egypt	31	39	23
Nigeria	30	42	17
Cuba	27	30	23
Israel	20	29	10
Panama	17	26	7
United States	12	20	3
Yugoslavia	12	18	5
Brazil	11	14	7
India I	10	14	5
Dominican Republic	10	15	4
West Germany	7	11	3
Philippines	6	9	2
Average	*19*	*25*	*12*

low emphasis on this value among Filipinos, West Germans, Brazilians, people in the Dominican Republic and India is especially noteworthy.

Job or Work Situation

As can be seen from Table VIII:11, the Kibbutzim and Israel rank high with their problems of placing so many newcomers. In Egypt there

TABLE VIII:11

REFERENCES TO JOB OR WORK SITUATION

Country	Average	Hopes	Fears
Kibbutzim	36%	51%	20%
Egypt	31	42	20
Israel	23	35	10
Dominican Republic	18	25	10
Panama	16	26	6
India I	14	22	6
Yugoslavia	11	20	2
Nigeria	11	19	2
Cuba	9	14	4
Philippines	9	11	7
United States	8	10	5
West Germany	6	10	2
Brazil	5	8	2
Average	*15*	*23*	*7*

is great concern about finding a decent job. But by and large, it is significant that the worry about not obtaining a better or steady job is relatively low in nearly all of the countries studied.

Social Values

Table VIII:12 shows that the people in the Kibbutzim stand out above all others in their concern for social responsibilities in the community.

TABLE VIII:12

REFERENCES TO SOCIAL VALUES

Country	Average	Hopes	Fears
Kibbutzim	57%	63%	51%
Nigeria	14	14	14
Israel	7	10	4
Egypt	6	9	2
India I	5	8	2
United States	4	5	3
Cuba	4	4	3
Yugoslavia	3	4	2
Philippines	3	5	1
West Germany	3	3	2
Panama	2	3	1
Dominican Republic	2	2	1
Brazil	2	1	2
Average	*9*	*10*	*7*

This concern drops to less than one out of ten persons for Israel as a whole. It will also be seen how small the spread of concern about such matters is on either side in most countries and that it is almost non-existent in Brazil, the Dominican Republic, West Germany, and Panama.

International-World Situation

As can be seen from Table VIII:13 the fear of war enters the personal reality worlds of people much more than does the hope for peace. The possibility of war, along with the possibility of bad health, are the major threats to well-being or chances for development in any direction. War as a fear, along with the devastation war brings, is especially high in the Philippines, among the Kibbutzim members, the West Germans, Israelis, and Yugoslavs, where past experience with war is a fresh memory, as well as among Americans who know that they would be the primary target of any nuclear attack. But for seven of the countries listed, only

TABLE VIII:13

REFERENCES TO INTERNATIONAL-WORLD SITUATION

Country	Average	Hopes	Fears
Kibbutzim	36%	23%	48%
West Germany	33	15	50
Israel	20	12	27
Yugoslavia	18	8	27
United States	17	10	24
Philippines	12	—	23
Cuba	4	3	5
Egypt	3	2	4
Brazil	2	1	3
Panama	2	—	3
Dominican Republic	1	—	1
Nigeria	1	—	1
India I	—	—	—
Average	*11*	*6*	*17*

5 percent or less are concerned with the international and world problems either as hopes or as fears: they apparently feel they simply do not have to bother about these problems. In India, less than 1 percent had any such concerns, even though the study was made just a few months before the Indian-Sino border incident.

Political Concerns

Table VIII:14 shows that there is no appreciable concern of the individual with political affairs except in Cuba and the Dominican Republic, which had recently gone through political crises and were concerned with political stabilization. The fears of some Germans concerning political instability and of some Nigerians concerning regional and tribal factionalism are reflected in the data. Among the specific code items included in this general political category is that concerning freedom of speech and freedom of religion, which we never found mentioned by more than 3 percent either as an aspiration or a worry. And throughout all countries there was practically no mention of any fear of a Communist threat or take-over.

Concern with Preserving Status Quo

Two points are worth noting in Table VIII:15—while the desire to preserve the status quo is found as a part of the reality worlds of some Americans, still nine out of ten Americans are not satisfied with

TABLE VIII:14

POLITICAL CONCERNS

Country	Average	Hopes	Fears
Cuba	15%	15%	15%
Dominican Republic	9	9	9
West Germany	5	1	8
Egypt	4	4	4
Kibbutzim	4	3	4
United States	4	2	5
Nigeria	3	—	5
Israel	2	2	2
Panama	2	1	2
Philippines	1	—	1
Brazil	1	—	1
India I	—	—	—
Yugoslavia	—	—	—
Average	*4*	*3*	*4*

TABLE VIII:15

CONCERN WITH PRESERVING STATUS QUO

Country	Average	Hopes	No fears
United States	12%	11%	12%
Egypt	6	—	11
India I	5	2	8
Israel	5	4	6
Cuba	5	1	9
Kibbutzim	4	6	2
Nigeria	4	—	8
West Germany	3	4	2
Yugoslavia	3	2	3
Brazil	3	1	4
Philippines	2	—	3
Panama	1	1	1
Dominican Republic	—	—	—
Average	*4*	*2*	*5*

things as they are; and about one out of every ten Cubans and Egyptians say they have no fears or worries, probably revealing their satisfaction with the post revolutionary conditions.

Tables VIII:16 and VIII:17 tell in a different way the same story heard in comparing both the volume and nature of personal concerns in each country. Again the variation in the range of people's aspirations and worries is seen as well as the accents given when replies were grouped into our general categories. While the story has by now become a familiar one, some of the highlights shown in the tables are worth repeating.

In the *Kibbutzim,* the comparatively minor emphasis on personal economic matters is notable; in *Israel,* economic affairs began to loom large, along with family interests and worry about the impact of the international situation on personal lives. *Nigerians* were even more preoccupied with their economic problems but at the same time more than average mindful of health, family, and personal values and character. However, they showed practically no personal concern for international problems. By contrast, in the two other large, "emerging" nations studied, *India* and *Brazil,* the total concerns of the people dropped appreciably: family references and personal values, even economic concerns, declined, while in India good health almost disappeared as an aspiration.

TABLE VIII:16

PERSONAL HOPES BY COUNTRY

	Personal hopes									
Country	Economic	Family	Health	Values & character	Job/work	Social	International	Political	Status quo	Total
Brazil	68%	28%	34%	14%	8%	1%	1%	—%	1%	*155%*
Cuba	73	52	47	30	14	4	3	15	1	*239*
Dominican Republic	95	39	17	15	25	2	—	9	—	*202*
Egypt	70	53	24	39	42	9	2	4	—	*243*
India I	70	39	4	14	22	8	—	—	2	*159*
Israel	80	76	47	29	35	10	12	2	4	*295*
Kibbutzim	41	74	24	59	51	63	23	3	6	*344*
Nigeria	90	76	45	42	19	14	—	—	—	*286*
Panama	90	53	43	26	26	3	—	1	1	*243*
Philippines	60	52	6	9	11	5	—	—	—	*143*
United States	65	47	48	20	10	5	10	2	11	*218*
West Germany	85	27	46	11	10	3	15	1	4	*202*
Yugoslavia	83	60	41	18	20	4	8	—	2	*236*

TABLE VIII:17

PERSONAL FEARS BY COUNTRY

Country	Economic	Health	Family	International	Values & character	Job/work	Social	No fears	Political	Total
Brazil	30%	42%	17%	3%	7%	2%	2%	4%	1%	108%
Cuba	47	42	24	5	23	4	3	9	15	172
Dominican Republic	82	29	25	1	4	10	1	—	9	161
Egypt	46	42	30	4	23	20	2	11	4	182
India I	51	23	19	—	5	6	2	8	—	114
Israel	55	58	44	27	10	10	4	6	2	216
Kibbutzim	33	52	48	48	45	20	51	2	4	303
Nigeria	65	64	27	1	17	2	14	8	5	203
Panama	57	64	37	3	7	6	1	1	2	178
Philippines	38	25	30	23	2	7	1	3	1	130
United States	46	56	25	24	3	5	3	12	5	179
West Germany	51	51	14	50	3	2	2	2	8	183
Yugoslavia	33	60	26	27	5	2	2	3	—	158

In the "rich" *United States* economic aspirations and fears were mentioned almost as frequently as they were in "poor" India. The desire for good health was expressed more frequently than anywhere else and family references remained high, with the international situation a personal worry to one out of every four Americans. Somewhat in contrast, in another "advanced" country, *West Germany,* economic matters shot up in frequency and health was high as a concern, but there was little emphasis on the family or on social values, while the threat of adverse international developments worried about half the West German people.

Individuals in the relatively new and Communist nation of *Yugoslavia* had many more personal hopes than personal fears and these centered around economic matters, health, and family. A quarter of the Yugosolavs were apprehensive about the turn international affairs might take and none expressed any personal concern about political matters.

In the *Dominican Republic,* just recovering from a political revolution which had ousted a corrupt dictator, practically everyone had some aspiration for a better deal in economic life as well as a fear that things might not improve—concern so pervasive that it tended to minimize all others. *Cubans*, too, were involved with economic, health, and family matters, but among them the stabilization of their successful revolution was a concern for about one out of seven people. *Panamanians*, like the people in the Dominican Republic, nearly all had aspirations for economic advancement, but they were not as apprehensive as their island neighbors that these would not occur. *Filipinos* had relatively restricted concerns. In *Egypt* there was a noticeable rise in the number of people interested in a decent job.

National Concerns

The specific code items combined into the general categories with reference to *national* hopes and fears were as follows:

POLITICAL
As hope
>   Honest government
>   Efficient government
>   Balanced government
>   Democratic or representative government
>   Socialistic government
>   Freedom
>   Law and order
>   National unity
>   Political stability, internal peace and order
>   Miscellaneous—political

As fear
>   Dishonest government
>   Inefficient government
>   Communism
>   No democracy or representative government
>   Fear country will become socialistic
>   Lack or loss of freedom
>   Lack of law and order
>   Disunity among people of the nation
>   Political instability, chaos, civil war
>   Miscellaneous—political

GENERAL ECONOMIC
As hope
>   Economic stability
>   Miscellaneous—economic (general)
>   Improved or decent standard of living
>   Improved standard of living through technological advances
>   Employment
>   Miscellaneous—economic (national)
>   Social security
>   Housing
>   Agrarian reform

As fear

    Economic instability

    Deterioration/inadequate standard of living

    Miscellaneous—economic (general)

    High or increased taxes

    No improvement/inadequate standard of living

    No improvement/inadequate standard of living—no technological advances

    Failure to preserve present standard of living

    Unemployment

    Miscellaneous—economic (national)

SOCIAL

As hope

    Social justice

    Eliminate discrimination—race, caste, color, religion

    Eliminate discrimination—class, economic status

    Education

    Improved labor conditions

    Control of labor

    Public health

    Limited population growth

    Sense of social and political responsibility and awareness

    Morality, ethical standards, religion, honesty, self-discipline

    Miscellaneous—social matters

As fear

    Social injustice

    Continued discrimination—race, color, religion

    Continued discrimination—class, economic status

    Inadequate educational facilities and schooling

    Poor or unfair working conditions

    Abuses by labor

    Unlimited population growth

    No sense of social and political responsibility or awareness

    Lack of morality, ethical standards, honesty, religion, self-discipline

    Mechanization, standardization, materialism, conformity

    Miscellaneous—social matters

INTERNATIONAL, PEACE

As hope

    Peace

    Disarmament

    Lessening of cold war

    Better relations with Communist bloc

    Friendly relations with all countries

    Better world

    Maintain neutrality

    Help other nations

    Increased foreign trade or exports

    Miscellaneous—international relations

As fear
> War
> Continued armament
> No lessening of cold war
> Be isolated from other nations
> Inability to maintain neutrality
> Miscellaneous—international relations

INDEPENDENT STATUS
As hope
> Be militarily strong
> Be world power
> Enhancement of status and importance
> Be important in regional affairs
> Exert moral or ideological leadership
> National independence
> Miscellaneous—importance of nation
As fear
> Not to be world power
> Lose or have no status or importance
> Fail to exert ideological or moral leadership
> Lack or loss of national independence
> Threat, aggression—Communist power
> Threat, aggression—any foreign power
> Miscellaneous—status of nation

MAINTAIN STATUS QUO (HOPE)
NO FEARS

Table VIII:18 shows the overall, across-the-board frequency with which comments referred to the different headings in our general categories.

TABLE VIII:18

AVERAGE OF NATIONAL CONCERNS BY GENERAL CATEGORIES

Concern	Average of hopes and fears	Average of hopes	Average of fears
General economic	48%	66%	30%
Political	34	31	36
International, war-peace	23	18	27
Social	21	28	14
Independent status	14	12	15
Keep status quo or no fears	3	1	4

Again, as with the individual concerns, references to economic affairs lead the list when the average of the total sample is computed. But apprehensions about unstable political situations are more frequently mentioned than are worries about economic matters. Improvement in social conditions and responsibilities is found twice as frequently in the hope column as in the column for fears, while it is clear that only a very tiny fraction of people want their nation to stay as it is. The variations of these concerns among the different people studied should again give further insight into the different reality worlds of national groups.

Economic Concerns

It will be seen from Table VIII:19 that aspirations are higher than fears throughout the list and that this is especially true among Yugoslavs,

TABLE VIII:19

ECONOMIC CONCERNS FOR NATION

Country	Average	Hopes	Fears
Kibbutzim	67%	83%	50%
Dominican Republic	63	84	42
Nigeria	62	81	43
Israel	62	79	44
West Germany	57	69	44
Panama	54	74	33
Cuba	50	75	24
India I	47	70	24
Yugoslavia	47	81	12
Brazil	46	58	34
Egypt	44	58	29
United States	37	45	29
Philippines	33	52	14
Average	*51*	*70*	*32*

who are apparently more sanguine than any other people about economic development. The great emphasis that people in the Dominican Republic give to economic problems again reflects the desperate situation they were in at the time of our study. The high frequency with which members of the Kibbutzim mention economic development is in sharp contrast to the low emphasis that they give economic matters in their personal lives—their emphasis is on the welfare of the state with all sharing equally in advances made. It will also be noticed that Americans are lower than any other people in the frequency with which they mention aspirations relating to economic advances.

Political Concerns

Table VIII:20 shows that people in the Dominican Republic easily top the list of both hopes and fears, having just ousted a dictator and

TABLE VIII:20

POLITICAL CONCERNS FOR NATION

Country	Average	Hopes	Fears
Dominican Republic	76%	78%	74%
Nigeria	60	50	69
Kibbutzim	56	62	49
Cuba	39	18	59
West Germany	38	49	27
Philippines	36	37	34
Yugoslavia	33	47	19
Panama	32	22	41
Israel	29	35	23
Egypt	26	26	26
Brazil	20	16	24
United States	18	13	23
India I	15	9	20
Average	*37*	*36*	*38*

desperately hoping for and anxious about a stable, future democratic government. The worry of Cubans that their revolution might fail is again clearly reflected, as is the apprehension of Nigerians about the consequences of regional and tribal factionalism that so stand in the way of the achievement of national unity. Political fears are also high among members of the Kibbutzim who are trying to preserve their own way of life in a larger macrocosm. Political worries are lower among Yugoslavs than among all other people: comments reflect the sense of relief that centuries of antagonism between different nationalities are now over and that they all live in a united country. It will be noticed that both in the United States and in India anxieties about political matters are greater than aspirations. The comments show that in both countries there is a confidence in the political system but while in India there is frequent mention of a fear that another form of government may replace their socialism, in the United States the fear reflected from comments is that American private enterprise may be gradually eroded by socialism.

International Situation, War-Peace

The wide range in differences found in Table VIII:21 is, of course, due either to the effect of past experience or, as among Americans, with

TABLE VIII:21

REFERENCES TO INTERNATIONAL SITUATION, WAR-PEACE

Country	Average	Hopes	Fears
Kibbutzim	91%	94%	87%
Israel	71	69	72
United States	58	59	57
West Germany	56	42	70
Yugoslavia	55	31	79
Egypt	32	29	35
Philippines	28	10	45
Panama	15	7	23
India I	14	3	25
Nigeria	12	12	11
Brazil	12	5	19
Cuba	9	7	10
Dominican Republic	6	2	9
Average	*35*	*28*	*42*

a threat of being a target for nuclear attack. Among nearly all people the threat of deteriorating international relations is more of a self-conscious fear than a positive hope for improved international relations. The ratio of fears to aspirations is much higher in Germany, Yugoslavia, and the Philippines, all of whom, of course, remember the devastation of World War II.

When people who express a fear of war either as a personal or a national fear are separated out from the general category of "international, war-peace," the extent to which war haunts people in different nations is more clearly revealed (see Table VIII:22).

Except for the United States, the six countries that lead the list have recently experienced war on their own territory. The six peoples who mention war-peace less frequently have not experienced the full impact of modern war and apparently feel a future conflict would not be a particular threat to them. It is especially noteworthy that in India not even one out of every twenty-five people expresses any fear of war, in spite of the difficulties India had already had both with China and Pakistan.

In reviewing the specific code items one finds almost no mention of the techniques or mechanisms proposed to avoid war or to maintain peace: "disarmament," for example, is never mentioned by more than 3 percent of the people in any country, "foreign trade," "regional integrations," and the like are usually even less frequently mentioned. This lack of concern on the part of the public regarding means for achieving desired goals will be discussed in later chapters.

TABLE VIII:22

SPECIFIC REFERENCES TO FEAR OF WAR,
PERSONAL PLUS NATIONAL

Country	Total fear
West Germany	113%
Yugoslavia	103
Kibbutzim	80
United States	72
Philippines	66
Israel	56
Egypt	26
Panama	22
Brazil	21
Nigeria	11
Dominican Republic	9
Cuba	4
India I	3

Social Values

The outstanding position of the Kibbutzim members is by now a familiar story. Table VIII:23 shows the much greater frequency with which hopes for social improvement are expressed than fears that such

TABLE VIII:23

REFERENCES TO SOCIAL VALUES

Country	Average	Hopes	Fears
Kibbutzim	77%	89%	65%
Nigeria	52	66	37
Israel	50	70	30
Egypt	28	36	19
United States	27	33	21
Panama	23	31	15
India I	17	19	14
Yugoslavia	17	31	2
West Germany	16	16	15
Cuba	15	21	8
Brazil	14	19	8
Philippines	11	13	8
Dominican Republic	9	14	4
Average	27	35	19

improvements will not be made; this is especially true in Yugoslavia, Cuba, and Brazil. It is also noteworthy that there is such a sizable difference in social concerns among the people of the two most advanced nations on the list, the United States and West Germany, with very few West Germans concerned about such matters.

Independent Status

It is not surprising to find that the three peoples who head the list in Table VIII:24 are the Egyptians, members of the Kibbutzim, and

TABLE VIII:24

REFERENCES TO INDEPENDENT STATUS

Country	Average	Hopes	Fears
Egypt	41%	44%	37%
Kibbutzim	38	46	30
Israel	27	37	16
Nigeria	16	24	7
West Germany	15	11	19
Philippines	13	9	17
Cuba	12	13	11
India I	9	9	8
United States	8	4	11
Yugoslavia	6	6	5
Panama	5	3	6
Dominican Republic	5	1	8
Brazil	4	4	3
Average	*15*	*16*	*14*

the Israelis. In addition to feeling that Israel is a threat to their sovereignty, Egyptians are highly aware of the recent Anglo-French invasion of their territory which was called off by the United Nations with the strong support of the United States. West Germans and Filipinos are also more anxious than most about the independence of their country, the former worried about its exposed position, the latter remembering long Japanese occupation of their relatively remote island home. The self-conscious aspiration of Nigerians for the future of their newly independent land is also reflected in the comparison.

Maintenance of Status Quo

Table VIII:25 makes it clear that people in all countries want to move ahead. Only in Cuba did any sizable proportion of people have no fears and worries for the country at the time our study was made.

TABLE VIII:25

MAINTENANCE OF STATUS QUO FOR NATION

Country	Average	Hopes	No fears
Cuba	8%	2%	14%
United States	6	7	4
Israel	4	1	6
India I	4	—	7
Yugoslavia	3	—	6
Philippines	3	—	6
Egypt	3	1	4
Nigeria	2	—	4
West Germany	2	2	1
Brazil	2	1	2
Panama	1	—	2
Dominican Republic	1	—	2
Kibbutzim	1	1	—
Average	*3*	*1*	*4*

Tables VIII:26 and VIII:27 give us at a glance an idea of both the range and nature of national concerns. Only some of the highlights of the results already reported more in detail are mentioned here.

Among members of the *Kibbutzim,* references to the social problems facing their country, as well as to international problems and the preservation of the nation's independent status, were higher than in any other population group. *Israelis* were also very high on these categories. *Egyptians* were even more worried about their independent status than were the people of Israel.

Both *Americans* and *West Germans* were characterized by their fear of deteriorating international relationships that might lead to war, a concern also shared by most *Yugoslavs,* who expressed fewer worries than any other group studied that they would not achieve their economic goals.

Again it is seen that while *Nigerians* expressed a concern for the economic, political, and social stabilization and development of their country, even these matters were comparatively infrequently mentioned by people in the two other large underdeveloped nations studied, *Brazil* and *India,* the latter being particularly unperturbed about the country's economic plight. The corrupt and unstable political situation that obtained in the *Philippines* at the time of our study is again reflected in the Filipinos' relatively high concern for political matters. The apprehension of *Cubans* and people in the *Dominican Republic* that their revolutions may not prove successful is also apparent once more.

TABLE VIII:26

NATIONAL HOPES BY COUNTRY

Country	Economic	Political	Social	International	Independent status	Status quo	Total
Brazil	58%	16%	19%	5%	4%	1%	*103%*
Cuba	75	18	21	7	13	2	*136*
Dominican Republic	84	78	14	2	1	—	*179*
Egypt	58	26	36	29	44	1	*194*
India I	70	9	19	3	9	—	*110*
Israel	79	35	70	69	37	1	*291*
Kibbutzim	83	62	89	94	46	1	*375*
Nigeria	81	50	66	12	24	—	*233*
Panama	74	22	31	7	3	—	*137*
Philippines	52	37	13	10	9	—	*121*
United States	45	13	33	59	4	7	*161*
West Germany	69	49	16	42	11	2	*189*
Yugoslavia	81	47	31	31	6	—	*196*

Summary

1. There are wide variations in the total *volume* of concerns expressed by people in different nations, reflecting the degree to which a people are self-consciously striving either to protect gains made or to improve their present situation. At one extreme are people like those in the Kibbutzim, Israel, Nigeria, West Germany, and Yugoslavia, who appear involved and enthusiastic, while at the other extreme are people like the Brazilians and Indians, who appear apathetic or who, like the Americans, are relatively complacent.

2. Considerable differences were found in the *range* of issues, problems, potentialities, and threats of concern to people in different countries. Members of the Kibbutzim, Israelis, and Nigerians showed the widest spectrum of interests and Filipinos, Indians, and Brazilians the narrowest spectrum.

3. The *concentration* or *focus* of concerns also varies between the people of different nations, with least focus in the Dominican Republic, the country which was most troubled at the time of our study.

TABLE VIII:27

NATIONAL FEARS BY COUNTRY

Country	International	Political	Economic	Social	Independent status	No fears	Total
				National Fears			
Brazil	19%	24%	34%	8%	3%	2%	90%
Cuba	10	59	24	8	11	14	126
Dominican Republic	9	74	42	4	8	2	139
Egypt	35	26	29	19	37	4	150
India I	25	20	24	14	8	7	98
Israel	72	23	44	30	16	6	191
Kibbutzim	87	49	50	65	30	—	281
Nigeria	11	69	43	37	7	4	171
Panama	23	41	33	15	6	2	120
Philippines	45	34	14	8	17	6	124
United States	57	23	29	21	11	4	145
West Germany	70	27	44	15	19	1	176
Yugoslavia	79	19	12	2	5	6	123

4. The comparison of *personal concerns* expressed by people in different countries shows that hopes are mentioned more frequently than fears except on the topics of health and the international situation, where the reverse is true. By and large, hopes and fears go together—where one is high the other is also, the most notable exception being the case of people in Yugoslavia who exhibit few worries that their economic position will not improve.

Personal economic references were low among Kibbutzim members; family references low among Brazilians and West Germans; health references lowest of all in India; references to personal and social values outstandingly high in the Kibbutzim and low in West Germany, the Philippines, Brazil, and the Dominican Republic; the implications of the possibility of war high or low depending on a people's experience with modern war or their sense of its threat to them. Only in Cuba and the Dominican Republic did any appreciable minority of people mention problems of a political nature as being of any personal concern to them.

5. As for *concerns for the nation,* aspirations for improved economic positions lead the list by far with relatively few people apparently feeling some advances would not be made. When people looked at the political situations in their countries, their anxieties slightly outweighed their hopes, especially in Cuba. Wide variations were found in the number of people in various countries mentioning the international situation—ranging from 71 percent in Israel to 6 percent in the Dominican Republic. While over half of all respondents in Nigeria expressed a concern for social values, less than one out of ten did so in the Dominican Republic. The independent status for the nation was mentioned most frequently by Egyptians, Israelis, Nigerians, and West Germans.

CHAPTER IX

Ratings Compared

This chapter continues the overall comparisons of results obtained in all the countries studied. The comparisons here are of the various ratings given on the ladder and of the ratings and concerns expressed to indices of each nation's socioeconomic development.

COMPARISON OF RATINGS

Ratings are compared here in step-by-step fashion: beginning with the present, then seeing where these came from in terms of past ratings, then where people think they and their countries are headed and what the overall shifts are. This should add to the insights given in the earlier chapters where the standing of people in each country was reviewed separately. After listing what has been found, some generalizations can be drawn from the facts.

Present Ratings

Table IX:1 shows the mean personal and national ratings given by rank order of mean personal ratings.

Here it will be seen again how high the people in the Kibbutzim rate themselves on the personal ladder and also how relatively high Americans and Cubans are. The low personal and national ratings of Indians and citizens of the Dominican Republic also stand out. The low mean rating the Polish people give themselves clearly reflects their feeling of being hemmed in by circumstances beyond their control.

It is only among the people in the Kibbutzim where the personal ladder ratings are significantly higher than the mean ladder rating given the nation, whereas the mean national rating is significantly higher than the mean personal rating in the majority of the nations studied: in Yugoslavia, Nigeria, Panama, the Dominican Republic, West Germany, India, Cuba, Brazil and Egypt. Among three peoples—those in the United

TABLE IX:1

MEAN PRESENT RATINGS *

Country	Personal	National
Kibbutzim	7.0	5.3
United States	6.6	6.7
Cuba	6.4	7.0
Egypt	5.5	5.9
Israel	5.3	5.5
West Germany	5.3	6.2
Japan	5.2	5.3
Yugoslavia	5.0	6.8
Philippines	4.9	5.1
Panama	4.8	6.0
Nigeria	4.8	6.2
Brazil	4.6	5.1
Poland	4.4	— †
India I	3.7	4.9
Dominican Republic	1.6	2.7
Average	*5.0*	*5.6*

* As indicated previously, a difference of 0.2 in ladder ratings is significant at the .05 level.

† It will be remembered that the questions concerning national aspirations could not be asked in Poland.

States, Israel, and the Philippines—the mean personal and national ratings show no significant difference. The rank order correlation of the personal and national ratings is 0.55, significant at the .05 level.

Shifts in Ladder Ratings from Past to Present

Table IX:2 compares the mean personal and national ratings both on the past and the present.

The extent of the shift from the past to the present—where people thought they had come *from* five years ago—is shown in Table IX:3.

People in all countries except the Philippines and the Dominican Republic felt they had gone up the ladder of life during the past five years. All except the Filipinos felt the nation had gone up, although the shift assigned the nation upward by the Brazilians is statistically insignificant and the advance given Americans for the United States is small. The rank order correlation between the shifts in personal and national ratings is 0.71, significant at the .01 level.

People in the majority of the countries surveyed felt that the upward

TABLE IX:2

MEAN PAST AND PRESENT RATINGS

Country	Personal		National	
	Past	Present	Past	Present
Kibbutzim	6.3	7.0	4.5	5.3
United States	5.9	6.6	6.5	6.7
Cuba	4.1	6.4	2.2	7.0
Egypt	4.6	5.5	3.5	5.9
Israel	4.7	5.3	4.0	5.5
West Germany	4.1	5.3	4.1	6.2
Japan	4.6	5.2	4.2	5.3
Yugoslavia	4.3	5.0	4.9	6.8
Philippines	4.9	4.9	6.1	5.1
Panama	4.5	4.8	5.0	6.0
Nigeria	2.8	4.8	4.0	6.2
Brazil	4.1	4.6	4.9	5.1
Poland	4.0	4.4	—	—
India I	3.4	3.7	3.5	4.9
Dominican Republic	1.6	1.6	1.7	2.7
Average	*4.3*	*5.0*	*4.2*	*5.6*

TABLE IX:3

SHIFTS IN MEAN LADDER RATINGS FROM PAST TO PRESENT

Personal		National	
Cuba	2.3	Cuba	4.8
Nigeria	2.0	Egypt	2.4
West Germany	1.2	Nigeria	2.2
Egypt	0.9	West Germany	2.1
United States	0.7	Yugoslavia	1.9
Yugoslavia	0.7	Israel	1.5
Kibbutzim	0.7	India I	1.4
Israel	0.6	Japan	1.1
Brazil	0.5	Panama	1.0
Japan	0.6	Dominican Republic	1.0
Poland	0.4	Poland	—
India I	0.3	Kibbutzim	0.8
Panama	0.3	United States	0.2
Philippines	0.0	Brazil	0.2
Dominican Republic	0.0	Philippines	— 1.0
Average	*0.8*	*Average*	*1.4*

trend for their nation was greater than the upward trend for themselves from the past to the present. The shift in national ratings was higher than the shift in personal by the following amounts:

Cuba	2.5
Egypt	1.5
Yugoslavia	1.2
India I	1.1
Dominican Republic	1.0
Israel	0.9
West Germany	0.9
Panama	0.7
Japan	0.5
Nigeria	0.2

Only in three countries was there a greater trend up on the personal ratings than on the ratings given the nation from the past to the present. The shift in personal ratings was higher than the shift in national ratings by the following amounts in:

Philippines	1.0
United States	0.5
Brazil	0.3

There was no significant difference in the shift from past to present among members of the Kibbutzim.

Comparison of Present and Future Ratings

Table IX:4 shows the mean present and future ratings on both the personal and national ladders.

The extent of the shifts between the mean present and the mean future ratings is shown in Table IX:5.

It will be apparent at a glance that people everywhere expect both their own future and the future of the nation to improve during the next five years. The rank order correlation between the shifts in the personal and national ratings here is 0.66, significant at the .01 level.

In the following countries, the shift in the mean rating from present to future on the personal side is higher than the shift for the nation:

Egypt	0.9
Philippines	0.8
Nigeria	0.6
United States	0.5
Panama	0.5
Brazil	0.2
Cuba	0.2

TABLE IX:4

MEAN PRESENT AND FUTURE RATINGS

Country	Personal		National	
	Present	Future	Present	Future
Kibbutzim	7.0	7.9	5.3	6.5
United States	6.6	7.8	6.7	7.4
Cuba	6.4	8.4	7.0	8.8
Egypt	5.5	8.0	5.9	7.5
Israel	5.3	6.9	5.5	7.5
West Germany	5.3	6.2	6.2	—
Japan	5.2	6.2	5.3	6.4
Yugoslavia	5.0	6.7	6.8	8.6
Philippines	4.9	6.7	5.1	6.1
Panama	4.8	7.0	6.0	7.7
Nigeria	4.8	7.4	6.2	8.2
Brazil	4.6	7.3	5.1	7.6
Poland	4.4	5.5	—	—
India I	3.7	5.1	4.9	6.7
Dominican Republic	1.6	5.8	2.7	7.0
Average	*5.0*	*6.9*	*5.6*	*7.4*

TABLE IX:5

SHIFTS IN MEAN RATINGS FROM PRESENT TO FUTURE

Personal		National	
Dominican Republic	4.2	Dominican Republic	4.3
Nigeria	2.6	Brazil	2.5
Brazil	2.7	Nigeria	2.0
Egypt	2.5	Israel	2.0
Panama	2.2	Cuba	1.8
Cuba	2.0	Yugoslavia	1.8
Philippines	1.8	India I	1.8
Yugoslavia	1.7	Panama	1.7
Israel	1.6	Egypt	1.6
India I	1.4	Kibbutzim	1.2
United States	1.2	Japan	1.1
Poland	1.1	Poland	—
Japan	1.0	Philippines	1.0
Kibbutzim	0.9	United States	0.7
West Germany	0.9	West Germany	—
Average	*1.9*	*Average*	*1.8*

The shift in mean rating from present to future for the nation is higher among the following three peoples:

Israel	0.4
India	0.4
Kibbutzim	0.3

No significant differences between personal and national shift in mean rating are found in Japan, Yugoslavia, or the Dominican Republic.

Overall Shift from Past to Future

Table IX:6 shows the differences between the mean past and future ratings people gave both themselves and their countries. The rank order correlation here is 0.85.

TABLE IX:6

OVERALL SHIFT IN MEAN RATINGS FROM PAST TO FUTURE

Personal		National	
Nigeria	4.6	Cuba	6.6
Cuba	4.3	Dominican Republic	5.3
Dominican Republic	4.2	Nigeria	4.2
Egypt	3.4	Egypt	4.0
Brazil	3.2	Yugoslavia	3.7
Panama	2.5	Israel	3.5
Yugoslavia	2.4	India I	3.2
Israel	2.2	Panama	2.7
West Germany	2.1	West Germany	—
United States	1.9	Brazil	2.7
Philippines	1.8	Japan	2.2
India I	1.7	Kibbutzim	2.0
Kibbutzim	1.6	United States	0.9
Japan	1.6	Philippines	0.0
Poland	1.5	Poland	—
Average	2.6	*Average*	3.2

The low mean shift from the past through the present into the future among Poles again reflects the sense of personal frustration of a people who must carry on in a social and political context that is not of their own choosing.

The shift in these mean ratings from the past through the present to the future is higher for the nation than for the self by the following amounts in:

Cuba	2.3
India	1.5

Yugoslavia	1.3
Israel	1.3
Dominican Republic	1.1
Japan	0.6
Egypt	0.6
Kibbutzim	0.4
Panama	0.2

The shift from past to future was higher on the personal ratings than on those assigned to nation by the following amounts in:

Philippines	1.8
United States	1.0
Brazil	0.7

There was no significant difference between the personal and national shift upward for Nigerians who, as already seen, were very high in both instances.

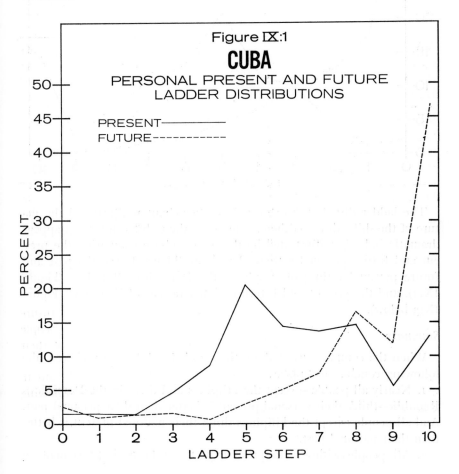

Figure IX:1
CUBA
PERSONAL PRESENT AND FUTURE LADDER DISTRIBUTIONS
PRESENT————
FUTURE----------

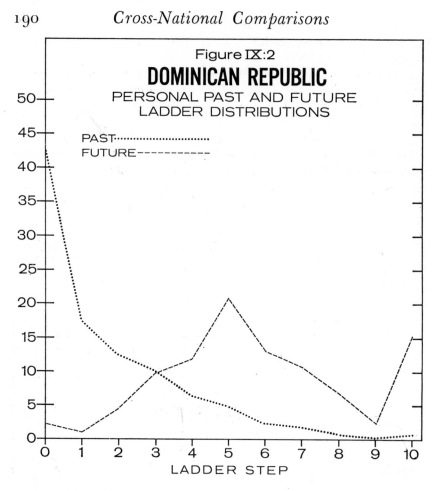

Figure IX:2
DOMINICAN REPUBLIC
PERSONAL PAST AND FUTURE LADDER DISTRIBUTIONS

PAST·················
FUTURE----------

LADDER STEP

The ladder distributions shown in earlier chapters illustrated the nature of the shifts discussed here. Sometimes these shifts in ratings appear dramatic indeed as illustrated by the figures above comparing the present and future personal ratings of Cubans (Figure IX:1), the past and future personal ratings of people in the Dominican Republic (Figure IX:2), and the present and future national ratings of Yugoslavs (Figure IX:3 below).

Summary

When the comparisons of the ratings and the shifts are reviewed, the following conclusions appear.

1. Nearly all people—except the Filipinos and those in the Dominican Republic—think their personal present is better than their personal past. And all people except the Filipinos think their national present is better than their national past.

2. All people without exception expect significant improvement in

the future both for themselves and for their nations. Hope here seems universal.

3. Most people tend to rate the nation higher than they rate themselves. The single consistent exception is the members of the Kibbutzim, who place themselves significantly higher than their country on the past, the present, and the future.

4. The greatest shifts upward from the past to the present on the personal ladder occurred in Cuba and Nigeria—recently independent nations. And where the personal present rating is higher or about the same as the present national rating, the highest personal ratings were also given for the past—in the Kibbutzim, the United States, Israel, the Philippines, and Japan.

The smallest shift upward from the past to the present on the personal ratings occurred in the Dominican Republic, the Philippines, Panama, India, and Poland. It was in these countries that people sensed least personal progress had been made during the past five years with Filipinos, and with those in the Dominican Republic feeling no progress had been experienced in their own lives.

5. The greatest shift up from past to present on the national ladder ratings was found among people whose nations had in one way or an-

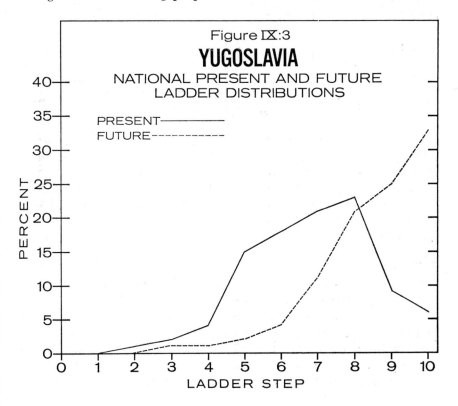

other recently experienced a rebirth—in Cuba where the shift upward was by far the highest, in Egypt, in Nigeria, in West Germany, and in Yugoslavia. The only exception to the noticeable shift up among people who had recently undergone political change was found in the Dominican Republic where at the time of our survey people were still in a postrevolutionary turmoil and state of instability.

The lowest shifts upward from past to present were found in Brazil and the United States where the trends upward are hardly significant and, of course, among the Filipinos who felt their nation had gone down a whole step on the ladder during the past five years. A high correlation of 0.71 significant at the .01 level was found between the rank order of the shifts in the past to present personal and national ratings.

6. The greatest shifts upward from present to future on the personal ratings, where hope was apparently highest, were found among the people in the Dominican Republic, Nigeria, and Brazil.

The smallest shifts in the upward direction from the present to the future on personal ratings were found, except for Poland, in countries where the personal rating for the present was already significantly high— in West Germany, the Kibbutzim, Japan, and the United States. The rank order correlation between the personal past to present shift and the personal present to future shift was negative, −0.24.

7. As far as the national ratings are concerned in the comparison of the present to the future, here again people in the Dominican Republic appear outstandingly hopeful for their country, followed by people in Brazil, Nigeria, and Israel, who also held more than average optimism for the nation.

While all people expect their nation to progress in the next five years, least relative progress was foreseen by Americans who rated their country high for the present and seemed to feel that it would continue a steady growth.

The upward shifts on the personal and national ratings from the present to the future tend to go together, with a high correlation of 0.66 between the rank order of personal shifts and national shifts from the present to the future. However, the rank order correlation between the shifts in the national past to present ratings and the present to future ratings was low (0.27), revealing that people apparently do not feel that what happened in the past is a good basis upon which to predict what will happen in the future with respect to their countries.

8. The greatest overall shifts in the national ratings were found in countries that had been more or less recently established or have become recently independent—especially Cuba, the Dominican Republic, Nigeria, Egypt, Yugoslavia, and Israel. The ratings in Cuba, the Dominican Republic, and Egypt reflect the exuberance brought about by revolu-

tionary change which has been long overdue; the shift in the ratings for Israel reflects the enthusiasm for the creation of the new state, whereas the ratings in Nigeria show the enthusiasm with which people greeted national independence within the British Commonwealth.

9. The overall shift in personal ladder ratings from past to the future tend to be higher than average in these same countries—especially in Cuba, the Dominican Republic, and Nigeria. The correlation between the rank orders of overall shifts in personal and national ratings is extremely high, 0.85, while again there is an insignificant correlation between the present personal standing and the overall shift in personal ratings (0.28).

10. One might forecast trouble ahead among a people like the Brazilians when there is great personal and national expectation deriving from a past that shows very little sense of improvement *unless* some drastic reforms occur that will confirm expectations and give some feedback that can be directly experienced.

It is also important to point out that especially among people who feel they have made great progress in realizing personal or national goals, whose sense of progress makes them optimistic about their future, who feel they are finally on their way to a better life, if future events do not confirm their expectations, if the anticipated consequences of their action do not result in satisfying experiences, then disillusionment will inevitably set in, bringing with it a desire for other changes. *If* we had found a people who had little hope for the future, who foresaw little or no improvement, then we would expect despair to set in with trouble ahead. But none of the nations studied fit this pattern.

Obviously it would be most valuable—both in terms of understanding and in terms of policy—if repeat studies could be made in such places as Cuba, the Dominican Republic, Nigeria, and Egypt to see what expectations did and did not seem to have been met, what the resulting consequences were on the reality worlds of the citizens, and which citizens in the different educational and occupational brackets were affected.

LADDER RATINGS AND SOCIOECONOMIC INDICES

Curiosity naturally arises as to how the ratings people give themselves and their nations on the ladder are related to the indices used by economists to measure the stage of development people are in. Since no single index is alone reliable as a measure of development, the practice is to combine various indices into one. The index used here employed the following indicators.[1]

General Welfare
    1. GNP per capita in U.S. dollars in 1961
    2. Number of doctors per 10,000 persons, circa 1958

Communications

 3. Number of vehicles per 1,000 persons, circa 1958

 4. Number of telephones per 1,000 persons, circa 1959

 5. Number of radios per 1,000 persons, circa 1959

 6. Newspaper circulation per 1,000 persons, circa 1959

Industrialization

 7. Energy consumption per capita, circa 1959 (Kg. of coal equivalent)

 8. Percent of the economically active population in the nonagricultural sectors (includes those employed outside of services)

Urbanization

 9. Percent of the population in cities over 100,000, circa 1959

Education

 10. Percent of the population literate, circa 1957

 11. Primary school enrollment ratio

The countries were ranked for each of the eleven indicators, and their relative standings were then converted to a 1.0 to 0.00 scale. The indicators within *each* of the five sectors were then combined (for example, the four indicators of "Communications" were combined into one) and put on a 1.0 to 0.00 scale. Finally, the five sections were combined and represented on the 1.00 to 0.00 scale.

The socioeconomic index thus obtained was:

United States	1.00
West Germany	.71
Israel	.67
Japan	.60
Poland	.45
Cuba	.35
Panama	.31
Yugoslavia	.19
Philippines	.17
Dominican Republic	.16
Brazil	.16
Egypt	.14
Nigeria	.02
India	.00

The rank order correlations with the ladder ratings are:

NATIONAL		PERSONAL	
present	.47*	present	.67†
past	.39	past	.56*
future	.15	future	.11

* Indicates significance at the .05 level.

† Indicates significance at the .01 level.

As would be expected, the correlation of the present personal rating with the socioeconomic indices is highest of all—in other words, an individual's personal experience now. Next in order is the person's estimate of his own ladder rating in the past and then a significantly high correlation between the present rating of the nation and its socioeconomic index. When it comes to the future, both for the individual and the nation, any clear-cut relationships break down.

The relationship between the ratings people gave themselves for the present and the socioeconomic index for their nation is shown in Figure IX:4.

1. People in the four most highly developed countries give themselves low present ratings *relative to* their favorable position as measured by objective indices.

2. People in all the less-developed countries, except the Dominican Republic, give themselves high present ratings *relative to* their unfavorable position as measured by objective indices.

The relationship of the index to the ratings people gave themselves for the future is shown in Figure IX:5.

1. The ratings people assign themselves for the future in all the less-developed countries are dramatically high *relative to* their present unfavorable positions as measured by objective indices.

2. The ratings people in the two most highly developed countries (United States and West Germany) assign themselves for the future are low *relative to* their very favorable positions, while the ratings given by people in the two other highly developed nations (Israel and Japan) are modest.

The relationship between the ratings people gave their nation at the present time and the socioeconomic index for the nation is shown in Figure IX:6.

1. People in the most advanced nations (United States, West Germany, Japan, and Israel) subjectively rate their nation *relatively low* in terms of what they regard as an ideal country.

2. People in all of the less-developed nations subjectively rate their nation *relatively high* in terms of what they perceive as an ideal state.

3. Except for the Dominican Republic, people who give their nation the relatively highest rating in comparison to "objective" indices are those where there has been either (a) the more or less recent establishment of a new independent state (i.e., Yugoslavia, Nigeria, India) or (b) a recent revolution that has brought major political change (i.e., Cuba, Egypt).

4. The present low level of morale in the Dominican Republic (personal rating of 1.6) represents a nation where the vast majority of people have suffered under a dictatorial regime so recently overthrown that

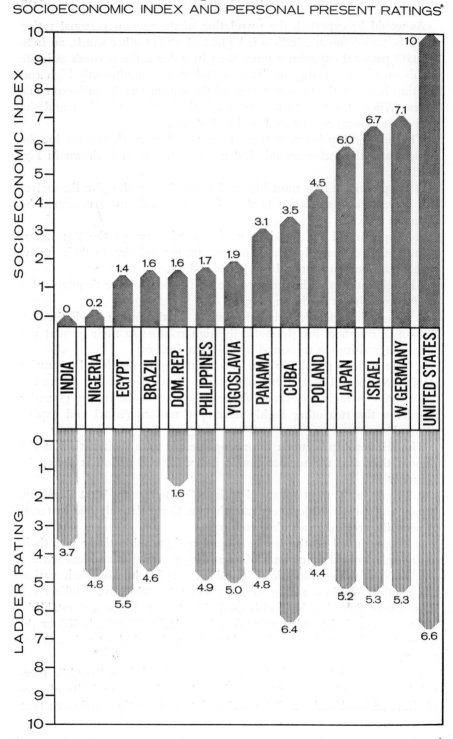

Figure IX:4
SOCIOECONOMIC INDEX AND PERSONAL PRESENT RATINGS*

*In order to facilitate easy comparison between the two sets of figures, Socioeconomic Index figures have been multiplied by 10 to create a 1-10 scale.

Figure IX:5
SOCIOECONOMIC INDEX AND PERSONAL FUTURE RATINGS*

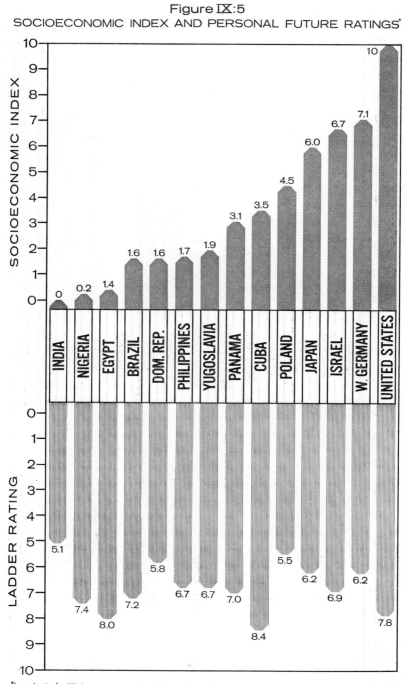

*In order to facilitate easy comparison between the two sets of figures, Socioeconomic Index figures have been multiplied by 10 to create a 1-10 scale.

Figure IX:6
SOCIOECONOMIC INDEX AND NATIONAL PRESENT RATINGS*

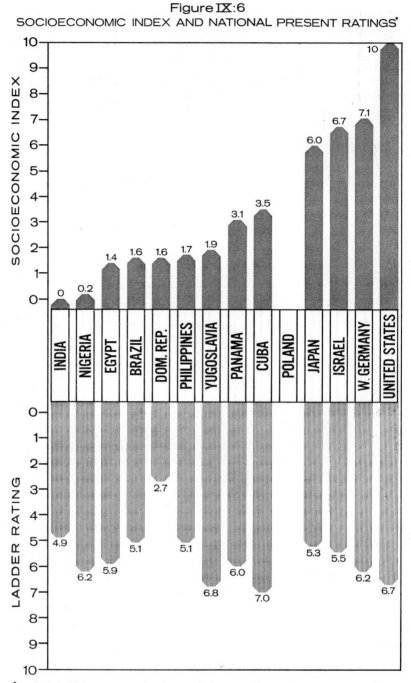

*In order to facilitate easy comparison between the two sets of figures, Socioeconomic Index figures have been multiplied by 10 to create a 1-10 scale.

the change expected (future national rating is 7.0) has not had time to be confirmed.

5. The remaining countries not mentioned above (i.e., Brazil, Panama, and the Philippines) represent nations where most people do not have the sense of desperation from their "objective" conditions and where there is no overriding national goal or unity to provide a focus of hope.

Figure IX:7 illustrates the relationship between the socioeconomic index and the rating given the nation for the future.

1. Again, as with the national present rating, people in the most advanced nations rate the future of their country relatively low in terms of what they regard as an ideal country. (It will be remembered that because of a misunderstanding no future rating for the nation was obtained in West Germany.)

2. And again, as with the rating given the nation for the present, but this time including the Dominican Republic, people in all of the less-developed nations subjectively rate their nations relatively high—and quite high—in terms of what they regard as an ideal state. All foresee a bright future.

The relationship between the socioeconomic indices and the amount of overall change from past to the future on both the personal and national ladder ratings generally shows, not surprisingly, a much greater subjective change in countries with the lower indices. The rank order correlation between socioeconomic indices and overall shift in personal ratings is -0.46 (significant at the 95 percent level), and the correlation with the overall shift in national ratings is -0.41, which nearly reaches the same level of significance: the lower the socioeconomic index, the greater the tendency for a larger shift in overall ratings.

In order to get some idea of the relationship between the developmental index and the total volume of concerns expressed by people in the different countries as reported in the last chapter, countries were rank ordered by their total concerns and this was correlated with their ranking on the socioeconomic index. A positive correlation, then, would indicate that the higher the socioeconomic index, the more likely are people in a country to have a greater volume of concerns. The correlations below show that the relationship between the socioeconomic index and the volume of hopes, both personal and national, is positive but modest while the relationship with the volume of fears, both personal and national, is significant (at .05 level).

Socioeconomic index with

Personal hopes	0.24
Personal fears	0.46
National hopes	0.25
National fears	0.51

Figure IX:7
SOCIOECONOMIC INDEX AND NATIONAL FUTURE RATINGS*†

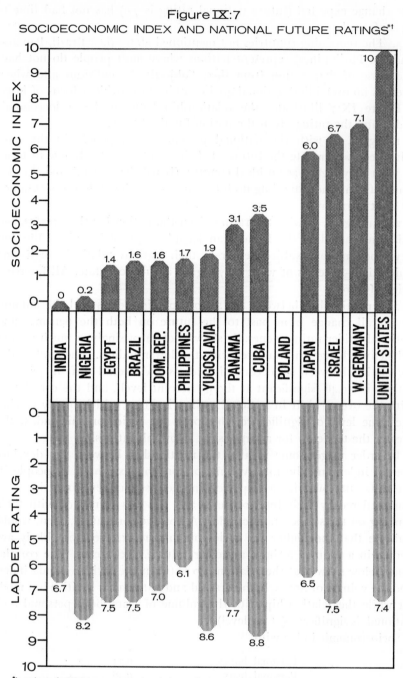

*In order to facilitate easy comparison between the two sets of figures, Socioeconomic Index figures have been multiplied by 10 to create a 1-10 scale.

†Note that no rating was obtained for German future.

The question arises as to what, if any, relationship exists between the developmental index of a country and the concerns expressed by the people in that country for matters that would presumably be most closely related to national development—economic and social concerns. Table IX:7 brings together the volume of items expressed in the general economic categories on both the personal and national questions and the total percentage of comments in our general category of "social" concerns relative to national problems.

TABLE IX:7

SOCIOECONOMIC INDEX AND ECONOMIC AND SOCIAL CONCERNS

| Country | Index | Economic Concerns | | Social Concerns |
		Personal	National	National
United States	1.0	111%	74%*	54%
West Germany	.71	136	113	31
Israel	.67	145	123*	100
Cuba	.35	120	99	29
Panama	.31	147	107	46
Yugoslavia	.19	116	93*	33
Philippines	.17	98	66†	21
Dominican Republic	.16	177	126†	18
Brazil	.16	98	92	27
Egypt	.14	116	87	55
Nigeria	.02	155	124	103
India I	.00	121	95	39

* In these countries, economic concern was exceeded by the general category of international, war-peace.

† In these countries, economic concern was exceeded by political concerns.

It will be seen here that there is by no means a clear-cut relationship between concern for economic matters, either at the personal or national levels, and the objective indices of a country's socioeconomic status. The rank order correlation between the index and personal economic concerns was 0.01, with national economic concerns, −0.05; and with national social concerns, −0.01—all indicating a complete lack of any relationship. With the general social category, a positive relationship is helped by the highest social concern in poor Nigeria and the low social concern in rich West Germany, but is upset by the low concern in poor India, Brazil, and the Dominican Republic, and relatively high social concern in rich United States and Israel.

Summary

The relationships between the stage of a people's development, as measured by objective indices and their subjective ratings of their own or their nation's standing in terms of the ideals they set for themselves, reveals the extent to which these subjective ratings are determined by the psychological context, the frame of reference within which such ratings are made. The standards of judgment upon which the ratings are based are rooted in the reality worlds that in turn derive from an individual's own background and experience.

People in highly developed nations have obviously acquired a wide range of aspirations, sophisticated and expensive from the point of view of people in less-developed areas, who have not yet learned all that is potentially available to people in more advanced societies and whose aspirations concerning the social and material aspects of life are modest indeed by comparison. This will be seen more clearly in the next chapter where the concerns of people in "rich" and "poor" nations are contrasted. People must learn what to want as they must learn everything else. And obviously they must also learn how to satisfy these wants, a process that is often discouragingly slow, painful, and disappointing in terms of the visions ahead.

CHAPTER X

Rich Countries, Poor Countries

While the reality worlds of people who live in countries which differ widely in economic development have already been described, the gap between the quality of experience and the pattern of hope of "rich" people and "poor" people can be brought into bolder relief by more direct comparisons of the two groups.

The psychological problem involved is essentially that of discovering the experiential, subjective consequences that low and high standards of living produce; the relationship of the "reality" of the state of society as measured by "objective" indices to the "vision" of what the society both is and ought to be, held by the people who compose it. By pooling and contrasting the averages and overall data obtained from the studies of different people in different nations, we can discern some of the effects that socioeconomic development or the lack of it have on people's concerns and on their estimates of where they stand on the ladder of life with respect to their ideal.

It has become clear by now that when, for example, one person rates himself as being at step 8 on the ladder at the present time he is using a completely different frame of reference in making his rating than is another person who also rates himself at step 8 whether he lives in the same or a different culture.

The last chapter showed how subjective the ladder ratings were for people both with respect to themselves and their countries. Nevertheless, if the ratings given by people in the three countries sampled which have the highest socioeconomic index are separated and compared to the ratings given by people in three of the poorest countries in our sample, as indicated by Table X:1, people in rich countries are found to rate themselves significantly higher on the present, the past, and the future and to rate their nations higher on the past and the present, but not on the future. However, when the shifts in the ratings are examined, it turns out that the shift upward is significantly higher among people in

TABLE X:1

Comparison of Ladder Ratings and Shifts in Ratings
Among People in 3 Poor Countries and
People in 3 Rich Countries

Country	Economic index	Personal				National			
		Past	Present	Future	Shift	Past	Present	Future	Shift
RICH									
United States	1.0	5.9	6.6	7.8	1.9	6.5	6.7	7.4	0.9
West Germany	.71	4.1	5.3	6.2	2.1	4.1	6.2	——	——
Israel	.67	4.7	5.3	6.9	2.2	4.0	5.5	7.5	3.5
Average		*4.9*	*5.7*	*7.0*	*2.1*	*4.9*	*6.1*	*7.5*	*2.2*
POOR									
Brazil	.16	4.1	4.6	7.3	3.2	4.9	5.1	7.6	2.7
Nigeria	.02	2.8	4.8	7.4	4.6	4.0	6.2	8.2	4.2
India	.00	3.4	3.7	5.1	1.7	3.5	4.9	6.7	3.2
Average		*3.4*	*4.4*	*6.6*	*3.2*	*4.2*	*5.4*	*7.5*	*3.3*
Differences in averages		*1.5*	*1.3*	*0.4*	*−1.1*	*0.7*	*0.7*	*0.0*	*−1.1*

poorer nations both on the personal ratings and the ratings assigned the nation.

As shown in Chapter VIII, the total volume of concerns people expressed had no clear-cut relationship to the socioeconomic index of their country. Similarly, the range of concerns seemed to show no high correlation with the stage of a nation's development. For example, while among Indians and Brazilians both the volume and range of concerns expressed were found to be low; in Nigeria, on the other hand, both the volume and range of concerns were high. Furthermore, there seemed to be no significant difference between the volume of hope expressed and the volume of fears expressed between the people in the three rich countries and the three poor countries.

THE MEANING OF "A DECENT STANDARD OF LIVING"

At the time of the Constitutional Convention of the American colonies, James Madison wrote "The man who is possessed of wealth, who lolls on his sofa or rolls in his carriage, cannot judge of the wants or feelings of the day laborer. The government we mean to erect is intended to last for ages." [1] Webster's International Dictionary defines "standard of living" as "a minimum of necessities, comforts, or luxuries which is accepted or, regarded as essential to maintaining a person, class, or race, in his or its customary or proper circumstances." Obviously, what one person perceives as "customary" or "proper" will be enormously different from what another person considers customary or proper, whether they live in the same country or not.

In order to demonstrate what the phrase "decent standard of living" actually refers to among the people of different countries and in order to help us "judge of the wants or feelings" of people in different societies from our own, excerpts have been taken from the comments of people in all countries except Poland. The comments cited below were some of those classified under our code item as the aspiration for an "improved or decent standard of living for self or family; sufficient money to live better or to live decently; freedom from debt; make ends meet; relief from poverty; not suffer want, hunger, etc." The illustrations are meant to be representative and are not selected merely because some of them are dramatic. A few more quotes are listed from people in countries with which the reader is perhaps somewhat less familiar, so that he can get the flavor and feeling of a people's ongoing, naïve, unanalyzed, and completely subjective definition of what he or she means by a "decent standard of living."

India—Socioeconomic index, 0.00

My main wish is that my land produce enough so that I may be able to repay my debts as I have to pay a great deal of money to money-lenders now. I should some day like enough money to educate my children. (A sixty-year-old Hindu of moderate education)

I should like above all to know that I could live a life without the possibility of starvation. I should also like to get some education and then get a job as soon as possible. (twenty-two-year-old man who is a Harijan earning 60 rupees, about $12 a month)

I would like to construct a well and set up an electric pump on my land. I also need enough manure to get the maximum yield from the land. (thirty-eight-year-old owner-cultivator now earning about $35 a month)

The main thing I wish for is to have some money at my disposal so I could marry off my daughter. I also need to have better produce from my land so I can repay the money-lender. If I get these wishes then my life will be very comfortable. (fifty-year-old illiterate, owner-cultivator, earning about $20 a month)

I should like to have a water tap and a water supply in my house. It would also be nice to have electricity. My husband's wages must be increased if our children are to get an education and our daughter is to be married. (forty-five-year-old housewife, family income about $80 a month)

I want a son and a piece of land since I am now working on land owned by other people. I would like to construct a house of my own and have a cow for milk and ghee. I would also like to buy some better clothing for my wife. If I could do this then I would be happy. (thirty-five-year-old man, illiterate, agricultural laborer, income about $10 a month)

I wish for an increase in my wages because with my meager salary I cannot afford to buy decent food for my family. If the food and clothing problems were solved, then I would feel at home and be satisfied. Also if my wife were able to work the two of us could then feed the family and I am sure would have a happy life and our worries would be over. (thirty-year-old sweeper, monthly income around $13)

I would like to be able to build a house so I would not have to live with my parents. I would also like to purchase a cow. I have a wife but I would like to have one more. (thirty-year-old unskilled worker earning $35 a month)

I hope in the future I will not get any disease. Now I am coughing. I also hope I can purchase a bicycle. I hope my children will study well and that I can provide them with an education. I also would sometime like to own a fan and maybe a radio. (forty-year-old skilled worker earning $30 a month)

I am a sweeper working in a municipal corporation. At present I am not given any money for overtime. And I do not get any woolen clothes in the winter. Other Harijans working in Bombay and Delhi get woolen garments. If I could get woolen garments and a little more money, then I would be contented. (twenty-seven-year-old illiterate, monthly income $18)

I wish my son could be employed in a factory on a regular basis. Then my old age would be saved from rotting and he could support the family in my absence. I hope the government will start some cottage industry in our village so that we can earn a living. (sixty-year-old laborer earning about $18 a month)

I should like to save enough money to marry off my daughters. I wish I had some land to cultivate so that I could have some regular income and save money to buy the necessities of life and get the burden of my daughters off of my shoulders. (sixty-two-year-old shoemaker, monthly income around $20)

I wish that I could get a grant from the government so that I could buy a number of buffaloes and start a milk route in the nearest city. Then if

I could make a profit I might open up a shop for my son and I would be very happy. (sixty-seven-year-old farmer, monthly income $25)

I wish my son could be employed in some factory with regular pay so that we could all live and eat better. Then I could marry him also. I wish him to marry into a nice family, but he cannot marry a good family girl if he is unemployed. (thirty-five-year-old housewife)

I wish I could be given a small loan by the government to start my own small scale cottage industry. I would then buy raw material and hire a few people from my village to make baskets and sell them in the market at reasonable prices so that I could have better food to eat and could support my family. (twenty-nine-year-old basketmaker)

I wish that I had some money so that I could repair my house so that we could at least have a roof over us. As it is now, I am not safe from strong winds and rains. (sixty-year-old midwife, monthly income around $15)

The government once gave us some land but we have had no money to cultivate the land. We have no bullocks. I would like at least two bullocks. I also need money to dig a well. A well is necessary for me. The government should take an interest in repairing and constructing a water tank for our village. (sixty-year-old owner-cultivator, income $20 a month)

Nigeria—Socioeconomic index, 0.02

I would have enough money to educate my children and have an apartment of our own to live in (forty-three-year-old illiterate man)

I wish we had a decent house to live in and that I could train my children to be drivers, carpenters, or ministers of religion. (seventy-two-year-old illiterate agricultural worker)

I wish we could have a house of our own. Also I would like my children to be educated so their standards would be higher than ours have been. It would be nice to see my children prosper during my lifetime. (forty-year-old housewife living in the city)

Any man without money is as useless as a dustbin. I am badly off financially despite my responsibility as head of a large family with my parents and various relatives as well as my children depending on me. All I want is to earn a little more money. (twenty-five-year-old worker)

I am struggling to amass enough money for the maintenance of my dependents. That is my main concern and if I knew that they could be cared for I would be content. (thirty-year-old farmer)

I want to work hard and save enough money to establish some sort of trade that I can carry on. Also sometime I would like a house of our own in the township. (thirty-year-old agricultural worker)

All I want is enough food to eat and some clothes to wear. I would then be happy. (fifty-eight-year-old agricultural worker)

I am in dire poverty. I just have no means of subsistence. (twenty-eight-year-old man living in rural area)

At the present time, I am badly worried because I do not have any financial standing at all when I compare myself to my fellow men. I must somehow earn money if I am going to marry for at my age I am supposed to have been married and have children. (thirty-six-year-old city worker)

My main worry about the future is how I will get enough money to train my children to some skilled trade. (sixty-four-year-old urban worker)

I want more money so I can sometime have a house of my own to live in and better dishes of food. (seventy-six-year-old man living in the city)

My immediate relations depend on me but I cannot give them the financial assistance they need. Also I do not have enough money to maintain my own family or train my children. (thirty-five-year-old worker)

Egypt—Socioeconomic index, 0.14

I want to be a happy peasant living far from other people's problems. I would also like to bring my sons home who now work as servants in Cairo and Suez and I would like to have enough money to be able to feed them. (forty-five-year-old tenant farmer)

My main wishes are to have enough food to eat and enough decent water to drink. (forty-year-old agricultural worker)

I should like to live in contentment but I cannot do this as long as I am so much in debt. I see that I must struggle until I am dead in order to provide for my children. (sixty-four-year-old city barber)

I would like to graduate from a college and then find a respectable job so I could accumulate enough money to open a store. (twenty-one-year-old student)

I want to marry a rich and educated man who will give me a high standard of living. (twenty-two-year-old student)

I would like just enough money to know that we could continue living as we are. Then I will also encourage my sons to get an education and tell them all the mistakes I have made in the past and how to avoid them in their own future. (thirty-seven-year-old skilled rural worker)

I want to have enough money to take care of my family decently. I hope my children will have an easy life without troubles and will be able to finish their education. I want my family to be able to live without the need of help from anyone else after my death. (forty-year-old government officer)

I would like to have better health so that I can get rid of the diseases I now have. I also would like to have a better room than the miserable one I live in and to have better clothes for myself and my two daughters. I ask God to improve my social situation. (forty-four-year-old woman)

I want to own some land and acquire some domesticated animals and have equipment enough to take care of the land. I would also like to acquire a new wife. (thirty-five-year-old agricultural worker)

I would like to live in a house instead of this one room. I would like to be able to buy two kilos of meat instead of only half a kilo and to buy a whole box of cigarettes instead of buying only one or two cigarettes every now and then. (fifty-year-old unskilled worker)

I would like to have more sons to help me in my farming. I also hope I will stay healthy and sometime be able to buy a cow. I would also sometime like to have electricity. (twenty-five-year-old agricultural worker)

I wish we had electricity here and that I could sometime have a refrigerator and a radio. I also want my children to go to school so that they will not be as ignorant as I am. (thirty-eight-year-old villager)

I want enough money to buy clothes, sheep, and goats and to improve my land. I would like more money for my children to enable them to seed their land properly. (forty-eight-year-old agricultural worker)

I wish my husband owned more land. If we could have five feddans instead of two we would be well off. I also wish we had three cows instead of the one we now own. I also wish I could have a radio. I also wish my four daughters could be married and that one of my sons could become an engineer. (thirty-two-year-old woman)

I am extremely poor and do not have enough money to provide even the essentials. I badly need some new clothes and I would like a better room than this miserable one I live in. I would also like to get rid of the diseases I have so often. (forty-five-year-old woman living in the city)

I would like to build a room to live in instead of having to live with my brother-in-law. I have let my oldest son go to work on the farm with his father so the youngest son could go to the nearest school. I need clothes for all my children. (forty-year-old village woman)

I would like to own a piece of land to work for my own and have a sheep, also a cow to help me at my work with the land. I would like to have a clean house with two rooms and a separate place for the animals so they would not have to live with us. (forty-year-old woman)

I wish we had more land and two more cows. I also wish we had something that would get rid of the pests which now destroy our crops. (twenty-five-year-old farmer)

I would like to earn more money every day since I now have six children but the case is hopeless for the time being. I would also like to be able to rent land and work on it with my children and have some cows and buffaloes. (forty-five-year-old woman)

I would like my husband to be free from debts and my children to finish school and get jobs in an office. I wish we had electricity and water in the house instead of having to pump it all the time. I also wish we had two or even three cows. (thirty-two-year-old woman)

I would like a small amount of land with a small house built on it. I wish I could always have a cup of tea and cigarettes when I wanted them. I hope that my children can finish their studies and that one of them can be a doctor. (forty-year-old agricultural worker)

I dream of being a landowner and not having to work for anybody. I want to own a cow to help me in the field and to supply me with milk. I want my old parents to be able to rest now and not have to work all day long. I want to own a house of two rooms. (twenty-eight-year-old agricultural worker)

I want to own two or three acres instead of renting them. I also want to buy another buffalo so I will have two. I would like to buy a gold necklace and earrings for my wife and I wish my children could have a university education. (fifty-three-year-old tenant farmer)

Brazil—Socioeconomic index, 0.16

If my husband only had a better job we could live better. Now we have very hard times and are hardly able to buy food. (married woman living in the city)

I work one day and spend all I earn the next day. If I die, my family will be helpless. Somehow I must be more secure. (forty-year-old married man who is a soldier)

I hope my husband and son can keep their jobs. They have sometimes been unemployed and we have suffered from hunger and thirst. It was bad. (housewife living in the city)

I want to improve my standard of living by being able to work with cattle. Then everything would be better. Some day I might even be able to buy a truck. (fifty-year-old merchant living in small town)

I wish I had many things because I have many children and I don't own anything. What I would like would be a sewing machine, some clothes, a cow to give milk to the children. I work and when I am sick I am hardly able to buy food. (forty-year-old housewife living in a small town)

I would be content if I had a small farm with my own house. Then I could grow crops. I think that would be enough for me. (forty-year-old married man who is merchant in a village)

All I want is that my children should never be short of a dish of food and that they will not starve if I get sick. (forty-year-old housewife living in village)

I would like to own a big industry and provide jobs to many workers. I would like to have a job of importance and own a house. I would like to be able to sell my bicycle shop and make a great deal of money from that. (thirty-year-old married man living in city)

I would like to fix up my house and get my furniture repaired so it would be pretty. I would like to make a million in a lottery so my dreams would come true and I could buy a car for my husband. (thirty-eight-year-old married woman who is a seamstress)

I want to make my house better and also improve my land. When I die I hope to leave my children trained to some occupation they will choose. But it will take money to accomplish this. (thirty-year-old married man, a barber)

I ask God for help and peace at home. If poor people have health they still have everything. I wish that I could earn enough money so I wouldn't have to worry about the next day because life is so hard now. I would like to be a civil servant. We poor people fight and fight and seem to have less each day because prices are higher every day. (fifty-year-old married man who is a mason)

I hope to be able to educate my children. My son must go to grade school and I am afraid there will be no place for him in public schools and my husband is not able to pay for a private school. (married woman living in city)

Above all I want a good job. The government should look after us be-cause living in the country today is no joke. The cost of living is too high —especially for people like me and it gets higher all the time. I have six children and earn only a little. I have some corn and a few pigs but that's all I have. If I need material of any kind I don't have money to buy it. (thirty-eight-year-old agricultural worker)

I would like to have a sewing machine but I have no money to buy it. (twenty-eight-year-old women who is an agricultural worker)

I would like to buy some cattle for milk. I want to own a piece of land to grow grass for the cows and sell the milk to Nestle. (married man who is government official living in small village)

I hope the prices of cloth and food will go down. These are the things we need most. I wish my husband had a good job. He is now a brick-layer and a carpenter but finds no job and has to work in agriculture. (thirty-five-year-old married woman living in village)

I hope the person who owns the sewing machine I use will not take it away from me. For then I would be helpless. With this machine I maintain myself and my daughter. (thirty-year-old married woman who is a seamstress)

I don't want to be rich. I want only to be able to have lunch and dinner and not become too tired. I would like to have work which is not real hard. (twenty-seven-year-old agricultural worker)

I want an ox to plow the land. I would like to own a little piece of land and not have to live on other people's land giving them money. (twenty-five-year-old married man, agricultural worker)

I work a whole year on the land for other men and at the end of the year they can't pay me and are not satisfied. I work the whole year long and they get all the money I earn. With what I earn for a day I can buy only a kilo of flour. It would take over three days of my wages to buy a kilo of meat. There is no point in this. The poor just can't get along. (twenty-five-year-old married man, agricultural worker)

Dominican Republic—Socioeconomic index, 0.16

Since I am so poor, I need a house and some money as I am suffering terrible hunger. There are days when we don't even eat at all for lack of ways of getting money. (fifty-seven-year-old farmer)

I should like to have enough food for my children. If I have this, I would feel happy with my life. (twenty-two-year-old housewife)

I would like to raise my children so they will be equipped to cope with the future and will become something in life. I requested the government to have this house given to me to live in because I am a victim of Tru-jillo's tyranny which took my husband's life for political reasons. I should like my children to be able to get ahead and the government grant me a pension because my husband was assassinated under Trujillo. (forty-three-year-old woman who works in domestic employment)

To be happy in the future I want only one thing: to be able to give my children a good education. But I now lack economic resources for this. (twenty-three-year-old woman who is domestic servant)

My main desires are to have a place to work where I can produce money to take care of my children's needs. With this I would feel very happy. I would also like to legalize the deeds for a little house I have built without permission from the government just as other people in this area have done. (twenty-three-year-old housewife)

My greatest wish is that there would be industries in our country in which I could work and produce money for my family, if possible in my native town. I would hope that I could get a job in these industries and earn money and not let my family go hungry so much. I would like to have enough money to put up a little house on this empty lot which is located in front of this little hut where I am now living in such crowded and poor conditions. (sixty-year-old day laborer)

I should like a house for my family to live in because the one where I am now living does not have the necessary sanitary facilities and I do not own it. I have a hope that I might get some money to make my life better and less wretched than the one I am leading at present. To feel happy, I should also like to have a radio to listen to the news and to lots of music. (seventy-year-old housewife)

My problem is that I haven't been able to pay what is owing on my house because my husband has no work and we are afraid we will lose what we have invested in it and they will take our house away and we shall have no place to go with our children. (forty-eight-year-old housewife)

If I don't get some economic help soon I don't know what I shall do because these children of mine are going to fall dead with hunger. We are eating very badly now and if things keep going this way hunger may do us in. I would like to be able to educate my children. (twenty-five-year-old woman living on small pension)

I would be happy if we had a hut of our own. But now neither my husband or I have good work. I haven't worked for several years and my mother's plot of land was taken away from her by the Trujillo administration and she was almost killed. I am worried because I can't raise my children decently. (thirty-seven-year-old housewife)

I want above all else to get out of my present state of wretchedness. As you can see yourself, I am living in a tiny room without water or light and we have a hard time finding enough to eat. In fact we don't eat every day. It would make me happy to know that my son did not have to bear this misery. (thirty-year-old mason)

I am head of a family with eight children. I have no work and cannot support them. I am afraid my children might get sick and I might have to buy medicine for them and I would not have the money to do this. In the hospitals they give people only a little dirty water. I am afraid of always being out of work, of having no home and of living in misery. (thirty-five-year-old carpenter)

The Philippines—Socioeconomic index, 0.17

I want to have a steady job so I can support my family without worrying about where to get money the next day. (thirty-eight-year-old man who manages a restaurant)

I want to have plenty of money so I can buy plenty of clothes and shoes and also eat good food and be able sometime to travel to America. (thirty-year-old woman who is an unskilled worker)

I would like to be able to help my family more and provide for their daily needs, giving them money, shelter, and food. I also wish I could give my children the best education, even a college education if that were possible. (fifty-six-year-old farm tenant)

My dream is that every year there will be a good harvest so among us farmers we won't be so hard up for money. (fifty-one-year-old farm owner)

I would like to have some economic security for that is the only way I can get any peace of mind. I should like a job that was steady enough so that I will not have to keep begging from my children who are all married. (fifty-five-year-old skilled worker)

I would like to have a little business of my own so my life would be light and easy. I would like to buy some real estate, some jewelry, and maybe a house of my own. (twenty-eight-year-old unskilled worker, female)

I would like to have money so that I could send my children to school. I would also buy them some nourishing food so we would all become healthy. (thirty-five-year-old professional woman unemployed)

I wish to have money enough to provide for my grandmother and myself sufficiently. I hope to have this old house remodeled into a more modern one. I would like to invest some money in a small farm so that we do not have to worry for our food in case I don't work. (twenty-five-year-old unskilled worker)

What I want is to have a greater yield from our farms and our woven products so that we will not be too hard up in our living. (thirty-three-year-old married woman)

I wish I could improve my farm like the farms I see in the American movies, complete with electric power and a water system. (married man, small farmer)

I am already an old man. I have been poor all my life. I am a widower. All my children are married but living miserably. Therefore I only wish that before I die I could help them improve their living conditions, have their own farms, and be able to send their children to school. I would like them to be able to give their children the things they did not get when they were kids such as education and better living conditions. (seventy-four-year-old retired worker)

The harvest I get is hardly enough to feed my family. Therefore I wish that someday I might be able to acquire more government land to make my farm bigger. (fifty-three-year-old farmer)

I hope to be able to raise plenty of rice and be able to sell some of it. With the money I intend to buy land or maybe occupy myself with cock-fighting once in a while. I also wish to buy a car of my own. (twenty-three-year-old tenant farmer)

I would like to improve our chicken houses and our piggery to help increase our income. Someday I would like to have a house completely furnished. (twenty-three-year-old housewife living near a village)

Yugoslavia—Socioeconomic index, 0.19

I would like to have new furniture, a nice wardrobe, and an apartment in Belgrade and to have a paved street in front of where I live. (forty-six-year-old farmer)

Above all I would like to have an apartment of my own where my husband and I and our seven children could live. (wife of a skilled worker)

I would like to be able to dress nicely and to have some oxen and some pigs and build a little house. (forty-year-old farmer's wife)

I wish we had some cattle to help us cultivate our land. I would also like to buy a sewing machine as a dowry for my daughter. (forty-three-year-old farmer's wife)

I wish we could repair our house and have many things in it, including a cupboard. I would like also to be able to preserve food for the winter. (twenty-seven-year-old farmer's wife)

I would like to be able to build one additional room as a bedroom on our house. (thirty-nine-year-old skilled worker)

I would like to be able to move out of the city and raise chickens and have a pigsty. (fifty-seven-year-old widower)

I wish we could finish fixing our house and get some new furniture and a better wardrobe and even buy a piece of land to add to what we have. (forty-year-old farmer)

What I want most of all is a motorcycle. (forty-eight-year-old farmer)

I wish I didn't have to rent rooms in my apartment and could live here just with my family. (fifty-year-old housewife)

Panama—Socioeconomic index, 0.31

My greatest hope for myself is to have a place to build a new home and to work on the land because I have always lived from farming and that is my art. I hope to go on working so that someday I will be able to save enough for this and have a cow and a horse as I progress. If I could have my own new little house and secure work I would be happy. (sixty-five-year-old owner of small farm)

I should like to have money enough to educate my children and keep them all in good health. I should especially like to educate my oldest daughter because she is so eager to learn and to go to school and her father can't support us all the way we would like. Sometimes we are even lacking food in the house. (forty-five-year-old housewife)

I hope that my wife and I will stay healthy and that I can continue to support myself and that God will help us. I do not want to be dependent upon others. As long as I can earn my daily bread I shall be happy. (eighty-year-old farmer)

I hope always to have work because my mother and I are alone and have no one to help us. As long as I can work I can support my mother and me. I also hope that if my mother dies from her ailing heart I will have money enough to give her a proper funeral. (a woman who is forty-nine and a cook)

I hope industries will be built near by so that more people can be more steadily employed. I also hope that some schools will be put up and there will be no trouble about children getting an education and learning to read and write. (fifty-four-year-old unskilled worker)

I hope there will be more advancement and progress and that someday I can have a house built of concrete and live comfortably. (twenty-five-year-old construction worker)

I hope that I shall continue to have no financial problems for at present I am able to meet my financial obligations without owing anyone. But I would like a greater equity in a home of our own. (thirty-eight-year-old skilled worker)

Cuba—Socioeconomic index, 0.35

My greatest aspirations are to have my own house and my own business. (twenty-seven-year-old white chauffeur)

I would like to live with the basic necessities of life but not necessarily richly. I want my own house and to see my children learn some useful occupation. (housewife, white, forty-five years old)

I would like to possess such material goods as furniture—better furniture and an automobile and be able to educate my children. I should also like to travel every three or four years at least. (white woman, thirty-eight years old, well educated)

I want an income which will permit me to live and dress well and also one which would permit me to travel from time to time. (thirty-seven-year-old white woman who is a teacher)

My life's aspirations are to live with a few more comforts, to be an individual, to have my own house, automobile, and a productive business. (thirty-five-year-old commission agent)

I would like to have a small business to do the type of work which would give me enough money to have a house of my own so that my children could be comfortable and have all that is necessary—a radio, TV, bathroom and other personal things. I would like an automobile in order to be able to travel. (thirty-six-year-old carpenter)

I want to have my own house and a salary which would permit me to live in comfort and be able to educate my children well and travel all over Cuba and sometimes to other countries. (forty-five-year-old unskilled worker)

My ambition is to have my economic problem sufficiently solved to educate my children, to have my own house, an automobile, and to be able to afford entertainment and read good books. (thirty-four-year-old carpenter)

I want to have a great many nice clothes, go to many fiestas, to have an automobile, to have money to pay for all my pleasures and to travel. (twenty-eight-year-old carpenter)

I would like to have economic security enough to meet all of my expenditures and have my children complete a good education which will permit them to live honestly. I want to be able to travel, to entertain, and to have a good library in order to strengthen my knowledge. (fifty-year-old insurance agent)

I want a job which will give me enough money to send my children to school, to buy a new house, to be able to dress my family well and to enjoy such diversions as horseback riding. (thirty-seven-year-old teacher)

I would like an economic position which would give me the necessities of life and also some comforts such as my own house, a TV, an automobile. I want to give my children an education and I want to travel all over the world and go to many fiestas. (thirty-eight-year-old bartender)

Israel—Socioeconomic index, 0.67

I hope to have a position that will fulfill all my daily needs and let me realize various wishes that come up from time to time even if they are not included in the daily routine. For instance: a comfortable apartment and one large enough to be a "last stop" even when the family grows, the ability to buy suitable clothing for my family, to educate my children, to have some entertainment, and home improvements but all within the bounds of convenience and not things that are luxuries. (twenty-eight-year-old middle-class native of Israel)

I want to live in a better house in the city and in a good neighborhood. I want an electric refrigerator and a washing machine and better beds. I wish I had money to educate my son. I would also like some free time at home so I can take care of the house which is now neglected. Also the vacation I get every year is far too short. (forty-eight-year-old widow working as cleaning woman)

My aspiration is to achieve independence and to give my family the maximum of a happy life so there will always be enough money to buy the vital necessities. I want to be able to live on my salary without scrimping and without any debts. I want to be self-employed and not a wage-earner and not be dependent upon someone else. (thirty-five-year-old clerical worker)

If one's husband earns only 260 pounds a month ($125), that's no life. For things to be all right one needs a good income and the children must be well taken care of. A person should be able to read the papers every day, go to the movies and the theater once a month, have a circle of friends. All that takes money. If you have the proper conditions then the children also develop differently. I want to be able to go to the cafe with friends and enjoy myself with groups of people. But if I am less than they are from the point of view of money then I cannot go with them. (thirty-five-year-old woman whose husband is white-collar worker)

I hope that my economic conditions will be such that I won't have to worry about bread and that I can have a car parked by the house. I want to succeed in supporting two or three people. I don't want to be rich but I do want to be above the average. (twenty-eight-year-old skilled worker)

I want to earn a living that will take care of the needs a person has. For instance, a person who has been a poultry farmer for twenty years should be able to have a secure income for his old age. What is needed is a good house and decent furniture. I am interested in developing a poultry farm because it will be a good means of support. I hope I can have an easier life and will not have to work hard in my old age. I would like to enjoy more culture, to see more movies and plays, to read more books and newspapers. I'd like to be able to visit all sorts of places in the country. I still haven't been to Jerusalem. (fifty-two-year-old farmer)

I hope to be able to provide for the children's future so they will all have an education and so that my son will be able to go to the university as he wants to. I should also like to travel abroad and see my family in the United States and in Russia. (fifty-eight-year-old skilled worker)

My wife and I plan to work so that we will be able to get settled and rent an apartment and buy furniture. I want also to get a car. I don't want a lot of children because our financial conditions will not allow it. I would like a three-room house, nice furniture, with a radio, sofa, closet, table, easy chairs. I don't aspire to a life of luxury and extravagance. (twenty-one-year-old army officer)

I would like to live in my own home and not in a rented apartment. I would like my own car. I don't want to be just a laborer for someone else. I would like to be a high official or the manager of a plant. I would like suitable entertainment such as being able to go to the movies, the theater, dances, and trips to the seashore, and participate in sport and chess competitions. (twenty-seven-year-old skilled worker)

Furnishing the house is important for me as is my son's education and upbringing. I bought him an accordion and I'm hoping to buy a bookcase. I have a library of 500 books. Maybe at Passover I'll buy a bookcase for it. I'd be happy if there were more people in our neighborhood for then our business would do well. (fifty-year-old cooperative grocer)

I'd like my standard of living to improve in comparison with what I had abroad. Today I feel I've gone down a lot even though I've come up since I came to this country. There are still lots of things that I'd like to have such as a larger house, a better social environment, and a good and secure education for my children. (thirty-nine-year-old married woman from Eastern Europe whose husband is skilled worker)

I'd like to open a workshop for copper work and craftwork because that is what I deal in. If I open such a workshop I'll buy machines and hire people and in that way I'll be sure of making a good living in the future. I'd buy a nice house near the workshop, a house with three or four rooms. As the business progresses I hope to buy a truck that will help me in my work because I market my goods in all parts of the country. I hope to be able to take a tour abroad. I'd like to see the world. (twenty-three-year-old small shop owner)

My hope is that the Jewish agency will give me a large sum of money so that I will be able to develop my farm and also add another room to the house. I would like 25 acres of land, 50 Holland cows, 100 head of sheep, and about 300 hens. I would like the yield from my farm to be so high that I could open a marketing cooperative. After I get financially established I'll give back to the agency twice as much as it gave me. (forty-one-year-old farmer)

I'd like to be so rich that I could buy myself a private car and a big, pleasant apartment. I wish I had a maid who could help me with the housework so that I could have more time for my children. I hope we will be able to help our relatives out financially so they can come here. (forty-four-year-old married woman, whose husband is a farmer)

West Germany—Socioeconomic index, 0.71

I'd like to see a little of the world. I'd like to see the Rhine once. I want to travel, to dress up, to live in hotels and be able to sleep as long as I want to. (fifty-five-year-old woman, husband a clerk)

I'd like to be able to work independently. I want a house in a quiet, clean part of town. I want a car and would like to be able to travel in Germany and abroad just as I want to. (thirty-seven-year-old medical worker)

I hope we can keep the basis of existence we have established and always be free from financial worries. We do not want a luxurious life but a normal and decent living. This includes a modern apartment. I hardly dream of building a house of our own but it would be really fine if we ever got that far. (sixty-two-year-old housewife, husband a salesman)

As a mason, I want to have at least a house of my own. I help to build so many houses while I myself live in rather modest quarters. I want our house to be furnished with all modern conveniences such as a bathroom. I would also like to have a garden. Maybe I'll find a way of getting it. Also I hope for a secure old age. I also want a television set. (thirty-six-year-old bricklayer)

I would like to have a house of my own so that we would no longer be dependent upon other people. Also I would like to make an extended tour through Italy or to the North Sea. I would like to furnish my apartment beautifully and also have a car. I would like to dress according to the latest fashion. I wish my husband could set up the business he wants, that of an automobile repair shop of his own. Then we would be very happy. (twenty-eight-year-old woman who is a saleswoman)

I would like to have a house of my own and a garden in a quiet location. I hope to be able to keep my small shop and that business will improve. (thirty-six-year-old grocer)

I'd like to have a little family house with a nice flower garden and lots of fruit trees. I want enough money to get along easily and not have everyday worries. I would like to make a nice trip to the Italian lakes. (fifty-one-year-old housewife)

I'd like to win in the lottery once. Then I'd have a house built for the children, one that I was not ashamed of, and we would take a long vacation trip as a family. (seventy-two-year-old retired miner)

I hope my shop will flourish so that I can afford a big car and not have to work so hard. I want to travel through Germany and live in good hotels. I want a nicer apartment with television, gas heating, a refrigerator. Then I'd be most content. (forty-two-year-old plumber)

I want a bigger apartment with a balcony and bathroom on the first floor if possible. I want to take a nice trip to the Tyrol and not have to be careful with every mark I'm spending. (forty-year-old government worker)

At first I'd take a long rest from work and do nothing, not even cook my own meals but go to a restaurant. I'd like to have enough money to furnish a house of my own and have a car to drive wherever I wanted to. (thirty-eight-year-old nurse)

I'd like to earn so much money that I could buy a house of my own with a garden, go traveling during my vacation, taking a long trip every two years. (twenty-six-year-old warehouse worker)

United States—Socioeconomic index, 1.00

I hope that when I retire I will have enough money to travel, not necessarily in top style. We have had a nice comfortable home life raising our children and have enjoyed it. Now I'd like to do a few different things, like traveling. (fifty-two-year-old insurance agent)

I want to see that my children are happily married and financially secure. I want enough money to travel and go back to school and study and learn to be a psychologist. (forty-nine-year-old mechanic)

USA i-dex= 1,00

If I could earn more money I would then be able to buy our own home and have more luxury around us, like better furniture, a new car, and more vacations. (twenty-seven-year-old skilled worker)

These days one has to work so hard, there is always someone pushing you. I would like a slower pace in living, more time for the simplicities of life. I'd like to put my four sons through college so they don't have to work as hard as I have. I would be a fool if I didn't want more money and a nice house to live in, a new car, and a chance to travel. (forty-six year-old skilled worker)

I'm getting pretty old. I would like to see twenty more years. I would like a little more money. My pension ain't enough for travel. Never been to New York. My wife and I got enough to live on, but we can't go no-where. Dreams are for the youngsters. I can't think of anything more I want. (sixty-eight-year-old house painter)

Materially speaking, I would like to provide my family with an income to allow them to live well—to have the proper recreation, to go camping, to have music and dancing lessons for the children, and to have family trips. I wish we could belong to a country club and do more entertaining. We just bought a new home and expect to be perfectly satisfied with it for a number of years. (twenty-eight-year-old lawyer)

I would like a reasonable enough income to maintain a house, have a new car, have a boat, and send my four children to private schools. (thirty-four-year-old laboratory technician)

I wish we had enough money to live independently from our son and take a trip to Europe. We would like enough things to be emotionally independent and do the interesting things we enjoy doing. (fifty-year-old druggist)

I would like financial security and enough to be able to quit work and stay home with the children. (thirty-four-year-old bus driver)

I just get by. If I was in better shape and had more money, everything would be better. I'd like a good standing in life. There just ain't enough money around here. All the people on this street are miserably poor and some are on relief. (seventy-two-year-old Negro worker)

I would like a new car. I wish all my bills were paid and I had more money for myself. I would like to play more golf and to hunt more than I do. I would like to have more time to do the things I want to and to entertain my friends. (Negro bus driver, twenty-four years old)

I would like to be completely free to trade and spend my money in any establishment. I would like very much to have my own house and a

Cadillac in the garage. I want all my kids to go through college and my wife to live in a comfortable home. I enjoy hunting and fishing but have little time to do them now. (forty-eight-year-old Negro farmer)

If I had more money I could build a home, get married, move out of the city, and take a long vacation. I would like to be able to take my bride to Europe. (twenty-six-year-old clerk)

The reader will quickly have seen the increased sophistication and complexity of the requirements for a "decent or improved standard of living" as one moves up from countries with low developmental indices to those with higher indices. For a typical Indian, a decent or improved standard of living may mean aspiring to ownership of a bicycle, a bullock, or the opportunity for his children to learn to read and write, whereas for an American, a decent or improved standard of living may mean having a Cadillac, modern farm equipment, or sending all of his children through college. Clearly a way of life that an Indian, a Nigerian, or a Brazilian might rate as 8 or 10 on the ladder, an American would probably rate at 0 or 1.

The focus on the problem can again be made sharper if the personal concerns as classified into our general categories of people in the three richest nations of our sample are compared to people in three of the poorest nations of our sample. These comparisons are shown in Tables X:2 and X:3.

Table X:2 shows very clearly that people in the rich nations in our sample are significantly more concerned about international problems of war and peace as hopes and, even more especially, as fears. But it will be noted that by and large the differences between the percentages of the three peoples in poor countries from each other and the people in the three rich countries from each other are greater than the average difference between the three rich and the three poor countries. This is especially noticeable with respect to the concern for health: among Indians both aspirations for better health and fear of poor health are exceedingly low, whereas in Nigeria they are exceedingly high.

Table X:3 again shows the huge difference between people in the three rich and the three poor countries of our sample with respect to their relative concern about international issues of war and peace. The three rich peoples in our sample are also somewhat more concerned both about political affairs and maintaining an independent status for their country, while the people in the three poorest nations are somewhat—but not overwhelmingly, by any means—more concerned with the general economic problems facing their countries. Again, as with personal concerns, the differences between the percentages of the three poor people from each other and the three rich people from each other are

TABLE X:2

COMPARISON OF 3 RICH AND 3 POOR PEOPLES ON PERSONAL GENERAL CATEGORIES

(No sign indicates rich higher; — indicates poor higher)

| | Rich | | | | Poor | | | | |
General category	United States	West Germany	Israel	Average	Brazil	Nigeria	India	Average	Percentage difference *
HOPES									
Personal values	20%	11%	29%	20%	14%	42%	14%	23%	−3%
Personal economic	65	85	80	77	68	90	70	76	1
Job or work	10	10	35	18	8	19	22	16	2
Health	48	46	47	47	34	45	4	28	19
Family	47	27	76	50	28	76	39	48	2
Political	2	1	2	2	——	——	——	——	2
Social	5	3	10	6	1	14	8	8	−2
International, war-peace	10	15	12	12	1	——	——	——	12
Status quo	11	4	4	6	1	——	2	1	5
FEARS									
Personal values	3	3	10	5	7	17	5	10	−5
Personal economic	46	51	55	51	30	65	51	49	2
Job or work	5	2	10	6	2	2	6	3	3
Health	56	51	58	55	42	64	23	43	12
Family	25	14	44	28	17	27	19	21	7
Political	5	8	2	5	1	5	——	2	3
Social	3	2	4	3	2	14	2	6	−3
International, war-peace	24	50	27	34	3	1	——	1	33
None	12	2	6	7	4	8	8	7	0

* A difference of 3 percent is significant at the .05 level.

by and large greater than the average of the differences between the three rich and the three poor peoples.

CONDITIONS FOR THE BLOSSOMING OF CERTAIN ASPIRATIONS

It has often been pointed out—by Marx and Lenin, among others—that if people are pushed down by poverty they cannot be expected to

TABLE X:3

COMPARISON OF 3 RICH AND 3 POOR PEOPLES ON NATIONAL GENERAL
CATEGORIES

(No sign indicates rich higher; — indicates poor higher)

General category	Rich				Poor				
	United States	West Germany	Israel	Average	Brazil	Nigeria	India	Average	Percentage difference *
HOPES									
Political	13%	49%	35%	32%	16%	50%	9%	25%	7%
Economic	45	69	79	64	58	81	70	70	−6
Social	33	16	70	40	19	66	19	35	5
International, war-peace	59	42	69	57	5	12	3	7	50
Independent status	4	11	37	17	4	24	9	12	5
Status quo	7	2	1	3	1	—	—	—	3
FEARS									
Political	23	60	23	35	24	69	20	38	−3
Economic	29	18	44	30	34	43	24	34	−4
Social	21	11	30	21	8	37	14	20	1
International, war-peace	57	44	72	58	19	11	25	18	40
Independent status	11	16	16	14	3	7	8	6	8
None	4	—	6	3	2	4	7	4	−1

* A difference of 3 percent is significant at the .05 level.

show much interest in anything except their daily bread. What a person regards as a minimum standard of living in his own terms is presumably required before other interests and concerns can unfold and blossom forth. In other words, some conditions related to the assurance of a decent standard of living as subjectively defined seem necessary and primary for most individuals before they feel they can afford the luxury of other interests and aspirations.

In order to check this hypothesis, people in all countries who said they were worried about or fearful of a "deterioration in or inadequate standard of living for themselves or their family" were sorted out and then compared to people who were not worried about a deterioration in or inadequate standard of living with respect to certain personal aspirations as these were classified in our general categories. These two groups of people—those worried about an inadequate standard of living and those not worried about it—were then compared in the three highest countries on our socioeconomic index and three of the lowest countries with respect to the personal aspirations expressed.

Table X:4 indicates the percentage of people in the three high in-

TABLE X:4

PERCENTAGE OF PEOPLE WORRIED OR NOT WORRIED WHO EXPRESS CERTAIN
ASPIRATIONS COMPARED IN HIGH AND LOW INCOME COUNTRIES

(High = United States, West Germany, Israel; low = Brazil, Nigeria, India)

Aspiration	Worried		Not Worried	
	High	Low	High	Low
Personal worth	4%	1%	2%	1%
Self-development	7	10	4	8
Health of family	37	4	13	4
Job or work	23	14	10	17
Happy family life	35	24	14	8
Own health	70	33	27	12
Children's welfare	55	48	25	29
Ownership	55	55	21	37
Total %	*25*	*41*	*75*	*59*
Total n	*1099*	*4619*	*3300*	*6718*

come countries who said they were worried about an inadequate standard of living and who also expressed the different aspirations we classified. It also compares them to the people in three of the lowest income countries who were also worried about an inadequate standard of living and expressed the same aspirations. The table includes comparable figures for those in both the high and low income countries who said they were not worried about an inadequate standard of living. Table X:5 indicates the differences between the aspirations of people in high and low income countries who said they were worried or not worried about their standard of living.

It will be noted at once from Table X:4 that there is a very significant difference between the percentage of people in the low income countries and the high income countries who actually expressed a worry about an inadequate standard of living or a deterioration in their present standard—a ratio of 25 percent to 41 percent.

Table X:5 shows that in the three high income countries, significantly more people who said they were worried about an inadequate standard

TABLE X:5

RANK ORDER OF DIFFERENCES BETWEEN HIGH AND LOW COUNTRIES IN ASPIRATIONS
EXPRESSED BY THOSE WORRIED OR NOT WORRIED ABOUT STANDARD
OF LIVING

(No sign means people in *high* income countries express aspiration more frequently; − means people in *low* income countries express aspiration more frequently)

Worried		Not worried	
Aspiration	Percentage difference *	Aspiration	Percentage difference †
Own health	37%	Own health	15%
Health of family	33	Health of family	9
Happy family life	11	Happy family life	6
Job or work situation	9	Personal worth	1
Children's welfare	7	Children's welfare	−4
Personal worth	3	Self-development	−4
Ownership	0	Job or work situation	−7
Self-development	−3	Ownership	−16

* A difference of 4 percent is significant at the .05 level.
† A difference of 2 percent is significant at the .05 level.

of living or a deterioration of the present standard were also more concerned than were people in three low income countries with the health of themselves and their families, with having a happy family life, with improving their job or work situation, and with the welfare of their children. In other words, in the low income countries, if people are worried about their standard of living, this worry tends to blanket out aspirations concerned with health, happy family life, job improvement, and children's welfare. These might be regarded, then, as "luxury" concerns, as aspirations poor people in poor countries have only if and when their standard of living is secure and shows some signs of improvement. In rich countries, however, people have learned both to want and expect these aspects of a good life and thus good health, happy family life with opportunity for children, together with a good job tend to be seen more as part of the definition of a decent standard of living.

Table X:5 also shows that among the people in high income countries who are not worried about their standard of living, there was still more concern for their own and their family's health and for a happy family life but that among these people in high income countries not worried about their standard of living, there was not as much concern as among people in poor countries about problems of ownership, job or work situation, their children's welfare, or self-development—these latter presumably not areas of frustration for them if they were not anxious about their standard of living.

In order to discover the contrast between people in the richest nation of the world, the United States, and people in the poorest nation in the sample and one of the poorest nations of the world, India, the same comparison was made on these two isolated populations and is shown in Tables X:6 and X:7.

Table X:6 shows that twice as many Indians as Americans were actually worried about a deterioration in or inadequate standard of living

TABLE X:6

COMPARISON OF AMERICANS AND INDIANS WHO ARE WORRIED OR NOT WORRIED ABOUT STANDARD OF LIVING AND WHO EXPRESS CERTAIN ASPIRATIONS

	Worried		Not worried	
Aspiration	United States	India	United States	India
Personal worth	4	——	1	1
Self-development	3	4	1	6
Health of family	34	1	10	2
Job or work situation	15	16	7	26
Happy family life	40	3	13	4
Own health	88	3	27	2
Children's welfare	55	33	22	33
Ownership	54	51	17	43
%	20	*41*	*80*	59
Total n	*545*	*2326*	*2203*	*3394*

for themselves or their families. Table X:7 shows the large differences between Americans and Indians who said they were worried about an inadequate standard of living or a deterioration of the present standard and who also expressed other aspirations. Many more Americans than Indians who were worried about their standard of living were also concerned about their own and their family's health, a happy family life, and their children's welfare—these aspects of living being a part of what they have learned is a high standard of living. Among Indians not worried about their standard of living, there is more concern than among Americans not worried about their standard of living with their children's welfare, the job or work situation, and the ownership of some property—items that Americans not worried about the standard of living can presumably take more for granted.

TABLE X:7

RANK ORDER OF DIFFERENCES BETWEEN AMERICANS AND INDIANS IN ASPIRATIONS EXPRESSED BY THOSE WORRIED OR NOT WORRIED ABOUT STANDARD OF LIVING

(No sign indicates Americans express aspiration more frequently; — indicates Indians express aspiration more frequently)

Worried		Not worried	
Aspiration	Percentage Difference *	Aspiration	Percentage Difference †
Own health	85%	Own health	25%
Happy family life	37	Happy family life	9
Health of family	33	Health of family	8
Children's welfare	22	Personal worth	0
Personal worth	4	Self-development	—5
Ownership	3	Children's welfare	—11
Self-development	—1	Job or work situation	—19
Job or work situation	—1	Ownership	—26

* A difference of 5 percent is significant at .05 level.
† A difference of 3 percent is significant at .05 level.

In order to obtain some idea of the relationship between "primary" and "luxury" concerns and the total volume of concerns expressed by the people in a country, countries were rank ordered according to the percentage of total personal hopes, of total personal fears, of total national hopes, and of total national fears. Rank orders were then made in each of the four categories according to the extent of the people's concern with luxury aspirations or worries, which conservatively included, in the case of personal hopes and fears, all items except those dealing with economic, health, or family (including, then, personal worth and self-development, job or work situation, children's welfare, political and social concerns, ownership, and international problems) and, in the case of national concern, all those except economic and political aspirations or worries (including, then, social problems, the international area of war and peace, and independent status).

The following rank order correlations, then, are between the total volume of concerns expressed and the extent to which luxury concerns were mentioned:

Between volume of *personal hopes* and luxury concerns 0.67

Between volume of *personal fears* and luxury concerns 0.49

Between volume of *national hopes* and luxury
concerns   0.68
Between volume of *national fears* and luxury
concerns   0.33

The first three correlations are significant at the 95 percent level of confidence and indicate that the greater the total number of personal hopes, personal fears, and national hopes, the more likely are people to be concerned with the luxury items as here rather arbitrarily defined; whereas the fewer the total number of personal hopes and fears or national hopes, the less likely are people to be concerned with such luxury items. It will also be noticed that there is a higher correlation on the side of hopes than on the side of fears. The expansion of the people's reality world to include a broader volume of concerns simply means an extension in their vision of what to aspire to and what to worry about, of what either they or their nation might be or might become.

Summary

1. Both in terms of their economic and social development, as measured by "objective" indices and in terms of their aspirations as expressed by their people, nations might be roughly differentiated into those that are in a stage of *premobilization,* such as India and Brazil, a stage of *mobilization,* such as Yugoslavia and Israel, or a stage of relative *maturity,* such as the United States and West Germany.

2. Psychologically, this mobilization of a nation means an extension of what people learn to want out of life as they perceive new potentialities for increasing both the range and the quality of their satisfactions. What a people in a mature nation may regard as a primary requirement for a decent standard of living, such as good health, may be regarded by people in a premobilized nation as a luxury item and not a requirement for their definition of what constitutes a decent standard of living.

Once a people are awakened, their very backwardness can serve as an incentive for their strivings, if they sense the potentialities available to remedy their lot, as appears to be the case, for example, among Nigerians and Egyptians. This is implicitly revealed in the relatively high ladder ratings people in underdeveloped countries assign for themselves and the nation for the future, providing them targets to aim for.

3. In the stage of mobilization as compared to premobilization, the emphasis is more on increasing the range of satisfactions, whereas in the stage of maturity as compared to mobilization, the emphasis is more on the quality of satisfactions, as "quality" is defined by the people in a culture.

4. In this process, it is clear that the developed nations of the West

with their relative abundance of material goods and their use of technology to ease the burdens of life serve as models by means of which people in less-developed nations learn to define and expand their wants. It is relatively rare that a people do not sooner or later learn to define their goals in terms of Western standards—the people of the Kibbutzim, perhaps a passing microcosm in the present stage of world history, are the prize example.

CHAPTER XI

Person and Nation

The problem here is to ferret out from the data the relationships and interdependencies between the concerns and estimates a person expresses for his own life and those he sees for his nation. To what extent are the reality worlds of individuals impinged upon and influenced by the national context? To what extent are people ego-involved in national affairs? To what extent do personal loyalties or frustrations overlap with loyalties and frustrations relating to national goals?

In a sense the problem was stated many years ago by Alexander Hamilton in the Federalist papers, when he wrote:

> It is a known fact in human nature that its affections are commonly weak in proportion to the distance or diffusiveness of the object. Upon the same principles that a man is more attached to his family than to his neighbourhood, to his neighbourhood than to the community at large, the people of each State would be apt to feel a stronger byass towards their local governments than towards the government of the Union; unless the force of that principle should be destroyed by a much better administration of the latter.[1]

There are various ways to look at the information gathered from the different countries to get some insight into the strength or weakness of an individual's "affections" concerning his nation and the extent to which he regards his problems as national problems and national problems as his problems. The account of the procedures used and findings obtained may at times appear a bit tortuous or repetitive but it is essential to look at the data from a number of angles to get at the central problem.

CORRELATIONS BETWEEN PERSONAL AND
NATIONAL LADDER RATINGS

Table XI:1 brings together and compares the correlations obtained on past, present, and future ladder ratings, both individual and national. The table is arranged by rank order of correlations on present ratings.

TABLE XI:1

CORRELATIONS BETWEEN PERSONAL AND NATIONAL RATINGS

Country	Present	Past	Future
Nigeria	.40	.38	.44
Cuba	.38	.35	.41
Japan	.31	.23	.33
India I	.30	.30	.29
West Germany	.30	.31	—
Dominican Republic	.28	.32	.33
Yugoslavia	.21	.26	.30
Panama	.18	.21	.24
Kibbutzim	.16	.08	.14
Brazil	.15	.22	.26
Egypt	.14	.24	.27
Philippines	.13	.15	.09
Israel	.12	.23	.14
United States	.08	.10	.18

It will be seen at once that these correlations are high in most countries where there has been recent and major political change, such as Cuba and the Dominican Republic; where independence has been achieved in the lifetime of the respondents, as in Nigeria and India; where there has been major overhaul in the governmental structure of the country, as in West Germany and Japan; or where, as in Yugoslavia, various nationality groups have been brought together into a new nation.

It will also be noticed that the correlations for the past in both Egypt, where a new revolutionary government more or less recently took over, and Israel, a newly formed state, are also indicative of a positive relationship between personal and national ratings but that these have dwindled in the ratings for the present. In both of these instances, one gets the feeling from the information gathered and from personal visits that the national élan and the personal opportunities and enthusiasms for participation in the formation of the new nation have definitely diminished over the past few years.

The rank order correlations of the personal and national ratings on all countries were: past, 0.57; present, 0.55; and future, 0.46—all significant at the 95 percent level of confidence and confirming the impression that there is a definite tendency for personal and national estimates to be positively related.

It is also significant in this connection to look at the percentage of people who were unable to give any ladder ratings either for themselves or for the nation. Several observations may be made from the figures in Table XI:2. One sees how relatively difficult it is for people to

TABLE XI:2

PERCENTAGE OF "NO ANSWER" ON LADDER RATINGS

Country	Personal				National			
	Past	Present	Future	Average	Past	Present	Future	Average
United States	1%	1%	8%	3%	6%	3%	10%	6%
West Germany	4	3	20	9	11	10	—	11
Japan	14	11	33	19	31	29	43	34
Yugoslavia	1	1	2	1	1	1	2	1
Brazil	21	19	44	28	34	30	47	37
Nigeria	6	5	27	13	16	16	28	20
India I	18	15	22	18	29	27	29	28
Israel	2	2	11	5	6	4	10	7
Kibbutzim	3	1	7	4	3	2	7	4
Egypt	1	2	1	1	2	2	4	3
Philippines	1	1	5	2	1	1	4	2
Cuba	1	3	3	2	2	2	3	2
Dominican Republic	2	2	3	2	4	3	4	4
Panama	3	2	11	5	6	4	9	6
Average	*6*	*5*	*14*	*8*	*11*	*10*	*14*	*12*

project themselves into the future both on the personal and national levels—an appreciable 14 percent on the average were unable to give either a personal or national rating for the future. One also sees that nearly twice as many people are unable to rate their country for the past and the present as are able to place themselves on the ladder, obviously because of the complexity of such a rating and the many unknown and indeterminate factors involved. The high percentage of "no answers" is also seen in the three major underdeveloped countries studied, India, Nigeria, and Brazil, where the situation both for the individual and the nation is relatively unstructured and uncharted.

The degree to which personal and national ratings correlate of course tells us nothing about the similarity of the mean ratings or the extent to which they may parallel each other. Figures XI:1 and XI:2 show the mean ratings of the two countries where the correlations were highest, Nigeria and Cuba, while Figures XI:3 and XI:4 show the ratings of the two people where the correlations were lowest, Americans and members of the Kibbutzim. In all these cases, roughly similar trends can be noted between the mean personal and national ratings as we go from the past through the present to the future.

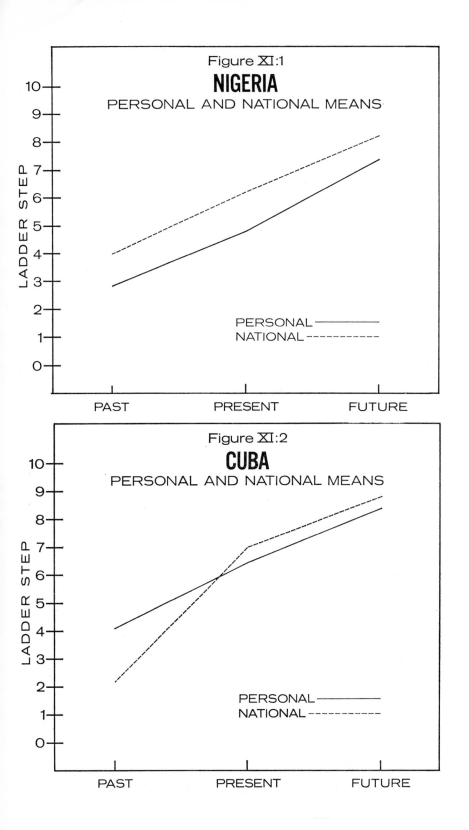

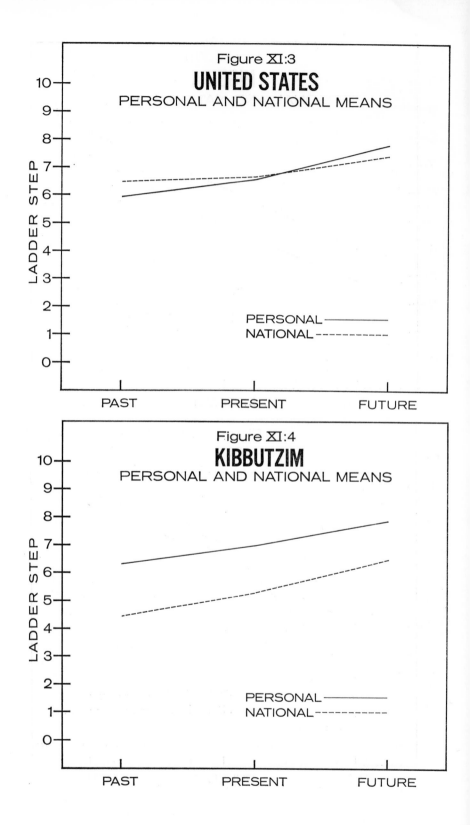

RATINGS AND CONCERNS

In order to learn something about the broad relationship between the extent to which people share common concerns either in their personal lives or with respect to the nation and the ladder ratings they gave, a separate rank order was made of the frequency of mention of all code items with respect to personal hopes, personal fears, national hopes, and national fears, and then a rank order was made of the average ladder ratings for the past, present, and future of all people who had mentioned the items in each of the four categories. A rank order correlation between these columns was calculated.

A positive correlation, then, means that the more people who share concerns, the higher is their average ladder rating. In other words, the extent to which people have common concerns tends to raise their ladder ratings, presumably because there is a sense that these shared concerns are sources of satisfaction or are concerns which people feel they will make progress in achieving. In the case of fears, a positive correlation between shared concerns and higher ladder ratings means that the fears are not extremely important, operationally, or that people feel the sources of the fears will diminish or be remedied without too much difficulty. A negative correlation means that the more people who share concerns, the lower is their average ladder rating. In other words, the extent to which people have common concerns tends to lower their ladder ratings, presumably because there is a sense that these shared concerns are sources of dissatisfaction or are concerns which people feel they will not make progress in achieving. An insignificant correlation means that there is no relationship between the extent to which people share a concern and their ladder rating.

On the basis of these relationships, we may differentiate six different states of mind:

1. *Sense of accomplishment:* A positive correlation between concerns as ranked by frequency of mention and by past ladder ratings associated with specific concerns.
    A. *Hopes based on gains:* the more frequently mentioned the hope, the higher the past ladder rating associated with it.
    B. *Fears not related to gains:* the more frequently mentioned the fear, the higher the past ladder rating.
2. *Sense of discouragement:* A negative correlation between concerns as ranked by frequency of mention and as ranked by past ladder ratings associated with specific concerns.
    A. *Hopes not based on gains:* the more frequently mentioned the hope, the lower the past ladder rating associated with it.

B. *Fears based on few gains:* the more frequently mentioned the fear, the lower the past ladder rating associated with it.

3. *Sense of satisfaction:* A positive correlation between concerns as ranked by frequency of mention and as ranked by present ladder ratings associated with specific concerns.

A. *Hopes a source of satisfaction:* the more frequently mentioned the hope, the higher the present ladder rating associated with it.

B. *Fears not operative enough to be a source of dissatisfaction:* the more frequently mentioned the fear, the higher the present ladder rating associated with it.

4. *Sense of frustration:* A negative correlation between concerns as ranked by frequency of mention and by present ladder ratings associated with specific concerns.

A. *Hopes not a source of satisfaction:* the more frequently mentioned the hope, the lower the present ladder ratings associated with the hope.

B. *Fears a source of frustration:* the more frequently mentioned the fear, the lower the present ladder rating associated with that fear.

5. *Sense of expectation:* A positive correlation between concerns as ranked by frequency of mention and as ranked by future ladder ratings that tend to be associated with specific concerns.

A. *Hopes a source of anticipation:* the more frequently mentioned the hope, the higher the future ladder rating that tends to be associated with that hope.

B. *Fears not operative enough to be a source of anxiety:* the more frequently mentioned the fear, the higher the future ladder rating that tends to be associated with that fear.

6. *Sense of anxiety:* A negative correlation between concerns as ranked by frequency of mention and as ranked by future ladder ratings that tend to be associated with specific concerns.

A. *Hopes not a source of expectation:* the more frequently mentioned the hope, the lower the future ladder rating that tends to be associated with that hope.

B. *Fears a sense of anxiety:* the more frequently mentioned the fear, the lower the future ladder rating that tends to be associated with that fear.

The personal and national concerns and ratings are shown in Tables XI:3 and XI:4. In the left column (accomplishment, satisfaction, and expectation) are listed those countries in which there is a positive correlation. All correlations above 0.3 have been considered a trend. All countries in the right column (discouragement, frustration, and anxiety) are countries in which there is a negative correlation: correlations below

−0.3 have been considered a trend, and the others are marked with the degree of confidence indicated above. The top row (accomplishment and discouragement), then, is related to past ladder ratings; the middle row (satisfaction and frustration) is related to present ladder ratings; while the bottom row (expectation and anxiety) is related to future ratings.

TABLE XI:3

PERSONAL CONCERNS AND RATINGS *

Accomplishment (past)		Discouragement (past)	
Hopes based on gains	*Fears not related to gains*	*Hopes not based on gains*	*Fears based on few gains*
Nigeria †† Brazil	Yugoslavia West Germany	India †	Panama ††
Satisfaction (present)		Frustration (present)	
Hopes a source of satisfaction	*Fears not operative enough to be a source of dissatisfaction*	*Hopes not a source of satisfaction*	*Fears a source of frustration*
Egypt	Yugoslavia † Egypt Brazil Israel United States	India	Dominican Republic Cuba
Expectation (future)		Anxiety (future)	
Hopes a source of anticipation	*Fears not operative enough to be a source of anxiety*	*Hopes not a source of expectation*	*Fears a source of anxiety*
Yugoslavia	United States Dominican Republic	Brazil †† India † Egypt Dominican Republic	Brazil India Panama Cuba

* The rank order correlations on which this table is based will be found in Appendix E3.
† Indicates significance at the .05 level of confidence.
†† Indicates significance at the .01 level of confidence.

TABLE XI:4

NATIONAL CONCERNS AND RATINGS *

Accomplishment (past)		Discouragement (past)	
Hopes based on gains	*Fears not related to gains*	*Hopes not based on gains*	*Fears based on few gains*
West Germany †	United States ††	Panama †	
Brazil	Israel ††		
India	Philippines ††		
Yugoslavia	Brazil		
	Panama		
	Egypt		

Satisfaction (present)		Frustration (present)	
Hopes a source of satisfaction	*Fears not operative enough to be a source of dissatisfaction*	*Hopes not a source of satisfaction*	*Fears a source of frustration*
Egypt	Philippines †	Brazil	West Germany †
Panama	Egypt		Brazil
West Germany	Panama		
	India		
	Cuba		
	Israel		

Expectation (future)		Anxiety (future)	
Hopes a source of anticipation	*Fears not operative enough to be a source of anxiety*	*Hopes not a source of expectation*	*Fears a source of anxiety*
Yugoslavia	India	Brazil	
Egypt	Israel		

* The rank order correlations on which this table is based will be found in Appendix E3.

† Indicates significance at the .05 level of confidence.

†† Indicates significance at the .01 level of confidence.

Within each of the six blocks shown in the tables, hopes and fears have been considered separately but are put within the same block because they seem to point, psychologically, to rather the same conclusion. For example, in the "accomplishment" block, if it is true that the more frequently mentioned the hope, the higher the ladder rating that tends to be associated with that hope, while the more frequently mentioned the fear, the higher the ladder rating associated with that fear, then ladder ratings are going to be high regardless of whether one is talking about hopes or fears.

What these tables mean for each country is summarized in the following brief sketches:

United States. The personal fears Americans share are not operative enough to be a source of frustration with the present or any anxiety concerning the future. The national fears shared by Americans are not related to the gains they feel the nation has made.

West Germany. The personal fears the people in West Germany share are not due to a sense of lack of accomplishment, while the fears the West Germans do have for their nation are a source of frustration with the present. The hopes shared for the nation are a source of satisfaction with the present and are based on a sense of national accomplishment.

Yugoslavia. The shared personal fears of the Yugoslavs are not operative enough to be a source of frustration with the present and there is no feeling that these personal fears are based on lack of accomplishment. The national hopes shared by the Yugoslav people are based on a sense of accomplishment and both the personal and national hopes shared are sources of positive and desirable expectations concerning the future.

Brazil. Both the personal and national hopes Brazilians share are based on a sense of accomplishment but do not serve as sources of expectation concerning the future. Furthermore, the national hopes shared are not a source of satisfaction with the present and the national fears shared are not based on a sense of lack of accomplishment.

Nigeria. Here the only significant finding—and it is highly significant —is that personal hopes are based on a sense of accomplishment.

India. While shared national hopes are based on a sense of national accomplishments, the personal hopes Indians share are not based on a sense of personal accomplishments. Furthermore, the shared personal hopes are neither a source of satisfaction with the present nor a source of expectation about the future. While the shared personal fears are a source of anxiety about the future, the shared national fears are not operative enough to be a source of dissatisfaction with the present or of anxiety about the nation's future.

Israel. Both the personal and national fears shared by Israelis are not operative enough to be a source of frustration with the present, nor are the shared national fears based on any sense of lack of accomplishment. Shared national fears are not operative enough to be a source of dissatisfaction with the present or of anxiety about the future for the people of Israel.

Egypt. For Egyptians, both the personal and national hopes they have are a source of satisfaction with the present, and both the personal and national fears they share are not sufficiently functional to be a source of dissatisfaction with the present. While the national hopes shared are a source of satisfaction with the present and of anticipation about the national future, the personal hopes shared are not a source of expectation about the personal future.

The Philippines. On the personal side there is no significant relationship one way or the other between the concerns people have and their ratings. On the national side, however, the fears shared by Filipinos are not based on a sense of lack of accomplishment, are not operative enough to be a source of dissatisfaction with the present nor a source of anxiety about the future.

Cuba. For the Cuban people at the time of the survey, the personal fears they shared were a source of anxiety about the future as well as a source of frustration with the present. The fears they shared for the nation were not, however, operative enough to be a source of dissatisfaction with the present.

The Dominican Republic. For people in the Dominican Republic, the personal hopes they share do not appear to function as a source of positive expectation or anxiety about the future. But the personal fears shared by people in the Dominican Republic are a source of frustration with the present but are not operative enough to be a source of anxiety about the future.

Panama. The personal fears that Panamanians share are based in part on a sense of little accomplishment and are a source of anxiety about the future. The fears they share for the nation are not based on a sense of small accomplishment and are not operative enough to be a source of frustration concerning the present. The hopes they share for the nation are a source of satisfaction with the present, but are not based on any sense of gains made.

A second method employed to learn more directly what interdependence there was between concerns and ratings was to look at the average national ratings given by people who mention different personal concerns and then to see what average personal ratings were given by people who expressed different concerns for the nation. The illustrations here will be confined to instances where personal ladder ratings deviated by at least 0.5 steps among people who expressed certain concerns for their country. The detailed results of this analysis, indicating where the ladder ratings of people who expressed a given concern deviated by at least 0.5 steps from the mean rating of all people in the country, are given in Appendix D3, since a recital of all the findings here would be tedious.

United States. Lower present personal ratings were assigned themselves by people who hoped for employment, and higher present ratings were assigned by those whose hopes included a desire for a better morality, maintenance of the status quo, and reduction of international tensions.

West Germany. Higher past, present, and future ratings were found among those who said they feared national disunity—indicating that this concern was not sufficiently operational at the time to lower personal ratings.

Yugoslavia. Higher personal future ratings and a greater overall shift upwards from past to future were found among those who hoped for technological advances, better housing and transportation, and greater industrial growth.

Brazil. Higher past, present, and future personal ratings were assigned themselves by people who said they were worried about Communism within the country—showing this is presumably not a major operational concern.

Nigeria. Higher present and future ratings among those who hope for the attainment of the status of a Republic for the country.

India. Higher future rating and greater overall change in personal ratings among those who are fearful of disunity within the nation or loss of national independence, again indicating that these are not intense enough to affect personal ratings adversely.

Israel. Lower future ratings and less overall shift up among those who hope all discrimination will be eliminated in Israel.

Egypt. Lower future ratings and less overall shift up among those who fear there will be no improvement in standard of living.

Philippines. Higher present ratings and greater overall shift upward among those whose hopes for the nation include assurance of national independence or economic stability.

Cuba. Lower present ratings and less shift upwards among those whose fears for the nation include unemployment, inadequate standard of living, or Communism—indicating that these fears *are* operational in lowering personal ratings.

The Dominican Republic. Lower future rating and less overall shift upwards among those who fear there will be no development in the sense of social and political responsibility of the people.

Panama. Lower present rating but a higher future rating and a great shift upward among those who fear political instability—indicating an increased optimism that political stability will be achieved.

OVERLAPPING BETWEEN PERSONAL AND NATIONAL CONCERNS

In order to probe still further the relationship between personal and national hopes, personal and national fears, the data were viewed in two other ways.

In the first place, the ratio was obtained of the total percent of personal hopes mentioned by at least 5 percent of the people when divided by the number of code items mentioned by 5 percent. These ratios were then arranged in rank order by decreasing size, meaning that the smaller ratios represented a greater concentration of concerns. The same was done with personal fears, national hopes, and national fears. Then, instead of making a rank order correlation between personal hopes and personal fears and national hopes and national fears, a correlation was obtained between *personal* hopes and *national* hopes and *personal* fears and *national* fears. The first correlation was 0.77, the second, 0.59, the former significant at the 99 percent level, the latter at the 95 percent level. In other words, the higher the concentration of personal hopes, the higher the concentration of national hopes; and the higher the concentration of personal fears, the higher the concentration of national fears. There is, then, a tendency for a clustering effect to operate, pulling both personal and national hopes or fears together to a relatively similar degree.

We used a second method to learn something more about the comparison of the concern people have on the personal side with their concern expressed for the nation on the same general category—in other words, how much of their national concern spills over as a personal concern, or how "personalized" or how distant a national concern is. To do this we calculated indices based on the following formula:

$$\frac{\text{Average national concern}}{\frac{(\text{National hopes} + \text{National fears})}{2}} \times \frac{\frac{\text{Personal hopes}}{\text{National hopes}} + \frac{\text{Personal fears}}{\text{National fears}}}{2}$$

This apriori device should give us an indication of both the spread and the intensity of the relationship between personal and national concerns.

To illustrate the way the formula works, let us take the example of the general category item concerned with the international situation, war-peace, and substitute in the formula above the figures obtained from the data for two different countries, West Germany and Brazil. In such cases the two indices would be obtained as follows:

$$\text{West Germany} \qquad \frac{42 + 70}{2} \times \frac{\frac{15}{42} + \frac{50}{70}}{2} = 30.0$$

$$\text{Brazil} \qquad \frac{5+19}{2} \times \frac{\dfrac{1}{5}+\dfrac{3}{19}}{2} = 2.1$$

In this illustration the reality of the concern expressed about the international situation, war-peace, on the national code is seen to be much greater for Germany than for Brazil in terms of personal involvement and spread within the population. The indices thus obtained on all the general categories where the personal and national concerns could be compared are given in Table XI:5. Table XI:6 gives the rank order of

TABLE XI:5

INDICES BY COUNTRIES AND CATEGORIES

Country	Political	Economic	Social	International, war-peace	Status quo unconcern	*Average*
United States	3.3	56.1	14.1	17.1	13.7	21
West Germany	6.0	67.7	9.7	30.0	4.0	23
Yugoslavia	0.0	88.7	35.8	16.5	0.8	28
Brazil	0.4	47.3	13.4	2.1	3.0	13
Nigeria	2.2	81.3	43.8	0.5	1.7	26
India	0.4	67.1	16.5	0.3	2.5	17
Israel	2.1	70.1	25.6	19.5	10.0	25
Kibbutzim	3.6	38.7	109.6	36.2	3.0	38
Egypt	4.0	61.4	37.1	2.9	4.1	22
Philippines	0.5	63.8	8.0	7.2	0.8	16
Cuba	21.2	73.3	34.6	4.2	4.6	28
Dominican Republic	9.0	97.1	11.1	0.3	0.0	24
Panama	1.5	79.5	16.9	1.0	0.3	20
Average	*4.2*	*68.6*	*28.9*	*10.6*	*3.7*	*23*

the average of all indices. The same data are included in the two different tabular forms in order to make comparison easier.

If the meaning of these figures is spelled out in the different countries in terms of what people are aware of and concerned about, what their personal involvement is in national problems, the description runs as follows:

United States. Although the greatest concern is with economic problems, as it is in all countries except the microcosm of the Kibbutzim, it is less than average. There is more concern in the United States than in any other country for preserving the status quo; there is more concern

TABLE XI:6

RANK ORDER OF AVERAGE OF ALL INDICES

Country	Average of indices
Kibbutzim	38.2
Yugoslavia	28.4
Cuba	27.6
Nigeria	25.9
Israel	25.4
Dominican Republic	23.5
West Germany	23.4
Egypt	21.9
United States	20.9
Panama	19.8
India	17.4
Philippines	16.1
Brazil	13.2

than average with international affairs and considerably more involvement with social responsibilities than in the other advanced Western nation, West Germany.

West Germany. Next to the people in the Kibbutzim, West Germans have a higher concern about international problems, including war and peace, than people in any other country studied, obviously because of the split in their country and their position vis-à-vis the Soviet Union. While there is more than average concern for political affairs, there is very little mention of social responsibilities, indicating, as noted before, that at the time of the survey West Germans were rather underdeveloped in the area of social awareness and involvement.

Yugoslavia. Yugoslavians have a very high concern and awareness with economic problems and are definitely above average on the social problems facing the nation. They are not the slightest involved in the political area, but they have a greater personal involvement in national concerns than any other people except Kibbutzim members.

Brazil. Overall, the people of Brazil are less personally involved in national problems than the citizens of any other country studied. Brazilians are low in all categories; at the time of the study, they were little able to become personally concerned about national problems of an economic, social, political, or international nature.

Nigeria. The Nigerians are very high in their economic concerns and, next to members of the Kibbutzim, higher than any other group in their sense of social responsibility. Their personal involvement in international affairs is extremely low.

India. In spite of the problems facing India, the Indian people show only average concern about economic problems, less than average on social affairs, and practically none in the political or international area. The average of all their indices is extremely low.

Israel. On the overall scale, Israelis are high especially in the international area. Their involvement in maintaining the status quo is also high, doubtless indicating their eagerness to hang on to what they have achieved in nationhood.

The Kibbutzim. Members of the Kibbutzim are highest of all in their average overall indices with an outstanding and unique personal involvement with social values and, as we have already seen in earlier chapters, with very little concern for the economic area, which is well taken care of in their communal life. Their personal concern with international problems, with war, and with peace is higher than that of any other group.

Egypt. Egyptians have only an average personal concern in the economic area, but they are above average in the area of social responsibilities. They have slightly more than average concern in maintaining the status quo, doubtless because of the new state which they are eager to maintain.

Philippines. Personal involvement in social problems is less than for any other nation in our sample. At the time our study was made, the Filipinos were generally unconcerned in all areas.

Cuba. Cubans were generally a highly concerned people and higher than any other country studied in the political area. They also showed above average involvement in wanting to maintain the status quo; doubtless, like the Egyptians, they want to hold on to the gains made by their revolution. They showed less than average concern with international problems.

Dominican Republic. Personal involvement in economic problems is greater than in any of the other countries. They were also high in the political area, since they had recently become aware of political situations and possibilities. They showed practically no involvement in international problems.

Panama. Except for higher concern than average in the economic area, Panamanians were lower than average in all other categories, with practically no personal concern about political or international problems.

As seen from Table XI:5, there is greatest personal involvement in the economic problems of the nation as measured by the overall average of the indices. Next in line, but a considerable jump down, comes personal involvement in social problems, then another jump down to the area of international problems and war and peace, with involvement in the political area being extremely low.

THE EFFECTS OF EDUCATION

A test of Hamilton's contention that "affections are weak in proportion to the distance or diffusion of the object" was made in the last survey conducted in this series of studies, the second survey in India. People were asked to fill in the question "How important to you personally is your ————?" by mentioning different prescribed groups or concepts with which they might identify themselves. They were furthermore asked in each instance to rate the importance of the group on the ladder. The groups or concepts, together with the mean ladder ratings, are shown in Table XI:7. It should be remembered that this particular

TABLE XI:7

MEAN RATINGS AND "NO ANSWER" ON PERSONAL
IMPORTANCE OF IDENTIFICATIONS

Identification	Mean rating	"No answer"
India	9.2	14%
Family	7.9	15
State	7.8	19
Language group	6.9	22
United Nations	6.4	61
The Commonwealth	5.2	66
Caste	4.2	19

study was done just after the Sino-Indian border conflict, when a sense of nationalism was unusually high. It should also be pointed out that many Indians are unlikely to give a frank evaluation of the importance of caste to a stranger since this identification is officially discouraged and often laden with emotional overtones an Indian would not care to share except with his most intimate friends and relatives.

Identification with India at the time of the study is clearly higher than any other identification, while the United Nations and The Commonwealth are clearly distant and diffuse, shown not only by the low ladder ratings but by the fact that six out of ten people were unable to make any rating at all.

When these identifications are examined by educational groupings within the Indian population, huge variations appear. Table XI:8 shows the percentage of people in different educational levels who assigned a ladder rating of 8 or more to the importance of the various identifications, while Table XI:9 indicates the percentage of people in each group who were unable to give any ladder rating at all. Clearly for the illiterates—four fifths of the total Indian population—both the United

TABLE XI:8

IDENTIFICATIONS BY EDUCATION, PERCENTAGE RATINGS AT 7 OR ABOVE

	Illiterate	Under matriculate	Matriculate	Intermediate graduate or above
India	19%	39%	18%	24%
Family	19	38	18	25
State	19	42	18	21
Language group	18	43	19	20
United Nations	4	27	26	43
The Commonwealth	3	24	24	49
Caste	29	39	15	17

TABLE XI:9

PERCENTAGE OF "NO ANSWER" ON IDENTIFICATIONS

Identification	Illiterate	Under matriculate	Matriculate	Intermediate graduate or above
India	33%	7%	1%	2%
Family	31	9	1	1
State	42	10	2	3
Language group	49	13	4	3
United Nations	93	63	22	7
The Commonwealth	96	71	29	11
Caste	37	13	2	2

Nations and The Commonwealth are almost meaningless, while caste is a more important source of loyalty. Among the best educated people, both the United Nations and The Commonwealth stand out in their importance above all other identifications.

In order to check the relative influence of educational background on concerns, the total sample of cases was sorted out by education and socioeconomic status, by education and age, and by education and urban or rural dwelling. In this way we were able to learn what percentage of people in each sub-category had expressed different concerns. We shall consider here the general categories dealing with aspirations for the nation: *international* (peace, disarmament, lessening of cold war, better relations with Communist bloc, maintain neutrality, etc.); *independent status* (national independence, be important in regional affairs, be militarily strong, etc.); *social* (social justice, eliminate discrimination, better education, improved labor conditions, public health, etc.); *political* (honest, efficient, balanced. or representative government, freedom, law and order, political stability, national unity, etc.); and *economic* (economic stability, improved or decent standard of living, employment, housing, social security, etc.). Table XI:10 gives the percentages and is based on over 23,000 card units.

TABLE XI:10

ASPIRATIONS FOR THE NATION BY EDUCATION AND OTHER VARIABLES

Variable	Inter-national	Independent status	Social	Political	Economic	N*
BEST EDUCATED						
Income: upper	30%	22%	34%	42%	70%	881
middle	23	18	37	33	68	900
lower	35	13	37	48	66	231
Age: 50+	38	26	43	37	60	329
49–30	30	19	38	40	66	870
29–	22	17	31	4	74	848
Dwelling: rural	17	12	27	38	64	750
urban	35	23	41	38	70	1313
MIDDLE EDUCATED						
Income: upper	36	14	33	33	67	1191
middle	44	17	35	28	69	1480
lower	29	17	41	44	69	1297
Age: 50+	47	15	37	30	60	705
49–30	42	16	36	33	66	1872
29–	26	18	37	37	73	1475
Dwelling: rural	27	15	33	36	66	1467
urban	43	17	39	33	69	2605
LEAST EDUCATED						
Income: upper	18	7	25	31	72	1058
middle	15	9	24	20	69	4509
lower	10	7	27	35	71	11598
Age: 50+	16	7	22	30	64	4401
49–30	12	8	28	32	72	8090
29–	9	9	26	29	73	4877
Dwelling: rural	7	6	24	29	70	12315
urban	23	11	32	35	72	5084

* The small variations in the totals for each educational group in the different sub-groups are due to incomplete returns on some background data.

With respect to a concern for the nation's *international* situation, the least educated people are much lower than either the middle educational group (those with the equivalent of at least some high school education) or the best educated group (those with some university education) in all socioeconomic and age categories as well as among both rural and urban dwellers. Except among the low income people, there is greater concern for the nation's international problems among those with average education than among those with high education: even in the United States with its high proportion of the population who have been to or graduated from college and where 59 percent of all Americans expressed a concern for international affairs, there is no appreciably greater concern among the best educated and those with moderate education (see Table XI:11).

TABLE XI:11

PERCENTAGE OF PEOPLE IN THE UNITED STATES IN THREE EDUCATIONAL GROUPS (BY INCOME) WHO EXPRESS CONCERN FOR INTERNATIONAL PROBLEMS

Income	Low education	Middle education	High education
Low	47%	61%	51%
Middle	53	64	65
High	58	64	66
Total %	*32*	*49*	*19*

Concern for international problems goes up with income among those with least education; people in urban areas are significantly more concerned about international problems in all educational categories, with urban persons of low education even more concerned than the best educated rural people. It has also been noted that there is a greater concern for international affairs in all educational groups among older people, practically doubling in each educational category when the youngest and oldest groups are compared.

There is less concern for the nation's *independent status* among the least educated groups in all socioeconomic and age groups while among the best educated people this concern increases with economic status, with age, and with urbanization.

The effect of education on the *social* concerns for the nation again shows that the least educated are less concerned in all categories. However, those living in cities tend to be more sensitive to social problems than those living in rural areas, irrespective of education. The people most concerned about the nation's social problems are older people with high education.

While the least educated people are somewhat less concerned about *political* matters than others, there are some important exceptions: only 4 percent of all well-educated young people express any political interests while poorly educated people who live in cities are considerably higher than many of their better educated compatriots, for example

than the middle educated, middle income group where the difference between these two sub-samples is significant at the 99 percent level of confidence (Chart 1, Appendix C).

When it comes to a concern for the nation's *economic* welfare, however,
consistent differences by education almost disappear and age becomes
more of a factor, with older people in each educational group having
fewer economic aspirations for the nation.

Summary

This review of the interplay of personal aspirations and worries with
the hopes and fears the same people have for their country, points to
the following conclusions:

1. Among peoples whose countries have recently experienced radical
political changes which discarded an outmoded and unpopular government (i.e., Cuba and the Dominican Republic), there is high personal
involvement with national problems, including great political concern,
as shown by the relatively high correlations between personal and national ratings and the relatively high scores on our indices. Personal
worries remain a source of frustration with the present while the estimate assigned the nation's position is affected by whether or not people
have faith that revolutionary gains will be stabilized. Among people so
involved in their domestic affairs, there is little personal concern expressed for the nation's international stance.

2. Among a people who are in the process of achieving national independence at a time when they are still underdeveloped economically
(i.e., Nigeria), there is also high personal involvement in national
affairs as indicated by the high correlation between personal and national ratings and the relatively high participation index. This involvement is particularly operative in the economic area but practically non-
existent in the area of international affairs. Personal hopes are strongly
rooted in the sense of accomplishment in the past, and high personal
ratings are given by those who rather confidently look forward to the
national independence of their nation, to political stability, and to an
improved standard of living with accompanying social gains.

3. Among a people whose nation achieved independence some years
ago and who still have hardly become aware of and begun to solve the
problems connected with their economic and social development (i.e.,
India), there is an unusually high proportion of people who are unable
to assign either themselves or their nation a rating on the ladder of life.
There is little personal involvement with national problems, as measured
by our indices, and complete uniformity in national ratings by people
who express different personal concerns. While there is a sense that the
nation's progress is based on its accomplishments and while worries
for the nation are not intense enough to be a source of dissatisfaction

and anxiety, the personal hopes people have are not based on a sense of gains made in their individual lives and are not a source of confident expectancies for the future.

4. Among a people who have been united into a nation for a long period but who are still very backward in their economic and social development after a stormy political history which has still not become stabilized (i.e., Brazil), there is little personal involvement in national problems of any kind. A third of the people find it impossible to assign their nation a rating for the past or present while nearly half are so be-wildered about things to come that they cannot assign the nation a rat-ing for the future. In this context, the personal worries people have are a source of anxiety while their hopes for the nation are not well enough founded to be either a source of satisfaction with the present or of antici-pation concerning the future. In spite of continued political turmoil and economic crisis, those who say they fear Communism do not regard this possibility as sufficiently likely to let it alter their optimistic ratings for the nation.

5. Among a people who have recently become united into an inde-pendent state after centuries of division into various nationality groups and who have strong, popular centralized leadership (i.e., Yugoslavia), there is high personal involvement with respect to the economic and social problems facing the country. Personal participation in the national effort assumes the shape of working within an administrative framework where the goals are essentially means to achieve the fixed aims laid down by those in power and in whom the people appear to have great confi-dence and faith. The people who appear most ego-involved in achieving the administrative goals laid down assign themselves higher personal ratings. In this situation, the hopes people express for the nation are based on a sense of accomplishment. Personal and national hopes are a source of anticipation of the future, while personal worries are not in-tense enough to be a source of dissatisfaction.

6. Among a people of a newly created nation which has brought to-gether people from many lands who share a religious conviction (i.e., Israel), there is a sense of considerable personal involvement in national affairs although our correlations indicate that this is decreasing. Because of the sense of success in achieving a high standard of living, a stable social democracy, and the capacity of the state to absorb new people and integrate them into ongoing activities, the worries people have are not a source of dissatisfaction to them or of anxiety concerning the nation's future.

7. In the world's most economically advanced nation where economic and social advances are still proceeding apace and where the people have enjoyed democratic political stability for a hundred years (i.e., United States), there is relatively little personal involvement in the national

arena except in the international area. The worries most people have are not intense enough to be sources of dissatisfaction with the present or of anxiety about the future and the fears people express for the nation are not based on a sense of lack of past accomplishment.

8. Among people who have recently experienced the ravages of war (i.e., Yugoslavia, West Germany, Israel, The Philippines) or, (as with Americans) who know the consequences for them of another war in which they might be a major belligerent, there is more personal involvement in the problems the nation faces in the international arena of world affairs and the maintenance of peace. On the other hand, among people who have neither directly suffered from recent war on their territory or who are not involved as major protagonists in any potential East-West conflict (i.e., India, Nigeria, Brazil), there is very little personal interest in world affairs as these affect their countries.

9. People who have at least the equivalent of some secondary education demonstrate a greater interest in certain aspects of their nation's affairs than those less well educated; the difference in the concerns of educated and uneducated being by far the greatest with respect to the more psychologically remote, less tangible, less immediate area of the nation's international relationships and its independent status. Education also consistently affects the concern a person has in the social problems confronting the nation more than does his economic status, his age, or whether he lives in the city or the country. Differences in concern by education diminish in the political area and disappear entirely when it comes to aspirations regarding the nation's economic situation, a tangible, immediate, and pressing concern for the least educated, of whom two thirds are in the low income group (Appendix B2).

There does not seem to be any progressively greater concern for the nation's problems with the degree of higher education; the "awakening" to national affairs apparently occurs at the secondary level and is not deepened or broadened by higher education within the sample as a whole.

Part Four

STRIVINGS, SATISFACTIONS, SITUATIONS

CHAPTER XII

Who Are the Satisfied?

The function of this chapter is essentially to provide a snapshot to find out where people think they stand at the present time on the personal ladder rating, to find out which individuals rate themselves high or low, and what the concerns are of those who put themselves at different points on the ladder of life. After this has been done, by way of a footnote, some related material from our survey of the United States will be reviewed to give a bit more insight on the psychological requirements for "satisfaction."

GROUPING LADDER RATINGS

People were separated into three groups by the ladder ratings given on the personal present: *low* (Steps 0, 1, 2, 3), *middle* (Steps 4, 5, 6), and *high* (Steps 7, 8, 9, 10). The overall distribution thus obtained is shown in Table XII:1. It should be emphasized again that these ratings must all be viewed within the cultural ethos at the time the surveys were made. It will be noted, for example, that at the time of our survey in Cuba, slightly a year after Castro's revolution, nearly half of the Cuban people rated themselves in the high group.

As shown in Chapter IX, the highest correlation (.67) between the socioeconomic indices of development and ladder ratings was with the rating people gave themselves on the present. A rank order correlation of the percentage of people in the countries sampled who placed themselves in our top rating group with the socioeconomic indices is .60 and that with people who placed themselves in our bottom group is −.74, the former figure significant at the 95 percent level of confidence, the latter at the 99 percent level. This is further evidence that people in poorer countries regard themselves as underdeveloped in terms of their own definitions of what a full life would be.

RATINGS AND DEMOGRAPHIC BACKGROUND

Table XII:2 shows the percentage of people in the overall sample who fall into the different rating groups according to their education,

TABLE XII:1

DISTRIBUTION BY RATING GROUP

(N = 25,115)

Country	Low	Middle	High	No answer	Developmental index
United States	7%	41%	51%	1%	1.00
West Germany	14	59	24	3	.71
Israel	19	50	29	2	.67
Cuba	9	43	45	3	.35
Panama	26	54	18	2	.31
Yugoslavia	21	57	21	1	.19
Philippines	24	54	21	1	.17
Dominican Republic	84	13	1	2	.16
Brazil	28	35	18	19	.16
Egypt	17	51	30	2	.14
Nigeria	28	46	21	5	.02
India	39	42	4	15	.00
Total %	*31*	*42*	*20*	*7*	

their income level, their occupation, their dwelling, and their sex and age.

It is abundantly clear from Table XII:2 that the interrelated variables of education, income, and occupation sharply differentiate the people who fall into the three groups based on the ladder ratings they gave themselves at the time the studies were made. There is also a tendency for people living in urban centers to rate themselves somewhat higher than those living on the land, and for older people to appear somewhat more resigned to their status in life. In the overall picture, men and women rate themselves about the same.

It is revealing to look at the extremes: groups where the highest percentage of people put themselves in the top bracket or in the bottom bracket. The tables from which these figures are taken, giving demographic background by countries, will be found in Appendix D2. I am including in the list of extremes only groupings where the number of cases was at least 100.

The rank order of groups with the largest percentage of *high* ladder ratings is:

United States—upper educational	63%
United States—upper income	63
Cuba—upper income	56
Israel—upper educational	55
Israel—upper income	54
Cuba—upper educational	51

TABLE XII:2

LADDER GROUPINGS BY DEMOGRAPHIC BACKGROUND

Demographic background	Low	Middle	High
EDUCATION			
High	11%	43%	46%
Middle	18	54	28
Low	32	48	20
INCOME			
High	11	49	40
Middle	18	54	28
Low	37	45	18
OCCUPATION			
Prof./bus./tech.	8	44	48
Mgr./official	10	45	45
White collar	18	43	39
Skilled	26	52	22
Unskilled	38	44	18
Farmers	37	48	15
Nonlabor	33	41	26
Housewife (if no head of household)	30	57	13
DWELLING			
Urban	23	50	27
Rural	31	46	23
SEX			
Male	29	47	24
Female	27	48	25
AGE			
–29	28	48	24
30–49	29	49	22
50+	25	46	29

The groups with the largest percentage of people in the *low* ladder rating brackets are:

Dominican Republic—low income	90%
Dominican Republic—rural	90
Dominican Republic—low educational	87
India—low income	58
India—under thirty years of age	50
Brazil—low income	47

Obviously, when one speaks of better educated and upper income people in the United States or in Israel, one is often talking about the same individuals. Likewise, the low income, rural, and poorly educated people in the Dominican Republic are largely drawn from the same sample, 94 percent of the low educational group, for example, being also in the lowest economic bracket (Appendix B2).

It is also revealing to learn where the ratios of the percentage of people in different groups within different countries differ appreciably from the overall average. This is shown in Table XII:3 where, for purposes of clarity, figures which reveal appreciable differences were selected from the data in Tables 21 and 23 of Appendix D2.

In reading Table XII:3 it is important to emphasize again that the interest is in ratios of groups within different countries and not with absolute percentage figures. Looking at these ratios, various conclusions stand out with respect to the different countries studied.

United States. There is considerably less spread among those who rate themselves in the top group when differentiated by education, income, or rural-urban—indicating the relative uniformity of the feeling of Americans that they are high on the ladder of life. At least four out of ten people in what is for the United States the low income group are found in the top bracket of the ladder rating, while only six out of ten upper income people rate themselves there. Differences between those who live in cities or on the land disappear completely.

Israel. There is a greater than average spread by income and education among those who rate themselves in the top group.

Cuba. At the time the survey was made, there seems to have been a common denominator of fervor after the revolution with very little spread by education or income among those who put themselves in our top bracket.

Yugoslavia. The relative economic security people feel is reflected again in the smaller spread between high and low income groups who rate themselves either in the top or bottom categories while the emphasis on the value of education is reflected in the greater than average spread by this variable both among those who rate themselves in the top and the bottom brackets.

The Philippines. A greater than average spread both by income and by rural-urban among those who put themselves in the top bracket.

The Dominican Republic. Where the vast majority of people rate themselves extremely low, as seen before, there is a much greater than average spread of those who put themselves in the bottom category according to their income and their education, variables which are, of course, closely interrelated.

Brazil. Considerably more men than women put themselves in the lowest bracket and fewer place themselves in the top bracket; those who

TABLE XII:3

WHERE RATIOS OF GROUPS WITHIN COUNTRIES DIFFER APPRECIABLY FROM OVERALL AVERAGE

Variable	Percent in low group							Percent in top group								
	Overall	Yugoslavia	Dominican Republic	Brazil	Egypt	Nigeria	India	*Overall*	United States	Israel	Cuba	Yugoslavia	Philippines	Brazil	Egypt	Nigeria
EDUCATION																
High	*11*	6	21	3			29	*46*	63	55	51	56		60		
Middle	*18*	9	57	13			28	*28*	52	35	46	32		38		
Low	*32*	24	87	37			49	*20*	42	18	46	18		20		
INCOME																
High	*11*	16	35	6			19	*40*	63	54	56	30	48	51		
Middle	*18*	14		30			40	*28*	50	30	49	27	18	22		
Low	*37*	24	90	47			58	*18*	40	13	43	19	9	15		
DWELLING																
Urban	*23*		24	12	28	36		*27*	52				30	28	38	20
Rural	*31*		41	20	30	49		*23*	51				18	18	28	23
SEX																
Male	*29*		41		28	47	24							17		24
Female	*27*		28		35	41	25							27		12
AGE																
−29	*28*				35	50	24									18
30–49	*29*				27	45	22									20
50+	*25*				25	41	29									34

live in the cities are found more frequently in the top category and much less frequently than rural people in the lower category. Furthermore, both the top and bottom brackets show that Brazilians vary more than average in placing themselves according to their education and their income.

Egypt. Those in rural areas are found more frequently in the lowest bracket, less frequently than city dwellers in the top bracket. Here the study, to repeat, must be regarded as a preliminary pilot study.

Nigeria. There is less than average spread by rural-urban but more than average spread between men and women, with more men than women feeling they are in the top bracket and fewer saying they are in the low bracket. A difference by age shows up in Nigeria with younger people found more frequently in the low category, less frequently in the top one.

India. Where a large proportion of people are found in the low bracket, sex, age, and place of residence are related to placement: more men than women, more younger people than older people, more rural than urban, feel they are low in the hierarchy. The ratio of placement varies greatly by education and income.

Somewhat more general conclusions can be drawn from Table XII:3:

1. In both the rich, private enterprise, "welfare" nation of the United States and the poorer, socialist nation of Yugoslavia, the differential placement by income is less than average. Apparently in each country there is a relative sense of economic security even among the low income groups; they know that no matter how bad their economic plight may be compared to their compatriots they still will not personally suffer unduly. This is in marked contrast to countries like Brazil, the Philippines, or busy Israel, where lower income people are more severely affected subjectively by the discrepancies of their socioeconomic status than their wealthier compatriots.

2. Except for Nigeria, people living in rural areas of undeveloped or poor countries rate themselves appreciably lower than average on the ladder. Nigeria differs from Brazil, Egypt, and India in this respect for several reasons: the population in Nigeria classified as "urban" is chiefly found in towns rather than in large cities, and among Nigerians in both towns and cities extremely close ties are maintained with clans and other groups found in rural areas from which people have migrated. Thus, the identification of many people living in urban areas to "urban" values is extremely tenuous.

3. While differences by sex are generally insignificant, in Brazil it appears that the breadwinning males in a nation suffering rapid inflation felt more frustrated than women did, while in India, too, more men than women were found in the lowest bracket.

4. Age differences, too, are usually small but appear in the two poor countries of Nigeria and India where the unfulfilled ambitions of the younger people are reflected in the higher proportion who put themselves in the low bracket.

RATINGS AND CONCERNS

In order to learn what differences there were in the aspirations and fears of people in the different ladder rating categories, the percentage in each of the rating groups who expressed the different concerns grouped into the general categories was found for the total sample of all countries (see Table XII:4).

TABLE XII:4

<small>Percentage in Total "World" Sample in High, Middle, and Low Groups who Express Different Concerns *</small>

	As hopes			As fears		
General categories	High	Middle	Low	High	Middle	Low
PERSONAL						
Values and character	29%	22%	17%	10%	8%	6%
Economic conditions	68	75	84	40	48	63
Job or work situation	19	21	20	5	6	6
Health of self or family	41	31	21	52	47	35
Family references	53	52	45	28	26	23
Political references	4	2	3	6	3	3
Social references	6	6	5	5	5	2
International references	5	3	1	16	11	4
Want status quo or have no fears	6	2	1	10	6	4
NATIONAL						
Economic	64	73	72	29	32	35
Political	35	30	37	39	36	41
Social	35	32	24	16	16	12
International	32	20	8	38	33	19
Independent status	17	14	8	17	18	13
Preserve national status quo or have no fears for nation	3	1	0	5	4	5
N	*5066*	*10593*	*7682*	*5066*	*10593*	*7682*

* Because of the large number of cases involved in the tabulations, differences are significant at the .05 level if they are even 2 percent.

Those who rate themselves in the higher bracket tend to be more concerned about everything, both in terms of their aspirations and their worries, than do people who rate themselves in the lower bracket, except with respect to their own and the nation's economic problems. People who rate themselves relatively high are especially more concerned about health, both as a hope and a fear, have more aspirations in the areas of personal values and character and family life, and are much more concerned on both the personal and national fronts about international problems. Although the number of people who want to preserve the status quo or who express no fears for themselves is small throughout, the ratio is, of course, greater among those with higher ratings.

People who rate themselves at the lower end of the ladder are much more concerned about economic problems, as already seen so often in earlier chapters. The difference between them and people who rate themselves at the upper end of the ladder is especially great with respect to their fears and worries. While people who give themselves a high rating still mention economic aspirations more frequently than any other, they mention economic fears and worries much less frequently than they do concern for health, a situation that by no means obtains among those who are in the lower rating group. This confirms the earlier finding that concern for the fulfillment of survival needs is a total experience, which preempts the energies and consciousness of individuals so pressured and repels concerns for other things, including even health, let alone such "remote" preoccupations as aspirations for the nation on the international front.

Since the fear of war appeared more frequently than any other concern for the nation (p. 278, Chapter XIII) and was so frequently mentioned as a personal concern, as shown in earlier chapters, the question naturally arises as to whether or not there are any differences in the mean ladder ratings of those who express this fear and those who do not. Table XII:5, based on our total sample of over 19,000 people, indi-

TABLE XII:5

MEAN LADDER RATINGS BY FEAR OF WAR

Time	Express fear of war	Do not express fear of war
NATIONAL		
Past	4.3	4.1
Present	5.8	5.6
Future	7.7	7.4
PERSONAL		
Past	4.1	4.0
Present	5.1	4.8
Future	7.0	6.8

cates that the answer is in the negative: those who mention war as a fear do not give lower national or personal ladder ratings.

Furthermore, when the mean ratings of those who mentioned fear of war in each country are examined, in no single instance did the people of a nation who expressed a fear of war give lower ratings than those who did not. The slightly higher mean ratings of those who did express a fear of war seen in Table XII:5 are largely due to the fact that people in the poorer nations who rated themselves lower on the ladder generally were those least concerned about war (p. 181, Chapter VIII). While this particular concern was not analyzed with other factors controlled, the evidence indicates that fear of war in and of itself is, on the whole, *not* a sufficiently operational and dominating fear to lower a person's estimate of where he is on the ladder, where he will be, or where the nation is or will be.

I wondered what the personal present rating would be for those people in India for whom a new code category of "resigned to fate or God's will —nothing worse can happen" was introduced. The mean ladder rating of the fifty-eight people who were so classified shows that they were, apparently, really somewhat more "resigned" since they put themselves at the personal present at 5.0 as compared to the personal present rating of 3.7 for the Indian sample as a whole.

SOME INGREDIENTS OF SATISFACTION

In order to learn something more about variables that might be involved in producing the psychological matrix experienced as "satisfaction," I included in our study of the United States, along with our Self-Anchoring Scale questions, several other questions designed to learn more about the constituents of this state of mind.[1] All evaluations were obtained by use of the ladder device.

I include some of the results here, since they give greater depth to our snapshot when the camera is focused on the United States.

Some Dimensions of Satisfaction

One of the questions asked and separated in the interview from the self-anchoring questions by a number of other questions was a head-on inquiry as to how satisfied people were:

> Some people seem to be quite happy and satisfied with their lives, while others seem quite unhappy and dissatisfied. Now, look at the ladder again. Suppose that a person who is entirely satisfied with his life would be at the *top* of the ladder, and a person who is extremely dissatisfied with his life would be at the *bottom* of the ladder.
>
> Where would you put yourself on the ladder at the present stage of your life in terms of how satisfied or dissatisfied you are with your own personal life?

The mean rating on this question was 7.6. The mean rating of Americans on the personal present for the Self-Anchoring Scale, as already reported, was 6.6, lower by a whole point. This is doubtless because in the self-anchoring questions people had been encouraged to dream about the ideal life for themselves, thus creating the highest aspirations they could which were still realistic in their own terms.

To learn more of what this self-estimate might mean, I asked the following series of questions, designed both to elucidate a person's estimate of himself and what he felt were some of the psychological relationships he had with his environment. The order of the questions reported below has been rearranged here to put them in the rank order of the mean rating given by Americans in 1959.

Now, I am going to ask you some questions which you can easily answer by looking at the ladder I showed you before.

After I ask you each question, just point to the place on the ladder you think is appropriate for you *now*. Don't be hesitant or embarrassed in putting yourself near the top or near the bottom of the ladder *if* that is the way you happen to feel. Just give your first reaction without thinking too much about it.

	Mean Rating
How important would you say *religion* is in your life. If religion is extremely important, use the top of the ladder; if it is not at all important, use the bottom.	8.5
Now, how about the *respect* you have for yourself *as a person* —that is, your feelings of being a worthwhile and worthy person, as contrasted to a feeling that you are a failure and don't amount to much. Think of worthwhileness as the top, sense of failure as the bottom.	8.1
To what extent do you feel there *is* a good deal you can do *yourself* to make your life happier and more satisfying than it is, as contrasted to the feeling that there *isn't* very much you can do about it yourself. Let the top of the ladder stand for being able to do a good deal for yourself, the bottom stand for a feeling of rather complete helplessness.	7.6
How about your *confidence* in yourself in general—that is, how sure you feel of yourself. Think of the top of the ladder as complete confidence in yourself, the bottom as not being at all sure of yourself.	7.4
Would you say that, by and large, you enjoyed yourself *yesterday?* Let's see, yesterday was: _____. Think of the top as having enjoyed yourself a lot, the bottom as not at all.	7.3

*Mean
Rating*

Now, how about the extent to which you feel you have an *opportunity* to do what you would *like to do,* as contrasted to the feeling that you are doing only what you have *"got"* to do. Think of the top of the ladder as being completely free to do what you want to do, the bottom as doing only what you have to do.   7.0

How would you rate yourself as to how *successful* or unsuccessful you have been in terms of achieving your own goals and aims in life? Think of the top of the ladder as being completely successful, the bottom as being entirely unsuccessful.   6.7

To what extent do you feel your life is full of *troubles* or *obstacles?* This time think of the *top* of the ladder as indicating a person whose life is mainly a whole series of problems and obstacles he is facing and the *bottom* as a person *without* troubles or obstacles.   4.3

To what extent are you *worried* or *afraid* that things might get worse for you and your family; that is, to what extent are you anxious that such things as your financial situation, your security, your health, your social position, your opportunities, etc., *might* become worse than they are now? This time think of the *top* of the ladder as indicating you are extremely worried; the *bottom* indicating you are not at all worried.   4.1

When these dimensions are correlated with the personal present ladder ratings, it turns out that "success in achieving goals," "satisfaction with life," and "extent of opportunity to do what one likes" are, not surprisingly, most closely related to the personal present self-anchoring rating since the meaning involved in these questions is closest to the meaning of the Self-Anchoring Scale itself. The extent to which a person felt he had worries and troubles was, of course, negatively related, and the evaluation that showed by far the least correlation was that concerned with the importance of religion (see Table XII:6).

When the dimensions were correlated with each other, it was found, as expected, that there was a close association, although the correlations with "worries" and "troubles" were somewhat lower than others. The lowest correlation of all was that concerning the "importance of religion" to self-evaluations on all other dimensions: religion seemed to have little effect on the way people perceived themselves, in spite of the very high rating this dimension received. The respect a person had for himself received a mean rating that was second only to religion, and this rating

TABLE XII:6

CORRELATION OF DIMENSION RATINGS WITH PERSONAL PRESENT
SELF-EVALUATIONS

Dimension	Correlation with present personal rating
Success in achieving goals	0.39
Satisfaction with life	0.36
Extent of opportunity to do what one likes	0.32
Ability to do things oneself to increase satisfaction	0.29
Confidence in oneself	0.28
Enjoyment of previous day	0.25
Respect for oneself	0.21
Importance of religion	0.11
Extent of troubles or obstacles in life *	−0.25
Worry or fear that things might get worse *	−0.27

* Top of scale indicated many worries and troubles.

on self-respect correlated highly with other dimensions, particularly with self-confidence, success in achieving goals, and general satisfaction. (The correlations are shown in Table 52, Appendix F2.)

Sensed Deficiencies

After learning what people regarded as their worries and frustrations, I asked them specifically about a number of factors that common sense, psychological understanding, and extensive pretesting all indicated might be widespread sources of discontent. After evaluations on a list of items were obtained, people were asked whether or not they expected that these deficiencies would be remedied in the next few years. The questions asked, together with the results, are shown below.

Nearly all of us, of course, want many things in life that we don't have. Sometimes our wants concern the material goods of life, sometimes they concern opportunities, sometimes they concern psychological or what are sometimes called spiritual satisfactions.

Will you tell me from the list on this card those items which seem to you particularly deficient in *your own* life now—that is, those which you really feel would make a big difference in your own happiness, even though you may already have mentioned these to me in answering my earlier questions.

You may name as many as you like that you feel are *really important* to you.

Area of deficiency	Do not now have (percent of total sample)	Expect to have (percent of those indicating deficiency)
Greater economic or financial security	56%	78%
Better education than I now have	53	39
More pay, larger income	48	79
Greater faith in God or religion	43	94
Being of more service to other people	42	90
Better home to live in	41	86
More leisure time and chance to enjoy leisure	39	78
More opportunities for my own personal development	36	76
Better health	35	65
Ability to get more enjoyment out of life, greater capacity to be satisfied with things as they are for me now	33	82
Happier home and family life	27	84
More interesting work; more congenial job	26	66
More exciting life	21	59

Two observations should be made. For one thing, it will be seen that an insufficient education was regarded by over half the people as a deficiency and that there was greater pessimism about improving this state of affairs than there was on any other of the items mentioned, obviously because once a person's formal education ceases and he assumes job and family responsibilities, he finds it difficult to better his education. Among the 39 percent of the people who did feel they could acquire more education, are doubtless found the millions of Americans who attend adult education classes, take extension courses, and the like. A second important item is the desire for better health, which, as seen before, is a major concern of Americans and was mentioned by 40 percent of them as a personal fear. The somewhat lower figure obtained here is doubtless due to the fact that people were asked to indicate what their deficiencies were *at the moment* and did not, as in our striving scale, place concerns in a larger temporal context. Still, about 40 million adult Americans indicated that their health at the moment was not what they would like it to be, which is a high figure and one that reveals the health standards Americans have.

People who felt themselves deficient in the different items generally gave significantly lower than average personal present self-ratings, while those who expected to overcome their difficulties tended to give higher ratings for the future than the present. The lowest ratings were given, as expected, by those who foresaw no chance of alleviating their deficiencies in the future. (See Tables 53, 54, and 55 in Appendix F3 for personal ratings by deficiencies indicated.) Some of the more specific relationships brought out in the analysis are: The desire for "greater faith in God or religion" showed no significant deviation from the sample as a whole; those who did not expect to obtain more education did not seem particularly concerned about it as judged by their average ratings, but those who felt they would obtain more education were more optimistic about the future; those who checked any of the items dealing with economic betterment rated themselves significantly lower, particularly if they saw no improvement ahead.

Further Obstacles to Satisfaction

This probing of deficiencies that made for dissatisfaction was continued by asking another question which was deliberately designed to overlap somewhat with the previous question but which included in addition an individual's estimate of the role his place in society might play in his feeling that he was being held back. The questions asked, together with the results, are shown below.

Which of the following things, if any, do you feel may be keeping you from having a more satisfying life than you are having now?
Indicate as many as you feel really concern you.

Item	Percent	Personal rating		
		Past	Present	Future
Total sample	*100%*	5.9	6.6	7.8
Lack of training and education	42	5.6	6.3	7.6
Lack of opportunity; not getting the right breaks in life	20	5.4	5.5	7.2
Lack of ability	16	5.4	6.1	7.5
Lack of any clear and positive aim in life	12	5.8	6.1	7.5
Own ambitions and the high goals I have set for myself	12	5.5	6.5	7.9
The circumstances in the United States that now restrict the chances of people who are in my station in life	9	5.6	5.4	7.3
The group, class, race, or religion I am in	6	5.9	5.3	7.7
Family background	6	5.4	5.7	7.4
None of these	21	6.3	7.2	8.1

Again a lack of training or education looms large, while social place-ment and social status were important for less than 10 percent of the total of all Americans. However, the fact that such items are not impor-tant for the vast majority undoubtedly increases their importance for the small minority who do feel they are denied their proper role as individuals because of socially discriminating factors.

Except for the people who felt their dissatisfaction was caused by their own high ambitions and goals, those who checked the other items they felt were hampering them rated themselves considerably lower on the personal present of the Self-Anchoring Scale than did the rest of the population. And it is not surprising to find that people who checked none of the items listed rated themselves significantly higher on the past, the present, and the future. It was the small minority of people who felt their placement in society or circumstances in the United States held them back who gave the lowest personal present ratings, compared to the total population, together with the 20 percent who checked the item that they were not getting the proper breaks in life.

Some Demographic Differences

In his review of the American data, W. Peter Janicki made a thorough analysis of the background factors related to all the questions concerning the sources of satisfaction and dissatisfaction. I will highlight here only some of his findings.[2]

With respect to *age,* as one would anticipate, young people might be characterized as actively seeking opportunities and expecting to realize future aspirations, while older people tend more to feel that they have been successful and appear to have leveled off their expectations for the future.

Occupational differences show a noticeable change in outlook as one goes "down" the occupational hierarchy according to commonly accepted standards: among people in the less prestigious occupations, there were lower self-estimates on success, opportunity, and ability, with people per-ceiving their own deficiencies and increasing their worries. Among the "higher" occupational groups, on the other hand, such psychological factors as setting their own goals and aspirations too high play a more important role in the concept of satisfaction. People with better *educa-tion* rated themselves higher than others in terms of the opportunities they felt they had to improve their positions, and they thus expressed a higher degree of self-confidence. However, a person's level of education seemed to make little difference in his rating concerning the extent to which he enjoyed life, his self-respect, or the degree to which he felt he was successful. Those in the lower educational brackets—which means, of course, that they were lower at many other levels—indicated a greater importance of religion and a sense of having more troubles than others.

With respect to the *economic level* a person had attained, one finds, as would be expected, that those in the higher income bracket had higher self-ratings, particularly with respect to the sense of opportunity they felt they had, their ability to do things for themselves, the success they had attained, their confidence in themselves, and their enjoyment of life. Significantly, however, there was one single item that did not show any difference among people at different economic levels—the rating on self-respect.

As shown in Chapter IV, at the time of our study the *Negro* American represented a very special group. Negroes rate themselves lower than whites with respect to the opportunity they feel they have, how successful they have been, how much they can do for themselves, and how much they enjoy life. And, of course, they rate themselves higher than do white people in terms of the troubles and worries that confront them. They also give religion a more important rating than do their white compatriots. But it is significant that here, too, there are no appreciable differences between Negroes and whites in the degree to which they respect themselves or in their degree of self-confidence. By 1959, the time of our survey, Negro Americans had apparently been able to shed the lack of self-respect that had so long haunted many of them vis-à-vis the white norms they had learned. And their bright hopes for improvement in their lot have bolstered their self-confidence. The effects of discrimination against the Negro are shown in a number of items: while only 7 percent of white respondents felt that any circumstances in the United States restricted their chances, 28 percent of Negroes did feel so; while only 2 percent of white respondents felt that "the group, class, race, or religion I am in" were obstacles to them, 38 percent of Negroes answered affirmatively, and while nearly 25 percent of all white respondents found it unnecessary to check any of our items concerned with factors they felt were holding them back, only 7 percent of Negroes believed none of the items were relevant to their own lives.

Although there are differences in the satisfaction, the sources of satisfaction, and the deficiencies felt between different groups of people in America, it should be emphasized that by and large these differences are relatively small and that there is a basic similarity of outlook in the American population. Such a situation can probably obtain only in a society of plenty and one which is becoming increasingly a welfare society where even the most "downtrodden" people still have hope that they will share what is available within the country. It was shown in Chapter IV that even the most frustrated group of Americans—the Negro Americans—expected a marked improvement in their situation.

One can also conclude that there is a clear-cut tendency for those who know what they want in life to be more optimistic in their outlook. Both the people who felt that "lack of clear and positive aims in life" kept them back and those who felt dissatisfied because of their own "ambitions and high goals," were from a similar demographic background, consisting more of young people, those relatively well educated, but from a variety of economic levels. But while those who felt they lacked a clear aim in life revealed a rather pessimistic outlook with a below-average present rating and a sense of achievement over the past five years of only 0.3 on the ladder, those who felt their dissatisfaction was due in part to their own high goals and ambitions rated themselves higher and had a sense of achievement of 1.0 on the ladder compared to five years ago.

As already seen, the importance of religion is felt rather uniformly among all Americans, but it is considered most important among the relatively lower educational and socioeconomic groups whose religious faith doubtless makes their positions more acceptable to them.

On the whole, it appears that if Americans feel they have an adequate income and social position, then they likewise feel there are relatively few external aspects of life that are holding them back, and they tend to look inward toward their own goals and ambitions as the limiting factors in their personal progress. On the other hand, persons less fortunate in educational and socioeconomic background found causes both within themselves and within their environment to account for their dissatisfactions.

Summary

Our data confirm the truth of Aristotle's observation that happiness comes from "the exercise of vital powers along lines of excellence in a life affording them scope."

People denied a scope for their lives because they live in poorer countries or are less favored by the social environment of richer countries are less satisfied and by and large by no means resigned to their situations. An apparent characteristic of man is never to be satisfied, always to want to experience some new value satisfactions, as well as to protect those he already enjoys. In a world where more and more people are becoming aware of what other people have and thus of what is potentially available to them, they perceive and assess their own situations in terms of the relative differences between what is and what might be for them in terms of their own purposes.

If a new quality of "excellence" or a new type of satisfaction is consistently experienced, then it does become a part of the "neutral" world, is assumed and loses its original value satisfaction until it is threatened or otherwise brought into awareness. Hence the lack of any absolute correlation between "objective" indices or evaluations and a person's own estimate of himself. But people are propelled by their own human, appetitive design to push on toward new experiences that will enable them to "exercise their vital powers" and experience the desired consequences of action they intend will enrich the range or quality of their satisfactions. Satisfaction comes from attaining a goal through action based on choice—a never-ending process of transforming a potential desire into an experiential reality.

CHAPTER XIII

Bracketing Human Concerns

In gathering the information for this study, probably a larger sample of the world's population has been interviewed than ever before on the questions of people's aspirations and worries. It should be revealing if data from all countries are pooled and the results projected to the total population sampled. This will give an idea of what it is that people in general are trying to move toward and move away from.

In order to do this, the rounded population figures for the countries in our sample (except Poland) were added as of the time the studies were made. The following are the number of millions of people in each of the twelve countries:

India	438
United States	180
Brazil	70
West Germany	56
Nigeria	34
Philippines	27
Egypt	26
Yugoslavia	19
Cuba	7
Dominican Republic	3
Israel	2
Panama	1
Total	*863*

Taking the world's population as approximately three billion people, the population of the nations in our sample represents roughly 30 percent of the total. No attempt was made at the beginning of my program to obtain a sample of the world's population by region, and it turns out that North America is overrepresented, containing nearly a quarter of our sample but only about 10 percent of the world's population; likewise, the sample of Asia is somewhat overrepresentative, containing 65 percent in this sample, while the world's proportion in Asia is around 56 percent.

In order to learn what the concerns were for the 863 million people represented in the twelve samples combined, the percentage of people whose responses were classified in each item of the code was weighted according to the population of each country. Thus, percentages in code items for the Indian people were given a weighting of 438, for the United States, 180, for Israel, 2, etc. Table XIII:1 gives the rank order of per-

TABLE XIII:1

RANK ORDER OF PERSONAL CONCERNS

Concern	Rank order (millions)
Hoping for improved or decent standard of living	549
Hoping for welfare and opportunities for children	262
Fearful of deterioration of present standard of living	259
Fearful of ill health, accident, death of self	222
Hoping for good health of self	144
Fearful of ill health, accident, death in family	133
Hoping for good job, congenial work	132
Hoping for a house of their own	124
Hoping for own land or farm	123
Fearful about children's welfare or opportunities	109
Hoping for happy family life	99
Fearful of war	83
Hoping for own business	62
Hoping for health of family	62
Fearful of unemployment or inability to work	58
Hoping for happy old age	47
Hoping to be useful to others, public service	46
Hoping for modern conveniences	45
Hoping for welfare of relatives, being with relatives	44
Hoping for recreation, travel, leisure	40
Hoping for self-development and improvement	40
Fearful of separation from relatives, not living up to expectations from them	36
Hoping for employment	36
Fearful of unhappy family life	35
Hoping for resolution of religious, ethical problems	34
Hoping to lead good, decent life	32
Fearful of poor or uncongenial work	32
Fearful of being dependent on others	28
Hoping for peace in international situation	26
Fearful of not having own business or improving it *	26
Hoping for acceptance by others	26

TABLE XIII:1 (*Continued*)

RANK ORDER OF PERSONAL CONCERNS

Concern	Rank order (millions)
Hoping to maintain status quo	23
Hoping for emotional stability and maturity	23
Hoping for success	23
Hoping for wealth	18
Fearful of not owning land or improving it *	18
Fearful of being unable to provide dowry for daughters *	18
Hoping to be able to marry daughters and provide dowry *	18
Fearful of not being able to get a house	18
Fearful of being alone	15
Fearful of general economic instability	15
Fearful of no self-improvement or development	14
Resigned to Fate or God's will, nothing worse can happen *	13
Fearful of not being accepted by others	11
Fearful of being a failure in job or work	10
Fearful of being emotionally unstable and immature	9
Fearful of inadequate standard of living for whole nation	9
Fearful of becoming antisocial, taking to crime	8
Fearful of inequality of opportunity based on race, color	8
Hoping for social security	7
Hoping to achieve sense of own personal worth	7
Hoping for equal opportunities	6
Fearful of lack of freedom	6
Fearful of militarism and armaments	6
Fearful of not being useful to others	5
Fearful of achieving no sense of personal worth	5
Fearful of aggression or domination by Communist power	4
Fearful of no social security	4

* Refers to special problems added to original code.

sonal concerns, Table XIII:2 gives the rank order of concerns for the nation. All items mentioned by at least four million people, or 0.5 percent of the total population sampled, are included. Each table is so set up that aspirations can be quickly differentiated from fears.

Several conclusions emerge from this listing of the concerns expressed by a sample of nearly a third of mankind.

1. Man seems to be a creature of hope: "hope springs eternal" or, as the Psalmist said, "But I will hope continually."

2. The fears, worries, and apprehensions people express are, of course, by definition, that their desires will not be obtainable, that conditions

TABLE XIII:2

RANK ORDER OF NATIONAL CONCERNS

Concern	Rank order (millions)
Fearful of war	372
Hoping for improved or decent standard of living	182
Hoping for technological advances	154
Hoping for peace	126
Hoping for employment	106
Fearful of Chinese aggression *	96
Fearful of dishonest government	91
Hoping for better education throughout nation	88
Fearful of economic instability	87
Hoping for economic stability	79
Hoping for agrarian reform	62
Hoping for improved sense of social and political responsibility on part of the people	58
Fearful of disunity among people of nation	50
Fearful of Communism	49
Fearful of unemployment	46
Fearful of political instability	44
Fearful of no improved or inadequate standard of living	42
Hoping for better public health	40
Fearful discrimination will not be eliminated	36
Fearful of Kashmir-Pakistan problem *	35
Hoping discrimination will be eliminated	33
Fearful of threat, aggression, domination by Communist power	32
Fearful of lack of moral, ethical standards among people	31
Hoping for honest government	30
Hoping for social justice	30
Hoping for national unity	29
Fearful of lack of national independence	28
Hoping for national independence	27
Hoping for national prosperity through planning *	26
Hoping for better moral, ethical standards	25
Hoping for better world re international situation	25
Hoping for reunification of the country *	25
Fearful of population problem	25
Hoping for efficient government	23
Hoping nation will enhance its status and importance	21
Fearful of threat or aggression by some foreign power	21
Hoping for political stability	21
Hoping housing situation will be improved in country	21
Fearful standard of living in country will deteriorate	20
Hoping for improved labor conditions	19

TABLE XIII:2 *(Continued)*

RANK ORDER OF NATIONAL CONCERNS

Concern	Rank order (millions)
Hoping for democratic or representative government	18
Fearful of social injustice	17
Hoping to maintain status quo	15
Fearful no technological advances will be made	14
Fearful about lack of freedom	13
Fearful about lack of law and order	13
Fearful planning may fail *	13
Fearful there will be no rural development *	13
Hoping nation will become a world power	13
Hoping for increased foreign trade	11
Hoping for law and order	11
Hoping for modern amenities for people	11
Hoping nation will be militarily strong	10
Hoping for fewer taxes *	10
Hoping cold war will lessen	10
Hoping for social security for nation	10
Fearful of poor or unfair working conditions	9
Fearful of inefficient government	9
Fearful of consequences of Nehru's death *	9
Fearful of inadequate educational facilities	8
Fearful of no democratic or representative government	8
Fearful of high or increased taxes	8
Fearful of continued armament	7
Hoping for friendly relations with all countries	7
Hoping for disarmament	6
Fearful of no sense of social and political responsibility	6
Hoping for freedom	6
Hoping for socialist government	5
Hoping Tito will maintain health and position *	5
Hoping country will provide moral or ideological leadership	4
Fearful of natural disasters *	4

* Refers to special problems added to original code.

beyond their control will interfere and prevent the hopes from being realized: war, a deterioration in their standard of living, and illness are the major sensed impediments to the realization of hopes or the undercutting of gains already made.

3. At the present stage of human and societal development, the vast majority of both hopes and fears revolves around the complex of well-

being as this is rather simply defined: a decent standard of living; opportunities for children; technological advances within the nation which will increase economic development; good health; a good job; a house, land, or business of one's own; a happy home life; better educational facilities in the country, etc. Wealth per se is a desideratum for only 2 percent of all people sampled.

Relatively few hopes are more idealistic or sophisticated, although such items as a desire for an improved sense of social and political responsibility, being useful to others, and the aspiration for self-development are mentioned by at least 5 percent of the population sampled. But concerns for greater social justice, better moral standards, the resolution of moral or ethical problems, leading a good and decent life, achieving a sense of personal worth, freedom, and self-discipline appear to be *self-conscious* concerns for only a very tiny minority throughout the world. Nevertheless, it may well be that these percentages, small as they are, actually are higher than might have been found if a comparable study had been made on the people who inhabited the globe two thousand years ago, and may be smaller than those that would be found in another comparable study done two thousand years hence. One must never lose sight of the fact that this study, as well as any other done by the social scientist, occurs at a specific point in time in the long history of mankind.

SOME INGREDIENTS OF A "STANDARD OF LIVING"

People in the richer countries more than people in the poorer countries tended to include the fulfillment of other aspirations in their definition of a decent standard of living. Preoccupation with a low standard of living, as reflected by the socioeconomic indices, so preempted the reality worlds of people that they did not indulge themselves in aspirations about other aspects of life. Any single, overriding fear can be a total experience and crowd out all other concerns.

The question here is this: do people now by and large include in their conception of a decent life other aspirations than those concerned purely with the provision of the basic necessities for living? Apparently the answer is "Yes."

Table XIII:3, based on the data from all countries, shows that those who are worried about an inadequate standard of living or a deterioration of the present standard are significantly more concerned than those not worried about it with having a happy family life, good health for themselves, opportunities for their children, and the ownership of some property (house or land). In other words, if people are worried about their standard of living, the frequency with which they mention their aspirations for these other aspects of life are significantly increased,

TABLE XIII:3

Percentage of Those who are Worried (or Not Worried) About Inadequate Standard of Living or Deterioration in Present Standard and Who Have Certain Other Aspirations *

	Worried		Not worried	
Aspiration	%	N	%	N
For sense of personal worth	2	157	2	303
For self-development				
and self-improvement	8	717	6	964
For health of family	10	944	7	1098
For job or work situation	18	1689	15	2324
For happy family life	25	2396	*14*	2155
For own health	*36*	3497	*17*	2723
For children's welfare	*43*	4084	27	4268
For ownership	55	5276	*31*	4790
Total N		9575		*15,594*

* The differences between the percentages are significant at the .05 level when they are 4 percent with a total of 2000 cases; 3 percent with 3000 cases; 7 percent with only 500 total cases. Figures that are significantly different are italicized.

while if they are not worried about their standard of living they have fewer frustrations concerning the potential realization of these aspirations.

One can therefore conclude that the overall picture in the world today is one of people definitely aware that living should consist of more than subsistence: a happy home life, good health, opportunities for children, and some ownership are among the essential ingredients people feel are potentially available to them and that they deserve in their search for a good life.

CONCERNS AND CIRCUMSTANCES

In order to get some idea of the psychological factors that generate and nourish different concerns, all the general categories of concerns were analyzed with respect to the interrelated background factors of education, socioeconomic status, age, and rural or urban dwelling: these circumstances can point at least roughly to the psychological variables brought into play. We sorted out the percentage of people in the various sub-groups of the population who expressed the different concerns covered by the general categories. The personal aspirations of the various groupings are found in Table XIII:4. From this table and from the

TABLE XIII:4

Personal Aspirations by Education and Other Variables *

Variable	Values and character	Personal economic	Job and work	Health	Family	Political	Social	International	Status quo	N
BEST EDUCATED										
Income: upper	28%	58%	23%	22%	59%	2%	12%	5%	4%	881
middle	31	55	31	21	51	3	10	5	1	900
lower	40	57	28	26	54	2	13	3	8	231
Age: 50+	23	57	11	37	46	2	12	7	10	329
49–30	31	60	19	27	59	3	10	5	3	870
29–	33	53	40	12	54	2	12	3	1	848
Dwelling: rural	22	45	23	16	57	3	9	2	2	750
urban	36	63	28	26	54	2	12	7	4	1313
MIDDLE EDUCATED										
Income: upper	25	66	17	37	55	2	7	5	9	1191
middle	27	71	22	34	55	2	6	9	3	1480
lower	36	75	29	31	58	3	11	5	3	1297
Age: 50+	23	66	10	45	42	2	5	9	8	705
49–30	25	73	18	39	61	2	7	8	6	1872
29–	39	71	35	22	57	3	10	4	2	1475
Dwelling: rural	32	69	22	27	52	2	11	4	3	1467
urban	28	72	23	38	58	2	6	8	6	2605
LEAST EDUCATED										
Income: upper	18	74	17	30	50	4	6	3	6	1058
middle	14	72	14	26	42	1	6	3	2	4509
lower	18	83	18	30	47	2	4	1	1	11598
Age: 50+	16	73	11	34	41	2	4	3	3	4401
49–30	16	82	16	30	50	2	5	2	1	8090
29–	19	80	23	22	43	2	5	1	1	4877
Dwelling: rural	16	79	17	26	43	2	4	1	1	12315
urban	20	79	18	35	53	2	6	3	3	5084

* The personal fears that lead to essentially the same conclusions will be found in Table 49, Appendix E2.

earlier reports of national aspirations one discovers where the different background factors play a role. But it should be emphasized once more that these and many other factors actually function together in a symphonic, interdependent fashion, and that in describing variables separately one must always bear in mind that they lie within a complex, subtle psychological matrix which secondary and tertiary "breakdowns" only crudely reveal.

It seems fair to conclude that of all the factors on which information was obtained, education is the most important, although, as will be seen, there are various situations where education is either irrelevant or less relevant than other variables. But Table XIII:4 shows that education increases the concern for personal values and character, for personal social values especially among people in the low income group, for family life and for the type of job or work situation a person wants, particularly if he is young. An education beyond the primary school level increases concern for the nation with respect to its international stance, its independent status, and the social or political problems it faces.

A low socioeconomic status, as shown over and over again, creates immediate aspirations for improvement, particularly among the least educated where this economic concern rises to 83 percent of the total "world" sample, 50 per cent of whom are classified in the low income, low education group. A higher economic status decreases the interest in personal economic situations among the least educated, increases a concern for preserving the status quo and reduces the interest in personal values and character among the middle and best educated groups.

The factor of age is of special importance with regard to the job or work situation among younger people, especially well educated young people, while older people develop a concern for health, for the nation's international problems, and for preserving the status quo. As so often seen, it is also people under fifty years of age who express greatest interest in family matters.

Marked differences are found between the concerns of people living in cities and those living in rural areas: urbanites in all educational groups are more concerned with health, are more sensitive to the nation's international problems and the importance of its independent status. Among the least educated people, those living in cities express more interest in aspirations for their families. A greater proportion of well-educated urbanites than of well-educated rural people are concerned with personal values and character.

Several conclusions stem from these findings. For one thing, people must learn what to want the way they must learn everything else. They must learn both the potential range and the potential quality of experiences that might be theirs if things were different. In this respect, education beyond the grammar school level clearly increases the aspirations of the world's population. Interrelated with the degree of formal education itself is, of course, the whole complex of informal educational processes involved with the greater exposure those with at least moderate schooling are likely to have to all mass media of communication, which so sensitize them both to problems and to potentialities.

It is also apparent that an urban environment increases horizons of awareness of potentialities available both to individuals and to nations; this is a direct result of the greater exposure of urbanites to mass media as well as to greater social participation and involvement in a wider variety of problem situations.

The data give no indication that an individual's economic position per se has any wide-ranging effect on concerns or differentiates people into classes which have consistently contrasting and opposing attitudes. As Marx and Engels themselves constantly reiterated, the "class struggle" requires the education of the "proletariat" to the consequences of their conditions.

The educational process—whether formal or informal—affords an opportunity for a person to become aware of new potentialities, of both new aspirations and new means of attaining goals. A person becomes aware of new reasons for circumstances in which he finds himself and perceives new ways of improving them. He learns how to act more effectively to carry out his purposes. His reality world thus becomes extended to include an awareness of a wider range of those economic, social, and political factors which, on the one hand, may be a threat to his values, and of those which, on the other hand, might serve as instruments to help make his values become more real.

CHAPTER XIV

The Politically Elite:
Comparisons of Parliamentarians
and the Public

During recent years there has been an understandable and deserved emphasis on studying the elite groups in a country and determining how their perceptions differ, if at all, from that of the public at large. The problem one confronts in such an undertaking is, of course, the problem of definition. And this problem of determining what an elite group is becomes multiplied if the interest is in cross-national comparisons.

In order to have some standard criteria for the selection of elite groups in many countries, it occurred to my associate, Lloyd Free, that one could use members of the legislative bodies of a country as representatives of the elite.[1] Not only do parliamentarians tend to represent the elite on a variety of standards, but they also obviously would be expected to have somewhat more of a sense of responsibility, somewhat more informed judgments, than an elite selected by most other criteria.

I report here comparisons of parliamentary and public replies on our Self-Anchoring Striving Scale in six different countries. I have deliberately omitted here any interparty comparisons of the legislators in different countries since such comparisons would be too peripheral to our main interest here.[2] In each country, the aim was to obtain a sample of one hundred members of that nation's legislative body, carefully selected so that there would be proper representation by party, by region of the country, and—where it was important—by seniority. Interviewing was conducted by the most experienced members of the organizations involved. The six countries studied were:

	Date	Number of Interviews
United States	Spring 1958	98
West Germany	Spring 1958	100
Brazil	January 1961	100
Nigeria	Spring 1963	100
India I	Spring 1958	103
India II	Jan.–Feb. 1963	100
Philippines	Spring 1960	100

In pretesting this method, Mr. Free soon found that the questions on our Self-Anchoring Scale dealing with personal concerns turned up rather unrealistic replies, since legislators, being politicians, tended to give answers that were politically colored, rather resembling campaign speeches they might make to their constituents. On the other hand, the replies given to the questions concerning national hopes and fears and the ratings assigned the nation on the ladder appeared realistic indeed. It is with these replies that I deal here.

CONCERNS

Table XIV:1 compares the general categories of hopes and fears for the nation expressed by the public and the legislative body of that nation. Table XIV:2 lists the specific code items under which comments of the public or the parliamentarians were classified.

Here, in brief, are the pictures shown in each country from the figures in Tables XIV:1 and XIV:2.

United States. American Congressmen are considerably more alarmed than the public about the threat of Communism to the independent status of the country and more eager that America achieve some ideological leadership in the Cold War, even though they are much less concerned than the public about international affairs including the threat of war. They are also more concerned about domestic problems of social justice.

West Germany. Members of the Bundestag are much more worried about internal political problems of the nation than is the public at large. They are also more concerned about the problem of German reunification and about the possible loss of freedom and democracy, and they are less concerned than the public about international affairs and much less troubled by the fear of war and its devastation.

Brazil. Brazilian legislators are much more concerned than the public about Brazil's independent status and they want the country to become an important world power with technological advances. They are considerably more concerned about internal political affairs in the country.

TABLE XIV:1

Comparison of Public and Parliamentarians
on General Categories *

General categories	United States Public	Parl.	West Germany Public	Parl.	Brazil Public	Parl.	Nigeria Public	Parl.	India † Public	Parl.	Philippines Public	Parl.
HOPES												
General economic	45%	41%	69%	67%	58%	69%	81%	91%	72%	59%	52%	107%
Social	33	32	16	24	19	28	66	65	21	44	13	22
Independent status	4	31	11	18	4	47	24	67	16	17	9	39
Political	13	17	49	78	16	37	50	69	5	76	37	33
International, war-peace	59	38	42	32	5	5	12	17	3	5	10	5
Status quo	7	1	2	—	1	1	—	—	—	—	—	1
FEARS												
International, war-peace	57	30	70	44	19	7	11	15	49	30	45	10
General economic	29	21	44	18	34	24	43	41	24	19	14	28
Political	23	27	27	60	24	47	69	63	17	92	34	77
Social	21	12	15	11	8	13	37	33	12	41	8	24
Independent status	11	31	19	16	3	9	7	13	6	16	17	19
No fears	4	2	1	—	2	32	4	8	10	2	6	11

* Columns total more than 100 percent because of multiple answers to specific items in each general category; also any one general category may total more than 100 percent because of multiple answers to specific items which it brings together. A difference of at least 10 percent is required for significance at the .05 level. All statistically significant differences are in italics.

† India public figures are based on India II survey done at same time as the parliamentary study.

The Brazilian people as a whole are more worried about their economic problems, and a greater proportion of them express a hope for economic stability.

Nigeria. Members of the Nigerian Parliament are much more concerned than the public about achieving and maintaining the independent status of the country and having Nigeria achieve some regional leadership. They are also more sensitive than the public to the difficul-

TABLE XIV:2

(No sign means parl. higher; — means parl. lower)

Items	Parl.	Public	Difference
UNITED STATES			
National Hopes			
Ideological leadership	19%	1%	18%
Social justice	13	——	13
Peace	27	48	−21
National Fears			
Loss of democracy	13	——	13
War and devastation	27	64	−37
WEST GERMANY			
National Hopes			
Reunification	72	44	28
Social justice	14	3	11
Employment	3	13	−10
Peace	21	37	−16
Economic stability	8	24	−16
National Fears			
No reunification	27	5	22
Loss of freedom	17	6	11
Loss of democracy	11	1	10
Economic instability	8	18	−10
War and devastation	38	99	−61
BRAZIL			
National Hopes			
National independence	22	2	20
Technological advances	33	15	18
Become world power	19	2	17
Improved standard of living	31	20	11
Enhance national status	10	——	10
Economic stability	14	28	−14
National Fears			
Have no fears for nation	32	2	30
War and devastation	4	19	−15
NIGERIA			
National Hopes			
Technological advances	83	42	41
Become a republic	42	9	33
Employment	54	31	23
Achieve regional leadership	15	2	13

TABLE XIV:2 (*Continued*)

SPECIFIC CODE ITEMS WHERE VARIATION BETWEEN PUBLIC AND
PARLIAMENTARY AT LEAST 10 PERCENT

(No sign means parl. higher; — means parl. lower)

Items	Parl.	Public	Difference
NIGERIA (*Continued*)			
National independence	18	6	12
Have modern amenities	12	31	−19
Public health	13	39	−26
National Fears			
Disunity among leaders or government	21	6	15
Unemployment	33	19	14
No fears for nation	15	4	11
No technological advances	14	4	10
Public health	——	13	−13
Failure to preserve present standard of living	10	25	−15
Political instability	35	51	−16
INDIA *			
National Hopes			
Have socialist government	26	1	25
Have democratic government	27	1	26
National unity	13	1	12
Employment	2	17	−15
National Fears			
Loss of democratic government	17	1	16
Continued discrimination	15	1	14
Political instability	12	1	11
Chinese aggression	25	45	−20
National disunity	17	4	13
PHILIPPINES			
National Hopes			
National independence	33	6	27
Technological advances	46	24	22
Efficient government	12	——	12
Employment	22	11	11
Honest government	10	34	−24
National Fears			
Communism from within	34	17	17
War and devastation	9	46	−37

* Figures from second India survey made at same time as parliamentary study.

ties of achieving unity among sectional leaders and the urgency of solving general economic problems, including unemployment. The Nigerian people, on the other hand, are more concerned than the legislators with public health and having modern amenities, and they are more fearful of the consequences of a lower standard of living and political instability.

India. The outstanding difference between members of the Indian Parliament and the public is the very much greater concern parliamentarians have with internal political problems facing the nation, including the attainment and assurance of a unified, democratic government along socialist lines. While they seem more sensitive than the public to the social problems confronting India, including ridding India of its ancient discriminatory practices, they are less concerned than the public about strictly economic problems, as well as about international problems, including Chinese aggression and the urgency of maintaining peace.

It is interesting to compare the two surveys made in the Lok Sabha (House of the People) of Indian parliamentarians after approximately a five-year interval. These are given in Table XIV:3.

TABLE XIV:3

COMPARISON OF THE TWO INDIAN PARLIAMENTARY STUDIES,
1958 AND 1963

Concern	1958	1963	Difference *
NATIONAL HOPES			
Be militarily strong	1%	10%	9%
Improved standard of living	17	25	8
Socialist government	19	26	7
Agrarian reform	†	7	7
Prosperity through planning	†	5	5
National unity	9	13	4
Democratic government	25	27	2
Technological advances	30	25	−5
Eliminate discrimination	16	9	−7
Public health	10	——	−10
Sense of social and political responsibility	17	7	−10
Educational opportunities and facilities	23	12	−11
Exert ideological and moral leadership as a nation	15	1	−14
To attain the position of a world power	15	——	−15
Social justice	20	3	−17
Total	*217%*	*170%*	

TABLE XIV:3 (*Continued*)

COMPARISON OF THE TWO INDIAN PARLIAMENTARY STUDIES,
1958 AND 1963

Concern	1958	1963	Difference *
NATIONAL FEARS			
Chinese aggression	*	25	25
Continued discrimination	1	15	14
Pakistan/Kashmir	*	11	11
Fear consequences of Nehru's death	*	7	7
Deterioration in standard of living	3	13	10
Dishonest government	12	14	2
No moral, ethical, or religious standards	6	6	0
Loss of democratic government	18	17	−1
Lack of social and political responsibility	12	11	−1
Fear of Communist danger from within India	10	8	−2
Inefficient government	21	10	−11
National disunity and political instability	41	29	−12
Total	*124%*	*166%*	

* A difference of 14 percent between the two studies is required for statistical significance at the .05 level.

† Not included in 1958 code.

It will be noted here first of all that there is a decrease in the total percent of hopes and an increase in the total percent of fears over this five-year period, revealing more limited aspirations, with somewhat increased anxiety, and possibly a greater realism that accompanies political and international responsibility. Although most of the differences here do not meet the requirement of a 14 percent difference for statistical significance, still there is an apparent trend for Indian parliamentarians to give less emphasis to matters of national status, and they had by 1963 almost abandoned the hope of attaining the position of a world power. On the other hand, their attention has turned somewhat to the rather rougher side of politics, namely, building up the military. Except for the fear of continued discrimination, social values and public welfare play a less important role in 1963 than they did in 1958. In general, there seems to be a greater tendency to assume that the government will move ahead efficiently and that the political situation will remain stable.

The Philippines. Tables XIV:1 and XIV:2 show that members of the Philippine Legislature are much more interested than the public in assuring the independence of the country and resolving its economic problems. They are eager for an efficient government that would cut down the threat of Communism, even though a considerably smaller percentage of parliamentarians than of the public were willing to admit that the government at the time was corrupt. However, the percentage of Filipino legislators who expressed fears concerning the internal political

TABLE XIV:4

COMPARISON OF MEAN LADDER RATINGS OF PUBLIC AND PARLIAMENTARIANS ON
NATIONAL STANDING

(No sign means present higher than past or future higher than present; — means
past higher than present or present higher than future)

Country	Past	Present	Future	Past to present	Present to future	Overall
BRAZIL						
Parl.	3.5	5.1	7.6	1.6	2.5	4.1
Public	4.9	5.1	7.6	0.2	2.5	2.7
Difference *	−1.4	0.0	0.0	1.4	0.0	1.4
WEST GERMANY						
Parl.	3.9	5.3	6.4	1.4	1.1	2.5
Public	4.1	6.2	——	2.1	——	——
Difference	−0.2	−0.9	——	−0.7	——	——
UNITED STATES						
Parl.	7.2	6.6	7.5	−0.6	0.9	0.3
Public	6.5	6.7	7.4	0.2	0.7	0.9
Difference	0.7	−0.1	0.1	−0.8	0.2	−0.6
PHILIPPINES						
Parl.	3.6	4.7	6.1	0.9	1.4	2.3
Public	6.1	5.1	6.1	−1.1	1.1	0.0
Difference	−2.5	−0.4	0.0	2.0	0.3	2.3
INDIA II						
Parl.	4.0	4.9	6.0	0.9	1.1	2.0
Public	3.1	4.6	6.5	1.5	1.9	3.4
Difference	0.9	0.3	−0.5	−0.6	−0.8	−1.4
NIGERIA						
Parl.	3.3	5.8	7.8	2.5	2.0	4.5
Public	4.0	6.2	8.2	2.2	2.0	4.2
Difference	−0.7	−0.4	−0.4	0.3	0.0	0.3

* Difference of 0.5 significant at .05 level in all cases.

situation of the country was over twice as high as the percentage of Fili-pino citizens expressing such fears. The legislators in the Philippines, too, were considerably less concerned than the public about interna-tional problems including war and its devastation.

LADDER RATINGS

Table XIV:4 compares the mean ladder ratings of the public and the parliamentarians on the standing assigned the nation at the present time as well as five years ago and five years hence.

It will be noted that there is considerable similarity in the ratings assigned the nation by both the parliamentarians and the public. How-ever, there are several differences: American Congressmen started with a higher rating for the United States in the past, hence the progress they see the country making is less than that of the public; members of the Western German Bundestag gave the nation a significantly lower rating for the present; members of the Indian Parliament in 1963 were more sanguine with regard to the past but less so with respect to the future; members of both the Brazilian and the Philippine legislatures were opti-mistic about overcoming what they regarded as the low points in their past; and the ratings assigned by Nigerian legislators, while lower for the past, were about the same as the public for the present and future.

The ratings given India by the two parliamentary studies separated by the five-year interval are compared in Table XIV:5. It will be no-

TABLE XIV:5

COMPARISON OF LADDER RATINGS GIVEN INDIA BY
INDIAN PARLIAMENTARIANS IN 1958 AND 1963

(No sign means 1963 higher; − means 1958 higher)

Time	1958	1963	Difference *
Past	2.6	4.0	1.4
Present	3.7	4.9	1.2
Future	5.3	6.0	0.7
Past to present	1.1	0.9	−0.2
Present to future	1.6	1.1	−0.5
Overall change	2.7	2.0	−0.7

* A difference of 0.72 between the two studies is significant at the .05 level.

ticed that all of the 1963 ladder ratings for India are higher than those assigned the nation five years earlier, but that the differences between the 1963 ratings assigned the past, present, and future are less than the differences obtained in 1958. In 1963, the past looks better than it did at the time but the present doesn't quite measure up to the earlier prediction. All of this seems to indicate the general feeling that India has made some progress even if not as much as anticipated.

COMPARISON OF THE BETTER EDUCATED WITH PARLIAMENTARIANS

The question naturally arises as to how the concerns the lawmakers have for their country compare to the concerns of the better educated members of the population. Table XIV:6 compares the average public concern for each of the general categories with the concern of the better educated group in each country. Since the term "better educated" varies so much by the general educational level in each country, the criteria used to define "better educated" should be borne in mind. In the United States, Brazil, and the Philippines, the group includes those people who have had at least some college education; in West Germany, those who have completed secondary education; in Nigeria, those with at least some secondary education; and in India, those who were at least intermediate graduates.

Table XIV:7 is essentially a shorthand comparison between Tables XIV:1 and XIV:6 indicating where the parliamentarians and the better educated differed from the public at large. It will be noticed from Table XIV:7 that in the United States, Nigeria, and India, the better educated people are concerned about a somewhat wider variety of problems facing the nation than are the legislators. It is also noteworthy that in India, parliamentarians are much more concerned about internal social and political affairs (Table XIV:1) than are the better educated (Table XIV:6), while in unstable Brazil an even higher proportion of the best educated than of parliamentarians are worried about political instability in the country. It is also significant that the better educated are seldom less concerned than the public at large with respect to the overall general categories, while in all countries except Nigeria the legislators tend to be less preoccupied than the public with the international issues of war and peace.

Summary

1. By and large, the legislators of a nation tend to view the nation's problems in rather the same way as does the public and to rate the country's standing from the same subjective base.

2. Legislators show somewhat more concern with their country's position—either with respect to its ideological, world, or regional leadership,

TABLE XIV:6

COMPARISON OF BEST EDUCATED GROUP IN COUNTRIES WITH TOTAL SAMPLE *

Concern	United States		West Germany		Brazil		Nigeria		India †		Philippines	
	Average	Best educated	Average	Best educated	Average	Best educated	Average	Best educated	Average	Best educated	Average	Best educated
HOPES FOR NATION												
General economic	45%	52%	69%	80%	58%	83%	81%	86%	72%	79%	52%	61%
Social	33	42	16	24	19	31	66	74	21	27	13	20
Independent status	4	8	11	6	4	42	24	40	16	31	9	13
Political	13	21	49	62	16	53	50	56	5	19	37	45
International, war-peace	59	63	42	42	5	6	12	20	3	5	10	7
Status quo	7	6	2	3	1	—	—	1	—	5	—	—
FEARS FOR NATION												
International, war-peace	57	54	70	70	19	22	11	12	49	57	45	26
General economic	29	33	44	50	34	39	43	50	24	31	14	21
Political	23	37	27	45	24	53	69	84	17	32	34	54
Social	21	27	15	18	8	17	37	43	12	23	8	12
Independent status	11	17	19	29	3	17	7	12	6	12	17	20
No fears	4	5	1	—	2	6	4	2	10	6	6	3

* Significant differences are in italics. The difference in percentage required for significant at .05 level varies according to the number of cases in the total and in the best educated group as defined. For the United States, Nigeria, and India this is 6 percent, for the Philippines 8 percent, for Brazil 14 percent, and for West Germany 13 percent.

† India public figures used here based on India II survey done at the same time as this parliamentary survey.

TABLE XIV:7

COMPARISON OF PARLIAMENTARIANS AND BEST EDUCATED ON GENERAL CATEGORIES

(+ indicates parliamentary significantly higher than public, or best educated group in the country significantly higher than the national average; − indicates parliamentary significantly lower than public; blank space means no significant differences)

General Categories	United States		West Germany		Brazil		Nigeria		India		Philippines	
	Parliamentarians	Best educated	Parliamentarians	Best educated	Parliamentarians	Best educated	Parliamentarians	Best educated	Parliamentarians	Best educated	Parliamentarians	Best educated
HOPES												
General economic		+			+	+	+		−	+	+	+
Social		+						+	+	+		
Independent status	+				+	+	+	+		+	+	
Political		+	+	+	+	+	+	+	+	+		+
International, war-peace	−		−					+				
Status quo												
FEARS												
International, war-peace	−		−		−				−	+	−	−
General economic			−		−			+		+	+	
Political		+	+	+	+	+		+	+	+	+	+
Social		+						+	+	+	+	
Independent status	+	+								+		
No fears						+						

or, as in the case of the more self-consciously nationalistic and developing countries, with respect to the assurance of its independence.

3. Parliamentarians on the whole exhibit a greater sensitivity to the problems of achieving and insuring an efficient, balanced, and stable government. This is particularly true in all the underdeveloped nations covered here: Brazil, Nigeria, India, and the Philippines.

4. The problem of maintaining peace on the international front is high among both public and parliamentarians in the two advanced nations and low among both the public and parliamentarians in all the less developed countries, which were more concerned with their domestic

problems. However, with the exception of Nigeria, parliamentarians in all countries are less concerned than the public with the problem of avoiding war and its devastation. In Nigeria, few people anywhere are bothered about such matters.

5. In the underdeveloped nations of Brazil, Nigeria, and the Philippines, parliamentarians are more aware than the public of the need to lift the nation up economically through greater technological advancement. The problem had not yet become a greater focus of interest for Indian parliamentarians by 1963.

6. The overall picture indicates that the legislators showed a somewhat narrower range of concern than did the most educated citizens in the countries studied. The main reason for this finding is very matter-of-fact: parliamentarians, being elected from local districts, in large measure must utilize their positions to get attention to and benefits for the problems facing their local constituents, and they thus become diverted from giving greater consideration to overall national issues.

Part Five

CONCLUSIONS

CHAPTER XV

The Patterning of Concerns

In this chapter, some of the systematic conclusions our findings point to will be bracketed. In pulling the threads together I shall again try not to get lost in the details of all the data that tabulating and computing machines pour out with such enticing ease and shall stay at a level of accounting appropriate to the problem at hand, using a vocabulary that may be helpful to social scientists in general, not a jargon restricted to the specialist.

One must always bear in mind that this study has dealt with an order of experience—experience as reported—that is one step removed from naïve, ongoing experience itself, and that any abstractions used to conceptualize our findings are man made and still further removed from first-person experience and behavior, the stuff of which psychology is made. Many of the conclusions will be seen as restatements of well-recognized principles, while others may have a fresher look.

The word "patterning" is deliberately included in the chapter heading to convey two reminders: first, that the genetic pattern of man gives him certain capacities and characteristics as a species of living matter but a pattern which—within limits—develops and unfolds according to circumstances and situations; second, that this development is a ceaseless process, a "becomingness" that follows an irreversible sequence both for the individual and for the society of which he is a part.

The findings are systematically considered to answer the general question: What are the stages of the development of the concerns of large groups of people living in the modern nation-state?

PHASES OF DEVELOPMENT

It has become abundantly clear that the concerns of people are patterned largely according to the phases of development they are in both culturally and ontogenetically within their society. Except in certain critical situations such as war or revolution, the stage of social and political organization characterizing a nation appears more closely related to human concerns than it does to any ideology as such. While the conflicts of ideologies, with their different emphases concerning the use and organization of power, are obviously of the utmost importance for the psychologist as well as the political scientist, our current quest could be misleading if the emphasis were put on variations in ideologies rather than on variations in phases of development. The fundamental problem is the transformation of political and social systems along with the transformation of people.

The phases of development differentiated here are those the data seem to disclose. There is, of course, usually no clear-cut boundary between one phase and another: one is always dealing with process where phases flow into each other. The differentiations made here are meant to describe the psychological factors involved in the genesis of economic or political stages of development or brought about as the consequences of such development, without any implication of an artificial bifurcation between the individual and the society of which he is so integral a part. Nor is there any implication that all people begin in the first phase differentiated below and progress in orderly sequence through all phases. Some people—for example the Americans, West Germans, Yugoslavs, and Israelis—never were in Phase 1. My interest is in the process of development itself no matter what the status in quo, "the state in which anything is," among a particular people whose concerns were tapped at a particular point in their developmental process.

Sometimes the status in quo of most people in a nation-state, as in Brazil, is that of an underdeveloped people whose awareness and concern is confined to the major problems facing them: the establishment of an effective democracy, agrarian reform, or national unity. These are a people who feel they have made little progress during the past few years but who are still optimistic about the future, a people who would be ripe for rebellion if they lose confidence in existing governments to remedy their lot. In other countries, such as Panama, the picture is of a nation dominated by a few wealthy families, dependent on a powerful neighbor, with little in the way of dedicated democratic leadership and with an active dissident minority stirring up a people who sense little improvement in their personal lives during the recent past. In other places, such as Cuba or the Dominican Republic, there are examples of people who had just ousted tyrannical or outmoded dictators. Elsewhere, as in West Germany or Yugoslavia, the study is of people who are consolidating themselves under new governments after experiencing the ravages of war. In Nigeria and Israel, one deals with newly independent nations whose people are seething with aspirations; while in the United States the concern is with a people who are far along the scale of socioeconomic development, who seem to have built up for themselves a relatively neutral psychological world in which most of them are quite satisfied and confident.

In differentiating the phases of development, I shall give examples of various population groups in various countries which seem to be in the different phases as shown from our data and the observations made in those countries. In this placement, I am concerned with people who constitute the vast bulk of the population and am deliberately omitting the elite who differ so markedly from their less privileged compatriots in all the countries studied.

Phase 1. Acquiescence to circumstances. To give a reference point, we can start with the people in India who were found to be still unaware of their problems; who were too depressed to have many ambitions for themselves; who were unaware, too, of the possibilities of action at the national level to improve their welfare; whose passivity derives in large part from an ancient and widespread fatalism which still makes it possible for millions upon millions of Indians to accept their wretched lot. An unusually high proportion of the Indian people were unable to assign either themselves or their nation a rating on the ladder of life, and there was little personal involvement with national problems together with a complete uniformity in national ratings by people who expressed different personal concerns.

In this first phase, then, one sees a people who tend to lack confidence in their government to assist them in resolving their problems, whose aspirations for their nation are low, who regard as luxuries what those in more aware and developed societies regard as primary requirements, such as good health. In short, we see a people not yet psychologically frustrated or mobilized and not yet on the move from their backward, subject status to an active, participant status in the variety of benefits and opportunities the modern world offers and the responsibilities and self-disciplines it requires. This is the portrait of the great majority of Indian people and does not in any sense deny the importance for India's future development of the nucleus of dedicated and educated Indians, of advanced village leaders, and of sophisticated industrial workers.

Most Brazilians also appear to be in this slumbering stage, unaware of their backwardness. Rural Brazilians who do not live near large cities, as well as poorer urban Brazilians in the northeast section of the country, revealed little personal involvement in national problems of any kind. Like the majority of the Indian people, their concerns were focused on and restricted to survival needs. A rather large proportion of these Brazilians were also unable to assign themselves or their nation a rating on the ladder of life. The same backwardness holds for rural Filipinos in the remote villages who have not yet awakened to operative aspirations.

Phase 2. Awakening to potentialities. This is the phase in which people become aware of new possibilities to increase the range or quality of their satisfactions, when they acquire new aspirations and learn new purposes. In this phase, people become psychologically mobilized as they learn what they can want out of life.

The period of acquiring new frustrations has been labeled the "disturbed" phase: the phase when people discover that the assumptions and loyalties of their reality worlds are hemming them in and creating too rigid constraints. The data have continuously shown that frustration and worry are the other side of the coin of hope. So people goad themselves to be rid of these constraints and handicaps. In the case of backward people, their very backwardness can serve as an incentive for their strivings once they learn that the new satisfactions are available.

There is likely to be an interim period of relative social chaos, irresponsibility, and lack of discipline following the breakdown of established loyalties, institutions, and controls. Old group allegiances and the appeal of old symbols are weakened and there may be few, if any, roots in the past which people can cling to if newly emerging goals and new purposes are to be accepted. When such psychological moorings and the ties that bind are temporarily lost, it may take considerable time before any new and commonly shared significances can become articulated, accepted, and organized into some institutional form for control and enforcement. The transformation of a people, like the birth of political systems and nations, is not always easy.

In this phase of sensing more of the potentialities living can offer we can place the mass of Filipinos and Panamanians in the lower socioeconomic group, whether they live in the country or in cities; the bulk of the poorer urban Brazilians; many Yugoslav peasants; some of the more backward Negroes in the United States; most of the Oriental Jews who have recently migrated to Israel; most of the Egyptian *Fellahin;* and those Indian villagers who have been exposed to modern life in some way.

It is during this stage of development that the mass media serve an especially important function. People who may have been separated from each other by valleys, villages, distances, or language barriers can share experiences with radios (and the news from papers passed on by the literate) telling them what is going on in other people's worlds, holding up new vistas, and at the same time giving them a sense of contact with each other.

Phase 3. Awareness of means to realize goals: sensing the possibility that the new potentialities perceived can become real. A vision of a brighter future will lead only to despair or will be given up entirely unless there are some ways to start making the vision come true.

This is the period when faith must be engendered, "the substance of things hoped for; the evidence of things not seen," as St. Paul observed. Faith plays the crucial psychological role of holding values together and integrating purposes. While frustration and discontent are likely to be exacerbated by the initial problems of putting means to economic, social, and political development into effect, the new demands on people who are aware of means available to achieve their goals often kindle and nourish faith which is, after all, born of frustration. This state of affairs, of course, makes the political situation in a country a precarious one, especially if a parliamentary government stemming from an ignorant and politically inexperienced people is trying to cope with the situation. The overthrow of the parliamentary system in the Dominican Republic since our study was made is only one illustration of many such episodes likely to be repeated on the world scene until people and systems have had time to transform themselves as development proceeds.

Frustration and discontent are bearable as long as faith is in some way confirmed. And it would appear from the findings that when conditions are recognized as bad, any change which appears to be in a desired direction, which indicates a trend has started, gives a psychological lift to the individual far out of proportion to the alteration of objective conditions. This was brought out especially by the big shifts in ladder ratings from the past to the present and on to the future among people in many countries with a low socioeconomic index. On the other hand, when conditions are good, it takes a great deal of change in the desired direction before this change appreciably alters the psychological state of mind, or, as the psycho-physicists would say, is perceived as a "just noticeable difference." As many observers from de Tocqueville on have pointed out, impatience is likely to be greatest when a goal is just around the corner, not when it is still far off. Then time becomes more telescoped and more important and people become more apprehensive that the goals they feel they have almost reached may still elude them.

If people are underdeveloped and inexperienced in political organization, and if both the awareness of new potentialities and their faith in experiencing them have been brought about largely by strong and dramatic leadership which has ousted or checkmated an oppressive power structure, then the leader is likely to stay on not only as the titular head of state but, more important, as the ritualistic head of state. He represents in his person and authority the new significances, confidence, and faith people have acquired. The effective leader, such as a Tito or a Nasser, further solidifies his position by giving both himself and his program names that perpetuate allegiances and that serve as symbols for wide identification. Such leadership is likely to remain until some sense of power relationship involving more people is perceived as likely to insure more democratic government that will encourage the flow of development in desired directions. But the studies revealed that most people in the world today are rather unconcerned about political freedoms, including freedom of speech, if they have faith that their more primary concerns, such as those for a decent standard of living and a congenial family life with opportunities for children, seem possible in the foreseeable future. And it must also be remembered that millions of people in many lands are quite unaware of what "freedom" refers to and have no such concept to be concerned about.

Only when a number of people assign the same significance to a happening can one say there is something of "social" or "political" significance. The new values that emerge can themselves not be experienced until people also share the significances of the sequence of events that must take place, the steps required to provide the operational link for the fulfillment of the new values held up as a vision. Without common purposeful values and common sequential events there would be no social group. The Nigerians especially exemplify this aspect of this particular stage of development. The recent establishment of an independent republic was obviously an eventful achievement around which Nigerians could rally individually and allay in some measure the anxieties over half of them had about the dangers tribal and sectional loyalties held for any sort of unity.

The Nigerians as a whole provide a good example of this phase of awareness of new possibilities: not only was the total volume and range of their concerns almost twice the volume and range expressed by Indians, but over half of all Nigerians sensed that their personal progress depended on the nation's progress and nearly half of them revealed their awareness and expressed their hope that technological advances could be used as a means to raise the nation's standard of living.

During this period there is likely to be an intense sense of nationhood as people in underdeveloped and newly independent areas see the apparent success the formation of nation-states has brought other people in breaking down the restrictions of narrower loyalties stemming from linguistic, tribal, or sectional divisions and in providing more efficient means of achieving personal goals, including a sense of status and importance.

In the process of consolidating themselves into a nation-state, people are apt to have a sense of being pushed or pulled into the larger world without yet clearly knowing what role they can or want to play. Hence it is to be expected that they will tend to follow a policy of nonalignment and neutralism and that they will be suspicious of the economic aid they are so eager to obtain. For they do not want to be indebted to anyone; they do not want to feel under the tyranny of having to be grateful. Confucius said: "I never gave you anything so why do you hate me?"

The people in a number of other countries studied appear to be in this phase of development. Many of them recently released from colonial status or recently formed into new national groups reveal their sense of liberation, of freedom from old restraints, of roadblocks removed. They are eager to push ahead faster. The greatest overall shift in national ladder ratings was found among people who had experienced a rebirth, either having lately achieved independence or consolidated themselves into a new nation. At the time of our study, the Cubans in general were sensing new possibilities ahead as were the majority of Dominican people, including even those in the lower socioeconomic bracket in both urban and rural areas. The more sophisticated Egyptian and Indian farmers and workers could also be placed here, as could Brazilians and Filipinos of above average status as well as the majority of Negro Americans who are rapidly moving into Phase 4.

With the feeling that there is something that can be done to achieve the new aspirations learned, there is sometimes found a personal involvement in the search for means to achieve aspirations, as people become curious, willing, or eager to know what they can do to realize new ambitions. In such cases people find themselves faced with the choice of doing something or nothing and, if they choose to do something, they face the further choice of certain alternatives they perceive as available to them. To exercise this choice is self-rewarding: the results showed, for example, that people who are clear both about their goals and the means to achieve them are more optimistic in their outlooks than those who are not so clear. This is nicely illustrated among the Yugoslavs, a people who have become generally self-conscious about the role they might play as participant citizens to attain their goals. In Yugoslavia there was a high sense of personal involvement with national problems, a developing sense of personal participation for and commitment to a common welfare which was perceived to overlap with and contribute to individual welfare. While the Yugoslavs knew they still had a long way to go, they were experiencing sufficient progress in desired directions to engender a faith in their socialist system, and they had acquired a definite vision of a brighter future. Personal development in the nation's affairs was spreading to an increasingly wider base of the population. Intense regional rivalries and animosities which had separated the people for centuries had been replaced by identification with the new nation-state under a trusted and adored leader, producing a people who were proud of their country and its achievements. And Yugoslavs were apparently satisfied with their government's policy of nonalignment.

Phase 4. Assurance and self-reliance: experiencing intended consequences through action. "It is important that everyone feel strong and recognize the sources of his strength" observed E. B. White. The attainment of such a psychological state of affairs for an individual or a people can develop only after they have experienced the satisfaction that comes when some action in which they have voluntarily participated confirms their assumptions and brings them closer to their goals. Faith is then confirmed both in goals and in the means devised to attain them. And with this come the important by-products of assurance and self-confidence as well as a heightening of the feeling that self-direction is possible through responsible action.

The measure of the effectivity of a nation-state in providing an individual with a developing sense of surety is a very pragmatic one. The ideological wrapping within which such development occurs appears from our data much less important than the extent to which whatever "system" that obtains satisfies people and appears to them to promise further satisfactions. For example, rather uniform ladder ratings for the nation were found among all income groups both in the rich, private-enterprise, welfare state of America and in the much poorer Communist state of Yugoslavia. Few people in either nation showed much concern for extending the ideological leadership of their particular system as long as their independence was not threatened. By the time this fourth phase of development is reached, it appears that nationalistic passions become moderated, having run their course through the phases of awakening and sensing the possibilities ahead.

Modern Israel might be said to have become launched on its way in the third phase of development, and by now it may be taken as an example of a nation that has moved into the fourth phase. The people in that tiny and newly formed land appeared to be not only dedicated to making their dream come true but confident of their ability to do so. While there was a pervasive fear of war with the Arabs, this fear was not intense enough to be a source of dissatisfaction with the present or of anxiety about the future. Israelis seemed confident that the political, economic, and social arrangements they had established, along with their increasing use of technology, had been tested and were guaranteed to lead them on to experience more and more the favorable consequences they intend their actions to bring about.

Phase 5. Satisfaction and gratification: general satisfaction with a way of life achieved which promises continued development. It should be emphasized that this final phase of development is not a static stage where people feel they have attained Nirvana and within which they want no change from the status quo. It is, on the other hand, a stage in which people feel that the continual emergence they crave can and will occur if no drastic outside events upset the general forms of social, political, and economic life within which this emergence seems assured; people in this stage feel that while they have "arrived" they still have much further to go. In this phase there is a patience, maturity, and responsibility that does not characterize those who are widely and profoundly frustrated because their aspirations so far exceed their accomplishments or any foreseeable means to insure further accomplishments and satisfactions.

The pattern of concerns of the American people can serve as an example of this final stage of development, although the West Germans could also be classified as being in the fifth phase.

The total volume of concerns of the American people was relatively low, especially those related to their hopes and fears for the nation, except for the single overriding concern that war be avoided. On the personal side, there was unusual emphasis on good health. In other words, Americans appeared to be chiefly concerned with the two major threats they felt were most beyond their control, war and illness. But even these worries were not intense enough to be sources of frustration with the present or of anxiety about the future. Long experience in resolving frustrations appears to have produced general confidence, although it was found that Americans who were least fortunate in their educational and socioeconomic backgrounds felt external aspects of life were holding them back.

The data revealed that Americans were relatively low in their economic concerns both for themselves and for the nation: there was a rather uniform sense of economic security with little variation in the personal concern for economic matters shown in various economic brackets of the population. And very few Americans were worried about getting more congenial jobs, most of them apparently taking both economic progress and job opportunities for granted. On the side of political concerns, Americans were next to the bottom of the list of the people we studied but, of course, for very different reasons than the people found in last place, the Indians: Americans were by and large self-conscious, proud of, and satisfied with their political system and the way it works, while most Indians were not yet awakened to political problems.

While far outstripped by Kibbutzim members, Israelis, and Nigerians with respect to their social values, Americans expressed much more concern for their fellows than did the Germans, who despite their relatively high socioeconomic index still appeared underdeveloped in a sense of social responsibility. The universal attainment of security and of some sense of improvement can have the effect of encouraging social relationships and providing the possibility for an enlargement of the self. This is perhaps one reason why so many foreign observers report as a primary national characteristic of the American people their awareness of others, including their requirement for approval.

Americans, although optimistic both about their own and their nation's future, were modest in their predictions compared to less highly developed people. While the nation was rated about the same by all demographic groups, least relative national progress was foreseen by those who rated the nation highest and who felt its growth would be slow but steady. As pointed out earlier, once a people are generally satisfied, it takes considerable change before that change may be consciously noticed. This can of course work both ways: whether a change is in a desirable or undesirable direction, it must be of greater magnitude or duration before its impact is sufficient to be perceived. People who are generally satisfied are generally cautious. They want to be quite sure that any proposed actions will lead to the desired consequences or relieve frustrations that may be building up. This is the case, in America, except for the Negroes, who feel the only direction they can go is up, who are highly aware of even minor improvements in their lot, and who with every improvement quite understandably become more impatient for still more improvement.

Most Americans felt they personally had made considerably more progress over the past five years than had the nation as a whole. The correlation between personal ratings Americans gave themselves on the ladder of life and the rating they assigned the nation was insignificant and the lowest of all those obtained. Compared to people in other nations, most Americans, except the Negroes, seemed relatively satisfied; there appeared to be a lack of any profoundly felt common purpose or dedication to any common cause, a state of affairs that could engender complacency and further restrict interests to personal and community affairs and pleasures.

The processes involved in this final phase of development among any people are likely to continue until some major event or crisis transpires which creates major and widespread frustrations. Only then are people likely to become awakened to the inadequacy of the assumptions they have come to take for granted. And only then are they likely to propel themselves on to a self-conscious reappraisal of their assumptions and transform their reality worlds into a new patterning more appropriate in handling the transformation of circumstances.

It should be noted in passing, however, that people in some cultures or subcultures may seem to qualify for placement in this fifth stage of "satisfaction and gratification" who have not gone through earlier stages of development but appear to outside observers to be stuck at relatively primitive levels. The Masai of Kenya and Tanganyika might be regarded as such a pocket of contentment within their microcosm. There is, of course, every likelihood that once the boundaries of such a microcosm are penetrated by "advanced" cultures with the aspirations they intrude into people's minds, then the people within such a microcosm will alter the standards by means of which they judge satisfaction and revert to an earlier stage of development.

SOME ASPECTS OF DEVELOPMENT

In order to complete the story of the patterning of concerns, a few observations that stem from the data and cut across various phases of development deserve underscoring.

For one thing, it should be stressed again and again that all purposive behavior must be learned: for example, there was no indication that an individual's economic frustration in and of itself had sufficiently wide-ranging effect on his concerns to place him automatically into any psychological class identification. But there were instances where such frustrations had been focused on a course of action by an able leader —a Nehru, a Castro, a Tito, or a Nasser—who was able to articulate people's aspirations and buoy their hopes just as the founding fathers did in the early days of American independence. It is because people learn about Western standards that they realize they are underprivileged and underdeveloped.

It must likewise be emphasized that the standards and expectations by means of which people judge their own development are relative to their experience. The data supply an abundance of evidence confirming this conclusion. People in less developed countries have not yet learned all that is potentially available and their needs are modest indeed in comparison to those of people living in rich countries; a low socioeconomic status creates immediate aspirations for improvement especially among the least educated; a major national fear of Egyptians was foreign aggression from which they had recently suffered; people in the Dominican Republic craved political stability after the turmoil they had been through; Cubans were eager for tranquility and the consolidation of their revolution; Filipinos were interested in getting good government after the corruption in high places; all people who had experienced the ravages of war were concerned about war and peace, whereas those who had not shared such experiences were not worried about such problems unless they felt, as did Americans, that they would be major participants in another war; older people were especially concerned about their health, middle-aged people about their children, younger people, especially if they were well educated, about getting a good job; people living in cities and exposed to more stimulation were more sensitive than those living in rural areas to a wide range of potentialities and possibilities ahead both for themselves and their nations; people in a Kibbutz, whose reference group is one of high idealism, were much more concerned with social values than any other group studied.

Rather extravagant ratings were given by people in underdeveloped countries concerning their own and their nation's future, implying both a relative lack of knowledge of the high quality and wide range of standards possible and an ignorance or underestimation of the many difficulties ahead before their aspirations could be realized. In Cuba, for example, it was the poorest people who foresaw the brightest future both for themselves and their country. The ratings concerning the future among the more advanced, politically experienced, and more firmly established people were modest by comparison.

As was to be expected, the findings showed that the sense of accomplishment and surety a people felt was higher if their own experience had been rewarding and if they lacked any anxiety that the satisfactions they were now enjoying were threatened. Thus, individuals who were better-off not only tended to give themselves higher ladder ratings, but also placed more aspirations in front of themselves and were sanguine about the future: the Egyptian *Fellahin* were especially optimistic about the future because of the land reform program already launched; in Yugoslavia, the state employees and those not still struggling with the land were more certain of their own and of their country's development; among the highly developed and dedicated Israelis, the better-off people were more certain of the nation's progress than of their own personal progress. Castro's revolution confirmed the hopes of poorer people, while the sophisticated were more skeptical about its future benefits; the Filipino elite gave their country relatively low ratings since they, more than others, saw the need for political reforms at the time of our study and were not sure that such reforms would come about; likewise, in Panama it was the elite who perceived the inefficiency and instability of their government and most feared a Communist take-over.

In this process of experiencing intended consequences and developing a sense of surety, the important role of education continues. It must be remembered that the higher education being acquired by more and more people in all countries is itself a process of experiencing an intended consequence through voluntary action. It was found that by and large education was the most crucial single influence in widening the scope of people's concerns, not so much those involving the more immediate day-to-day standard of living but the more long-range aspects of personal development such as attaining a congenial job, achieving a satisfying set of values together with greater involvement in more overall social justice, more honest and efficient government, and a resolution of the international problems the nation must face.

As such concerns become interiorized within the individual, he becomes committed to attain his goals, at least in some measure during his lifetime. His better education, whether formal or informal, increases his sensitivity to different alternatives he perceives are available to him or that he himself may devise. He presses for improvement and reform within the system possibly faster than the legislators of his country whose concerns tend to be somewhat narrower and who must keep their eyes more on the special needs of their local constituencies. These studies have illustrated the well-known fact that if improvement and reforms are not sooner or later accommodated, impatience and frustration are likely to turn into revolt by the intellectual elite against the system itself.

The findings also point to another aspect of development, a caution to those who sometimes speak glibly about "national purpose"—a phrase which makes psychological sense only if it is taken to mean a common purpose shared by people living within certain national boundaries and one to which they are individually committed. Obviously during critical periods, such as wartime or other clearly perceived threats to national security or well-being, national purposes emerge and are sustained. Egypt may have such a national purpose in its pan-Arabism; Israel, in proving it is a viable state that can provide the necessary political and military structure for survival and growth. Yugoslavs seem to have as a national purpose the demonstration that their heretofore separate regions can successfully work out their brand of Communism independent of outside alliances; the United States might be said to have the purpose of preventing the spread of Communism. But it is hard to define the national purpose of most countries we studied. And it can be misleading indeed to attribute national purposes where none exist and to confuse national purpose with government policy, as is sometimes done implicitly. To indicate that a people appear to have no national purpose is, of course, not likely to be popular with the people involved, nor is it a point of view any circumspect leader is apt to mention. This is not to deny, however, that nationalism is clearly the real religion in most of the world today, commanding greater loyalty than any ideologies.

Finally, no matter how critical one may be of the values of Western society, it appears from the data that the potentialities and possibilities of a good life are defined in Western terms and that no developing people will choose to go in a different direction and no minority opposing the trend will be able to hold out for long. Werner Heisenberg has said that "the spirit of a time is probably a fact as objective as any fact in natural science." All the findings would indicate that the spirit of this century is one in which the standards of Western society clearly prevail.

This is all understandable enough. For the vast majority of people's hopes and fears were found to revolve around the complex of well-being rather simply defined in terms of a decent standard of living, a more secure family life with opportunities for children. In underdeveloped countries, an appreciable number of people hoped for technological advances which would speed improvements in their standards of living. Modern technology with all its faults obviously tends to alleviate the burdens people have borne for so many centuries and opens up more opportunities for more satisfactions in terms of greater security, better health, and self-development in a variety of ways. It is not until a people have achieved the high standard of living technology has made possible that they can begin to sense the huge new problems which emerge because of it and which so vex the more sophisticated observers of the modern scene.

CHAPTER XVI

The Human Design

In describing the differences found among people in any study of wide scope, it is all too easy to neglect basic uniformities which take diverse forms in different cultural settings. Differences between individuals or groups of individuals are often dramatic and easier to detect than the similarities they may obscure.

I conclude this study, therefore, with a statement of what seem to be the demands human beings everywhere impose on any society or political culture because of their very nature. For human beings have a genetically built-in design that sooner or later must be accommodated. I shall try here to orchestrate the diversities of mankind found in different societies into some systematic unity.

1. *The satisfaction of survival needs.* Any listing of the characteristics of any living organism must begin here. As noted in Chapter II, neurophysiologists have located and described in a most general way two built-in appetitive systems found in higher animals: one system propelling them to seek satisfying and pleasurable experiences, the other protecting them from threatening or unpleasant experiences. These two systems together can be thought of as the basic forces contained within all human beings which not only keep them and the species alive as their simple survival needs for food and shelter are gratified, but which are involved in the desire for life itself.

These appetitive systems of course become enormously developed, refined, and conditioned, especially in man, as new ways are learned to achieve satisfactions and avoid dangers and discomforts. But it has been noted over and over again that unless the survival needs are satisfied, a person devotes himself almost exclusively to fulfilling them. Most people in the world today were found to be still concerned with living a type of life that constitutes well-being on a relatively simple level with what amenities their cultures can provide.

2. *Man needs a sense of both physical and psychological security to protect gains already made and to assure a beachhead from which further*

315

advances may be staged. Man wants some assurance that one action can lead to another, some definite prehension which provides an orientation and integration through time. People invariably become embittered if they nurse a dream for a long time with no signs of it becoming a reality.

The story of evolution tells us that members of every species stake out some territory for themselves within which they can provide for their needs and carry on their living. The extent of this territory depends on what is required for the survival of the species and it is extended if it will contribute to such survival. In the present era the territories human beings stake out for themselves are largely bounded by the nation-state, a territorial unit rapidly replacing narrower geographical and psychological identifications but doing so just at the time when it is becoming more and more apparent that the concept of nation itself limits and threatens man's development in an age of increasing interdependence and highly developed weaponry.

3. *Man craves sufficient order and certainty in his life to enable him to judge with fair accuracy what will or will not occur if he does or does not act in certain ways.* As noted in Chapter II, people want sufficient form and pattern in life to be sure that satisfactions already enjoyed will be repeatable and will provide a secure springboard for take-offs in new directions. The fears, worries, and apprehensions people express are by definition that their desires will not be attainable or that conditions beyond their own control will so upset the order of things that aspirations will not be realized.

The conflict of old loyalties with emerging new loyalties in the case of developing people is bound to create uncertainties, doubts, and hesitations. If these people become frustrated and anxious enough they will do almost anything in a desperate attempt to put some order into apparent chaos or rally around the symbols and abstractions of a new order that promises to alleviate the uncertainties experienced in the here and now.

In stressing process and change, the desire of people to preserve the status quo when it has proved satisfying and rewarding and to protect existing forms against alteration must never be overlooked. And the craving for certainty would include the satisfactions that come from the sense of stability provided by our habitual behavior, including much of our social and political behavior.

4. *Human beings continuously seek to enlarge the range and to enrich the quality of their satisfactions.* I have frequently emphasized the ceaseless quest impelling man to extend the range and quality of his satisfactions through the exercise of his creative and inventive capacities. This is, of course, a basic reason why order of any kind is constantly being upset. Alfred North Whitehead expressed the point eloquently in his statements that "the essence of life is to be found in the frustrations

of established order" and that "the art of progress is to preserve order amid change, and to preserve change amid order." [1]

The distinguished British philosopher John Macmurray has used the phrase "the self as agent" as the title of his book analyzing the role of action in man's constant search for value satisfactions. And in a companion volume he has noted that "human behavior cannot be understood, but only caricatured, if it is represented as an adaptation to environment." [2] The search for an enlargement of satisfactions in the transactions of living can also be phrased as the desire for development in a direction, the desire to do something which will bring a sense of accomplishment as we experience the satisfaction of successfully handling new challenges. During a conversation in Beirut, a wise man once remarked to me that "people are hungry for new and good experiences."

It seems worthwhile to differentiate this search for value satisfactions into two varieties: (a) value satisfactions that are essentially new, different, more efficient, more reliable, more pleasurable, or more status-producing results of activity along familiar and tried dimensions, and (b) value satisfactions that are new in the sense of being emergent, new qualities people discover or create themselves for the first time, as does the child who tries out and relishes new experiences as his own developmental pattern unfolds. The former variety, like the growth on the limb of a tree, extends people's range, while the latter, like the new growth at the top of the tree, lets them attain new heights and see new vistas. The satisfactions sought by a newly developing people are at first most likely to be of the former type.

The particular value satisfactions man acquires are the result of learning. Some of the values learned will serve as the operative ideals of a people, others will be chiefly instrumental. People in rich countries were found to have learned to want and to expect many aspects of a good life that less favored people had not yet learned were possibilities. From this point of view one might say that the competition between social and political systems is a competition in teaching people what to want, what is potentially available to them, and then proving to them in their own private experience that these wants are best attainable under the system described.

5. *Human beings are creatures of hope and are not genetically designed to resign themselves.* This characteristic of man so clearly brought out in the results reported here stems from the characteristic just described: that man is always likely to be dissatisfied and never fully "adapts" to his environment.

Man seems continually to hope that the world he encounters will correspond more and more to his vision of it as he acts within it to carry out his purposes while the vision itself continuously unfolds in an irreversible direction. The whole process is never-ending. It is characteristic of man in his ongoing experience to ask himself "Where do I go from here?" Only in his more reflective moods does a person ask "Where did I come from?" or "How did I get this way?" Most of the time, most people who are plugged into the changing world around them are future-oriented in their concerns. Throughout this study it was found that few people indeed—no matter how unfavorable or how favorable their circumstances—resigned themselves to staying put: all people without exception expected an improvement in the future both for themselves and for their country.

6. *Human beings have the capacity to make choices and the desire to exercise this capacity.* Any mechanical model of man constructed by a psychologist or by anyone else is bound to leave out the crucially important characteristic of man as an "appetitive-perceptive agency." Perceptions are learned and utilized by people to provide various prognoses to weigh alternative courses of action to achieve purposes. Consciously or unconsciously, people are trying to perceive the probable relation between their potential acts and the consequences of these acts to the intentions that constitute their goals.

The human brain and nervous system has the capacity to police its input, to determine what is and what is not significant for it, and to pay attention to and reinforce or otherwise modify its behavior as it transacts in the occasions of living. In this sense, the human being is a participant in and producer of his own value satisfactions. The data here further demonstrate that people perceive only what is relevant to their hopes and fears and make their choices accordingly.

7. *Human beings require freedom to exercise the choices they are capable of making.* This characteristic of man related to freedom is deliberately worded as it is rather than as a blanket statement that "human beings require freedom," since the freedom people want is so relative to their desires and the stage of development they have attained. Human beings, incidentally, apparently require more freedom than other species of animals because of their much greater capacity to move about and to engage in a much wider variety of behavior.

While it seems true that maximum freedom is a necessary condition if a highly developed individual is to obtain maximum value satisfaction, it is equally true that too much freedom too soon can be an unbearable burden and a source of bondage if people, like children, are insufficiently developed to know what to do with it. For freedom clearly involves a learning of responsibility and an ability to take advantage of it wisely.

In these studies, few people indeed seemed to be self-consciously concerned with "freedom" as a category in the code. This is not because freedom is unimportant but because the coding had to follow the prevailing narrow, nonpsychological connotation of the concept, such as freedom of speech, of religion, and the like. But the concept of freedom is essentially a psychological and not a political concept. It describes the opportunity of an individual to make his own choices and to act accordingly. Psychologically, freedom refers to the freedom to experience more of what is potentially available, the freedom to move about and ahead, to be and to become. Freedom is thus less and less determined and more of a reality as man evolves and develops; it emerges and flowers as people learn what it can mean to them in terms of resolving their frustrations.

The authoritarian leadership sometimes required to bring about man's awakening and to start him on the road to his definition of progress appears to go against the grain of the human design once man is transformed into a self-conscious citizen who has the desire to exercise the capacity latent within him. The definition of freedom in the Soviet dictionary, *Ushakov*, as "the recognition of necessity" is limited to those periods in the life of an individual or a people when they are willing to let others define what is necessary and to submerge their own individuality.

8. *Human beings want to experience their own identity and integrity,* more popularly referred to as the need for *personal dignity.* Every human being craves a sense of his own self-constancy, an assurance of the repeatability of experience in which he is a determining participant. He obtains this from the transactions he has with other individuals.

People develop significances they share with others in their membership and reference groups. If the satisfaction and significance of participation with others ceases to confirm assumptions or to enrich values, then a person's sense of self-constancy becomes shaken or insecure, his loyalties become formalized and empty or are given up altogether. He becomes alienated or seeks new significances, new loyalties that are more operationally real.

9. *People want to experience a sense of their own worthwhileness.* A human being wants to know he is valued by others and that others will show that his own behavior and its consequences make some sort of difference to them in ways that give him a sense of satisfaction. When this occurs, not only is a person's sense of identity confirmed, but he also experiences a sense of personal worth and self-respect.

People acquire, maintain, and enrich their sense of worthwhileness only if they at least vaguely recognize the sources of what personal identity they have: from their family, their friends and neighbors, their associates or fellow workers, their group ties, or their nations. The social, religious, intellectual, regional, or national loyalties formed play the important role of making it possible for individuals to extend themselves backward into the past, forward into the future, and to identify themselves with others who live at more or less remote distances from them. Shared experiences are thus compounded into a bundle that can be conceptualized and felt in the here and now of daily living, thus making a person feel a functional part of a more enduring alliance. Man accomplishes such feats of self-extension largely through his capacity to create symbols, images, and myths which provide focal points for identification and self-expansion. After reviewing the lessons from history, historian Herbert Muller noted as one of the "forgotten simplicities" the fact "that men have always been willing to sacrifice themselves for some larger cause, fighting and dying for their family, tribe, or community, with or without hope of eternal reward." [1]

The process of extending the sense of self both in space and in time appears also to involve the desire that one's "presence" shall not be limited merely to the here and now of existence but will extend into larger dimensions. The almost universal desire people had that their children should enjoy more opportunities would appear in part to reflect this extension of self into the future. The value satisfaction obtained by an individual in being part of a community we found demonstrated in high degree among the members of the Kibbutzim whose personal goals in life so completely overlapped community goals in their identification.

10. *Human beings seek some value or system of beliefs to which they can commit themselves.* In the midst of the probabilities and uncertainties that surround them, people want some anchoring points, some certainties, some faith that will serve either as a beacon light to guide them or a balm to assuage them during the inevitable frustrations and anxieties living engenders.

People who have long been frustrated and who have searched for means to alleviate their situations are, of course, particularly susceptible to a commitment to a new system of beliefs or an ideology that they feel holds promise of effective action. Hence the belief in the rewards of nationalism was found by and large most widespread and intense among people for whom nationalism was a new way out of their difficulties. And the most widespread fear that national unity would not be achieved turned up in areas such as India and Nigeria where ancient belief systems bounded by tribal and regional loyalties linger on.

Beliefs are confirmed insofar as action based on them brings satisfying consequences, and they are denied with growing skepticism if disastrous results consistently occur because they are followed. For example, West Germans have apparently given up the thought of achieving status as a world power or spreading their ideological influence as a result of their total defeat in World War II.

Commitment to a value or belief system becomes more difficult among well-informed and sophisticated people who self-consciously try to reconcile what they believe with what they know and what they know with what they believe. In such circumstances, beliefs become more secular and less important as personal identifications. While most Americans felt religion was important, this belief had little relationship to the way they perceived themselves in terms of their self-respect, their self-confidence, and their satisfaction with life in general; it was the least educated, the poorest Americans, who felt religion was most important.

11. *Human beings want a sense of surety and confidence that the society of which they are a part holds out a fair degree of hope that their aspirations will be fulfilled.* If social mechanisms deny people satisfactions they aspire to in achieving potential goals, then obviously their frustrations and anxieties mount, they search for new means to accomplish aims, or, on the other hand, they make any sacrifice required to protect a society they feel is fulfilling their needs but is seriously threatened.

It cannot be stressed too strongly that any people will become apathetic toward or anxious about ultimate goals they would like to achieve through social organizations if they continually sense a lack of reliability in the means provided to accomplish these goals. Obviously any viable society must satisfy basic survival needs, must provide security, must insure the repeatability of value satisfactions already attained, and must provide for new and emerging satisfactions. The effective society is one that enables the individual to develop personal loyalties and aspirations which overlap with and are congenial to social values and loyalties, and which at the same time take full account of the wide range of individual differences that exist.

Such a social organization must, too, become the repository of values, must provide symbols for people's aspirations, must comprise customs, institutions, laws, economic arrangements, and political forms which enable an individual to give concrete reference to his values in his day-to-day behavior. If the gap between what society actually provides in terms of effective mechanisms for living and what it purports to provide becomes too great, the vacuum created will sooner or later engender the frustrations that impel people to seek new social patterns and new symbols. Whitehead wrote that "the major advances in civilization are processes which all but wreck the societies in which they occur:—like unto an arrow in the hand of a child. The art of free society consists first in the maintenance of the symbolic code; and secondly in fearlessness of revision, to secure that the code serves those purposes which satisfy an enlightened reason. Those societies which cannot combine reverence to their symbols with freedom of revision, must ultimately decay either from anarchy, or from the slow atrophy of a life stifled by useless shadows." [4]

Every social and political system can be regarded as an experiment in the broad perspective of time. The studies reported here have given us a few insights into different types of experiments in their different stages. Whatever the circumstances, the human design will in the long run force any institutional framework to accommodate it. This has been the case throughout human history. And few would deny that the varied pattern of experiments going on today hold out more promise of satisfying the human condition for a greater number of people than ever before.

Notes

Chapter I

1. A good recent review of the field of social psychology will be found in "Social Psychology: Problems and Trends in Interdisciplinary Relationships," by Muzafer Sherif, in *Psychology: A Study of a Science,* edit. Sigmund Koch (New York: McGraw-Hill, 1963), VI, 30–93. The best short history of social psychology will be found in "The Historical Background of Modern Social Psychology," by Gordon W. Allport, in *Handbook of Social Psychology,* ed. Gardner Lindsey (Cambridge, Mass.: Addison-Wesley, 1954), Ch. 1.

2. H. A. Murray, et al., *Assessment of Men* (New York: Rinehart, 1948), p. 466.

3. "Clues to an Understanding of Mind and Body," in *The Scientist Speculates,* ed. I. J. Good (London: Heinemann, 1962), pp. 71, 73.

Chapter II

1. A brief review of recent research in neurophysiology as related to the "appetitive systems" will be found in Hadley Cantril and William K. Livingston, "The Concept of Transaction in Psychology and Neurology," *Jl. of Individual Psych.,* 1963, XIX, 3–16, from which some of this discussion is taken.

2. *De Anima,* Book II, trans. R. D. Hicks (Cambridge: Cambridge University Press, 1907), p. 105.

3. *The Study of Man* (Chicago: University of Chicago Press, 1959), p. 56.

4. The concept of "value satisfaction" is treated more fully in Hadley Cantril, *The "Why" of Man's Experience* (New York: Macmillan, 1950). Chs. 2 and 3.

5. *Personal Knowledge* (Chicago: University of Chicago Press, 1958), p. 196.

6. "The Task Before Us," *Proceedings of the American Academy of Arts and Sciences,* 1954, LXXXIII, 98.

7. Doubt and Certainty in Science (London: Oxford Press, 1951), p. 107.

8. *Personal Knowledge,* p. 312.

9. *The Nature of Experience* (London: Oxford Press, 1959), p. 35.

10. This discussion is abbreviated from Hadley Cantril, "Transactional Inquiry Concerning Mind," in *Theories of the Mind,* ed. Jordan Scher (Glencoe, Ill.: The Free Press, 1962), pp. 330–54.

11. See Cantril and Livingston for a discussion of some of this research.

12. *The Passing of Traditional Society* (Glencoe, Ill.: The Free Press, 1958).

13. *Rambler,* No. 128.

14. "Psychometabolism," *Jl. of Neuropsychiatry,* 1962, III, Supp. 1.

15. *The Policy Implications of Social Change in Non-Western Societies* (Cambridge, Mass.: Center for International Studies, 1957).

16. See Robert L. Heilbroner, *The Future as History* (New York: Harper and Brothers, 1959).

17. See Clifford Geertz, "The Growth of Culture and the Evolution of Mind," in *Theories of the Mind,* pp. 713–40.

18. See Lucian Pye, *Politics, Personality, and Nation Building* (New Haven, Conn.: Yale University Press, 1962), Chs. 1, 2, and 3.

CHAPTER III

1. I am indebted to Dr. Franklin P. Kilpatrick for his assistance in creating this device. Previous descriptions of the method have appeared in F. P. Kilpatrick and Hadley Cantril, "Self-Anchoring Scaling, A Measure of Individuals' Unique Reality Worlds," *Jl. of Individual Psych.,* November, 1960, XVI, 158–73; Hadley Cantril and Lloyd A. Free, "Hopes and Fears for Self and Country," *The American Behavioral Scientist,* October, 1962, VI, Supp. 2; Hadley Cantril, "A Study of Aspirations," *Scientific American,* February, 1963, Vol. 208, No. 2, pp. 3–8. The idea of utilizing the self-anchoring technique with reference to the nation was originally proposed by Lloyd Free.

2. A discussion of some of the problems encountered in this type of research in underdeveloped areas will be found in a special issue of *Public Opinion Quarterly,* "Attitude Research in Modernizing Areas," 1958, Vol. XXII, No. 3.

CHAPTER IV

1. Per capita income is taken from P. N. Rosenstein-Rodan, "International Aid for Underdeveloped Countries," *The Review of Economics and Statistics,* 1961, Vol. XLIII, No. 2; percent of population outside agriculture and services from the *Demographic Yearbook 1960* (Twelfth Issue), United Nations, New York, pp. 373–90; automobiles per thousand was calculated on the basis of data in the *Statistical Yearbook 1961,* United Nations, New York, pp. 21–36 and 338–45; literacy from the *Demographic Yearbook 1960,* pp. 434–44; and life expectancy from the *Demographic Yearbook 1961* (Thirteenth Issue), United Nations, New York, pp. 622–41.

2. A full report of the United States study was written by W. Peter Janicki when he was a research associate with the Institute for International Social Research, under the title *America Speaks Up.*

CHAPTER V

1. The Self-Anchoring Striving Scale questions were part of a larger battery of questions used by Lloyd Free in his study of *Some International Implications of the Political Psychology of Brazilians,* Princeton, N.J., Institute for International Social Research, 1961.

2. For a more detailed report of Nigeria, see Lloyd Free, *The Attitudes, Hopes and Fears of Nigerians,* Princeton, N.J., Institute for International Social Research, 1964.

3. This is essentially an abstract of a longer report on this subject prepared by Albert H. Cantril, Jr., "The Indian Perception of the Sino-Indian Border Clash," *Public Opinion Quarterly,* 1964, XXVIII, 233–42.

4. See Lloyd Free, *Six Allies and a Neutral* (Glencoe, Ill.: The Free Press, 1959).

CHAPTER VII

1. A report of Lloyd Free's more inclusive study in Cuba appeared in *Attitudes of the Cuban People Toward the Castro Regime*, Princeton, N.J., Institute for International Social Research, 1960.

2. The Self-Anchoring Striving Scale questions were used by Lloyd Free, along with other questions and techniques, in his study of *The Dynamics of Philippine Politics*, Princeton, N.J., Institute for International Social Research, 1960.

CHAPTER IX

1. The index used here was adapted from indices developed in *The Politics of the Developing Areas,* eds. Gabriel Almond and James Coleman (Princeton, N.J.: Princeton University Press, 1960), and by Everett E. Hagen in "A framework for analyzing economic and political change," in *The Development of the Emerging Countries* (Washington, D.C.: Brookings Institution, 1962). I am especially grateful to Professor Hagen of the Department of Economics at the Massachusetts Institute of Technology for his assistance. The indices were compiled by Albert H. Cantril, Jr. Anyone familiar with the task of obtaining reliable statistics from a variety of countries knows how unreliable many officially reported figures are. For our purpose of obtaining a general picture and a rank order of the developmental status of the countries studied, the overall index computed is quite satisfactory without adjusting the official, published data obtained after consultation with experts who would be able to make intelligent guesses as to where published data were somewhat off. The sources used were: per capita GNP estimates, from P. N. Rosenstein-Rodan, "International Aid for Underdeveloped Countries," *The Review of Economics and Statistics,* 1961, Vol. XLIII, No 2.; other data were taken variously from the following: *Statistical Yearbook 1961* (Thirteenth Issue), United Nations, New York; *Demographic Yearbook 1960* (Twelfth Issue), United Nations, New York; *Demographic Yearbook 1961* (Thirteenth Issue), United Nations, New York.

CHAPTER X

1. Quoted in S. E. Morison and H. S. Commager, *The Growth of the American Republic* (New York: Oxford University Press, 1942), I, 290.

CHAPTER XI

1. Federalist Paper No. 17. *The Federalist,* ed. J. E. Cooke (Middletown, Conn.: Wesleyan University Press, 1961), p. 107.

CHAPTER XII

1. The material in this section is essentially a condensation of a chapter in a manuscript by Peter Janicki, *America Speaks Up* (Princeton, N.J.: Institute for International Social Research).

2. The numerous tabulations on which these observations are made are contained in Peter Janicki, *America Speaks Up.*

CHAPTER XIV

1. See Lloyd Free, *Six Allies and a Neutral* (Glencoe, Ill.: The Free Press, 1959). In addition to the legislative bodies studied and reported here, Mr. Free has also done parliamentary studies in Great Britain, France, Italy, and Japan. These are not included since I had no information in these countries based on the completion of the Self-Anchoring Striving Scale by a sample of the public.

2. Some of these comparisons will be found in Lloyd Free, *Six Allies and a Neutral.* See also his reports on *Attitudes of Philippine Legislators,* 1960; *Some International Implications of the Political Psychology of Brazilians,* 1961; and *The Attitudes, Hopes and Fears of Nigerians,* 1964, all issued by the Institute for International Social Research, Princeton, N.J. Further analysis will also be found in Albert H. Cantril, Jr., *Matrices of Parliamentarian Concern,* Dartmouth College Library, 1962.

CHAPTER XVI

1. *Modes of Thought* (New York: Macmillan, 1938), p. 119; *Process and Reality* (New York: Macmillan, 1929), p. 515.

2. *Persons in Relation* (London: Faber and Faber, 1961), p. 46.

3. *Uses of the Past* (New York: Mentor, 1954), p. 392.

4. *Symbolism: Its Meaning and Effect* (New York: Macmillan, 1927), p. 88.

Part Six

APPENDICES

Appendix A: Coding

1. THE COMPLETE CODE

Code for Questions 1(A) and 1(B): Personal Hopes and Aspirations; Personal Worries and Fears

The categories for personal hopes and aspirations are given on the left-hand side of the page — columns 1–6. The categories for personal worries and fears are given on the right-hand side of the page — columns 7–12.

CONCERNED WITH SELF AND/OR FAMILY

Own Personal Character

_____ Col. 1

1. *Emotional stability and maturity*—peace of mind, mental health and well-being; sense of humor, understanding of others, etc.; harmonious life.

2. *Be a normal, decent person*—leading a quiet life, harming no one.

3. *Self-development or improvement*—opportunity for independence of thought and action, for following through with own interests; further study; reading for non-leisure purposes; no "rut."

4. *Acceptance by others*—recognition of my status by others; to be liked, respected or loved (exception: where reference is restricted to family or marriage, code under Col. 4-1).

5. *Achieve sense of my own personal worth*—self-satisfaction; feeling of accomplishment; lead a purposeful life. (Note: recognition by *self* as contrasted to recognition by others.)

6. *Resolution of one's own religious, spiritual, or ethical problems.*

7. *To lead a disciplined life.*

8. *Miscellaneous* aspirations regarding one's own personal character.

Y. Nothing to code in this column.

_____ Col. 7

1. *Emotional instability and immaturity*—lack of peace of mind, of mental health or well-being; no sense of humor or understanding of others, etc.; life of disharmony.

2. Become *anti-social;* take to *crime.*

3. *No self-development or improvement*—getting in a "rut"; no opportunity for independence of thought and action, for following through with own interests; no further study or reading, etc.

4. *Not be accepted by others*—no recognition of my status by others; not be liked, respected, or loved (exception: where mention is restricted to family or marriage, code under Col. 9-5).

5. *No sense of personal worth*—feel personally inadequate; unable to achieve aspirations as to occupation or role in life; feel worthless; have no purpose in life.

6. *To be a person without character.*

7. *Miscellaneous* worries and fears regarding one's own personal character.

Y. Nothing to code in this column.

Personal Economic Situation

_____ Col. 2

1. *Improved or decent standard of living for self or family;* sufficient money to live better or to live decently; freedom from debt; make ends meet; relief from poverty; not suffer want, hunger, etc.

3. Have *own business;* ability to increase or expand one's business.

4. Have *own land or own farm.*
5. Have own *house,* apartment, or garden; or get better ones.
6. Have *modern conveniences,* such as a car, bathroom, fine or new furniture, fine clothes, large appliances such as washing machine, radio, television, etc.
7. Have *wealth*—money to do anything I/we wish.
8. *Miscellaneous* aspirations having to do with economic situation of self or family.
Y. Nothing to code in this column.

_____ Col. 8

1. *Deterioration in or inadequate standard of living for self or family;* not sufficient money to live better or to live decently; debt; poverty; suffer want, hunger, etc.

3. *Miscellaneous* worries and fears having to do with the economic situation of self or family.

Job or Work Situation

_____ Col. 3

1. *Good job, congenial work* for self, spouse, or other family member; independence in choice of occupation; pleasant, interesting job or work situation; chance of advancement.

2. *Employment*—steady work for self, spouse, or other family member.

3. *Success* in one's work for self, spouse, or other family member; make a contribution to one's field.
5. *Miscellaneous* aspirations regarding job or work situation.

_____ Col. 8 (Cont'd)

6. *Poor job, uncongenial work* for self, spouse, or other family member; no independence in choice of occupation; unpleasant, uninteresting job or work situation; no chance for advancement.

7. *Unemployment*—no steady work for self, spouse, or other family member; inability to find or hold a job; unable to work because of sickness or old age.

8. *Failure* in one's work for self, spouse, or other family member; contribute little or nothing to one's field.
9. *Miscellaneous* worries and fears regarding job or work situation.
Y. Nothing to code in this column.

Other References to "Self"

_____ Col. 3 (Cont'd)

7. One's own *health*—continued or re-
gained health (physical or mental)
for *self;* strength to enjoy life.
8. *Happy old age*—long and happy life;
peaceful, pleasant, secure old age.
9. *Recreation, travel, leisure time;* sports,
reading for pleasure, etc.
0. *Miscellaneous* aspirations involving
other references to "self."
Y. Nothing to code in this column.

_____ Col. 9

1. *Ill health, accident, death,* or continued
illness (physical or mental) for
self; no strength to enjoy life.
2. *To be dependent on others.*

3. *Miscellaneous* worries and fears involving other references to "self."

Other References to Family

_____ Col. 4

1. *Happy family life*—happy marriage;
pleasant home; love within family;
have a (good) husband or wife;
have children.

2. *Relatives*—concern for spouse, children, parents, or other relatives;
be close to them; keep them together or get them together again;
help or take care of them; live up
to their expectations.
3. *Health of family*—continued good
health or improved health (physical or mental) for members of
family.
4. *Children*—adequate opportunities for
them (including education); children themselves do well, be happy,
successful.
5. *Miscellaneous* aspirations regarding
family.

_____ Col. 9 (Cont'd)

5. *No or unhappy family life*—no husband,
wife, or children; no marriage or
unhappy marriage; no home or
unhappy home; no love within
family.
6. *Relatives*—separation from (or abandonment by) spouse, children,
parents, or other relative; not to
be able to help or take care of
them; not to live up to their
expectations.
7. *Ill health, accident, death,* or continued
poor health (physical or mental)
for members of family.
8. *Children* — inadequate opportunities
for them (including education);
children themselves do poorly, be
unhappy, unsuccessful.

0. *Miscellaneous* worries and fears regarding family.

Y. Nothing to code in this column.

CONCERNED ABOUT OTHER PEOPLE, COMMUNITY, OR NATION
Political

_____ Col. 4 (Cont'd)

7. *Freedom,* including specifically freedom of speech, of religion, of
occupation, of movement, etc.

_____ Col. 10

1. *Lack of freedom,* including specifically
lack of freedom of speech, of
religion, of occupation, or movement, etc.

Political (Cont'd)

_____ Col. 4 (Cont'd)

8. *Miscellaneous* aspirations having to do with the political situation.

Y. Nothing to code in this column.

_____ Col. 10 (Cont'd)

2. *No improvement in present government;* fear present government will continue.
3. *Political instability;* chaos; confusion; lack of internal peace; civil war; etc.
4. *Miscellaneous* worries and fears having to do with the political situation.

General Economic Situation

_____ Col. 5

1. *Economic stability* (in general); freedom from inflation; fair prices.
2. *Miscellaneous* economic aspirations not restricted to self or family.

_____ Col. 10 (Cont'd)

7. *Economic instability* (in general); inflation; unfair or high prices.
8. *Deterioration in or inadequate standard of living for nation or group* (not restricted to self or family)—people unable to live decently; poverty, want, hunger, etc.
0. *Miscellaneous* economic worries and fears not restricted to self or family.
Y. Nothing to code in this column.

Social

_____ Col. 5 (Cont'd)

5. *Social justice*—greater equality in the treatment, benefits, and opportunities afforded all elements of the population, irrespective of race, color, class, caste, religion, etc.; integration; fairer distribution of wealth; elimination of discrimination or exploitation.
6. *Future generations*—better prospects and opportunities. (Note: if restricted to "own children," code under Col. 4-4.)
7. *Social security*, including pensions, annuities, etc.
8. *Miscellaneous* aspirations having to do with the social situation.
Y. Nothing to code in this column.

_____ Col. 11

1. *Social injustice;* continued inequality in the treatment, benefits, and opportunities afforded various elements of the population; discrimination or exploitation based on race, color, class, caste, religion, etc.; continuing unfair distribution of wealth.
2. *Future generations*—no better prospects or worse prospects; no opportunities. (Note: if restricted to "own children," code under Col. 9-8.)
3. *No social security;* no pensions, annuities, etc.
4. *Miscellaneous* worries and fears having to do with the social situation.

Religion, Morality, Public Service

_____ Col. 6

1. *Desire to be useful to others;* ability and opportunity to serve the people, community, nation, world; or to hold public office.

2. *Miscellaneous* aspirations having to do with public service or with religion or morality where the reference is not restricted to self or family.

_____ Col. 11 (Cont'd)

7. *Not to be useful to others;* not to serve the people, community, nation, world.

8. *Spiritual, ethical, moral, or religious disintegration, deterioration, or complacency on the part of society.*

9. *Miscellaneous* worries and fears having to do with public service or with religion or morality where the reference is not restricted to self or family.

Y. Nothing to code in this column.

CONCERNED ABOUT INTERNATIONAL SITUATION AND WORLD

_____ Col. 6 (Cont'd)

5. *Peace*—maintenance of; no war; no threat of war.

6. *Better world*—more international cooperation; countries working together; more international understanding and responsibility; relaxation of international tensions; stronger U.N.; world government.

7. *Miscellaneous* aspirations having to do with the international or world situation.

_____ Col. 12

1. *War;* nuclear war; living in fear of war.

2. *Militarism and armaments; misuse of nuclear energy;* fallouts from nuclear tests.

3. *Threat, aggression, domination,* or conquest by Russia, Communist China, Cuba, or other Communist power; become a Communist satellite.

4. *Miscellaneous* worries and fears having to do with the international or world situation.

GENERAL

_____ Col. 6 (Cont'd)

9. *Maintain status quo* (in general); person is happy with things as they are now.

0. *Miscellaneous* aspirations that do not fit under any of the preceding categories.

X. Don't know; no answer.

Y. Nothing to code in this column.

_____ Col. 12 (Cont'd)

7. *Can't think of any fears or worries.*

8. *Miscellaneous* worries and fears that do not fit under any of the preceding categories.

X. Don't know; no answer.

Y. Nothing to code in this column.

Code for Questions 3(A) and 3(B):
National Hopes and Aspirations; National Worries and Fears

The categories for national hopes and aspirations are given on the left-hand side of the page — columns 18–24. The categories for national fears and worries are given on the right-hand side of the page — columns 25–30.

CONCERNED WITH NATIONAL SITUATION

Political

_____ Col. 18

1. *Honest government*—fair and just; no corruption or nepotism.

2. *Efficient government*—competent leadership and administration; effective party system; no excessive bureaucracy.

3. *Balanced government*—adequate system of checks and balances; no excessive power in hands of government; less central government; more power to states or provinces.

4. *Democratic or representative government*— maintain present democracy or become a democracy; have more democracy or more representative government.

5. *Socialistic government*—aspiration to become a socialistic or welfare state.

6. *Freedom*—with specific reference to freedom of speech, of religion, of occupation, of movement, etc.

7. *Law and order*—Maintenance of the public peace; decrease or no increase in crime, juvenile delinquency, etc.; fair courts, good or improved juridical practices, penal system, etc.

_____ Col. 25

1. *Dishonest government*—unfair and unjust; corruption and nepotism.

2. *Inefficient government*—weak, indecisive leadership and administration; no effective party system; excessive bureaucracy.

3. *Communism*—fear of the Communist danger or of the consequences of Communist control. (Note: if specific reference to the external threat from the U.S.S.R., Communist China, or other Communist powers, code under Col. 29-8.)

4. *No democracy or representative government;* loss of democracy; totalitarianism. (Note: if specific reference to Communism, code under Col. 25-3.)

5. *Fear country will become socialistic.*

6. *Lack or loss of freedom*—in general, or with specific reference to freedom of speech, of religion, of occupation, of movement, etc. (Note: If loss of freedom is specifically connected with Communism, code under Col. 25-3.)

7. *Lack of law and order*—failure to maintain public peace; prevalence of or increase in crime, juvenile delinquency, etc.; unfair courts; poor or unfair juridical practices, penal system, etc.

Political (Cont'd)

_____ Col. 18 (Cont'd)

8. *National unity*—absence of unrest, tensions, and antagonisms based on regional, class, caste, religious, etc., differences.

9. *Political stability, internal peace and order.*

X. *Miscellaneous* aspirations having to do with the national political situation.

Y. Nothing to code in this column.

_____ Col. 25 (Cont'd)

8. *Disunity among people of the nation*—unrest, tensions, antagonisms based on regional, class, caste, religious, etc., differences.

9. *Political instability, chaos, civil war.*

0. *High or increased taxes.*

X. *Miscellaneous* worries and fears having to do with the national political situation.

Y. Nothing to code in this column.

Economic

_____ Col. 19

4. *Improved or decent standard of living* (in general); greater national prosperity (in general).

5. *Improved standard of living* or greater national prosperity *through technological advances*—increase in rate of mechanization, use of modern scientific advances, nuclear energy; greater *productivity* in industry or agriculture; development of natural resources.

7. *Economic stability*; no inflation; fair prices.

8. *Employment*—jobs for everyone; no unemployment problem.

9. *Miscellaneous* aspirations having to do with the national economic situation.

Y. Nothing to code in this column.

_____ Col. 26

4. *No improvement in or inadequate standard of living* (in general); not be a prosperous nation (in general).

5. *No improvement in standard of living* or no increase in national prosperity *through technological advances; economic backwardness;* no industrialization; *low productivity* in industry or agriculture; no use of modern scientific advances or of nuclear energy; no development of natural resources.

6. *Failure to preserve present standard of living;* decrease in national prosperity.

7. *Economic instability;* inflation; unfair or high prices; depression; national bankruptcy.

8. *Unemployment.*

9. *Miscellaneous* worries and fears having to do with the national economic situation.

Y. Nothing to code in this column.

Social

_____ Col. 20

1. *Social justice* (in the most general, positive sense); greater equality for the good of all in the treatment, benefits, and opportunities afforded all elements of the population.

_____ Col. 27

1. *Social injustice* (in the most general sense); continued inequality in the treatment, benefits, and opportunities afforded various elements of the population.

Social (Cont'd)

_____ Col. 20 (Cont'd)

2. *Eliminate discrimination* and prejudice based on *race, color, caste, religion,* etc.; integration.

3. *Eliminate discrimination* or *exploitation* based on differences in *class* or *economic status* (e.g., with reference to the poor, the workers, the common people, etc.); fairer distribution of wealth, income, and opportunities regardless of class.

4. *Education*—more and/or better schools; technical and trade schools; fight ignorance and illiteracy.

5. *Improved labor conditions*—shorter working hours, etc.

6. *Control of labor*—no strikes or labor unrest or pressures; regulation of labor practices and labor unions.

7. *Social security*—adequate annuities, pensions, etc.; security for aged, handicapped, indigent.

8. *Housing*—adequate or improved housing conditions; no slums.

9. *Agrarian reform,* especially "land for the landless"; agricultural development; help for the peasants.

0. *Public health*—improved medical care; more doctors, hospitals; combat disease, epidemics; people healthy.

Y. Nothing to code in this column.

_____ Col. 21

1. *Limited population growth*—no excess of population; control of birth rate; emigration.

2. *Sense of social and political responsibility and awareness* on the part of the people; less complacency; people working for the common good.

3. *Morality, ethical standards, religion, honesty, self-discipline* on the part of the public generally.

_____ Col. 27 (Cont'd)

2. *Continued discrimination* and prejudice based on *race, color, caste, religion,* etc.; segregation.

3. *Continued discrimination* or *exploitation* based on differences in *class* or *economic status* (e.g., with reference to the poor, the workers, the common people, etc.); continuing unfair distribution of wealth, income, and opportunities based on class differences.

4. *Inadequate educational facilities and schooling;* lack of technical and trade schools; ignorance and illiteracy.

5. *Poor or unfair working conditions*—long working hours; forced labor.

6. *Abuses by labor*—strikes, labor pressures and unrest; abuse of power by labor unions; inadequate or no regulation of labor practices or labor unions.

_____ Col. 27 (Cont'd)

7. *Unlimited population growth*—excessive population; excessive birth rate; too much immigration.

8. *No sense of social and political responsibility or awareness* on the part of the people; complacency; people not working for the common good.

9. *Lack of morality, ethical standards, religion, honesty, self-discipline* on the part of the public generally.

Social (Cont'd)

_____ Col. 21 (Cont'd)

4. *Miscellaneous* aspirations having to do with social matters.

Y. Nothing to code in this column.

_____ Col. 27 (Cont'd)

0. Too much *mechanization* and *standardization; materialism; conformity.*

X. *Miscellaneous* worries and fears having to do with social matters.

Y. Nothing to code in this column.

CONCERNED WITH INTERNATIONAL SITUATION

International Relations, Cold War, Peace, etc.

_____ Col. 22

1. *Peace*—no war or nuclear war; freedom from fear of war or devastation.

2. *Disarmament, limitation of armaments,* control or banning of nuclear weapons; cessation of nuclear tests.

3. *Lessening of cold war;* reduction of tensions between East and West; coexistence.

4. *Better relations with Communist bloc* or individual members of Communist bloc.

5. *Friendly relations with all countries.*

6. *Better world*—more international cooperation in general (without specific reference to cold war); countries working together; more international understanding and responsibility; stronger United Nations; world government.

7. *Maintain neutrality*—keep aloof from conflicting ideologies, blocs, etc.; have no enemies; not take sides.

8. *Help other nations* (especially the underdeveloped); promote worldwide prosperity.

9. *Increased foreign trade or exports.*

0. *Miscellaneous* aspirations having to do with international relations, the cold war, peace, etc.

Y. Nothing to code in this column.

_____ Col. 28

3. *War;* nuclear war; living in fear of war; devastation from war's consequences (e.g., destruction, famine, imprisonment, etc.)

4. *Continued armament; no control or banning of nuclear weapons;* misuse of nuclear energy; continuation of nuclear tests; fear of fallout.

5. *No lessening of cold war;* no reduction of tensions between East and West; no coexistence.

6. *Be isolated* from other nations; no friends; foreign relations deteriorate.

8. *Inability to maintain neutrality* or to keep aloof from conflicting ideologies, blocs, etc.; make enemies; have to take sides.

0. *Miscellaneous* worries and fears having to do with international relations, the cold war, peace, etc.

Y. Nothing to code in this column.

Independence, Status, and Importance of Nation

_____ Col. 23   _____ Col. 29

3. *Be militarily strong.*

4. Maintain or attain the position of a *world power.*

       3. Not to maintain or attain the position of a *world power.*

5. *Enhancement of status and importance* of the nation in general in international affairs; play a more important role in international affairs and negotiations.

       4. *Lose or have no status or importance* in international affairs in general; no important role in international affairs or negotiations.

6. Play a more important role specifically in *regional affairs* or *of regional leadership.*

7. *Exert ideological or moral leadership;* exercise potential influence abroad for peace and freedom; convey own ideas and culture to rest of world; be a mediating power; bring about understanding or reconcile opposing views of nations.

       6. *Failure to exert ideological or moral leadership*—failure to exercise potential influence abroad for peace and freedom, to convey own ideas and culture to rest of world, to be a mediating power, or to bring about understanding and reconcile differing points of views between other nations.

8. *National independence*—attain or preserve independence or gain greater independence; freedom from interference or excessive influence from other powers; pursuing independent foreign policy; achieve economic self-sufficiency or independence.

       7. *Lack or loss of national independence*—to live on sufferance of others; be subject to interference or excessive influence from other powers; to have no independent foreign policy; economic dependence; have to accept foreign aid.

       8. *Threat, aggression, domination,* or conquest by Russia, Communist China, Cuba, or any other *Communist power;* become a Communist satellite.

       9. *Threat, aggression, domination,* or conquest by any *foreign power* (not specifically Communist).

0. *Miscellaneous* aspirations having to do with the independence, status, or importance of the nation.

       0. *Miscellaneous* worries and fears having to do with the independence, status, or importance of the nation.

Y. Nothing to code in this column.

       Y. Nothing to code in this column.

GENERAL

_____ Col. 24

5. *Maintain status quo;* content as things are; present trends satisfactory.

6. *No hopes* or aspirations for the country.

7. *Miscellaneous* aspirations for the country not covered by any of the preceding categories.

X. Don't know; no answer.

Y. Nothing to code in this column.

_____ Col. 30

6. *No fears* or worries for the country.

7. *Miscellaneous* worries and fears for the country not covered by any of the preceding categories.

X. Don't know; no answer.

Y. Nothing to code in this column.

2. INSTRUCTIONS FOR CODERS

(1) Coding is an essential step in transferring, by a kind of numerical shorthand, the thoughts expressed in an interview onto an IBM punch card. These cards are made up of 80 columns. In each column there are 12 different places where holes can be punched. The first ten such places are indicated by the numbers zero through nine; the eleventh and twelfth by the letters "X" and "Y," respectively.

The numerical code you will be using is made up of two indicators: a *column* number in front of the hyphen; and a *punch hole* indicator after the hyphen (either zero through nine, "X" or "Y"). Thus 8-1 means column 8, hole 1. You will note that this particular code designation (8-1, that is) has to do with personal worries and fears mentioned in reply to Question 1(B) and indicates specifically a reference to "deterioration in or inadequate standard of living for self or family." Every time that particular hole is punched in that particular column it means that the respondent has made a reference to that particular topic.

(2) In general, each separate idea expressed in answering a question should be coded once, and only once.

Sometimes this becomes a little confusing, however. Occasionally a respondent may express two thoughts in a single sentence. Suppose he says, for example: "I want enough money to live decently and buy a house." This should be coded twice. In the first place, it comes under:

2-1 Improved or decent standard of living for self or family; *sufficient money to live better or to live decently;* etc.

But it also comes under:

2-5 *Have own house,* apartment or garden, etc.

Consequently, there is a need for coding it both 2-1 and 2-5.

Similarly, if a reply on personal worries and fears is to the effect that "I may not be able to take care of my children because I might lose my job," this also should be coded twice, even though the two thoughts involved are expressed as inter-related by way of a casual connection, namely under:

9-8 *Children* — inadequate opportunities for them, etc.

and under

8-7 *Unemployment.*

In a few, very rare cases, a single thought may require double coding. For example, suppose a respondent mentions "good government" as one of his aspirations for the country — just "good government" without any further specification. Our code does not provide a "good government" category. However, 18-1 refers to "Honest government" and 18-2 to "Efficient government." Since good government is obviously a combination of honest government and efficient government, we would in this case code *both* 18-1 and 18-2.

On the other hand, sometimes the respondent may express what on the surface appear to be two ideas but which are so closely related that under our coding scheme they should be coded as one. Suppose he says: "I want enough money to live decently and stay out of debt." Both of these ideas are included in a single topic in our code and should be coded only once — namely, under:

2-1 Improved or decent standard of living; *sufficient money to live better or to live decently; freedom from debt;* etc.

To know how to deal with such situations you must obviously become thoroughly familiar with the coding scheme as a whole.

(3) The coding scheme for Question 1 (A), having to do with personal hopes and aspirations, and Question 1(B), having to do with personal worries and fears, is organized primarily so as to show how broad the respondent's concerns are, starting with himself as an individual, moving out to his family, then to his fellow-citizens, and finally to the international and world scenes. The general categories are as follows:

CONCERNED WITH SELF AND/OR FAMILY

    Own Personal Character

    Personal Economic Situation

    Job or Work Situation

    Other References to "Self"

    Other References to Family

CONCERNED ABOUT OTHER PEOPLE, COMMUNITY, OR NATION

    Political

    General Economic Situation

    Social

    Religion, Morality, Public Service

CONCERNED ABOUT INTERNATIONAL SITUATION AND WORLD

GENERAL

(4) In a somewhat similar way, the code for Question 3(A), dealing with national hopes and aspirations, and Question 3(B), having to do

with fears and worries for one's country, is so organized as to show whether the respondent is concerned only about his own country or extends his area of concern to the international or world situations. The major headings are as follows:

CONCERNED WITH NATIONAL SITUATION

Political

Economic

Social

CONCERNED WITH INTERNATIONAL SITUATION

International Relations, Cold War, Peace, etc.

Independence, Status, and Importance of Nation

GENERAL

(5) In your coding work you must proceed on the basis of what the respondent actually said, neither adding to it nor subtracting from it. For you to put one of his thoughts under a particular code item, he need not of course have used exactly the words listed in the code, if the thought he is getting at is basically the same. As one of his personal aspirations, for example, he may say: "I want to learn not to worry so much." This exact wording is not listed under the code; but his remark quite clearly comes under the heading:

1-1 Emotional stability and maturity — *peace of mind,* etc.

On the other hand, you must take into account only what the respondent himself said, accepting it at face value, and not reading anything into it by way of inferences. For example, just because you happen to know that there is a widespread fear of a Communist take-over in a particular country, you should not infer when a respondent expresses the fear of "loss of freedom" that he is necessarily talking about Communist control. The item should be coded under 25-6 ("Lack or loss of freedom"), not under 25-3 ("Communism") unless the respondent himself makes an explicit reference to Communism.

Similarly, when a respondent expresses a wish to be elected to the legislature or hold other public office, you may *suspect* that his motivation is to make money rather than to be of public service. Nevertheless, the item should be coded on the basis of what he said, not what you may guess about his motivation; namely, under 6-1:

"Desire to be useful to others; ability and opportunity to serve the people, community, nation, world; *or to hold public office.*"

(6) If there is a choice of coding a given remark under a more specific or a more general category, put it under the more specific one. If, for example, a respondent mentions the possibility of conquest and domination by Russia as one of his fears for his country, code it under 29-8 ("Threat, aggression, domination or conquest by the U.S.S.R., etc.") rather than under 29-7 ("Lack or loss of national independence").

(7) Occasionally remarks will be found in the interviews which are irrelevant or non-responsive to the question asked. For example, in reply to Question 1(A), one respondent had this to say:

"To appreciate what one has. Not to demand too much out of life, or more than life can give us."

While these philosophical comments may provide a good rule for living, they do not constitute "wishes and hopes for the future."

Another respondent, replying to Question 3(A), said:

"With the greatest optimism and the way things are now, I believe that a person being absent from the country for ten years, would not recognize it."

While this is an estimate of the future, it does not express any of the respondent's "wishes and hopes for the future of our country."

A third interviewee, in answering Question 1(B) about personal worries and fears, talked in this fashion:

"Now that I am growing old and don't have enough money to live happily, I work hard every day."

While this is a depressing statement of present fact, it is not a fear and worry about the future; it is a complaint rather than a fear.

Such irrelevant or non-responsive remarks as these should be ignored and not coded.

(8) When you come across a remark that, after careful study, you feel doesn't fit under any category in the appropriate code, you should code it miscellaneous, using the miscellaneous designation provided at the end of each subject matter area covered in the code. For example, suppose a respondent expresses as one of his personal aspirations in answer to Question 1(A) that the present government should continue in power. There is no such category in the code for personal aspirations, but the remark obviously fits under the subject matter area denominated "Political." It should therefore be coded 4-8 ("Miscellaneous aspirations having to do with the political situation").

It is essential in this case, however, that you make a verbatim notation of all such miscellaneous remarks on a separate form, in every instance identifying the remark by the number of the interview in which it appeared. A separate list should be kept for each miscellaneous designation under each separate subject matter area. The reason for doing this is to make it possible for us to go back, if enough items of a certain kind emerge, and set up a new category in the code, transferring the appropriate items out of the miscellaneous category.

(9) When you start coding, break up what the respondent has said in reply to a particular question into each separate thought, either by underlining or by slant marks. Then jot down on some scratch paper the code for each of these thoughts as you come to them. Your list in the

case of a particular respondent's reply to Question 1(A) might, for example, look something like this:

5-6

2-5

1-1

2-3

The next step is to write these code designations in the space provided, in the right-hand margin of the interview forms. At this stage, however, several complications arise. To start with, the columns must be listed in proper sequence, which is not the case in the listing you have made on the scratch paper; that is, Column 1 should appear at the top; Column 2 below that; Column 3 below that; etc.

In the second place, when there is more than one punch called for in a particular column (such as in the case of 2-5 and 2-3 above), the punch card operator must be able to tell very quickly that there are to be two or more punches when she comes to Column 2 — and these punches must be listed in proper sequence: that is, the 1 first, the 2 second, etc. For this reason, in transferring our notations to the margin of the interview form, we now combine 2-5 and 2-3 and write them this way: 2-3, 5. (If they are to be included in such a sequence, zero is treated as if it were ten; X is treated as if it were eleven; and Y as twelve. Thus, if your list included 2-0, 2-5, and 2-Y, it would come out this way: 2-5, 0, Y.)

In the third place, we need to tell the punch card operator when *nothing* has been mentioned in the interview that fits under a particular column. The code for Question 1(A), for example, covers six columns: Columns 1–6. In the example given above, the ideas expressed were confined to Columns 1, 2, and 5. No ideas were expressed coming under Columns 3, 4, or 6. To indicate this fact, we list the column number and put a "Y" after it (e.g., 3-Y, 4-Y and 6-Y).

Thus when we transfer our notations from the scratch paper to the right-hand margin of the interview form, the example given above would come out looking like this:

1-1

2-3, 5

3-Y

4-Y

5-6

6-Y

To be sure you list all the column numbers in sequence covering a particular question, write all the column numbers down first in the right-hand margin of the interview form; then fill in the appropriate punch numbers afterward.

(10) As you will note from the two codes (one covering the two parts

of Question 1; the other the two parts of Question 3), the columns devoted to these particular questions are as follows:

Question 1(A):	Columns 1–6
Question 1(B):	Columns 7–12
Question 3(A):	Columns 18–24
Question 3(B):	Columns 25–30

(Columns 13 through 17 are devoted to "ladder" ratings involving the respondent's personal life; and Columns 31 through 35 to ladder ratings regarding the country. The coding scheme for these matters was given in a separate document.)

(11) Sometimes a respondent may mix things up a bit and mention what is really a fear under that part of the question which asks about hopes, or vice versa. In such cases, code the remark for what it really is, even though it may appear under the wrong part of the question.

(12) If you are dubious about selection of the appropriate code number, discuss the problem with the coding supervisor. Do not discuss it with your fellow-coders — the only way in which we can obtain uniform coding is for the coding supervisor to make all decisions. If there is no time to discuss your problem with the coding supervisor, attach a slip of paper to the coded questionnaire, indicating the dubious item, which will be checked later.

(13) Also to insure uniformity, the coding supervisor should check a sampling of each coder's work every day the coding continues.

Appendix B: Samples Used

1. DETAILS OF EACH COUNTRY:
NUMBER OF CASES, COMPOSITION, WEIGHTINGS

Brazil

National modified probability cross-section samples of both urban and rural populations. Tabulations in text based on weighting the original 1142 rural interviews by 1½ on basis of new census data. Urban sample of 1026, making total card units 2739. All numbers are for card units in the different categories. Instituto de Estudos Sociais e Economicos, Ltda., Dr. Octavio da Costa Eduardo.

SEX
Male	1242
Female	1497

AGE
18–29	899
30–49	1250
50+	590

EDUCATION
High	35
Middle	223
Low	1040
Illiterate	1441

SOCIOECONOMIC
Upper	205
Middle	1443
Low	1091

DWELLING
Rural	1713
Urban	1026

Cuba

Two samples were obtained: (1) a cross-section of the adult population of Havana, 494 cases; and (2) a national cross-section of the urban population outside of Havana of 498 cases, which was duplicated to give proper weighting. Total card units of 1490. Because of the conditions under which the study was done, it was impossible to interview in rural areas, and the name of the organization that did the work, long since disbanded and out of the country, must remain anonymous.

SEX

Male	833
Female	633
No answer	24

AGE

20–29	610
30–39	412
40–49	256
50+	190
No answer	22

EDUCATION

Higher	201
Secondary	358
Elementary; none	875
No answer	56

SOCIOECONOMIC

High; upper middle	272
Lower middle	441
Low	769
No answer	8

CITY

Less than 5000	100
5000–10,000	71
10,000–20,000	162
20,000–50,000	334
Over 50,000	331
Havana	487
No answer	5

The Dominican Republic

National samples of both the urban and rural publics: the former with 396 interviews, the latter with 418. The original cards were weighted both for mortality and for the proper rural-urban ratio, yielding a total of 2442 card units, 558 urban and 1884 rural. International Research Associates, S. A. de C. V., of Mexico City.

SEX

Male	1588
Female	854

AGE

21–29	715
30–39	712
40–49	437
50+	578

EDUCATION

Some secondary	169
Some primary	1149
No schooling	943
No answer	181

SOCIOECONOMIC

Upper	190
Lower	2226
No answer	26

DWELLING

Rural	1884
Urban	558

Egypt

As indicated in the text, the study in Egypt must be regarded as a preliminary pilot investigation, especially because of difficulties encountered in interviewing in rural areas. The rural sample of 82 cases was weighted 9 times and added to the urban sample of 417 cases, giving 1237 card units. Supervised by Dr. Abdo Elkholy.

SEX

Male	848
Female	363
No answer	26

AGE

15–19	222
20–39	741
40+	188
No answer	86

DWELLING

Rural	820
Urban	417

India I

Probability sample of 2366 cases modified to include the proper proportion of Harijans (Untouchables) who might not be obtained on a pure probability basis since they must cluster in certain areas. The original rural sample of 1118 cases was weighted by 4, giving 5720 card units. In both Indian surveys, the number of women who could be interviewed was very small due to various customs that make it impossi-

ble or difficult to talk with women. Indian Institute of Public Opinion.
E. P. W. da Costa and J. S. Yogie.

SEX

Male	5188
Female	532

AGE

−30	2069
31–40	1585
41+	2041
No answer	25

EDUCATION

Higher	744
Matriculate	722
Under matriculate	2218
Illiterate	1997
No answer	39

INCOME

301+ rupees	489
151–300 rupees	896
75–150 rupees	1889
Under 75 rupees	2050
No answer	396

CITY

Rural	4472
5000–99,999	608
100,000+	640

India II

Modified probability sample of 2014 cases with rural interviews numbering 993 again weighted by 4. Total card units 4993. Indian Institute of Public Opinion. E. P. W. da Costa and J. S. Yogie.

SEX

Male	4718
Female	275

AGE

−30	1861
31–40	1562
41+	1570

EDUCATION

Higher	626
Matriculate	635
Under matriculate	2105
Illiterate	1627

INCOME

301+ rupees	365
151–300 rupees	958
75–150 rupees	1705
Under 75 rupees	1765
No answer	200

CITY

Rural	3972
5000–99,999	538
100,000+	483

Israel

Probability sample of 1170 cases. No weighting. Israel Institute of Applied Social Research. Dr. Louis Guttman and Dr. Aaron Antonovsky.

SEX

Male	578
Female	592

AGE

—29	282
30–49	567
50–64	252
65+	68
No answer	1

EDUCATION

University	145
Secondary or elementary complete	700
Elementary incomplete	325

INCOME

Upper	156
Middle	672
Lower	257
No answer	85

CLASS

Upper; upper middle	93
Middle	611
Lower	58
Working	340
No answer	68

REGION

Cooperative settlement	82
New urban community	213
Long settled urban	101
Tel Aviv; Haifa	676
Jerusalem	98

The Kibbutzim

Sample of 30 members in each of 10 Kibbutzim chosen on the basis of type of social or religious movement represented and within each Kibbutz by the date of original settlement in the Kibbutz. Total of 300 cases. Note that income does not apply to members of the Kibbutzim. Israel Institute of Applied Social Research. Dr. Louis Guttman and Dr. Aaron Antonovsky.

SEX

Male	167
Female	133

AGE

—29	112
30–49	139
50–64	46
65+	3

EDUCATION

Higher	56
Secondary or elementary complete	227
Elementary incomplete	17

CLASS

Upper; upper middle	35
Middle	68
Lower	2
Working	189
No answer	6

Japan

Probability sample of 972 cases. No weighting. Central Research Agency of Tokyo.

SEX

Male	439
Female	533

AGE

21–29	226
30–44	366
45–64	292
65+	88

EDUCATION

Higher	150
High school incomplete	234
0–9 years' schooling	588

SOCIOECONOMIC

Upper; upper middle	206
Middle	547
Lower middle; lower	219

Nigeria

Modified probability sample of 1200 cases. Weighted as follows to conform to best population estimates: Western rural cases duplicated; Eastern region rural cases weighted by 2½; Northern region, urban weighted by 2 and rural by 6, giving 2876 card units as a total. Market Research (Nigeria) Ltd., James R. Wilson and Dr. Gordon Wilson.

SEX

Male	2324
Female	552

AGE

21–29	967
30–39	990
40–49	473
50+	443
No answer	3

EDUCATION

Some secondary or university	407
Some primary	803
No school/literate	445
Illiterate	1215
No answer	6

SOCIOECONOMIC

Upper	102
Lower	2748
No answer	26

CITY

Rural	2054
5000–20,000	492
20,000–100,000	172
100,000+	158

REGION

West	580
East	700
North	1596

RELIGION

Moslem	1379
Christian	1383
Pagan	102
No answer	12

Panama

National cross-sections of 359 completed urban and 283 rural interviews. Original cards weighted both for mortality and rural-urban ratio, yielding a total of 1351 units, 565 urban and 786 rural. International Research Associates, S. A. de C. V. of Mexico City.

SEX

| Male | 662 |
| Female | 689 |

AGE

21–29	333
30–39	337
40–49	291
50+	390

EDUCATION

Some secondary	341
Some primary	750
No schooling	247
No answer	13

SOCIOECONOMIC

Upper	370
Lower	964
No answer	17

DWELLING

| Rural | 786 |
| Urban | 565 |

The Philippines

National cross-section of 500 adults. The original sample of 148 rural cases was replicated 6 times to produce a total of 1036 rural cards, added to 188 urban and 164 semi-urban to give a total of 1388 units. The Psychological Center, Dr. George Hodel.

SEX

| Male | 780 |
| Female | 608 |

AGE

21–30	517
31–40	316
41–50	224
51+	331

EDUCATION

College complete	246
College incomplete	287
High school complete	170
High school incomplete	136
Elementary complete	125
Elementary incomplete	215
No schooling	209

ECONOMIC

Upper	81
Upper middle	220
Lower middle	560
Lower	527

DWELLING

Rural	1036
Semi-urban	164
Urban	188

Poland

Nationwide samples of urban and rural populations over 18 years of age. Urban sample stratified by occupation. Urban sample of 978, rural of 486. Since the population divides approximately 50 percent urban and 50 percent rural, the rural sample obtained was replicated, giving a total of 1950 card units. All numbers are for card units in the different categories. Dr. Adam Sarapata of the Polish Academy of Sciences.

SEX

Male	929
Female	1021

AGE

18–29	674
30–39	481
40–49	335
50+	460

EDUCATION

Some higher	203
Some secondary	738
Some primary	1009

OCCUPATION

Farmers	679
Unskilled	147
Skilled; craftsmen	416
White collar	598
Others; students	95
No answer	15

DWELLING

Rural	972
Urban	978

United States

Modified probability sample of 1549 cases. Adjusted for call-backs in a standard procedure found to increase accuracy. (See Alfred Politz and Willard Simmons, "An attempt to get the 'not-at-homes' in the sample without callbacks," *Jl. Amer. Statistical Assoc.,* March 1949.) Men not at home the previous three days at time of interview weighted 4, not at home previous two days weighted 2, not at home previous day weighted 1⅓, at home three previous days weighted 1. Women not at home three previous days weighted 5, not at home two previous days weighted 2½, not at home previous day weighted 1⅔, at home three previous days weighted 1¼. Total of 2696 card units. American Institute of Public Opinion. Dr. George H. Gallup and Paul Perry.

SEX

Male	1283
Female	1413

AGE

21–29	461
30–49	1280
50–64	569
65+	359
No answer	27

EDUCATION

College	527
High school	1325
Grammar school	837
No answer	7

ECONOMIC

Upper	825
Middle	915
Lower	827
No answer	129

CLASS

Upper	59
Upper middle	412
Middle	1031
Lower middle	138
Lower	60
Working	960
No answer	36

RACE

White	2432
Non-white	264

RELIGION

Protestant	1706
Catholic	720
Jewish	139
Other; none	131

West Germany

National probability cross-section of 480 adults. DIVO, Peter Schmitt.

SEX

Male	219
Female	261

AGE

—29	81
30–39	100
40–49	91
50–59	118
60+	90

EDUCATION

Secondary	51
University	15
Grammar school	395
No answer	19

ECONOMIC

Upper	40
Middle	281
Lower	157
No answer	2

CITY

Under 2000	113
2000–10,000	127
10,000–100,000	107
100,000+	133

Yugoslavia

Modified probability sample of 1523 adults. No weighting. Institute for Social Sciences, Belgrade. Dr. Radivoj Uvalić and Professor Ilija Stanojcić.

SEX

Male	761
Female	762

AGE

21–29	361
30–49	715
50+	445
No answer	2

EDUCATION

High school or higher	214
Some high school; primary complete	397

Some primary	665
No schooling	236
No answer	11

ECONOMIC

Upper — nonfarmer	258
Upper — farmer	249
Lower — nonfarmer	717
Lower — farmer	185
No answer	114

DWELLING

Rural	727
Semi-urban	83
Urban	706
No answer	7

NATIONALITY

Serbian	685
Croatian	350
Slovenian	160
Other	327
No answer	1

2. RELATIONSHIP OF EDUCATION TO AGE,
SOCIOECONOMIC STATUS, DWELLING

In Tables 1, 2, and 3, N.I. indicates that information was not included for these categories.

TABLE 1

BETTER EDUCATED BY AGE, SOCIOECONOMIC STATUS, DWELLING (N's)

Variable	Brazil	Cuba	Dominican Republic	India I	Israel	Nigeria	Panama	Philippines	United States	West Germany	Yugoslavia	Total N
Total sample	2739	1490	2442	5720	1170	2876	1351	1388	2696	480	1523	*23875*
Better educated	35	201	19	467	146	16	24	533	527	15	80	*2063*
AGE												
−29	15	92	7	235	36	4	6	283	142	2	26	*848*
30-49	13	90	11	184	62	9	16	193	245	7	40	*870*
50+	7	16	1	46	48	3	2	57	129	6	14	*329*
No answer	0	3	0	2	0	0	0	0	11	0	0	*16*
SOCIOECONOMIC												
High	31	94	13	158	52	10	24	224	246	4	25	*881*
Middle	4	68	N.I.	294	68	N.I.	N.I.	263	161	10	32	*900*
Low	0	38	3	15	17	6	0	46	83	0	23	*231*
No answer	0	1	3	0	9	0	0	0	37	1	0	*51*
DWELLING												
Rural	7	67	0	144	N.I.	5	2	364	152	3	6	*750*
Urban	28	134	19	323	146	11	22	169	375	12	74	*1313*
No answer	0	0	0	0	0	0	0	0	0	0	0	*0*

TABLE 2

Medium Educated by Age, Socioeconomic Status, Dwelling (*N's*)

Variable	Brazil	Cuba	Dominican Republic	India I	Israel	Nigeria	Panama	Philippines	United States	West Germany	Yugoslavia	Total N
Total sample	2739	1490	2442	5720	1170	2876	1351	1388	2696	480	1523	*23875*
Medium educated	223	358	150	277	482	391	317	306	1325	51	194	*4074*
AGE												
−29	115	203	40	163	126	217	135	126	276	11	63	*1475*
30-49	86	126	85	84	229	164	134	111	734	25	94	*1872*
50+	22	23	25	29	127	10	48	69	300	15	37	*705*
No answer	0	6	0	1	0	0	0	0	15	0	0	*22*
SOCIOECONOMIC												
High	106	100	68	55	78	71	189	54	437	15	18	*1191*
Middle	117	122	N.I.	186	296	N.I.	N.I.	150	507	29	73	*1480*
Low	0	135	82	36	69	318	119	102	329	7	100	*1297*
No answer	0	1	0	0	39	2	9	0	52	0	3	*106*
DWELLING												
Rural	38	206	57	160	N.I.	261	64	210	427	14	30	*1467*
Urban	185	150	93	117	482	130	253	96	898	37	164	*2605*
No answer	0	2	0	0	0	0	0	0	0	0	0	*2*

TABLE 3

LOW EDUCATED BY AGE, SOCIOECONOMIC STATUS, DWELLING (N's)

Variable	Brazil	Cuba	Dominican Republic	India I	Israel	Nigeria	Panama	Philippines	United States	West Germany	Yugoslavia	Total N
Total sample	2739	1490	2442	5720	1170	2876	1351	1388	2696	480	1523	*23875*
Low educated	2481	875	2093	4937	542	2463	997	549	837	395	1237	*17406*
AGE												
−29	769	297	611	1665	121	742	187	108	41	67	269	*4877*
30-49	1151	433	966	2245	276	1287	470	236	298	150	578	*8090*
50+	561	132	516	1011	145	428	340	205	497	178	388	*4401*
No answer	0	13	0	16	0	6	0	0	1	0	2	*38*
SOCIOECONOMIC												
High	68	73	108	270	26	21	157	23	142	20	150	*1058*
Middle	1322	232	N.I.	1817	308	N.I.	N.I.	147	245	232	206	*4599*
Low	1091	564	1965	2849	171	2420	832	379	414	142	771	*11598*
No answer	0	6	20	1	37	22	8	0	36	1	110	*241*
DWELLING												
Rural	1668	679	1663	4140	N.I.	1786	718	462	328	187	684	*12315*
Urban	813	195	430	797	542	677	279	87	509	208	547	*5084*
No answer	0	1	0	0	0	0	0	0	0	0	6	*7*

Appendix C:
Significance of Differences

1. SIGNIFICANCE OF DIFFERENCES WITHIN SAME SAMPLE

Chart 1 shows the significance of differences within the same sample at the .10, .05, and .01 levels.

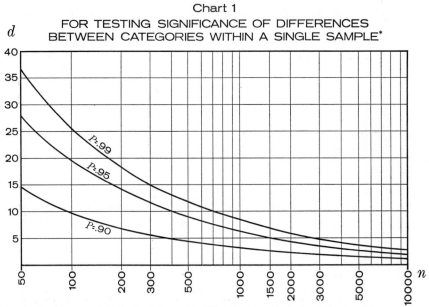

Chart 1

FOR TESTING SIGNIFICANCE OF DIFFERENCES
BETWEEN CATEGORIES WITHIN A SINGLE SAMPLE*

*Charts 1 and 2 prepared by Professor Samuel S. Wilks, Dept. of Mathematics, Princeton University.

Charts to facilitate the testing of the significance of differences between percentages are often useful to the research worker in public opinion polls, both in the design of his experiment and in the analysis of his results.

In the construction of Charts 1 and 2 the confidence limit approach has been employed to ascertain whether or not statistically significant differences occur *within* a sample (Chart 1) or *between* samples (Chart 2). Use of the confidence limit approach avoids the fallacious assumption in the computation of standard errors that an observed sample percentage is equal to the true population percentage.

It should be understood that the tests supplied by these charts are conservative, and that the charts are applicable only when the sampling has been done correctly.

As an example of the use of Chart 1, suppose the "yes" and "no" percentages to a given question in a sample of 3,000 cases are 38 per cent and 32 per cent, respectively. Locating n = 3,000 on the horizontal axis, it is seen that the vertical line representing n = 3,000 intersects the curve marked p = .99 at about 4½, this last figure being read from the vertical scale at the left of the chart. Thus, the 0.99 probability level critical difference is about 4½ per cent. Hence, the observed 6 per cent difference in the sample can be regarded as significant at the 0.99 probability level.

2. SIGNIFICANCE OF DIFFERENCES BETWEEN DIFFERENT SAMPLES

Chart 2 shows the significance of differences between two different samples at the 95 per cent level of confidence. Other charts for determining the confidence limits of survey samples will be found in Hadley

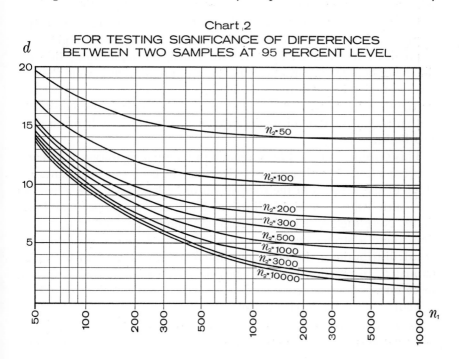

Chart 2

FOR TESTING SIGNIFICANCE OF DIFFERENCES
BETWEEN TWO SAMPLES AT 95 PERCENT LEVEL

Cantril, ed., *Gauging Public Opinion* (Princeton, N. J.: Princeton University Press, 1944), Appendix IV.

To illustrate the use of Chart 2, suppose the "yes" percentage to a certain question in a poll of 3,000 cases is 51 per cent, while the "yes" percentage to the same question in a second poll of 700 cases is 48 per cent. Taking $n_2 = 3,000$ and $n_1 = 700$ and locating the intersection of the respective curve and vertical line, it is seen that the critical difference is 4 per cent at the 0.95 probability level. The sample difference of 3 per cent is, therefore, of doubtful significance at the 0.95 probability level.

A more complete explanation of the meaning, use, and construction of these charts appears in an article by S. S. Wilks.[*]

3. SIGNIFICANCE OF DIFFERENCES BETWEEN LADDER RATINGS

Standard deviations (SD) were calculated for a sample of 444 separate ladder ratings in the American study. On the basis of this information, a plot of N (number of respondents per rating) against $(SD)^2/N$ indicated the limits within which 95 per cent of all such values lay for a selected range of N's. Using these lower and upper values of $(SD)^2/N$, differences between means required at three levels of significance ($p < 0.1$, $p < 0.05$, $p < 0.01$) were calculated. These are given in Table 4. Numbers in the table refer to "card units" since card units are indicated in the text.

Table 4 is used in the following way. If a group of respondents (represented by 1500 card units) is compared with another group of respondents (represented by 1500 card units), the table shows that the difference between means of 0.17 or less is not significant beyond the 0.05 level of probability. On the other hand, a difference of 0.27 or more will be significant beyond the 0.05 level of probability. It is not possible to state precisely the level of significance for values which lie between these two limits.

This empirical method for estimating minimum significant differences between means is rather conservative since in each case it assumes the value of the variants in the comparison to be least favorable, where, in fact, such values would be distributed between the upper and lower limits. Nevertheless, a possible exception should be pointed out. In a case where a strong negative correlation exists between any two compared distributions, the minimum difference would tend to be underestimated. In practice, however, such negative correlations are expected to be rare.

Table 5 gives the levels of significance from a comparable calculation

[*] S. S. Wilks, "Confidence Limits and Critical Differences Between Percentages," *Public Opinion Quarterly*, 1940, 4, 332-38.

based on the Israel sample, where the number of card units is the same as the number of respondents since no weighting of any kind was used.

Tables 4 and 5, together with the account of how they were calculated, were prepared by Dr. Peter Janicki in consultation with the late Professor Samuel S. Wilks.

TABLE 4

UNITED STATES SAMPLE:
MINIMUM SIGNIFICANT DIFFERENCES BETWEEN MEANS ON THE LADDER

Card units		Levels of significance*		
Group I	Group II	0.1	0.05	0.01
2000	400	0.21—0.35	0.26—0.41	0.34—0.55
	200	0.30—0.43	0.35—0.51	0.47—0.67
	150	0.33—0.46	0.39—0.54	0.52—0.71
1500	1500	0.14—0.22	0.17—0.27	0.23—0.35
	1000	0.16—0.25	0.19—0.30	0.25—0.39
	600	0.19—0.29	0.22—0.35	0.29—0.45
	400	0.22—0.36	0.26—0.43	0.34—0.56
	200	0.29—0.43	0.34—0.51	0.45—0.68
	150	0.33—0.48	0.39—0.57	0.52—0.75
1000	1000	0.16—0.25	0.21—0.30	0.27—0.39
	600	0.20—0.30	0.24—0.36	0.31—0.47
	400	0.23—0.37	0.27—0.44	0.36—0.57
	200	0.29—0.44	0.35—0.52	0.46—0.69
	150	0.34—0.49	0.40—0.58	0.53—0.76
600	600	0.22—0.34	0.26—0.41	0.35—0.54
	400	0.25—0.40	0.30—0.48	0.39—0.63
	200	0.31—0.47	0.37—0.56	0.48—0.73
	150	0.35—0.51	0.42—0.61	0.55—0.80
400	400	0.27—0.45	0.33—0.54	0.43—0.71
	200	0.32—0.52	0.39—0.61	0.51—0.81
	150	0.37—0.55	0.43—0.66	0.58—0.87
200	200	0.38—0.57	0.45—0.63	0.59—0.89
	150	0.41—0.61	0.49—0.72	0.65—0.95
150	150	0.45—0.64	0.53—0.76	0.70—1.00

* Below the first figure 95 percent of differences between means are not significant; above the second figure 95 percent of differences are significant.

TABLE 5

Israel Sample:

Minimum Significant Differences Between Means on the Ladder

Card units		Levels of significance*		
Group I	Group II	0.1	0.05	0.01
1000	1000	0.12—0.19	0.14—0.21	0.19—0.27
	600	0.15—0.21	0.18—0.24	0.23—0.32
	400	0.16—0.24	0.19—0.28	0.25—0.37
	200	0.20—0.33	0.24—0.39	0.31—0.51
	100	0.26—0.46	0.31—0.54	0.41—0.72
	50	0.35—0.65	0.42—0.77	0.56—1.01
600	600	0.15—0.23	0.18—0.28	0.24—0.37
	400	0.17—0.26	0.20—0.31	0.27—0.41
	200	0.21—0.34	0.25—0.41	0.33—0.54
	100	0.27—0.47	0.32—0.56	0.42—0.74
	50	0.37—0.66	0.43—0.79	0.56—1.02
400	400	0.19—0.29	0.22—0.35	0.29—0.46
	200	0.22—0.36	0.27—0.43	0.35—0.57
	100	0.28—0.49	0.33—0.58	0.44—0.76
	50	0.37—0.67	0.43—0.80	0.58—1.03
200	200	0.26—0.43	0.31—0.51	0.40—0.67
	100	0.31—0.53	0.37—0.64	0.48—0.84
	50	0.39—0.71	0.46—0.84	0.61—1.11
100	100	0.35—0.62	0.42—0.74	0.54—0.98
	50	0.42—0.77	0.50—0.93	0.66—1.22
50	50	0.48—0.90	0.57—1.04	0.76—1.41

* Below the first figure 95 percent of differences between means are not significant; above the second figure 95 percent of differences are significant.

Appendix D: Ladder Ratings

1. LADDER RATINGS BY DEMOGRAPHIC GROUPS BY COUNTRIES

TABLE 6

BRAZIL

Variable	Personal ladder ratings			National ladder ratings		
	Past	Present	Future	Past	Present	Future
SEX						
Male	3.6	4.2	6.8	4.8	5.2	7.6
Female	4.4	5.0	7.6	5.1	5.0	7.4
AGE						
18-29	3.9	4.8	7.5	5.1	5.2	7.4
30-39	3.6	4.3	7.2	4.9	5.3	7.6
40-49	3.8	4.2	7.0	4.9	4.9	7.6
50+	5.0	5.0	6.7	5.0	4.8	7.6
EDUCATION						
High	4.4	6.4	8.6	3.9	4.9	7.7
Secondary	4.8	6.0	8.3	4.2	5.2	8.1
Primary	3.9	4.7	7.3	5.1	5.2	7.4
No schooling	4.0	4.3	7.3	5.2	5.0	7.3
Illiterate	3.9	4.1	6.5	5.0	5.0	7.4
SOCIOECONOMIC						
1 (upper)	5.8	7.3	9.0	4.2	5.1	8.1
2	4.6	6.4	8.4	4.3	5.8	7.9
3	4.1	5.3	7.8	4.8	5.2	7.7
4	3.8	4.4	7.0	5.1	5.3	7.4
5 (lower)	4.0	3.9	6.6	5.0	4.8	7.4
CITY						
Rural	3.9	4.3	6.8	5.0	5.1	7.4
2000-50,000	4.1	4.9	7.6	4.8	5.0	7.3
50,000-500,000	4.5	5.6	8.1	4.9	5.0	8.0
500,000+	4.2	5.2	8.0	4.6	5.2	8.0

TABLE 7

CUBA

Variable	Personal ladder ratings			National ladder ratings		
	Past	Present	Future	Past	Present	Future
SEX						
Male	3.8	6.2	8.3	2.2	6.8	8.7
Female	4.4	6.5	8.4	2.1	7.0	8.9
AGE						
20-29	4.1	6.5	8.8	2.1	7.2	9.0
30-39	3.9	6.1	8.1	2.2	6.6	8.6
40-49	4.1	6.4	8.2	2.2	6.8	8.5
50+	4.3	6.4	7.7	2.2	6.8	8.6
EDUCATION						
High	5.0	6.5	8.4	2.6	6.2	8.1
Secondary	4.5	6.4	8.4	2.4	6.3	8.3
Elementary/none	3.7	6.3	8.4	2.0	7.2	9.1
SOCIOECONOMIC						
High; upper middle	5.5	6.7	8.2	2.8	6.1	7.5
Lower middle	4.1	6.4	8.3	2.2	6.7	8.6
Low	3.5	6.2	8.5	1.9	7.3	9.2
CITY						
−5000	3.8	5.3	7.7	2.5	6.3	8.7
5000-10,000	4.8	6.3	8.4	2.2	6.8	9.0
10,000-20,000	3.7	6.0	7.9	2.2	7.5	9.1
20,000-50,000	3.1	7.6	9.0	1.1	8.8	9.7
50,000+	4.0	6.3	8.7	2.4	7.0	9.0
Havana	4.9	6.0	8.0	2.6	5.6	7.8
RACE						
White	4.2	6.5	8.4	2.2	6.9	8.8
Negro	4.0	6.0	8.1	2.1	7.3	9.3
Mixed	3.5	5.9	8.2	1.9	6.7	8.8

TABLE 8

DOMINICAN REPUBLIC

Variable	Personal ladder ratings			National ladder ratings		
	Past	Present	Future	Past	Present	Future
SEX						
Male	1.4	1.5	6.0	1.6	2.6	6.9
Female	1.9	1.8	5.6	2.0	2.8	7.0
AGE						
21-29	1.5	1.6	5.6	1.6	2.8	7.1
30-39	1.6	1.6	5.9	1.7	2.6	6.9
40-49	1.4	1.6	6.4	1.4	2.6	6.7
50+	1.7	1.5	5.4	2.1	2.7	7.0
EDUCATION						
Some secondary	3.1	3.7	7.1	2.2	3.2	6.9
Some primary	1.6	1.6	6.3	1.6	2.6	7.4
No schooling	1.3	1.3	5.1	1.9	2.6	6.5
SOCIOECONOMIC						
Upper	3.5	4.3	7.5	2.2	3.9	7.5
Lower	1.4	1.4	5.7	1.7	2.6	6.9
DWELLING						
Rural	1.4	1.3	5.7	1.7	2.6	7.0
Urban	2.3	2.5	6.2	1.8	3.1	7.0

TABLE 9

EGYPT

Variable	Personal ladder ratings			National ladder ratings		
	Past	Present	Future	Past	Present	Future
SEX						
Male	4.4	5.4	7.9	3.5	6.0	7.7
Female	5.0	5.7	8.1	3.3	5.5	6.9
AGE						
15-19	4.2	5.9	8.3	3.6	5.9	6.9
20-39	4.4	5.0	7.6	3.0	5.5	7.1
40+	5.4	6.3	7.8	4.9	6.6	8.6
DWELLING						
Rural	4.7	5.4	8.0	3.5	6.1	7.7
Urban	4.5	5.8	7.9	3.5	5.5	7.2

TABLE 10

INDIA I

Variable	Personal ladder ratings			National ladder ratings		
	Past	Present	Future	Past	Present	Future
SEX						
Male	3.5	3.9	5.4	3.4	4.8	6.6
Female	3.5	4.0	5.5	3.7	5.0	6.7
AGE						
−30	3.2	3.8	5.5	3.3	4.7	6.6
31-40	3.3	3.8	5.2	3.4	4.8	6.5
41+	3.8	4.1	5.4	3.8	5.0	6.7
EDUCATION						
High	3.7	4.5	6.2	3.2	4.5	6.3
Matriculate	3.6	4.3	6.0	3.3	4.9	6.8
Under matriculate	3.5	3.8	5.2	3.8	5.0	6.8
Illiterate	3.0	3.2	4.1	3.5	4.9	6.4
INCOME						
301+ rupees	4.2	4.9	6.6	3.4	4.6	6.3
151-300 rupees	3.6	4.3	6.1	3.2	4.7	6.6
75-150 rupees	3.5	3.8	5.1	3.6	5.0	6.7
Under 75 rupees	3.0	3.0	4.3	3.4	4.9	6.6
CITY						
Rural	3.3	3.6	4.9	3.6	5.0	6.7
5000-99,999	3.5	4.1	5.8	3.3	4.8	6.6
100,000+	3.7	4.2	5.8	3.4	4.7	6.4
OCCUPATION						
Professional; student	3.6	4.5	6.4	3.2	4.6	6.6
Clerk; teacher	3.5	4.2	5.8	3.3	4.8	6.5
Skilled	3.2	3.7	5.3	3.7	5.1	6.8
Unskilled	2.9	3.2	4.2	3.5	4.8	6.7
Farm owner	3.4	3.7	4.8	3.4	4.8	6.5
Farm worker	2.9	3.1	4.3	3.6	4.9	6.9
Other	3.8	4.1	5.7	3.6	4.9	6.6

TABLE 11

ISRAEL

Variable	Personal ladder ratings			National ladder ratings		
	Past	Present	Future	Past	Present	Future
SEX						
Male	4.7	5.1	6.6	3.9	5.2	7.1
Female	4.8	5.5	7.2	4.1	5.8	8.0
AGE						
−29	4.9	5.4	7.7	3.8	5.3	7.3
30-49	4.5	5.3	7.0	4.0	5.7	7.7
50-64	5.1	5.4	6.2	4.0	5.5	7.5
65+	5.3	5.1	5.8	3.9	5.3	7.4
EDUCATION						
University	5.5	6.5	7.6	4.1	5.1	6.6
Elementary or secondary complete	4.9	5.5	7.1	3.9	5.5	7.5
Elementary incomplete	4.1	4.4	6.3	3.9	5.8	8.1
INCOME						
Upper	5.2	6.5	7.7	3.9	5.3	7.0
Middle	4.7	5.5	7.0	4.0	5.5	7.5
Lower	4.3	4.0	6.1	3.9	5.7	7.8
CLASS						
Upper; upper middle	5.7	6.8	8.1	4.3	5.6	7.3
Middle	4.9	5.7	7.2	3.9	5.5	7.4
Lower	4.4	3.2	4.9	4.3	5.6	7.4
Working	4.2	4.7	6.4	3.9	5.6	7.8
REGION						
Coop. settlement	4.8	5.3	7.4	4.1	5.7	7.8
New urban	4.4	4.5	6.4	3.6	5.3	7.7
Long settled urban	4.6	5.5	7.2	4.2	5.6	7.4
Tel Aviv; Haifa	4.9	5.5	7.0	4.1	5.6	7.5
Jerusalem	4.5	5.5	7.0	3.5	5.5	7.6

TABLE 12
KIBBUTZIM

Variable	Personal ladder ratings			National ladder ratings		
	Past	Present	Future	Past	Present	Future
AGE						
−30	6.0	6.8	8.2	4.7	5.5	6.9
30+	6.5	7.1	7.7	4.5	5.1	6.4

TABLE 13
JAPAN

Variable	Personal ladder ratings			National ladder ratings		
	Past	Present	Future	Past	Present	Future
SEX						
Male	4.5	5.1	6.1	4.2	5.3	6.4
Female	4.7	5.3	6.3	4.2	5.3	6.4
AGE						
21-29	4.8	5.4	6.6	4.1	5.2	6.4
30-44	4.4	5.1	6.3	4.3	5.3	6.4
45-64	4.6	5.2	6.0	4.1	5.3	6.4
65+	4.9	5.2	5.9	4.5	5.5	6.4
EDUCATION						
High	5.2	5.7	6.8	4.2	5.2	6.3
High school incomplete	4.7	5.4	6.5	4.3	5.4	6.6
−9 years' school	4.4	5.0	5.9	4.6	5.3	6.4
SOCIOECONOMIC						
Upper; upper middle	4.9	5.8	6.8	4.4	5.5	6.7
Middle	4.7	5.3	6.3	4.3	5.3	6.3
Lower middle; lower	4.1	4.3	5.4	3.9	5.0	6.2

TABLE 14

NIGERIA

Variable	Personal ladder ratings			National ladder ratings		
	Past	Present	Future	Past	Present	Future
SEX						
Male	3.0	4.8	7.4	4.0	6.1	8.2
Female	1.9	4.3	7.5	3.7	6.2	8.7
AGE						
21-29	2.5	4.5	7.3	3.7	6.1	8.1
30-39	2.7	4.7	7.4	4.1	6.3	8.4
40-49	3.1	5.0	7.8	4.3	6.3	8.3
50+	3.2	5.2	7.3	3.9	5.9	8.1
EDUCATION						
Some secondary	3.3	5.1	7.5	3.8	5.7	7.9
Some primary	2.9	4.5	7.4	3.7	5.9	8.2
No school/literate	3.4	5.4	7.7	3.3	5.2	8.7
Illiterate	2.5	4.6	7.2	4.3	6.4	8.3
SOCIOECONOMIC						
Upper	4.4	5.8	8.0	4.3	5.9	7.8
Lower	2.8	4.7	7.4	3.9	6.2	8.3
CITY						
Rural	2.8	4.7	7.4	4.0	6.3	8.4
5000-20,000	2.8	4.7	7.2	4.0	6.2	8.0
20,000-100,000	2.6	4.6	7.8	3.6	5.7	8.1
100,000+	3.1	4.7	7.4	3.5	5.1	7.8
REGION						
West	2.5	4.1	7.1	3.5	5.3	7.8
East	1.7	3.6	6.6	2.6	5.0	7.7
North	3.4	5.5	8.0	4.7	7.0	8.8
RELIGION						
Muslem	3.2	5.3	7.9	4.6	6.7	8.6
Christian	2.5	4.3	7.1	3.4	5.6	8.0
Pagan	2.0	3.8	7.5	3.9	6.2	7.5

TABLE 15

Panama

Variable	Personal ladder ratings			National ladder ratings		
	Past	Present	Future	Past	Present	Future
SEX						
Male	4.4	4.7	7.1	4.8	5.9	7.7
Female	4.6	4.9	6.9	5.1	6.1	7.7
AGE						
21-29	4.3	4.7	7.3	4.8	6.2	7.7
30-39	4.0	4.8	7.2	4.7	5.9	7.6
40-49	4.4	4.7	6.9	5.2	5.9	8.0
50+	5.3	4.9	6.5	5.1	6.1	7.5
EDUCATION						
Some secondary	5.1	5.5	7.7	4.5	5.5	7.4
Some primary	4.3	4.6	6.9	5.0	6.1	7.9
No schooling	4.5	4.4	6.2	5.3	6.4	7.8
SOCIOECONOMIC						
Upper	5.0	6.0	7.9	4.5	5.6	7.6
Lower	4.3	4.3	6.7	5.2	6.2	7.8
DWELLING						
Rural	4.5	4.4	6.7	5.2	6.3	7.8
Urban	4.6	5.3	7.4	4.6	5.6	7.6

TABLE 16

PHILIPPINES

Variable	Personal ladder ratings			National ladder ratings		
	Past	Present	Future	Past	Present	Future
SEX						
Male	4.8	4.8	6.5	6.0	4.9	6.1
Female	4.9	5.1	7.0	6.4	5.2	6.2
AGE						
21-30	5.0	5.0	7.3	5.9	5.1	6.3
31-40	4.2	4.2	6.5	5.9	4.5	5.9
41-50	4.8	5.0	5.9	6.7	5.1	5.9
51+	4.9	5.4	6.7	6.3	5.4	6.2
EDUCATION						
College complete	5.2	5.9	7.6	5.9	4.5	5.9
College incomplete	5.0	5.5	7.5	5.9	4.8	6.1
High school complete	4.9	5.0	7.0	5.7	5.2	6.5
High school incomplete	5.2	5.0	7.0	6.1	5.0	6.2
Elementary complete	4.4	4.3	6.5	6.2	4.5	5.7
Elementary incomplete	4.7	4.3	6.2	7.2	6.2	6.7
No schooling	4.4	4.3	5.2	6.0	5.1	5.7
ECONOMIC						
Upper	5.1	6.2	8.5	5.6	4.9	5.4
Upper middle	5.3	6.2	8.0	5.7	4.5	5.9
Lower middle	4.9	5.0	6.9	6.2	5.2	6.3
Lower	4.5	4.1	5.8	6.3	5.2	6.1
DWELLING						
Rural	4.8	4.8	6.6	6.2	5.1	6.2
Semi-urban	5.0	5.3	7.0	5.7	5.1	6.1
Urban	5.0	5.2	7.2	6.0	4.6	5.8

TABLE 17

POLAND

Variable	Personal ladder ratings		
	Past	Present	Future
SEX			
Male	3.8	4.3	5.4
Female	4.1	4.4	5.5
AGE			
18-29	3.8	4.5	6.1
30-39	3.9	4.3	5.6
40-49	3.9	4.3	5.2
50+	4.3	4.6	4.5
EDUCATION			
Some higher	4.4	5.1	5.8
Some secondary	4.2	4.7	5.8
Some primary	3.7	4.1	5.1
CITY			
Village (rural)	3.7	4.3	5.3
Up to 10,000	4.1	4.3	5.5
10,000-20,000	4.0	4.5	5.4
20,000-100,000	4.1	4.7	5.9
100,000+	4.4	4.6	5.6
OCCUPATION			
Farmers	3.7	4.1	5.0
Unskilled	3.3	3.7	5.0
Skilled; craftsmen	4.1	4.5	5.5
White collar	4.2	4.9	5.8
Others; students	4.5	4.8	6.6

TABLE 18

UNITED STATES

Variable	Personal ladder ratings			National ladder ratings		
	Past	Present	Future	Past	Present	Future
SEX						
Male	5.8	6.5	7.6	6.5	6.7	7.4
Female	6.0	6.6	7.9	6.4	6.6	7.4
AGE						
21-29	5.2	6.3	7.9	6.1	6.4	7.2
30-49	5.7	6.5	7.9	6.3	6.5	7.4
50-64	6.3	6.8	7.5	6.8	6.9	7.6
65+	6.9	6.5	6.6	6.9	7.1	7.5
EDUCATION						
College	5.8	6.9	8.5	6.2	6.5	7.3
High school	5.8	6.7	8.0	6.4	6.6	7.5
Grammar school	6.1	6.2	7.0	6.7	6.9	7.4
ECONOMIC						
Upper	5.8	7.1	8.0	6.4	6.7	7.4
Middle	6.0	6.6	8.2	6.5	6.8	7.5
Lower	5.8	6.0	7.3	6.5	6.6	7.4
CLASS						
Upper	6.9	7.2	8.3	7.8	7.6	8.1
Upper middle	6.1	7.4	8.2	6.6	6.8	7.5
Middle	5.9	6.8	8.0	6.2	6.6	7.5
Lower middle	5.3	5.7	7.3	6.3	6.6	7.6
Lower	6.4	4.6	5.5	6.0	6.8	7.8
Working	5.8	6.3	7.5	6.5	6.7	7.4
RACE						
White	6.0	6.7	7.9	6.4	6.7	7.6
Non-white	5.9	5.3	7.3	6.6	6.3	7.2
RELIGION						
Protestant	6.0	6.5	7.7	6.4	6.6	7.3
Catholic	5.9	6.7	7.8	6.6	6.8	7.8
Jewish	5.7	7.1	8.6	6.2	6.6	7.7
OCCUPATION						
Professional; business	6.1	7.1	8.2	6.3	6.6	7.3
White collar	5.4	6.6	8.2	6.5	6.8	7.7
Skilled	5.5	6.6	7.8	6.6	7.0	7.4
Unskilled	5.7	6.3	7.7	6.3	6.7	7.4
Farmer	6.3	6.5	7.7	6.0	6.0	7.3
Non-labor	6.8	6.3	6.4	6.9	7.2	7.6

TABLE 19

WEST GERMANY

Variable	Personal ladder ratings			National ladder ratings	
	Past	Present	Future	Past	Present
SEX					
Male	4.1	5.5	6.2	4.0	6.2
Female	4.0	5.1	6.2	4.2	6.1
AGE					
−29	3.5	5.3	6.7	4.1	6.4
30-39	3.7	5.3	6.5	4.0	6.1
40-49	3.8	5.2	6.1	4.0	6.0
50-59	4.3	5.1	5.7	4.0	6.0
60+	5.1	5.8	6.1	4.3	6.4
EDUCATION					
Secondary/university	3.8	5.5	6.5	4.0	6.2
Grammar school	4.1	5.3	6.1	4.1	6.1
ECONOMIC					
Upper	4.5	6.2	6.9	3.9	6.5
Middle	3.9	5.4	6.4	4.0	6.2
Lower	4.3	4.9	5.6	4.3	6.0
CITY					
−2000	4.1	5.2	5.9	4.1	6.1
2000-10,000	3.9	5.3	6.3	4.2	6.3
10,000-100,000	3.7	5.4	6.5	3.9	6.1
100,000+	4.2	5.3	6.1	4.1	6.1
RELIGION					
Protestant	3.8	5.3	6.3	4.0	6.0
Catholic	4.3	5.4	6.2	4.1	6.3

TABLE 20

YUGOSLAVIA

Variable	Personal ladder ratings			National ladder ratings		
	Past	Present	Future	Past	Present	Future
SEX						
Male	4.3	5.1	6.8	5.0	6.9	8.6
Female	4.3	5.0	6.7	4.9	6.8	8.6
AGE						
21-29	4.2	5.2	7.4	4.9	7.0	8.7
30-49	4.3	5.0	6.8	4.9	6.9	8.6
50+	4.6	4.9	6.1	5.0	6.7	8.4
EDUCATION						
High	4.8	5.9	7.5	5.0	6.8	8.4
Some high school	4.3	5.2	6.9	5.0	6.9	8.7
Some primary	4.4	5.0	6.7	4.8	6.9	8.6
No schooling	3.8	4.2	5.9	5.0	6.7	8.5
ECONOMIC						
Upper—nonfarmer	4.7	6.0	7.5	4.9	6.7	8.5
Upper—farmer	4.6	5.0	6.6	5.0	6.9	8.6
Lower—nonfarmer	4.3	5.0	6.9	5.0	7.0	8.8
Lower—farmer	3.7	4.3	6.0	4.7	6.8	8.5
DWELLING						
Rural	4.1	4.7	6.5	4.8	6.8	8.5
Urban	4.5	5.3	7.0	5.0	6.9	8.6
OCCUPATION						
State employee	4.7	5.9	7.5	5.2	6.9	8.6
Worker	4.3	4.9	6.9	4.8	6.8	8.6
Farmer	4.2	4.6	6.3	4.8	6.8	8.4
Housewife	4.3	4.9	6.6	4.9	6.9	8.7
NATIONALITY						
Serbian	4.4	5.2	7.0	5.1	7.1	8.8
Croatian	4.4	4.8	6.3	4.7	6.3	8.2
Slovenian	4.5	5.3	6.4	4.9	6.7	8.3
Other	4.0	4.8	6.8	4.8	6.9	8.7

2. LADDER GROUPINGS BY DEMOGRAPHIC GROUPS BY COUNTRIES

In Tables 21–23, N.I. indicates that information was not included for these categories; —— indicates that less than 0.5 per cent fall into the classification.

TABLE 21

HIGH PERSONAL PRESENT RATINGS

(Steps 7, 8, 9, 10)

Variable	Brazil	Cuba	Dominican Republic	Egypt	India I	Israel	Nigeria	Panama	Philip-pines	United States	West Germany	Yugo-slavia
SEX												
Male	17%	45%	1%	31%	4%	26%	24%	15%	20%	52%	28%	22%
Female	27	49	2	31	8	33	12	21	23	51	21	21
AGE												
−29	26	51	1	32	4	34	18	16	17	48	20	23
30-49	17	44	1	24	4	28	20	17	18	52	21	22
50+	29	55	2	43	5	29	34	20	33	52	29	20
EDUCATION												
High	60	51	21	N.I.	11	55	43	83	31	63	33	56
Middle	38	46	11	N.I.	4	35	24	23	21	52	20	32
Low	20	46	1	N.I.	4	18	21	15	12	42	25	18
SOCIOECONOMIC												
High	51	56	13	N.I.	15	54	41	32	48	63	40	30
Middle	22	49	N.I.	N.I.	4	30	N.I.	N.I.	18	50	22	27
Low	15	43	1	N.I.	2	13	21	13	9	40	24	19
DWELLING												
Rural	18	51	——	28	3	N.I.	23	15	18	51	26	16
Urban	28	40	5	38	9	30	20	21	30	52	23	26
Total sample	*2739*	*1490*	*2442*	*1237*	*5720*	*1170*	*2876*	*1351*	*1388*	*2696*	*480*	*1523*

TABLE 22

MIDDLE PERSONAL PRESENT RATINGS
(Steps 4, 5, 6)

Variable	Brazil	Cuba	Dominican Republic	Egypt	India I	Israel	Nigeria	Panama	Philippines	United States	West Germany	Yugoslavia
SEX												
Male	42%	45%	12%	50%	49%	52%	48%	58%	55%	41%	60%	58%
Female	45	42	14	56	51	50	53	52	55	42	63	56
AGE												
−29	43	41	12	51	46	48	47	58	61	46	70	57
30-49	45	46	14	58	51	52	53	54	50	39	65	56
50+	42	44	12	51	54	51	41	56	52	42	55	57
EDUCATION												
High	37	44	58	N.I.	60	42	38	17	48	32	60	38
Middle	49	48	32	N.I.	68	55	54	60	57	41	72	59
Low	43	42	12	N.I.	47	50	48	54	60	49	60	58
SOCIOECONOMIC												
High	43	38	52	N.I.	66	43	53	57	45	32	55	54
Middle	48	42	N.I.	N.I.	56	55	N.I.	N.I.	62	43	68	59
Low	38	46	9	N.I.	40	44	49	54	53	50	52	57
DWELLING												
Rural	41	41	10	52	48	N.I.	47	51	57	44	59	58
Urban	48	49	23	50	55	51	52	61	49	40	63	57
Total sample	*2739*	*1490*	*2442*	*1237*	*5720*	*1170*	*2876*	*1351*	*1388*	*2696*	*480*	*1523*

TABLE 23

LOW PERSONAL PRESENT RATINGS

(Steps 0, 1, 2, 3)

Variable	Brazil	Cuba	Dominican Republic	Egypt	India I	Israel	Nigeria	Panama	Philip-pines	United States	West Germany	Yugo-slavia
SEX												
Male	41%	10%	87%	19%	47%	22%	28%	27%	25%	7%	12%	20%
Female	28	9	84	13	41	17	35	27	22	7	16	23
AGE												
−29	31	8	87	17	50	18	35	26	22	6	10	20
30-49	38	10	85	18	45	20	27	29	32	9	14	22
50+	29	11	86	6	41	20	25	24	15	6	16	23
EDUCATION												
High	3	5	21	N.I.	29	3	19	——	21	5	7	6
Middle	13	6	57	N.I.	28	10	22	17	22	7	8	9
Low	37	12	87	N.I.	49	32	31	31	28	9	15	24
SOCIOECONOMIC												
High	6	6	35	N.I.	19	3	6	11	7	5	5	16
Middle	30	9	N.I.	N.I.	40	15	N.I.	N.I.	20	7	10	14
Low	47	11	90	N.I.	58	43	30	33	38	10	24	24
DWELLING												
Rural	41	8	90	20	49	N.I.	30	34	25	5	15	26
Urban	24	11	72	12	36	19	28	18	21	8	14	17
Total sample	*2739*	*1490*	*2442*	*1237*	*5720*	*1170*	*2876*	*1351*	*1388*	*2696*	*480*	*1523*

3. LADDER RATINGS BY CONCERNS BY COUNTRIES

TABLE 24

BRAZIL

Concerns	Personal ladder ratings			National ladder ratings		
	Past	Present	Future	Past	Present	Future
PERSONAL HOPES						
Happy family	4.4	5.6	8.1	4.9	5.1	7.1
Children	3.9	4.9	7.7	4.7	5.2	7.7
Health-family	4.1	4.7	7.2	5.0	4.9	7.1
Modern conveniences	3.3	4.7	7.3	4.5	5.0	7.7
Own house	3.8	4.5	7.7	4.8	5.1	7.6
Health-self	4.1	4.5	7.0	4.8	5.1	7.5
Employment	3.7	4.5	7.2	4.9	4.9	8.0
Own business	3.1	4.3	7.2	4.8	5.4	8.1
Improved std. of living	3.8	4.2	7.3	4.8	4.6	7.8
Wealth	4.1	4.2	6.9	5.2	5.2	6.7
Decent std. of living	3.9	4.1	6.9	4.9	5.1	7.6
Own land	3.6	3.7	7.0	5.3	5.0	7.4
PERSONAL FEARS						
Ill health-family	4.2	4.9	7.5	5.0	5.0	7.4
Children	4.3	4.8	7.5	5.0	4.9	7.3
Ill health-self	4.1	4.6	7.2	5.0	5.1	7.6
Unable to work; sick, old age	4.0	4.4	7.6	5.1	4.3	7.5
Inadequate std. of living	3.7	4.0	6.9	5.3	5.1	7.6

Concerns	National ladder ratings			Personal ladder ratings		
	Past	Present	Future	Past	Present	Future
NATIONAL HOPES						
Education	4.5	5.2	8.0	3.5	4.6	7.1
Efficient government	4.8	5.2	7.9	4.3	4.9	7.7
Technological advances	4.4	5.2	7.0	3.7	4.6	7.3
Social justice	4.8	5.1	7.4	3.9	4.4	7.1
Public health	4.7	5.0	8.0	4.0	4.4	7.6
Decent std. of living	5.0	4.8	7.8	4.1	4.4	7.3
Economic stability	5.2	4.6	7.4	3.9	4.5	7.3
NATIONAL FEARS						
Deterioration present std. of living	5.1	5.1	7.4	3.9	3.9	7.0
Communism	4.4	5.0	7.8	4.7	5.5	8.1
Political instability	4.9	5.0	7.6	3.8	4.5	7.1
Inadequate std. of living	5.0	5.0	7.3	4.0	4.6	7.1
War	4.9	5.0	7.6	3.9	4.6	7.5
Economic instability	5.2	4.8	7.3	3.6	4.4	7.1

TABLE 25

CUBA

Concerns	Personal ladder ratings			National ladder ratings		
	Past	Present	Future	Past	Present	Future
PERSONAL HOPES						
Success of revolution	1.7	8.3	9.6	0.7	8.8	9.8
Domestic tranquillity	3.4	7.2	8.8	1.1	7.7	9.1
Self-improvement	4.3	7.0	9.0	1.9	6.9	8.9
Acceptance by others	5.3	6.7	8.9	2.0	6.5	8.5
Health-self	4.0	6.4	8.5	2.1	7.0	8.9
Emotional stability	4.3	6.4	8.4	2.1	6.5	8.3
Decent std. of living	4.4	6.3	8.4	2.2	6.5	8.5
Own house	3.7	6.3	8.5	2.1	6.9	8.9
Health-family	4.1	6.3	8.5	2.3	6.7	8.8
Relatives	4.3	6.3	8.6	2.3	6.5	8.8
Happy family	4.7	6.2	8.6	2.2	6.6	8.7
Children	4.4	6.2	8.3	2.4	6.6	8.5
Recreation, leisure	5.0	6.1	8.1	2.7	6.3	8.2
Improved std. of living	3.5	6.1	8.2	2.1	7.1	9.2
Modern conveniences	4.2	6.0	8.4	3.4	6.2	8.1
Congenial work	3.6	5.8	8.2	1.9	6.8	9.0
Employment	3.5	5.2	8.5	2.0	4.1	9.1
PERSONAL FEARS						
Failure of revolution	2.7	7.3	9.4	1.1	8.0	9.4
Emotional instability	5.0	6.8	8.6	1.8	7.2	9.2
Ill health-family	4.2	6.7	8.7	1.9	6.8	9.0
No fears or worries	8.3	6.7	8.5	1.4	8.3	9.6
No self-improvement	4.2	6.7	8.7	2.1	6.4	8.8
Not be accepted	4.8	6.6	9.2	2.4	6.9	9.2
Unhappy family	4.9	6.4	8.3	2.1	7.2	8.6
Inadequate std. of living	5.1	6.3	8.1	2.8	6.5	8.6
Be alone	4.9	6.2	8.5	2.7	6.4	8.1
Ill health-self	4.4	6.1	8.2	2.4	6.6	8.7
Unemployment	3.9	6.1	8.6	2.4	6.9	9.0
Children unsuccessful	4.4	6.1	8.4	2.6	6.2	8.2
Relatives	4.0	6.1	8.8	2.4	6.6	8.9

Concerns	National ladder ratings			Personal ladder ratings		
	Past	Present	Future	Past	Present	Future
NATIONAL HOPES						
Success of revolution	1.3	7.8	9.6	3.7	7.1	8.8
Agrarian reform	1.2	7.3	9.2	2.7	6.8	9.0
Improved std. of living	2.1	7.1	9.0	3.8	6.5	8.6
Decent std. of living	1.9	6.9	8.9	4.3	6.2	8.5
Education	1.9	6.9	8.8	4.5	6.6	8.8
Domestic tranquillity	2.2	6.7	8.8	4.3	6.4	8.3
Technological advances	2.0	6.7	8.8	4.0	6.0	8.5
National independence	1.6	6.7	8.8	3.8	6.6	9.0
Employment	2.3	6.6	8.8	4.2	6.0	8.3
Social justice	2.0	6.5	8.4	4.3	6.4	8.0
Individual freedom	2.6	5.5	7.4	4.6	5.9	7.5
NATIONAL FEARS						
No fears or worries	1.7	8.0	9.5	3.4	6.8	8.4
U.S. aggression	1.0	8.0	9.6	2.9	7.2	9.5
Failure of revolution	1.8	7.6	9.5	3.9	6.4	8.8
Return to past	1.7	7.0	9.2	3.9	6.3	8.6
Aggression by any power	1.5	6.8	8.9	4.3	6.1	8.4
National disunity	2.5	6.4	8.3	4.5	6.5	8.5
Unemployment	2.7	6.3	8.4	4.6	5.6	8.0
Inadequate std. of living	2.6	6.0	7.8	4.9	5.6	8.0
Communism	3.9	3.9	5.6	6.0	5.4	6.9

TABLE 26

DOMINICAN REPUBLIC

Concerns	Personal ladder ratings			National ladder ratings		
	Past	Present	Future	Past	Present	Future
PERSONAL HOPES						
Be normal, decent	2.1	2.3	6.3	2.1	3.4	7.2
Happy family	1.8	2.1	6.2	2.2	3.2	7.5
Improved std. of living	2.0	1.8	6.0	2.0	2.9	7.1
Health-self	1.8	1.8	5.8	1.4	3.0	7.1
Children	1.7	1.8	5.9	1.8	2.9	6.9
Congenial work	1.4	1.7	5.8	1.8	2.9	6.9
Decent std. of living	1.3	1.5	5.6	1.5	2.4	6.8
Employment	1.5	1.5	6.1	1.5	2.8	7.1
Own business	1.6	1.4	5.8	1.7	2.2	7.3
Modern conveniences	1.1	1.4	6.2	1.5	2.7	7.1
Own house	1.2	1.3	5.7	1.7	2.6	6.9
Relatives	1.3	1.3	5.8	1.2	2.4	6.6
Own land/farm	1.2	1.0	5.5	1.8	2.3	6.8
PERSONAL FEARS						
Political instability	2.3	2.2	5.7	2.0	2.2	7.1
Ill health-self	2.1	1.9	6.3	1.7	3.0	7.2
Children	1.6	1.9	6.4	2.1	3.1	7.4
Ill health-family	1.7	1.8	5.3	1.8	2.8	6.9
Relatives	1.5	1.7	5.8	1.6	3.0	7.1
Unemployment	1.5	1.6	5.9	1.9	3.0	7.0
Deterioration present std. of living	1.6	1.6	5.8	1.8	2.6	7.4
Inadequate std. of living	1.4	1.4	5.7	1.6	2.7	6.8
Uncongenial work	1.0	1.3	5.6	1.4	2.4	6.4

Concerns	National ladder ratings			Personal ladder ratings		
	Past	Present	Future	Past	Present	Future
NATIONAL HOPES						
Social/political responsibility	2.3	3.1	7.3	1.7	1.4	5.2
Democratic/representative government	2.1	2.9	7.3	2.1	2.5	6.3
National unity	1.7	2.9	7.2	1.7	1.9	5.5
Political stability	1.9	2.8	7.3	1.7	1.7	5.8
Technological advances	1.8	2.8	7.0	1.6	1.8	5.9
Employment	1.7	2.7	6.9	1.4	1.4	5.4
Freedom	1.1	2.6	7.6	1.4	1.7	5.9
Improved/decent std. of living	1.6	2.5	6.7	1.5	1.4	5.8
Economic stability	1.3	2.4	6.3	1.3	1.3	5.6
Efficient government	1.3	2.3	7.1	1.4	1.4	5.9
Agrarian reform	1.2	2.0	7.7	1.4	1.9	5.6
NATIONAL FEARS						
War	2.1	3.4	7.7	1.6	1.5	3.4
No democratic/representative government	1.4	2.8	7.3	1.8	2.1	6.3
Unemployment	1.4	2.8	7.0	1.4	1.4	5.8
Communism	1.4	2.7	7.3	2.0	2.3	6.2
Inefficient government	1.8	2.6	7.6	1.3	2.1	6.4
Political instability	1.8	2.6	7.2	1.4	1.5	5.8
No improvement or inadequate std. of living	1.6	2.5	7.0	1.3	1.3	6.0
Economic instability	1.0	1.6	7.0	1.2	1.4	5.5

TABLE 27

EGYPT

Concerns	Personal ladder ratings			National ladder ratings		
	Past	Present	Future	Past	Present	Future
PERSONAL HOPES						
Useful to others	4.6	6.3	8.4	3.0	6.1	7.3
Congenial work	4.4	5.9	8.2	3.0	5.6	7.3
Acceptance by others	4.9	5.9	8.3	3.5	6.0	7.1
Emotional stability	5.0	5.8	7.9	3.1	5.1	7.2
Success	4.1	5.6	7.9	3.0	5.6	6.9
Health-self	5.2	5.6	7.5	4.4	5.9	8.0
Happy family	4.2	5.6	7.9	3.4	5.5	7.2
Wealth	4.5	5.5	7.4	3.4	5.4	7.3
Recreation, leisure	4.3	5.5	7.8	3.7	5.5	6.6
Children	5.1	5.5	8.1	3.7	6.1	8.1
Decent std. of living	4.5	5.4	7.9	3.6	5.8	7.1
Relatives	5.7	5.2	8.5	3.1	5.4	6.6
Own house	4.0	5.1	7.5	3.2	6.7	8.7
Sense of personal worth	3.6	4.3	8.6	3.0	6.2	7.2
Own land	3.5	3.9	9.3	2.4	6.8	8.9
PERSONAL FEARS						
Ill health-self	4.7	5.9	7.8	3.8	6.0	7.5
Failure	3.9	5.8	8.2	3.2	5.7	7.9
Unhappy family	4.2	5.7	8.0	2.9	5.6	7.2
Be alone	4.7	5.7	7.9	4.1	6.1	7.7
Uncongenial work	4.5	5.6	8.4	2.6	5.3	5.0
Not be accepted	4.0	5.4	7.5	3.5	5.6	7.6
No sense of personal worth	4.6	5.4	7.3	3.0	5.4	5.9
Inadequate std. of living	4.6	5.3	7.7	3.7	5.9	7.7
Unemployment	4.1	5.3	7.7	3.2	5.8	7.5
Ill health-family	5.4	5.3	8.3	3.6	5.8	7.4
No fears or worries	5.2	5.2	8.9	3.6	6.5	8.0
Relatives	4.3	4.9	7.6	3.6	6.4	8.5

Concerns	National ladder ratings			Personal ladder ratings		
	Past	Present	Future	Past	Present	Future
NATIONAL HOPES						
World power	3.6	7.2	7.4	4.6	5.8	8.5
National independence	4.1	6.7	7.8	5.0	6.3	8.6
Militarily strong	2.7	6.7	8.3	5.0	4.6	8.1
Peace	4.2	6.3	8.0	5.6	6.4	8.5
National unity	3.6	6.0	7.8	5.7	5.0	8.1
Technological advances	3.3	5.8	7.7	4.0	5.6	8.0
Public health	3.1	5.7	7.0	5.3	4.7	8.0
Social justice	3.6	5.6	7.9	5.2	4.8	7.8
Education	3.8	5.6	6.6	3.9	5.4	8.0
Improved std. of living	3.2	5.4	7.0	4.4	5.4	8.5
Democratic government	4.1	5.2	5.9	5.5	6.2	7.4
Enhance status	2.6	4.6	6.4	4.4	6.4	8.1
Freedom	3.3	4.4	4.7	5.3	6.8	8.5
NATIONAL FEARS						
Foreign aggression	3.6	6.6	7.8	4.4	5.3	8.3
Political instability	4.0	6.5	8.5	3.9	5.7	8.1
Inadequate educational facilities	3.2	5.8	6.4	4.6	5.5	7.9
No improvement std. of living	3.9	5.6	7.0	4.6	5.2	7.0
War	3.3	5.6	7.5	4.2	5.6	8.0
No technological advances	3.1	5.4	7.7	3.9	5.8	7.7
Communism	3.6	4.3	5.0	4.6	6.2	8.2
Dishonest government	2.4	4.1	6.9	4.7	4.7	8.1

TABLE 28

India I

Concerns	Personal ladder ratings			National ladder ratings		
	Past	Present	Future	Past	Present	Future
PERSONAL HOPES						
Self-development/ improvement	3.4	4.1	6.1	3.1	4.6	6.4
Happy family	3.4	4.1	5.6	3.1	4.5	6.3
Useful to others	3.5	4.1	5.8	2.9	4.5	6.2
Own business	3.3	4.0	5.9	3.5	4.9	6.6
Congenial work	3.0	3.9	5.6	3.5	4.9	6.8
Children	2.9	3.8	5.2	3.4	4.9	6.7
Relatives	3.1	3.7	5.3	3.0	4.7	6.5
Improved/decent std. of living	3.2	3.6	5.0	3.3	4.8	6.5
Own house	3.0	3.5	4.9	3.1	4.6	6.5
Own land/farm	3.1	3.3	4.4	3.3	4.6	6.2
PERSONAL FEARS						
No fears or worries	3.9	4.7	6.1	3.9	5.2	7.0
Not own business	3.7	3.9	5.7	3.6	4.9	6.7
Uncongenial work	3.4	3.9	5.2	3.3	4.6	6.3
Ill health-self	3.6	3.9	5.5	3.6	5.1	7.0
Ill health-family	3.4	3.9	5.4	3.8	5.0	6.9
Children	3.3	3.5	5.0	3.0	4.5	6.3
Deterioration/inadequate std. of living	3.2	3.4	4.9	3.2	4.6	6.4
Not own land/farm	3.1	3.4	5.1	3.2	4.5	6.2

Concerns	National ladder ratings			Personal ladder ratings		
	Past	Present	Future	Past	Present	Future
NATIONAL HOPES						
Prosperity through planning	3.4	5.0	6.9	3.5	4.1	5.6
Decent std. of living	3.6	4.9	6.7	3.5	3.6	5.7
Agrarian reform	3.5	4.8	6.7	3.3	3.6	5.0
Employment	3.4	4.8	6.7	3.5	4.0	5.6
Technological advances	3.3	4.7	6.5	3.4	3.9	5.5
Education	3.2	4.6	6.5	3.4	4.0	5.4
Enhance status	3.2	4.6	6.6	3.7	4.3	6.0
NATIONAL FEARS						
No fears or worries	3.9	5.2	7.3	3.2	3.9	5.4
Chinese aggression	3.5	5.0	6.7	3.5	4.2	5.7
Pakistan/Kashmir	3.4	4.9	6.8	3.6	4.1	5.8
No improvement/inadequate std. of living	3.3	4.8	6.6	3.5	4.0	5.8
Economic instability	3.7	4.8	6.4	3.6	4.0	5.5
Unemployment	3.2	4.8	6.6	3.5	3.9	5.3
Population growth	3.2	4.8	6.4	3.4	4.0	5.5
Lack/loss of independence	3.3	4.7	6.5	3.1	4.2	6.0
Dishonest government	3.2	4.6	6.3	3.6	4.0	5.5
Lack moral, ethical, religious stds.	3.0	4.4	5.9	3.3	3.9	4.9
National disunity	2.9	4.4	6.1	3.5	4.2	5.9

TABLE 29

ISRAEL

Concerns	Personal ladder ratings			National ladder ratings		
	Past	Present	Future	Past	Present	Future
PERSONAL HOPES						
Peace	4.8	6.0	7.2	4.0	5.5	7.6
Recreation, leisure	5.0	5.8	7.3	4.1	5.5	7.3
Self-development/ improvement	4.7	5.8	7.6	3.9	5.4	7.4
Happy family	4.8	5.4	7.4	3.9	5.5	7.5
Health-family	4.6	5.3	7.0	4.0	5.7	7.9
Children	4.6	5.3	6.9	4.0	5.7	7.7
Health-self	4.8	5.2	6.6	4.0	5.8	7.8
Relatives	4.5	5.2	6.9	4.0	5.8	7.8
Decent std. of living	4.6	5.1	7.0	3.9	5.6	7.6
Congenial work	4.0	5.1	7.0	3.9	5.6	7.5
Modern conveniences	4.2	5.0	7.2	4.0	5.7	7.7
Improved present std. of living	4.3	4.8	6.1	4.0	5.5	7.3
Own house	4.4	4.7	6.9	3.9	5.6	7.7
Employment	4.5	4.7	6.5	4.1	5.7	7.7
Own business	4.1	4.5	6.3	3.9	5.5	7.8
PERSONAL FEARS						
Ill health-self	4.7	6.5	6.8	3.9	5.6	7.6
War	4.8	5.9	7.3	3.9	5.4	7.4
Deterioration present std. of living	4.9	5.6	6.7	3.9	5.6	7.2
Ill health-family	4.6	5.5	7.1	3.9	5.7	7.7
Unhappy family	4.8	5.3	7.5	4.0	5.6	7.7
Children	4.4	5.0	6.9	3.9	5.7	7.8
Inadequate std. of living	4.5	4.8	6.6	3.9	5.6	7.5
Relatives	4.3	4.5	6.8	3.8	5.6	7.8
Unemployment	4.2	4.5	6.4	3.9	5.7	7.6

Concerns	National ladder ratings			Personal ladder ratings		
	Past	Present	Future	Past	Present	Future
NATIONAL HOPES						
Housing	4.1	5.8	7.9	4.4	4.9	6.5
Militarily strong	3.9	5.8	8.0	4.5	5.1	6.9
Employment	3.8	5.7	7.8	4.9	5.3	7.0
Education	3.9	5.7	7.6	5.0	5.2	7.1
Population increase	3.9	5.6	7.7	4.9	5.5	6.8
Economic stability	4.1	5.6	7.6	4.6	5.3	7.0
Technological advances	3.8	5.6	7.6	4.7	5.5	7.1
Improved/decent std. of living	4.0	5.5	7.5	4.8	5.2	6.9
Peace with Arabs	3.9	5.5	7.4	4.8	5.5	7.0
Peace	3.9	5.5	7.7	4.8	5.2	6.9
Increased foreign trade	3.7	5.4	7.4	4.7	5.4	6.9
Eliminate discrimination	3.8	5.3	7.4	4.7	5.2	6.4
Free secondary education	4.0	5.3	7.3	4.7	5.3	7.2
National independence	3.8	5.3	7.2	4.8	5.6	7.2
Cultural standards	3.7	5.2	7.4	4.9	5.7	7.2
Change election system	3.6	5.2	7.2	4.9	5.6	7.1
NATIONAL FEARS						
War	4.0	5.7	7.7	4.8	5.5	7.2
War with Arabs	4.0	5.6	7.5	4.7	5.3	7.0
Population decrease	3.9	5.5	7.3	4.8	5.4	6.9
High/increased taxes	3.9	5.4	7.2	4.2	4.8	6.5
No improvement or inadequate std. of living	3.9	5.3	7.3	4.6	5.4	7.3
No technological advances	3.7	5.3	7.4	5.0	5.5	7.0
Economic instability	3.9	5.3	7.0	4.6	5.2	6.6

TABLE 30
NIGERIA

Concerns	Personal ladder ratings			National ladder ratings		
	Past	Present	Future	Past	Present	Future
PERSONAL HOPES						
Resolve religious problems	3.2	5.5	8.4	4.0	6.6	8.7
Success	3.9	5.3	8.0	4.2	6.1	7.8
Modern conveniences	3.1	5.2	8.2	4.3	6.5	8.7
Improved/decent std. of living	3.0	5.1	7.7	4.2	6.4	8.5
Health-self	3.0	5.1	5.7	4.3	6.6	8.6
Happy family	2.8	5.0	6.8	3.9	6.4	8.5
Self-development/ improvement	2.8	4.9	7.6	4.0	6.1	8.2
Own business	2.9	4.8	7.5	4.0	6.2	8.2
Own land/farm	3.4	4.8	6.9	4.3	6.2	8.0
Own house	2.8	4.8	7.8	3.8	6.1	8.4
Happy old age	2.6	4.8	7.3	3.7	6.1	8.4
Congenial work	2.9	4.7	7.5	3.8	5.4	8.4
Children	2.6	4.7	7.5	3.6	6.0	8.2
Relatives	2.3	4.6	7.6	3.8	6.0	8.6
Useful to others	2.8	4.5	7.3	3.4	5.4	7.8
Wealth	2.4	4.1	7.3	3.8	6.1	8.0
Agricultural bounty	2.0	4.0	6.3	4.0	5.9	7.5
PERSONAL FEARS						
Fear of litigation	4.5	6.3	8.2	4.8	7.7	9.0
Fail religious goals	3.5	6.0	8.2	3.8	7.0	8.2
Insecurity/threat to property	3.6	5.5	8.1	4.5	7.0	9.1
Ill health-family	3.0	5.3	8.6	4.2	6.6	9.0
Unhappy family	3.0	5.1	8.0	4.3	6.4	8.6
Ill health-self	2.9	5.0	7.7	3.6	5.6	8.5
Children	2.7	4.9	7.6	3.8	5.7	8.3
Unemployment	3.2	4.9	7.9	4.4	6.5	8.6
Inadequate std. of living	2.8	4.8	7.6	3.9	6.2	8.3
No fears or worries	2.7	4.8	7.4	3.8	6.0	8.5
No self-development/ improvement	2.8	4.6	7.3	3.7	5.7	7.9
Relatives	2.4	4.6	7.6	3.4	5.8	8.3
Agricultural dearth	2.3	4.3	7.5	3.9	6.3	8.2

Concerns	National ladder ratings			Personal ladder ratings		
	Past	Present	Future	Past	Present	Future
NATIONAL HOPES						
Increased foreign trade	4.5	6.9	8.5	3.7	5.7	7.8
Independence, status-misc.	4.2	6.6	9.2	2.0	4.7	7.8
Improved internal trade	3.9	6.5	8.7	3.1	5.2	7.8
Law and order	3.9	6.4	8.8	3.2	5.2	7.7
Improved/decent std. of living	3.9	6.3	8.6	3.0	5.1	8.2

TABLE 30 (*Con...*)

	Past	Present	Future	Personal ladder ratings		
				Past	Present	Future
Political stability	3.6	6.2	8.7	2.6	4.9	8.2
Agricultural reform	3.9	6.2	8.2	3.0	4.9	7.5
Public health	4.1	6.2	8.3	2.9	5.0	7.6
Education	4.2	6.2	8.4	3.1	5.1	7.7
Employment	3.8	6.1	8.6	2.8	4.9	7.7
Republic status	4.1	6.0	8.5	3.2	5.3	7.9
Agricultural bounty	4.1	6.0	7.5	2.7	4.5	7.0
Technological advances	4.0	6.0	8.2	3.1	4.9	7.3
Modern conveniences	3.6	5.8	8.1	2.5	4.6	7.4
Moral, ethical, religious stds.	3.7	5.8	8.3	2.7	4.9	7.7
Honest government/ leaders	4.1	5.6	8.2	2.9	5.1	8.0
National unity	3.6	5.6	8.2	2.6	4.6	7.7
National independence	3.4	5.6	7.9	3.4	4.9	7.8

NATIONAL FEARS

	Past	Present	Future	Past	Present	Future
War	5.0	7.3	8.7	3.6	5.6	7.4
Lack moral, ethical, religious standards	4.0	6.7	8.9	3.0	5.2	8.1
No agricultural reform	3.6	6.3	8.7	2.4	4.8	8.1
Public health	3.9	6.2	8.7	2.9	5.0	8.2
Lack law and order	3.7	6.1	8.5	2.7	5.1	8.0
Political instability	4.0	6.1	8.3	3.1	5.1	7.6
Failure to keep present std. of living	3.9	6.1	8.3	2.8	4.8	7.6
Inadequate educational facilities	3.9	6.0	8.3	3.0	5.2	8.1
National disunity	3.9	5.9	8.1	3.0	4.8	7.3
Crisis-Western region	4.0	5.8	8.1	3.2	5.2	7.7
Discrimination/class, economic	3.2	5.8	8.3	2.3	4.6	7.6
No improvement or inadequate std. of living	3.7	5.7	8.3	2.5	4.3	7.1
Unemployment	3.4	5.7	8.0	2.4	4.3	7.1
Dishonest government/ leaders	3.9	5.6	8.1	2.8	4.8	7.7
Disunity-government/ leaders	4.0	5.5	8.0	2.6	4.4	7.4
Social injustice	3.5	5.5	7.9	2.7	4.7	7.4
High/increased taxes	2.9	5.3	8.4	1.9	4.2	7.7

TABLE 31

PANAMA

Concerns	Personal ladder ratings			National ladder ratings		
	Past	Present	Future	Past	Present	Future
PERSONAL HOPES						
Self-development/ improvement	4.3	5.2	7.5	4.0	5.3	7.5
Be normal, decent	5.1	5.0	7.1	5.2	5.8	8.3
Own business	4.6	4.9	6.8	4.8	5.7	7.5
Congenial work	4.5	4.9	7.3	4.9	5.9	7.8
Health-self	4.5	4.9	7.5	5.2	6.6	7.9
Emotional stability	5.0	4.8	7.4	4.5	5.2	7.8
Decent std. of living	4.4	4.8	6.9	5.0	5.8	7.4
Own house	4.1	4.8	7.0	4.6	6.1	8.1
Happy family	4.7	4.8	7.4	4.5	6.2	7.8
Children	4.1	4.7	7.1	4.9	6.1	7.9
Health-family	4.2	4.6	7.0	4.7	5.3	7.6
Improved present std. of living	4.3	4.6	6.9	4.9	6.1	7.9
Modern conveniences	4.0	4.5	7.3	5.0	6.1	7.5
Relatives	4.5	4.5	6.5	3.8	5.6	7.5
Employment	4.2	4.4	6.7	6.4	6.2	7.6
Own land	4.1	4.0	6.5	5.1	5.9	7.8
PERSONAL FEARS						
Children	4.6	5.0	7.1	4.6	5.6	7.4
Be alone	4.7	5.0	7.7	5.0	5.6	6.8
Ill health-self	4.5	4.9	7.1	4.8	6.1	7.6
Deterioration present std. of living	4.7	4.8	7.0	4.9	6.0	7.5
Unhappy family	4.9	4.7	7.6	4.4	5.6	7.8
Ill health-family	4.2	4.7	7.2	4.8	5.8	7.7
Relatives	4.3	4.5	6.6	4.4	5.7	7.5
Inadequate std. of living	4.2	4.4	5.9	5.0	5.8	8.0
Unemployment	4.4	4.3	6.6	4.8	5.8	7.6

Concerns	National ladder ratings			Personal ladder ratings		
	Past	Present	Future	Past	Present	Future
NATIONAL HOPES						
Economic stability	5.3	6.3	7.7	4.2	5.0	7.6
Education	4.9	6.3	7.8	4.1	4.7	7.2
Housing	4.7	6.1	8.0	4.4	4.7	7.1
Improved/decent std. of living	5.3	6.1	7.6	4.4	5.2	6.9
Employment	4.9	6.1	7.6	4.3	4.6	6.6
Agrarian reform	4.8	5.8	7.6	4.5	4.6	6.5
Improved system of roads	5.3	5.6	7.7	4.1	4.2	6.8
Technological advances	4.4	5.6	7.7	4.4	4.8	7.3
Public health	5.1	5.3	8.2	3.6	4.2	7.0
Efficient government	4.1	5.3	7.3	4.5	4.8	6.8
NATIONAL FEARS						
War	4.8	6.4	7.9	4.5	5.1	7.1
No improvement/ inadequate std. of living	4.5	5.9	7.7	4.0	5.3	7.3
Unemployment	4.9	5.8	7.6	4.5	4.7	6.9
Economic instability	4.9	5.7	8.0	4.2	4.4	6.8
Inefficient government	4.4	5.5	7.1	4.0	4.7	6.3
Communism	4.7	5.4	7.4	5.2	5.5	7.5
Political instability	5.6	5.4	7.5	4.5	4.3	7.6
Lack law and order	4.6	5.1	7.7	4.1	4.4	7.3

TABLE 32
PHILIPPINES

Concerns	Personal ladder ratings			National ladder ratings		
	Past	Present	Future	Past	Present	Future
PERSONAL HOPES						
Happy family	5.2	5.3	7.4	6.1	5.0	6.2
Success	5.1	5.3	7.0	5.4	5.0	6.2
Children	4.8	5.2	6.8	6.2	4.9	5.8
Wealth	4.6	4.8	6.4	6.4	5.7	7.0
Improved std. of living	4.7	4.7	5.7	5.6	4.4	4.8
Modern conveniences	5.5	4.7	6.6	6.8	5.4	6.3
Own house	4.7	4.5	6.5	6.0	4.8	5.6
Recreation, leisure	4.7	4.5	5.6	6.4	6.2	6.6
Own business	4.5	4.2	6.0	5.3	4.5	6.0
Decent std. of living	4.6	4.2	6.5	6.2	5.1	6.0
PERSONAL FEARS						
Ill health-family	6.1	5.8	7.1	7.0	5.2	5.7
Unhappy family	5.9	5.5	7.9	5.9	4.8	6.3
Children	4.5	5.4	6.5	6.2	5.1	5.8
Failure	3.9	5.1	7.2	5.3	4.9	5.9
War	5.4	5.0	6.7	6.7	5.3	6.3
Ill health-self	4.4	4.6	6.4	6.4	5.1	6.6
Inadequate std. of living	4.5	4.5	6.9	6.2	4.6	6.3
Deterioration present std. of living	4.6	3.9	5.8	5.6	4.2	5.0

Concerns	National ladder ratings			Personal ladder ratings		
	Past	Present	Future	Past	Present	Future
NATIONAL HOPES						
Peace	6.9	5.9	6.6	4.7	5.3	7.3
Improved present std. of living	6.2	5.3	6.6	4.9	4.9	6.5
Employment	6.7	5.3	6.3	5.3	4.8	6.9
Good government	6.5	5.3	6.1	5.1	5.1	6.9
Economic stability	6.1	4.8	6.3	4.8	5.4	7.6
National independence	5.5	4.6	5.2	4.3	5.5	7.5
Technological advances	5.6	4.5	5.7	4.9	5.1	7.4
NATIONAL FEARS						
War	6.6	5.4	6.7	5.0	4.6	6.3
Totalitarian aggression	6.4	5.3	6.8	4.4	5.1	7.1
Communism	5.8	4.7	6.0	4.6	4.8	7.1
No fears or worries	4.7	4.7	5.7	5.6	5.8	5.9
Bad government	5.7	4.6	5.6	4.7	5.2	6.5
National disunity	6.4	4.2	5.3	5.2	5.1	7.8
Economic instability	5.7	3.9	4.1	4.8	5.3	7.9

TABLE 33
UNITED STATES

Concerns	Personal ladder ratings			National ladder ratings		
	Past	Present	Future	Past	Present	Future
PERSONAL HOPES						
Maintain status quo	6.3	7.8	8.4	6.6	7.1	7.9
Emotional stability	5.7	7.1	8.2	6.1	6.4	7.4
Acceptance by others	6.0	6.9	8.1	6.4	6.3	7.5
Resolve religious problems	6.6	6.9	7.9	6.2	6.4	7.5
Health-family	5.7	6.9	7.9	6.3	6.5	7.4
Happy family	5.9	6.9	8.1	6.2	6.5	7.5
Children	5.7	6.7	8.2	6.3	6.5	7.4
Health-self	6.0	6.7	7.6	6.5	6.7	7.4
Happy old age	6.1	6.7	7.4	6.6	6.7	7.0
Relatives	5.8	6.6	7.8	6.3	6.7	7.8
Employment	5.4	6.5	8.0	6.6	6.7	7.7
Recreation, leisure	5.8	6.5	8.2	6.1	6.8	7.6
Congenial work	5.6	6.4	7.9	6.2	6.5	7.3
Peace	5.5	6.4	7.6	6.4	6.8	7.6
Decent std. of living	5.6	6.3	7.7	6.3	6.5	7.4
Improved present std. of living	5.5	6.0	7.2	6.2	6.5	7.2
Own house	5.4	6.0	7.9	6.3	6.7	7.6
Modern conveniences	5.1	5.7	7.5	6.5	7.0	7.8
PERSONAL FEARS						
Ill health-family	5.9	7.0	8.2	6.2	6.7	7.4
No fears or worries	6.3	6.9	8.1	6.8	7.0	7.8
Relatives	6.3	6.9	8.2	6.5	6.6	7.4
Dependency on others	6.2	6.8	7.4	6.5	6.6	7.3
Children	5.9	6.7	8.2	6.0	6.4	7.2
Ill health-self	5.8	6.7	7.7	6.4	6.7	7.5
War	5.9	6.6	7.9	6.4	6.8	7.7
Be alone	5.4	6.4	7.7	5.8	6.3	7.1
Unhappy family	5.6	6.3	8.0	5.7	6.1	6.7
Deterioration present std. of living	6.0	6.3	7.1	6.7	6.5	7.3
Inadequate std. of living	5.7	6.2	7.7	6.3	6.7	7.3
Unemployment	5.2	6.0	7.7	6.7	6.7	7.5

TABLE 33 (*Continued*)

Concerns	National ladder ratings			Personal ladder ratings		
	Past	Present	Future	Past	Present	Future
NATIONAL HOPES						
Maintain status quo	7.3	7.8	8.1	6.1	7.1	7.8
Technological advances	6.2	7.3	8.2	5.6	6.9	8.1
Improved std. of living	6.7	6.9	7.7	5.8	6.5	7.7
Employment	6.6	6.9	7.8	5.6	6.1	7.8
Peace	6.4	6.8	7.6	5.9	6.7	7.8
Better world	6.0	6.7	7.6	5.6	6.8	8.1
Public health	6.2	6.7	7.8	6.3	6.9	7.8
Improved labor conditions	6.2	6.5	7.6	5.7	6.5	7.5
Education	5.9	6.5	7.4	5.0	6.4	7.7
Reduction East-West tensions	6.3	6.5	7.3	5.8	7.3	8.2
Moral, ethical, religious stds.	6.4	6.4	7.7	6.0	7.2	8.1
Tax reduction	6.1	6.4	7.1	——*	——*	——*
Economic stability	6.1	6.3	7.1	5.7	6.9	8.0
Efficient government	6.4	6.3	7.2	6.1	6.8	8.2
Eliminate discrimination	6.0	6.2	7.0	5.8	6.5	7.8
NATIONAL FEARS						
Unemployment	6.6	7.3	7.7	5.5	6.0	7.4
Economic instability	6.4	7.1	7.3	5.8	6.6	7.6
Devastation/war	6.5	6.9	7.6	6.0	6.7	8.0
War	6.3	6.7	7.5	5.9	6.7	7.8
Communism	6.3	6.6	7.4	5.7	6.6	7.7
Threat of aggression	6.5	6.4	7.2	5.9	7.0	7.9

* Not cross-tabulated.

TABLE 34

West Germany

Concerns	Personal ladder ratings			National ladder ratings	
	Past	Present	Future	Past	Present
PERSONAL HOPES					
Happy family	4.2	6.0	7.0	4.3	6.8
Health-family	4.2	5.8	6.5	4.1	6.0
Keep present std. of living	4.3	5.8	7.0	3.8	6.3
Health-self	4.4	5.6	6.2	3.9	6.0
Improved std. of living	3.8	5.6	6.4	3.9	6.0
Children	3.8	5.6	6.0	4.3	6.0
Peace	4.0	5.5	6.6	4.1	6.2
Happy old age	4.3	5.4	5.8	4.1	6.3
Congenial work	3.8	5.4	6.6	4.0	6.3
Own business	3.8	5.3	6.3	4.2	6.5
Decent std. of living	3.9	5.2	6.2	4.3	6.1
Recreation, leisure	4.1	5.2	5.6	3.8	6.0
Employment	3.7	5.2	6.3	4.1	5.9
Modern conveniences	3.8	5.1	5.9	4.3	6.5
Social security	4.4	5.0	5.6	4.3	6.6
Own house	3.5	4.9	6.1	4.0	6.1
PERSONAL FEARS					
Deterioration present std. of living: nation	3.9	5.6	6.6	4.2	6.2
Deterioration present std. of living: person	4.0	5.6	6.6	3.8	6.2
War	4.1	5.5	6.5	4.1	6.2
Inadequate std. of living	3.8	5.4	6.3	4.0	6.2
Unemployment-nation	3.4	5.4	6.0	4.1	6.4
Ill health-self	4.0	5.3	6.3	4.0	6.1
Ill health-family	4.0	5.3	6.3	3.9	6.1
Unemployment-person	3.7	5.1	6.4	4.0	5.9
No social security	4.0	4.5	6.1	3.8	6.6

Concerns	National ladder ratings		Personal ladder ratings		
	Past	Present	Past	Present	Future
NATIONAL HOPES					
Improved present std. of living	3.8	6.4	3.9	5.4	6.6
Reunification	4.1	6.1	4.2	5.6	6.4
Peace	4.3	6.1	4.0	5.5	6.4
Employment	4.0	6.1	4.4	5.4	6.2
Housing	3.8	6.1	3.8	5.1	6.1
Technological advances	3.8	6.1	4.3	5.8	6.9
Social security	3.6	6.1	3.7	5.3	5.9
Economic stability	3.8	6.0	4.0	5.4	6.2
Decent std. of living	4.1	6.0	4.2	4.9	6.0
Better world	3.3	5.9	3.6	5.3	6.3
National independence	4.3	5.6	4.9	5.0	5.8
NATIONAL FEARS					
Unemployment	4.0	6.6	3.8	5.1	6.2
Lack personal freedom	4.1	6.5	4.2	6.1	6.7
Totalitarian aggression	3.7	6.4	3.6	5.6	6.6
Communism	3.9	6.4	4.2	5.7	6.5
Inadequate std. of living	4.0	6.2	3.7	5.5	6.4
National disunity	4.2	6.2	5.1	5.8	6.9
War	4.1	6.1	4.1	5.4	6.2
Devastation/war	4.2	6.1	3.8	5.2	6.2
Economic instability	4.1	6.1	4.0	5.2	6.3

TABLE 35
Yugoslavia

Concerns	Personal ladder ratings			National ladder ratings		
	Past	Present	Future	Past	Present	Future
PERSONAL HOPES						
Studies	4.4	5.9	7.9	5.2	7.2	8.9
Peace	4.7	5.6	6.8	5.3	7.2	8.8
Recreation, leisure	4.5	5.5	7.3	4.8	7.0	8.6
Happy family	4.5	5.4	7.2	4.9	6.8	8.6
Health-family	4.6	5.2	6.9	5.1	7.2	8.9
Children	4.3	5.1	7.1	4.8	6.9	8.7
Health-self	4.5	5.1	6.7	5.0	6.8	8.6
Own house	4.1	5.0	7.0	4.8	6.8	8.6
Modern conveniences	4.1	5.0	6.9	4.8	6.9	8.6
Relatives	4.7	4.8	6.6	4.7	6.6	8.4
Employment	4.2	4.7	6.8	4.7	6.7	8.5
More money	4.1	4.7	6.5	4.6	6.6	8.4
Move to town	3.9	4.6	6.9	4.9	6.7	8.6
Improved/decent std. of living	4.0	4.5	6.4	4.7	6.6	8.4
Remain a farmer	3.9	4.5	6.3	4.5	6.8	8.4
Social security	4.4	4.3	5.5	4.8	6.7	8.4
Decreased taxes	4.2	4.1	5.7	4.7	6.5	8.1
PERSONAL FEARS						
War	4.4	5.5	7.2	4.9	7.0	8.7
Unhappy family	4.3	5.4	7.4	5.0	6.9	8.6
Ill health-family	4.6	5.3	7.0	5.0	7.0	8.7
Ill health-self	4.3	5.0	6.7	4.9	6.9	8.6
Children	4.2	5.0	7.0	5.0	7.0	8.7
Poor crop	4.4	4.8	6.4	5.0	6.9	8.4
Not get apartment	3.8	4.8	7.1	4.7	7.0	8.6
Unemployment	4.0	4.7	6.4	4.6	6.4	8.3
Deterioration/inadequate std. of living	4.0	4.1	5.8	4.7	6.3	8.2

TABLE 35 (*Continued*)

Concerns	National ladder ratings			Personal ladder ratings		
	Past	Present	Future	Past	Present	Future
NATIONAL HOPES						
National unity	5.1	7.4	9.0	3.7	5.2	7.0
Education	4.7	7.0	8.8	3.8	5.0	6.7
Housing	5.0	7.0	8.8	4.3	5.3	7.2
Socialism	5.0	7.0	8.7	4.3	5.2	7.1
Industry	4.9	7.0	8.8	4.2	5.2	7.2
Transportation	4.8	7.0	8.8	4.2	5.3	7.2
Development of agriculture	4.8	7.0	8.7	4.3	5.1	7.0
Peace	5.0	6.9	8.7	4.4	5.1	7.0
Improved/decent std. of living	4.8	6.8	8.6	4.1	4.9	6.8
Technological advances	5.1	6.8	8.7	4.4	5.3	7.3
Employment	4.9	6.8	8.7	4.0	4.7	6.8
Public health	5.0	6.8	8.6	4.0	5.0	6.5
General development/ country	4.9	6.8	8.6	4.5	5.0	6.5
Electrification/villages	4.6	6.7	8.5	3.9	4.4	6.2
Economic stability	4.7	6.6	8.5	4.2	4.9	6.7
Improved housing conditions	4.4	6.5	8.4	3.9	4.7	6.7
Equalize salaries	4.6	6.5	8.2	4.2	4.8	7.0
Decreased taxes/ farmers	4.7	6.3	7.9	4.6	4.7	5.8
Tito's health/position	5.0	6.1	9.0	4.4	5.1	7.4
NATIONAL FEARS						
National disunity	4.9	7.2	8.8	4.0	4.8	7.1
Change Socialist system	4.9	7.2	8.9	4.5	5.3	7.4
Death of Tito	4.8	7.1	8.9	4.2	5.1	6.9
No fears or worries	4.9	6.9	8.5	4.2	4.8	6.1
Natural disasters	4.6	6.8	8.7	4.4	5.1	6.8
War	4.9	6.7	8.7	4.3	5.1	6.8
Occupation by another country	4.7	6.7	8.5	4.3	5.1	6.7

Appendix E:
Variations in Concerns

1. VARIATIONS OF CONCERNS BY DEMOGRAPHIC GROUPS BY COUNTRIES

In Tables 36–48, —— indicates that less than 0.5 percent fall into the category.

Concerns	Sex		Age				Education					Socioeconomic					City			
	Male	Female	18-29	30-39	40-49	50+	High	Secondary	Primary	No school	Illit.	1 (upper)	2	3	4	5 (lower)	Rural	2000-50,000	50-500,000	500,000+
PERSONAL HOPES																				
Values/character	15%	12%	14%	11%	17%	14%	33%	27%	12%	12%	13%	27%	23%	13%	13%	13%	10%	22%	23%	17%
Economic	76	61	70	73	69	57	67	58	70	69	67	56	53	65	70	70	68	68	63	73
Job/work	10	6	10	8	7	4	17	16	9	6	5	12	9	12	8	5	6	11	4	16
Health	28	40	27	35	38	43	8	21	29	31	43	21	31	22	35	40	36	32	39	24
Family	21	34	27	33	29	21	42	40	35	25	19	51	48	39	26	21	20	42	42	49
Political	—	—	—	1	1	—	—	2	1	1	—	—	1	1	—	—	1	—	—	1
Social	1	1	2	1	1	1	3	7	—	1	—	1	4	—	1	—	—	3	1	4
International	—	—	—	—	—	—	6	2	—	—	—	1	2	3	—	1	—	—	—	1
Status quo	1	2	1	1	3	2	6	5	2	1	1	11	7	2	1	1	1	2	5	3
PERSONAL FEARS																				
Values/character	9	6	8	6	9	6	11	11	6	6	8	11	6	9	6	8	8	8	7	5
Economic	39	22	29	31	37	24	33	31	35	38	23	23	31	33	30	28	28	31	29	43
Job/work	3	2	3	2	3	1	6	4	3	3	2	4	6	4	2	1	2	3	2	5
Health	38	46	43	46	42	37	47	52	45	45	37	52	50	47	42	39	39	47	47	57
Family	10	23	16	24	16	11	28	27	22	15	11	31	29	26	15	13	12	27	32	26
Political	2	1	1	1	1	1	—	2	1	2	2	3	3	2	1	—	1	—	—	4
Social	2	2	2	2	—	3	—	—	2	3	2	3	3	1	3	2	2	2	—	2
International	3	2	3	3	4	1	11	6	2	3	2	5	8	4	2	2	2	2	3	5
No fears/worries	5	3	3	4	4	7	14	9	5	4	3	11	10	6	4	2	3	4	9	9
NATIONAL HOPES																				
Political	22	12	15	15	17	20	53	28	20	20	10	35	39	21	17	10	13	22	23	28
Economic	65	52	56	63	62	48	83	73	67	62	44	75	72	71	59	48	52	65	71	74
Social	22	16	18	21	20	15	31	30	21	16	15	28	28	25	18	15	18	23	17	20
International	6	4	5	5	4	4	6	12	5	5	3	13	7	5	5	4	4	6	7	7
Indep., status	7	2	4	4	5	3	42	22	4	2	—	32	15	8	3	—	1	7	11	20
Status quo	1	—	1	1	—	1	1	1	1	1	—	1	3	1	—	—	—	1	1	1
NATIONAL FEARS																				
Political	29	21	23	27	24	24	53	44	22	29	15	55	46	36	23	17	22	29	29	30
Economic	40	30	34	36	37	30	39	41	38	37	29	33	37	41	35	36	36	30	30	35
Social	9	7	9	8	8	5	17	11	10	6	6	12	10	11	8	6	8	7	9	6
International	19	19	20	20	22	14	22	22	29	20	15	25	23	19	20	17	17	21	31	22
Indep., status	5	2	5	2	3	1	17	15	3	2	1	15	10	6	3	1	1	4	6	13
No fears/worries	2	1	2	1	2	2	6	3	2	2	1	3	3	2	2	1	1	1	5	5

TABLE 37

Cuba

Concerns	Sex		Age				Education			Socioeconomic			City					
	Male	Female	20-29	30-39	40-49	50+	High	Secondary	Elem/none	High/upper mid.	Lower mid.	Low	−5,000	5-10,000	10-20,000	20-50,000	50,000+	Havana
PERSONAL HOPES																		
Values/character	31%	28%	38%	24%	22%	24%	50%	44%	21%	40%	31%	26%	26%	21%	21%	25%	30%	39%
Economic	76	69	70	76	74	72	68	69	75	64	75	75	88	86	67	73	64	75
Job/work	18	8	17	15	10	6	17	15	13	15	11	15	22	14	15	11	15	13
Health	46	48	40	50	52	52	36	41	52	41	42	51	82	42	37	51	41	44
Family	48	59	57	52	54	40	66	53	49	59	53	50	46	61	42	45	47	65
Political	15	14	11	14	22	19	16	12	16	13	18	14	10	6	14	26	12	12
Social	4	5	4	3	6	6	11	4	3	7	4	3	—	—	3	4	3	7
International	3	3	2	5	6	2	6	4	3	3	4	3	—	3	3	1	4	6
Status quo	2	1	1	2	2	1	1	1	1	2	1	2	—	—	—	2	4	—
PERSONAL FEARS																		
Values/character	24	21	28	20	16	16	34	30	17	26	24	21	14	7	11	17	34	27
Economic	47	47	45	54	49	34	44	46	49	41	44	51	74	68	48	37	34	54
Job/work	6	2	6	3	2	4	6	6	3	5	2	4	4	6	3	3	4	6
Health	39	46	38	46	47	35	38	42	43	38	38	45	83	48	43	34	30	45
Family	21	28	27	20	16	20	34	28	21	29	22	23	14	34	16	11	23	37
Political	17	13	10	18	20	24	19	15	15	19	19	12	12	17	9	20	14	16
Social	3	3	3	3	3	5	7	3	3	4	4	2	—	6	—	—	5	5
International	5	5	4	4	4	7	7	5	6	4	5	5	—	—	5	5	5	5
No fears/worries	11	6	10	10	8	6	7	9	8	5	10	10	12	—	12	17	10	5
NATIONAL HOPES																		
Political	21	14	14	23	22	15	40	22	11	34	18	12	6	14	5	7	8	39
Economic	78	71	76	73	79	71	77	73	75	73	76	75	82	97	73	67	74	77
Social	21	20	24	23	20	13	41	26	15	33	19	18	8	34	17	12	20	30
International	7	7	7	8	6	10	13	10	5	10	7	6	—	1	1	5	3	14
Indep., status	14	10	13	14	12	12	25	16	8	21	13	9	6	6	5	11	14	18
Status quo	3	1	1	4	1	2	—	1	3	2	2	2	4	—	1	4	2	1
NATIONAL FEARS																		
Political	57	62	60	56	63	59	70	64	61	60	64	56	65	70	53	43	57	70
Economic	26	20	25	25	20	21	33	27	20	28	23	22	16	44	21	9	22	34
Social	8	8	10	8	6	7	15	12	6	12	9	7	4	13	3	4	7	14
International	8	11	8	9	10	16	10	12	3	6	8	2	4	6	1	4	1	

TABLE 38

DOMINICAN REPUBLIC

Concerns	Sex		Age				Education			Socioeconomic		Dwelling	
	Male	Female	21-29	30-39	40-49	50+	Some secondary	Some primary	No school	Upper	Lower	Rural	Urban
PERSONAL HOPES													
Values/character	13%	17%	13%	15%	18%	14%	27%	12%	16%	30%	13%	12%	23%
Economic	95	97	96	96	92	96	88	95	96	81	97	96	93
Job/work	27	21	30	27	19	20	27	26	23	25	25	22	34
Health	15	20	14	17	14	23	14	17	19	16	17	16	20
Family	34	47	40	45	38	31	49	43	30	56	37	36	48
Political	11	7	9	8	12	10	14	10	8	17	9	8	14
Social	3	2	2	3	4	1	7	3	—	8	2	2	3
International	—	—	—	—	—	1	1	—	—	1	—	—	—
Status quo	—	—	—	—	—	—	—	—	—	—	—	—	—
PERSONAL FEARS													
Values/character	5	4	6	2	7	4	5	6	2	2	5	4	5
Economic	81	83	82	88	77	77	55	82	86	67	83	82	79
Job/work	13	4	10	8	13	8	16	10	7	5	10	10	7
Health	28	31	31	29	20	35	29	30	32	36	29	28	34
Family	20	33	26	30	22	20	37	29	19	40	24	21	37
Political	10	8	6	12	13	9	21	14	2	21	8	7	17
Social	1	1	1	1	4	—	3	—	1	1	1	1	1
International	1	1	2	—	—	—	—	1	—	1	—	—	1
No fears/worries	—	1	1	1	—	1	—	1	—	1	—	1	2
NATIONAL HOPES													
Political	82	72	78	80	76	78	74	84	73	75	78	81	69
Economic	84	84	84	85	83	83	73	86	86	85	84	84	85
Social	14	15	19	13	13	10	24	12	17	21	13	13	19
International	2	2	2	2	2	3	6	3	2	6	2	1	7
Indep., status	—	1	—	1	—	1	2	—	1	1	1	1	1
Status quo	—	—	—	—	—	—	—	—	—	—	—	—	—
NATIONAL FEARS													
Political	76	72	73	78	72	73	78	80	69	81	74	74	75
Economic	41	46	50	44	39	34	23	50	38	32	44	45	34
Social	4	3	4	4	4	2	5	11	3	13	3	3	5
International	9	9	11	10	7	6	2	4	7	3	9	10	7
Indep., status	9	7	8	8	7	9	15	2	11	6	8	9	5
No fears/worries	2	1	1	3	2	2	1	1	3	1	2	2	3

TABLE 39

Egypt

Concerns	Sex		Age			Dwelling	
	Male	Female	15-19	20-39	40+	Rural	Urban
PERSONAL HOPES							
Values/character	39%	41%	48%	42%	32%	45%	29%
Economic	77	56	58	68	77	76	58
Job/work	40	47	50	56	19	35	54
Health	28	15	8	19	39	28	17
Family	52	56	59	55	48	51	57
Political	4	3	5	2	5	5	1
Social	11	8	11	12	6	7	14
International	2	3	5	3	——	2	1
Status quo	——	——	——	——	——	——	——
PERSONAL FEARS							
Values/character	21	31	34	23	19	20	31
Economic	51	33	40	49	45	50	38
Job/work	21	20	23	27	11	17	27
Health	39	54	49	44	38	44	39
Family	24	47	43	35	18	26	39
Political	4	4	5	4	4	4	5
Social	——	3	5	——	——	1	2
International	4	3	1	5	4	2	6
No fears/worries	11	——	——	4	18	12	2
NATIONAL HOPES							
Political	24	33	28	29	21	27	25
Economic	57	64	65	68	49	55	66
Social	36	40	45	41	28	34	41
International	28	31	43	27	24	29	28
Indep., status	49	38	46	48	40	50	34
Status quo	1	——	——	——	2	1	——
NATIONAL FEARS							
Political	23	34	37	29	16	22	34
Economic	28	33	34	31	24	26	35
Social	21	15	20	24	13	16	25
International	37	34	41	32	37	38	31
Indep., status	40	35	36	41	33	40	32
No fears/worries	4	1	2	2	7	5	2

Concerns	Occupation							City			Income				Education				Age		
	Other	Farm worker	Farm owner	Unskilled	Skilled	Clerk/teacher	Prof./student	100,000+	5000-99,999	Rural	−74 Rs.	75-150 Rs.	151-300 Rs.	301+Rupees	Illiterate	Under matric.	Matriculate	Higher	41+	31-40	−30
PERSONAL HOPES																					
Values/character	11%	7%	11%	8%	9%	28%	39%	22%	18%	12%	9%	14%	23%	26%	7%	10%	22%	33%	12%	13%	22%
Economic	70	79	79	75	68	57	46	67	63	71	79	70	64	58	77	72	62	54	66	72	66
Job/work	20	14	9	23	32	40	32	29	23	21	20	25	26	24	14	21	32	35	15	20	34
Health	5	2	2	4	3	3	5	3	4	4	3	3	4	4	2	3	4	5	4	4	3
Family	44	27	44	40	33	41	30	41	36	39	33	41	41	43	34	42	39	39	46	43	30
Political																					
Social	8	3	8	4	7	15	20	14	10	7	5	10	12	17	3	6	15	21	7	9	12
International																					
Status quo	1	2	1	2	3	1	2	2		2	1	1	1	3	2	1	2	2	2	2	1
PERSONAL FEARS																					
Values/character	6	2	2	4	6	10	13	9	7	3	3	7	8	10	3	3	9	11	3	5	10
Economic	42	56	59	58	48	42	32	47	41	50	59	48	41	36	57	46	42	38	47	45	48
Job/work	6	5	3	6	9	11	8	8	8	5	6	6	8	7	4	6	8	10	3	5	10
Health	23	19	16	21	29	21	17	16	21	24	20	22	18	14	21	25	20	16	25	21	17
Family	20	19	21	24	15	22	17	26	17	18	21	22	21	20	17	22	19	20	22	23	16
Political	1		1	1	1	1	1	1	2	2	1	2	3	2		1	3	1	1	2	2
Social	2		1	1	2	2	4	2	1					4				4	2	1	1
International	1					1	2	2						2				2	1		
No fears/worries	10	8	7	6	9	12	16	14	10	7	6	7	13	18	6	9	12	15	9	11	10
NATIONAL HOPES																					
Political	15	3	7	4	9	22	18	19	14	7	6	7	17	27	2	10	17	25	11	14	11
Economic	73	54	66	62	73	84	81	76	72	69	58	75	80	79	55	73	82	84	69	71	75
Social	22	12	15	15	18	29	35	26	23	16	14	19	29	33	9	19	30	34	20	22	23
International	4	1	3	2	6	7	6	6	5	3	3	3	6	7	3	5	6	7	2	5	5
Indep., status	10	5	7	9	15	16	21	17	13	8	5	10	17	22		10	14	22	10	10	14
Status quo																					
NATIONAL FEARS																					
Political	26	8	18	10	18	34	34	30	27	17	12	20	34	37	7	20	33	41	22	26	23
Economic	26	18	27	29	25	32	27	35	26	23	22	27	34	30	17	28	33	32	26	25	29
Social	16	8	14	16	20	18	24	22	18	13	13	16	20	21	12	14	21	23	16	16	17
International	28	14	20	21	36	45	36	34	34	23	18	32	37	34	13	33	36	38	23	30	33
Indep., status	11	3	4	5	8	18	16	14	10	8	6	9	15	14	2	9	16	17	7	8	14
No fears/worries	7	12	5	5	4	4	5	4	6	7	6	6	4	6	8	6	5	5	7	6	6

TABLE 41
Israel

Concerns	Sex		Age				Education			Income			Class				Region					Occupation						
	Male %	Female %	−29 %	30-49 %	50-64 %	65+ %	Univ. %	Elem. or Second. comp. %	Elem. incomp. %	Upper %	Middle %	Lower %	Upper; Upper mid. %	Middle %	Lower %	Working %	Coop. settlement %	New urban %	Long settled urban %	Tel Aviv; Haifa %	Jerusalem %	Prof. %	Business %	White collar %	Skilled %	Unskilled %	Farmer %	Other %
PERSONAL HOPES																												
Values/character	33	25	38	29	22	18	46	31	17	34	31	22	41	32	24	24	52	28	34	26	26	36	34	24	26	19	48	41
Economic	82	78	88	82	71	66	75	78	87	71	83	81	71	78	91	85	87	85	81	78	77	69	72	78	87	87	87	57
Job/work	41	29	49	35	23	18	45	35	31	38	36	34	48	33	36	37	35	39	34	33	41	40	32	31	32	44	43	30
Health	44	50	32	47	60	62	60	45	56	38	38	34	31	46	34	52	72	42	42	47	42	38	38	53	46	49	69	46
Family	70	83	77	82	67	65	66	78	78	73	79	73	73	76	85	78	78	84	71	75	71	74	74	79	80	77	77	—
Political	1	2	1	1	3	3	3	2	—	3	1	—	—	3	—	—	—	1	1	2	—	1	3	3	1	—	—	—
Social	11	10	7	11	13	7	13	11	6	13	12	7	13	11	2	10	29	11	10	2	4	15	12	8	9	6	25	7
International	13	12	6	14	16	12	18	13	8	16	14	8	18	14	5	11	5	5	14	16	8	19	15	13	12	6	9	15
Status quo	4	4	3	4	6	3	7	5	3	7	4	3	7	4	—	4	7	4	3	5	2	8	5	6	4	1	5	2
PERSONAL FEARS																												
Values/character	12	8	16	10	5	3	15	10	7	8	10	11	23	9	12	9	34	9	11	7	5	4	12	6	7	7	29	24
Economic	58	52	58	53	58	52	41	55	62	44	56	61	50	51	79	61	62	57	60	53	55	32	45	55	62	66	64	57
Job/work	15	6	16	12	3	2	15	10	8	15	10	7	17	10	12	10	27	9	8	9	9	12	—	9	9	11	26	—
Health	54	61	46	62	62	56	56	56	63	51	59	60	57	54	66	62	65	59	45	60	45	64	51	59	59	62	58	52
Family	39	49	51	47	33	27	36	44	50	37	45	44	47	43	52	43	60	55	41	39	46	37	36	39	50	49	53	57
Political	2	1	3	1	2	2	1	3	—	2	2	1	5	3	—	—	1	1	1	2	2	—	2	1	2	—	3	2
Social	4	3	1	5	4	—	8	3	3	8	3	4	8	3	5	3	1	5	2	2	3	6	4	2	2	2	10	4
International	29	26	23	30	27	21	40	29	17	40	30	13	42	29	12	23	15	25	30	30	19	47	32	27	28	16	20	20
No fears/worries	6	5	4	5	7	12	10	6	4	8	6	4	11	7	2	4	6	3	6	7	7	11	9	6	3	4	5	7
NATIONAL HOPES																												
Political	40	31	35	34	37	37	51	35	29	41	37	31	47	39	24	31	44	31	34	36	37	45	43	39	29	22	43	44
Economic	80	79	86	79	74	68	81	80	76	83	80	77	83	81	79	79	87	78	78	79	77	80	77	80	80	77	87	80
Social	70	69	68	71	71	66	76	70	67	77	73	66	76	68	62	73	85	60	67	66	61	75	75	68	67	67	77	65
International	70	69	72	70	68	57	76	72	61	77	72	59	76	71	62	70	74	60	65	73	65	71	75	68	67	66	71	70
Indep., status	42	32	36	38	38	27	50	38	28	47	38	27	53	39	35	31	45	27	32	39	41	49	44	32	35	28	43	35
Status quo	1	1	2	1	—	—	—	1	1	—	1	—	—	1	—	1	5	1	2	—	1	—	1	1	1	1	4	—
NATIONAL FEARS																												
Political	28	18	25	21	25	22	38	23	16	30	23	19	29	25	24	19	10	26	23	24	20	32	29	21	22	18	14	20
Economic	49	39	53	45	35	29	48	48	35	47	49	35	42	47	40	44	56	46	43	43	38	52	40	42	48	41	58	33
Social	33	27	29	29	27	22	43	31	22	28	32	28	45	29	35	31	31	36	34	30	16	30	37	26	27	31	27	33
International	68	77	78	73	69	59	70	73	73	76	74	73	68	74	74	73	65	75	76	76	76	67	76	72	73	73	70	67

TABLE 42

KIBBUTZIM

Concerns	Age −29	30+
PERSONAL HOPES		
Values/character	68%	54%
Economic	31	46
Job/work	53	49
Health	5	36
Family	71	75
Political	2	4
Social	56	66
International	12	29
Status quo	3	8
PERSONAL FEARS		
Values/character	54	39
Economic	20	41
Job/work	22	19
Health	30	64
Family	51	46
Political	3	5
Social	56	47
International	34	57
No fears/worries	4	——
NATIONAL HOPES		
Political	58	65
Economic	79	86
Social	85	92
International	92	95
Indep., status	43	47
Status quo	1	——
NATIONAL FEARS		
Political	42	53
Economic	48	51
Social	59	69
International	83	89
Indep., status	26	33
No fears/worries	——	——

TABLE 43

NIGERIA

Concerns	Sex		Age				Education				Socio-economic			City			Region			Religion		
	Male	Female	21-29	30-39	40-49	50+	Some second./univ.	Some primary	No school/lit.	Illit.	Upper	Lower	Rural	5000-20,000	20-100,000	100,000+	West	East	North	Moslem	Christian	Pagan
PERSONAL HOPES																						
Values/character	44%	32%	54%	38%	32%	34%	64%	48%	37%	31%	39%	42%	40%	45%	45%	43%	37%	41%	44%	41%	44%	16%
Economic	90	87	85	92	96	92	77	89	93	93	77	90	90	89	91	88	92	90	89	91	88	95
Job/work	20	12	30	17	10	4	44	28	14	6	38	18	18	20	17	23	17	20	19	14	24	8
Health	43	54	35	45	55	53	20	32	48	60	16	46	47	46	28	31	28	27	59	61	30	33
Family	74	83	72	80	73	77	71	82	68	76	69	76	75	73	81	87	88	90	65	68	83	83
Political			1				1	1								1			1			
Social	16	5	15	17	11	10	30	18	12	7	32	14	14	11	15	23	22	24	7	8	20	16
International	1		1			2			2		2				1	3			1			
Status quo		2																				
PERSONAL FEARS																						
Values/character	20	7	28	14	13	7	30	19	15	13	21	17	17	22	15	16	17	11	21	18	17	15
Economic	66	62	66	69	64	59	68	70	59	64	64	66	65	61	77	72	75	64	63	65	66	57
Job/work	3	1	4	2			7	3	1	1	10	2	2	3	4	7	5	2	2	2	3	
Health	61	77	59	68	63	68	44	61	64	73	32	65	66	68	57	44	41	62	74	72	57	63
Family	26	33	25	25	32	36	30	36	18	24	40	27	25	25	41	46	49	36	16	18	37	22
Political	5	4	4	3	7		5	5	8	3	7	5	4	4	5	11	9	2	4	5	4	3
Social	17	3	14	16	11	13	11	16	18	12	13	14	15	14	13	16	9	9	9	15	13	12
International	1		1	2			3		3		9	1	1	1	1	2	1	1	1	1	1	
No fears/worries	7	7	7	6	10	11	10	8	8	6	12	8	8	6	8	7	9	10	6	6	9	10
NATIONAL HOPES																						
Political	49	54	51	49	52	48	56	53	49	46	56	50	47	53	66	61	70	52	42	45	55	41
Economic	84	66	81	83	76	80	86	89	82	73	94	80	82	78	79	73	77	95	76	76	86	80
Social	68	59	64	69	67	63	74	71	64	61	68	64	65	69	72	63	64	69	66	62	71	53
International	13	11	15	12	11	7	20	12	14	9	24	12	12	15	10	14	11	13	12	10	15	10
Indep., status	24	24	28	25	18	21	40	29	18	18	39	24	23	26	26	39	23	21	26	23	27	7
Status quo							1										1					
NATIONAL FEARS																						
Political	73	53	66	72	65	69	84	77	68	59	80	68	68	68	76	72	80	72	63	62	78	42
Economic	46	32	39	48	39	47	50	55	36	36	73	42	43	41	49	53	52	70	29	32	55	33
Social	40	24	36	38	33	46	43	51	29	28	42	37	37	33	47	35	48	53	25	26	48	30
International	13	3	13	19	11		6		17	10	10	11	10	17		4	4	3	17	17	6	6

TABLE 44

PANAMA

Concerns	Sex		Age				Education			Socioeconomic		Dwelling	
	Male	Female	21-29	30-39	40-49	50+	Some second.	Some primary	No school	Upper	Lower	Rural	Urban
PERSONAL HOPES													
Values/character	25%	26%	30%	19%	19%	32%	31%	24%	21%	24%	25%	24%	28%
Economic	95	87	89	90	95	89	84	92	94	85	92	92	89
Job/work	31	23	30	25	29	23	28	27	23	22	29	24	29
Health	39	48	37	46	41	48	36	46	45	44	43	47	38
Family	45	61	60	60	51	43	57	57	34	60	50	48	60
Political	1	1	1	—	1	1	1	1	1	1	1	1	—
Social	4	1	3	2	3	2	3	2	3	4	1	1	4
International	—	1	—	—	1	—	—	1	—	1	—	1	1
Status quo	—	1	—	—	1	2	2	—	1	2	—	—	1
PERSONAL FEARS													
Values/character	10	5	14	4	5	5	10	5	9	5	7	7	8
Economic	62	52	59	55	60	54	56	62	43	49	59	53	62
Job/work	6	6	10	5	5	4	8	4	8	5	6	6	5
Health	61	67	66	66	71	57	61	68	58	64	64	64	65
Family	31	42	27	42	31	45	38	37	33	39	36	31	45
Political	3	1	3	1	—	3	2	1	4	5	1	2	1
Social	1	1	1	—	1	1	2	1	—	2	—	1	1
International	3	3	6	2	3	1	2	3	2	4	2	3	3
No fears/worries	1	2	1	2	1	1	3	—	—	3	1	3	3
NATIONAL HOPES													
Political	22	22	26	22	20	21	27	22	17	28	20	20	26
Economic	77	72	81	80	71	66	85	75	57	75	74	67	84
Social	30	32	27	36	33	30	30	33	29	35	30	34	27
International	8	6	5	7	10	5	11	6	4	11	5	5	9
Indep., status	4	2	3	2	4	3	5	3	1	6	2	2	4
Status quo	—	—	—	—	—	1	1	—	—	1	—	—	—
NATIONAL FEARS													
Political	39	43	42	48	36	38	58	38	25	56	35	32	53
Economic	33	33	39	31	36	27	36	34	23	36	32	28	39
Social	15	15	17	18	18	9	19	16	8	13	16	15	16
International	25	21	19	23	22	26	20	24	25	23	22	24	22
Indep., status	7	6	7	7	6	5	9	7	1	11	5	5	8
No fears/worries	2	2	1	1	3	3	—	2	6	1	2	3	1

TABLE 45
PHILIPPINES

Concerns	Sex		Age				Education							Economic				Dwelling			Occupation						
	Male %	Female %	21-30 %	31-40 %	41-50 %	51+ %	College comp. %	College incomp. %	High school comp. %	High school incomp. %	Elementary comp. %	Elementary incomp. %	No school %	Upper %	Upper mid. %	Lower mid. %	Lower %	Rural %	Semi-urban %	Urban %	Prof./business %	White collar %	Manual worker %	Farm owner %	Farm tenant %	Other %	No answer %
PERSONAL HOPES																											
Values/character	10	7	10	12	3	7	10	12	14	20	4	2	1	4	8	12	6	7	13	11	8	12	6	9	1	20	7
Economic	64	56	54	67	60	61	42	40	65	60	73	78	81	53	44	55	74	60	64	62	41	62	86	66	82	46	56
Job/work	7	8	15	4		4	16	26	18	7	2	1		10	11	7	4	8	8	7	26	18	14			17	1
Health	5	8	2	12	5	8	11	2	1	5	14	8	4	4	1	7	7	5	8	8	18	1	10			12	8
Family	52	53	49	56	58	49	62	60	68	46	27	41	47	58	67	57	40	52	49	55	58	55	47	49	43	47	58
Political												1				1				1		1			1		
Social	7	2	5	4	5	5	13	4	9	1	1	1		15	11	5		4	6	7	12	3	2	8		8	1
International										1						1										1	
Status quo							1	1						1		1				1						1	
PERSONAL FEARS																											
Values/character	4	5	5	1	1	1	1	8	2	2	1	1			4	4	1	2	3	4	6	3	2	1		4	
Economic	43	32	33	45	41	37	41	34	50	26	51	47	22	35	33	39	40	36	43	46	30	39	43	42	49	30	39
Job/work	7	8	15	4		4	16	12	8	7			3	10	11	8	4	8	4	7	21	7	8	8		4	2
Health	25	26	23	26	35	21	26	26	19	32	38	25	40	40	18	18	34	24	31	26	14	31	32	16	42	17	28
Family	27	34	26	32	43	27	62	35	45	21	16	30	9	31	39	34	23	31	26	30	36	41	33	16	13	31	32
Political	1	1		1	2	2	2	1	2	2				4								1					
Social		1	1				3								3			1	4	5	3	3				1	
International	22	23	24	19	26	22	11	23	12	38	22	24	34	7	20	25	24	24	23	18	15	23	20	33	34	18	26
No fears/worries	4	2		1	1	10	4	1		2	2	5	7	3	4	2	3	3	6	2	4	2	3	8		6	2
NATIONAL HOPES																											
Political	37	36	33	35	42	41	43	47	38	46	34	21	27	35	56	30	36	37	29	42	42	43	30	57	33	39	31
Economic	55	48	67	50	45	34	60	61	64	43	46	50	31	67	61	52	45	49	55	62	52	76	61	51	40	85	27
Social	17	9	12	12	15	17	27	13	3	18	14	10	7	12	19	14	10	15	8	10	29	12	4	8	8	13	11
International	4	18	8	12	11	13	3	10	13	16	8	18	8	4	5	13	11	9	20	12	5	3	12		5	6	11
Indep., status	13	4	6	6	8	17	17	9	15	13	1	1	7	31	13	7		9	10	10	20	15	9		5	5	24
Status quo																											5
NATIONAL FEARS																											
Political	41	25	37	38	36	25	57	51	33	28	14	22	13	48	42	42	20	31	37	48	50	55	32	34	23	33	22
Economic	16	12	13	19	14	11	23	20	17	21	2	6	7	20	19	15	11	13	15	22	21	24	9	9	13	17	10
Social	9	6	11	7	5	5	16	8	11	9	2	4	1	10	15	9	3	7	5	14	18	16	3		1	6	6
International	39	53	39	40	40	53	26	25	47	45	91	64	45	37	21	45	56	46	46	43	26	17	44	57	60	54	54

UNITED STATES

Column groups (left to right): Sex · Age · Education · Economic · Class · Race · Religion · Occupation

Concerns	Male	Female	21-29	30-49	50+	College	High school	Grammar	Upper (E)	Middle (E)	Lower (E)	Upper (C)	Upper mid.	Middle (C)	Lower mid.	Lower (C)	Working	White	Non-white	Protestant	Catholic	Jewish	Prof./business	White collar	Skilled	Unskilled	Farmer	Non-labor
PERSONAL HOPES																												
Values/character	16	23	16	20	21	31	17	18	21	20	17	29	29	18	23	23	16	21	13	21	15	17	27	22	14	18	21	20
Economic	67	63	71	69	57	68	68	59	63	68	66	51	65	64	72	70	68	64	76	64	69	70	63	73	71	67	63	47
Job/work	15	6	27	8	5	21	10	5	10	10	11	3	16	9	7	2	0	11	6	9	12	7	17	11	11	8	5	3
Health	42	53	33	51	53	45	49	50	48	51	45	56	46	50	51	52	47	50	33	47	51	63	49	55	46	43	52	54
Family	40	52	64	54	27	58	51	32	54	44	43	51	51	50	51	70	41	47	47	43	53	61	52	59	50	45	44	19
Political	3	1	2	4	2	2	2	1	3	3	2	1	1	3	2	2	2	5	2	2	3	—	3	3	1	1	—	—
Social	4	6	4	4	7	7	4	5	5	5	6	6	6	5	2	3	5	5	3	6	3	5	4	7	5	2	5	9
International	10	11	12	11	8	10	12	7	10	12	10	10	10	12	12	13	9	10	7	9	12	16	11	15	9	10	8	10
Status quo	11	11	6	10	16	7	11	13	15	8	10	12	10	12	7	3	11	11	8	11	14	8	12	15	11	10	9	17
PERSONAL FEARS																												
Values/character	3	4	4	4	2	9	2	1	5	3	2	12	5	3	7	—	2	4	4	3	3	7	7	6	2	2	2	2
Economic	47	44	48	46	47	45	47	44	44	51	43	34	45	41	57	52	50	46	41	45	48	40	43	52	49	53	39	29
Job/work	7	3	11	4	5	12	5	4	10	6	3	10	10	5	7	2	4	5	5	5	5	0	9	5	8	9	9	4
Health	52	59	53	56	56	54	59	51	59	60	49	58	56	57	59	45	54	58	32	52	63	68	60	70	58	49	48	44
Family	18	30	29	29	16	29	26	20	23	25	27	22	25	24	33	28	24	24	27	24	25	37	27	28	21	27	25	16
Political	6	3	5	5	4	4	5	3	5	6	3	14	5	6	4	1	3	5	6	5	4	2	7	5	3	3	4	6
Social	3	3	2	5	3	4	2	3	3	3	2	5	3	3	1	7	3	2	6	5	1	—	7	3	3	2	0	4
International	25	23	33	25	19	32	25	17	27	28	19	10	26	29	26	33	18	25	16	21	29	37	30	27	26	19	20	23
No fears/worries	12	11	6	12	15	8	11	15	13	9	11	15	11	12	6	8	13	11	14	14	8	1	8	8	12	14	12	22
NATIONAL HOPES																												
Political	15	12	15	14	11	21	11	10	16	12	11	24	18	16	7	17	8	13	11	13	12	16	18	16	11	8	14	17
Economic	48	43	48	45	43	52	45	40	48	44	39	29	50	46	62	25	41	45	44	44	46	57	49	59	47	45	31	35
Social	33	34	38	33	32	42	34	27	33	33	34	20	41	31	36	40	32	32	47	35	27	46	40	31	31	32	32	31
International	54	64	59	59	59	63	62	51	61	60	53	36	62	67	58	55	52	61	37	58	61	74	58	68	55	60	55	61
Indep., status	8	4	3	5	3	6	4	8	5	4	6	20	15	13	4	2	8	4	2	4	10	2	6	5	8	2	6	6
Status quo	5	5	5	7	7	6	6	8	7	7	6	9	8	5	8	2	8	7	2	5	4	5	6	5	8	7	6	6
NATIONAL FEARS																												
Political	25	21	25	25	17	37	23	15	26	26	18	27	27	26	15	17	19	24	14	23	20	29	30	29	18	17	28	20
Economic	33	26	30	31	27	33	30	25	30	32	27	12	32	31	39	22	28	29	29	28	21	21	36	32	31	24	26	26
Social	18	23	18	22	21	27	21	16	24	21	18	31	21	22	14	17	19	20	26	22	18	26	31	19	18	15	23	21
International	53	61	61	51	55	54	59	56	61	61	51	31	62	60	53	67	53	58	45	53	65	68	52	62	57	60	50	54
Indep., status	11	11	14	11	9	17	13	5	13	12	9	3	12	13	13	3	9	12	7	11	12	14	16	17	10	8	10	6
No fears/worries	4	4	3	4	4	5	3	4	5	4	5	5	5	4	4	—	3	3	7	4	4	—	4	4	5	5	1	4

TABLE 47
West Germany

Concerns	Sex		Age					Education		Economic			City			
	Male	Female	−29	30-39	40-49	50-59	60+	Secondary/university	Grammar	Upper	Middle	Lower	−2000	2-10,000	10-100,000	100,000+
PERSONAL HOPES																
Values/character	13%	8%	14%	11%	8%	15%	4%	14%	10%	5%	11%	12%	10%	11%	8%	13%
Economic	90	81	90	92	84	78	71	79	86	75	87	85	82	80	86	92
Job/work	16	4	15	10	9	11	3	6	11	5	10	10	11	7	16	6
Health	40	51	31	45	50	50	51	52	44	45	48	43	49	44	51	41
Family	20	33	36	24	37	24	16	39	25	33	29	21	20	21	37	29
Political	1	1		1	2	1	1	5	3	3	1	1	1	2		
Social	2	3	4	2	2	2	6	3	3	5	3	3	1	2	2	6
International	16	15	12	19	15	13	17	24	14	23	16	11	17	21	15	9
Status quo	4	3		4	3	2	9	4	4	8	3	4	5	5	4	1
PERSONAL FEARS																
Values/character	3	3	6	2	2	5	2	6	3		3	4	4	2	4	3
Economic	52	51	56	43	51	45	28	47	51	45	53	50	49	43	57	56
Job/work	3	2	1	3	1	5		5	2	3	2	3	1	2	2	1
Health	47	55	49	58	48	51	48	46	51	43	52	51	57	34	67	50
Family	6	21	16	20	9	15	9	18	14	18	13	16	14	17	17	9
Political	11	7	4	6	14	8	10	17	7	20	8	6	9	11	9	5
Social	3	2		1		3	6	5	2	8	1	3	2	2	1	3
International	50	50	54	53	51	46	48	56	49	53	53	45	52	41	55	53
No fears/worries	3	2	3	1	4	1	3	2	3	5	2	2	3	4	1	2
NATIONAL HOPES																
Political	55	44	57	52	46	42	50	62	47	45	52	45	36	38	69	54
Economic	78	62	72	77	71	75	50	80	69	80	73	61	66	69	70	71
Social	19	15	17	16	21	10	21	24	15	25	16	13	19	11	22	16
International	37	46	40	49	43	41	36	42	41	30	43	41	41	34	50	44
Indep., status	12	10	14	13	10	5	13	6	11	10	10	12	9	6	14	14
Status quo	2	3	3	3	2	2	2	3	2	5	3	1	3			
NATIONAL FEARS																
Political	30	25	24	25	35	24	29	45	24	43	28	21	21	21	37	30
Economic	48	40	51	49	42	46	30	50	44	45	45	42	36	43	51	45
Social	20	12	15	18	19	14	12	18	15	20	16	12	23	9	26	7
International	64	76	73	71	66	67	77	70	70	63	69	76	70	62	77	74
Indep. status																

Concerns	Sex		Age			Education				Economic				Dwelling		Occupation				Nationality			
	Male	Female	21-29	30-49	50+	High	Some High school	Some primary	No school	Upper—nonfarmer	Upper—farmer	Lower—nonfarmer	Lower—farmer	Rural	Urban	State employee	Worker	Farmer	Housewife	Serbian	Croatian	Slovenian	Other
PERSONAL HOPES																							
Values/character	24%	12%	32%	16%	9%	41%	21%	12%	6%	30%	7%	20%	10%	14%	22%	38%	22%	9%	7%	19%	20%	13%	15%
Economic	84	82	82	81	86	65	81	90	83	70	92	84	84	88	78	72	89	93	77	82	89	83	78
Job/work	23	18	24	20	17	21	19	19	24	18	25	17	28	25	15	20	17	29	17	22	21	12	19
Health	34	48	29	41	49	33	37	43	46	38	46	41	37	40	42	33	33	37	54	39	44	49	37
Family	53	67	62	66	49	68	56	59	60	66	59	60	64	56	64	67	56	54	70	65	58	39	61
Political				1			1					1			1	1	1			1			
Social	4	3	3	4	4	10	4	3	1	6	3	4	2	3	5	9	2	3	2	5	3	3	4
International	7	8	4	9	9	7	9	8	6	6	6	7	8	7	8	10	5	8	7	9	4	14	5
Status quo	3	1	1	2	3	1	2	2	2	2	3	2	2	2	2	1	2	3	2	2	2	2	1
PERSONAL FEARS																							
Values/character	7	3	11	3	3	12	5	3	2	7	6	6	2	4	6	11	4	3	1	6	5	3	3
Economic	33	33	32	29	39	22	26	39	37	22	46	30	39	40	27	21	32	45	31	33	34	30	33
Job/work	3	1	4	2	2	3	2	2	2	2	3	2	3	3	1	2	2	4	1	3	1	3	
Health	55	66	60	61	60	57	57	65	56	58	58	66	50	58	63	62	62	52	66	62	70	60	
Family	18	33	30	30	16	27	28	25	24	26	22	28	29	24	27	30	24	22	34	30	21	18	32
Political			1	2	4	1	2	2	4	2	2	3	2	2	3	3	1	3	3	3	1		
Social	3	2	26	27	27	42	31	22	20	40	21	26	25	23	31	37	25	20	27	27	23	31	4
International	27	27	3	27	27	4	4	3	4	4	1	3	5	3	3	4	4	3	3	1	4	7	30
No fears/worries	4	2	3	3	3	4	4	3	4	4	1	3	5	3	3	4	4	3	3	1	4	7	6
NATIONAL HOPES																							
Political	55	39	50	53	35	64	54	42	33	58	31	54	37	39	55	59	68	38	34	50	45	45	44
Economic	87	76	88	83	74	87	85	79	76	85	81	80	86	81	82	87	87	80	76	85	84	68	77
Social	31	31	35	32	27	39	30	31	25	39	31	31	27	30	32	39	30	29	30	33	36	23	26
International	29	34	32	32	30	33	36	30	30	34	27	33	35	32	32	31	30	29	34	32	31	32	29
Indep., status	8	4	6	7	3	12	5	5	1	11	4	6	2	4	8	14	5	3	3	6	7	6	2
Status quo																							
NATIONAL FEARS																							
Political	23	15	21	21	15	20	26	15	17	22	15	21	17	18	20	23	26	15	15	22	15	12	21
Economic	15	9	14	13	11	13	10	15	8	10	15	13	10	14	10	10	17	14	9	13	11	18	10
Social	2	1	2	2	1	4	3	2	1	1	2	2	1	2	2	3	2	2	1	2	2		1
International	76	81	83	78	77	80	79	79	76	80	80	80	80	77	81	82	75	76	82	81	82	71	75
Indep., status	8	3	7	5	6	14	7	6	1	9	3	6	2	4	7	9	7	2	2	5	4	4	8
No fears/worries	6	6	3	6		5	5		6	7	5	6	3	6	4	6	7	5	5	2	8	14	6

2. FEARS AND WORRIES BY EDUCATION

TABLE 49

Personal Fears and Worries by Education and Other Variables

Variable	Values & character	Economic	Job/work	Health	Family	Political	Social	International	No fears/worries	N
BEST EDUCATED										
Income: upper	9%	39%	11%	37%	28%	7%	4%	21%	7%	881
middle	12	41	13	30	29	5	3	18	8	900
lower	21	29	10	40	36	3	5	16	8	231
Age: 50+	5	42	2	41	22	8	3	20	12	329
30–49	9	39	7	39	33	7	4	19	8	870
−29	17	37	20	45	74	3	4	18	6	848
Dwelling: rural	9	36	13	26	33	4	5	15	4	750
urban	13	41	11	38	28	6	4	21	9	1313
MIDDLE EDUCATED										
Income: upper	8	42	7	52	31	5	3	16	9	1191
middle	8	47	7	50	30	4	2	23	7	1480
lower	14	51	7	45	30	5	5	12	7	1297
Age: 50+	3	47	3	52	21	4	2	20	10	705
30–49	6	44	6	51	35	6	4	20	8	1872
−29	18	49	9	45	29	4	3	13	6	1475
Dwelling: rural	13	45	7	43	27	5	4	14	7	1467
urban	9	47	7	53	32	5	3	19	8	2605
LEAST EDUCATED										
Income: upper	7	48	4	39	23	6	2	8	7	1058
middle	5	41	3	37	21	2	2	9	9	4509
lower	5	58	4	45	23	3	5	5	4	11598
Age: 50+	3	48	2	45	21	3	3	8	7	4401
30–49	5	54	4	45	25	3	4	6	5	8090
−29	8	54	6	38	21	2	5	5	5	4877
Dwelling: rural	5	53	4	40	20	3	4	4	6	12315
urban	6	52	4	49	30	3	4	10	6	5084

TABLE 50

NATIONAL FEARS AND WORRIES BY EDUCATION AND OTHER VARIABLES

Variable	Inter-national	Indep.; status	Social	Political	Economic	N
BEST EDUCATED						
Income: upper	32%	24%	17%	48%	31%	881
middle	33	30	16	49	28	900
lower	45	15	17	44	22	231
Age: 50+	34	22	16	45	32	329
30-49	37	22	20	48	30	870
—29	31	29	15	46	27	848
Dwelling: rural	26	23	11	53	21	750
urban	39	27	20	44	33	1313
MIDDLE EDUCATED						
Income: upper	37	15	17	45	34	1191
middle	50	21	17	33	33	1480
lower	34	14	21	47	32	1297
Age: 50+	49	14	16	30	27	705
30-49	44	16	18	41	35	1872
—29	35	19	20	45	33	1475
Dwelling: rural	30	19	19	45	30	1467
urban	48	16	18	38	34	2605
LEAST EDUCATED						
Income: upper	36	19	10	35	33	1058
middle	29	18	12	25	29	4509
lower	20	10	14	38	32	11598
Age: 50+	29	11	12	32	29	4401
30-49	23	12	14	37	32	8090
—29	21	15	13	34	32	4877
Dwelling: rural	19	12	12	35	31	12315
urban	36	13	15	35	34	5084

3. CORRELATIONS BETWEEN CONCERNS AND LADDER RATINGS

TABLE 51

RANK ORDER CORRELATIONS BETWEEN PERSONAL AND NATIONAL CONCERNS
AND MEAN LADDER RATINGS

	Personal		National	
Country	Hopes	Fears	Hopes	Fears
BRAZIL				
Past	.338*	.129	.456*	.314*
Present	−.044	.323*	−.377*	−.410*
Future	−.968††	−.500*	−.535*	.086
CUBA				
Past	.198	.071	.201	.079
Present	−.199	−.455*	.163	.304*
Future	−.134	−.563†	.294	.229
DOMINICAN REPUBLIC				
Past	−.161	−.292	.168	.185
Present	.098	−.425*	.023	−.083
Future	−.389*	.317	−.186	−.256
EGYPT				
Past	.022	.070	.282	.325*
Present	.383*	.313*	.414*	.389*
Future	−.353*	.115	.348*	−.175
INDIA I				
Past	−.582†	−.012	.562*	.293
Present	−.494*	−.095	.170	.330*
Future	−.706†	−.399*	−.188	.332*
ISRAEL				
Past	.278	−.178	.058	.866††
Present	.126	.304*	.154	.545*
Future	−.063	−.046	.046	.446*
NIGERIA				
Past	.990†	−.142	−.080	−.053
Present	.263	.030	−.130	.068
Future	.007	−.006	−.201	−.146
PANAMA				
Past	−.173	−.625††	−.591†	.321*
Present	.065	−.225	.303*	.393*
Future	−.108	−.358*	−.130	.048
PHILIPPINES				
Past	−.042	.000	.214	.893††
Present	.152	−.048	.000	.714†
Future	.203	−.048	.095	.643*
UNITED STATES				
Past	.241	−.016	.124	−.686††
Present	.080	.309*	.116	−.029
Future	.092	.336*	−.036	−.143
WEST GERMANY				
Past	.051	.558*	.609†	.025
Present	−.161	.021	.327*	−.642†
Future	−.127	.296		
YUGOSLAVIA				
Past	.060	.533*	.324*	.143
Present	.281	.642†	.241	−.232
Future	.336*	.275	.320*	.179

* = trend indicated.
† = significant at .05 level.
†† = significant at .01 level.

Appendix F: Data Concerning United States Sample

1. INFORMATION QUESTIONS, RESULTS AND GROUPINGS

1. "Could you please tell me if you happen to know who the following people are?"

	Percent correct
Marilyn Monroe*	85%
Perry Como*	80
Mickey Mantle*	79
Ernest Hemingway*	60
Marian Anderson*	57
Christian Herter	55
Charles de Gaulle	51
Nehru	42
Maria Callas*	39
Earl Warren	39
Harold Macmillan	33
William Fulbright	24

* Nonpolitical figures.

2. "Now, here are some abbreviations that you may or may not have heard of. Will you please tell me what the initials stand for?"

	Percent correct
U.N.	88%
G.O.P.	62
A.E.C.	21

3. "Have you heard or read of the North Atlantic Treaty Organization — NATO, that is?"
Of those in the above question who had heard or read of NATO, 78 percent responding "Yes," the next question asked was: "Do you

happen to know whether or not these countries are members of NATO?"

	Percent correct
U.S.A.	88%
Great Britain	85
Russia	57
Turkey	35
Sweden	27

4. "To your knowledge, has President Eisenhower ever met and talked with Nikita Khrushchev who is now Premier of Soviet Russia?"
   Of those 27 percent who answered "Yes," the question was then asked: "Can you tell me on what occasion, or under what circumstances, they met?"

	Percent correct
Geneva Summit Conference (1955)	13%

In order to obtain three groups of people according to their information level, an "information index" was constructed of the distribution of correct replies so that our best informed group consisted of 33 percent of the sample, the moderately informed of 33 percent, and the least informed of 34 percent. In calculating the index, the nonpolitical figures in question 1 (*) were not included, nor was the answer to the first part of question 3.

2. DIMENSIONS OF SATISFACTION

TABLE 52

PRODUCT-MOMENT CORRELATIONS OF DIFFERENT DIMENSIONS OF SATISFACTION

Item	Present rating	Success	Con-fidence	Self-respect	Oppor-tunity	Self-action	Enjoy-ment	Reli-gion	Troubles	Worries	Satis-faction
Personal present rating		.39	.28	.21	.32	.29	.25	.11	−.25	−.27	.36
Success in achieving goals	.39		.41	.41	.36	.25	.28	.15	−.26	−.23	.45
Confidence in oneself	.28	.41		.56	.32	.29	.21	.07	−.15	−.20	.31
Respect for oneself	.21	.41	.56		.32	.30	.22	.21	−.15	−.16	.39
Extent of opportunity to do what one likes	.32	.36	.32	.32		.46	.35	.06	−.29	−.20	.46
Ability to do things oneself to increase satisfaction	.29	.25	.29	.30	.46		.25	.08	−.21	−.21	.35
Enjoyment of previous day	.25	.28	.21	.22	.35	.25		.12	−.20	−.20	.38
Importance of religion	.11	.15	.07	.21	.06	.08	.12		−.05	.01	.18
Extent of troubles or obstacles in life*	−.25	−.26	−.15	−.15	−.29	−.21	−.20	−.05		.44	−.35
Worry that things might get worse*	−.27	−.23	−.20	−.16	−.20	−.21	−.20	.01	.44		−.24
Satisfaction with life	.36	.45	.31	.39	.46	.35	.38	.18	−.35	−.24	

*Top of scale indicated many worries and troubles.

3. PERSONAL RATINGS BY DEFICIENCIES EXPERIENCED

TABLE 53

LADDER RATINGS OF PEOPLE INDICATING DEFICIENCIES

Deficiency	Card units	Percent of total sample	Personal ratings		
			Past	Present	Future
Greater economic or financial security	1516	56%	5.8	6.2	7.6
Better education than I now have	1430	53	5.7	6.3	7.7
More pay, larger income	1285	48	5.7	6.2	7.7
Greater faith in God or religion	1145	43	5.8	6.4	7.6
Being of more service to other people	1125	42	5.8	6.4	7.5
Better home to live in	1098	41	5.7	6.2	7.7
More leisure time and chance to enjoy leisure	1060	39	5.8	6.2	7.7
More opportunities for my own personal development	983	36	5.8	6.2	7.6
Better health	954	35	6.1	6.0	7.0
Ability to get more enjoyment out of life; greater capacity to be satisfied with things as they are for me now	895	33	5.7	6.0	7.5
Happier home and family life	714	27	5.7	5.7	7.3
More interesting work; more congenial job	692	26	5.8	5.9	7.6
More exciting life	574	21	5.7	5.8	7.4
Total sample	*2696*	*100*	*5.9*	*6.6*	*7.8*

TABLE 54

LADDER RATINGS OF PEOPLE INDICATING DEFICIENCIES
AND EXPECTING TO ALLEVIATE THEM*

Deficiency	Card units	Percent†	Personal ratings		
			Past	Present	Future
Greater economic or financial security	1066	78%	5.6	6.3	8.0
Better education than I now have	507	39	5.3	6.3	7.7
More pay; larger income	943	94	5.5	6.3	8.0
Greater faith in God or religion	1020	94	5.6	6.4	7.7
Being of more service to other people	917	90	5.8	6.6	7.8
Better home to live in	855	86	5.5	6.2	8.0
More leisure time and chance to enjoy leisure	754	78	5.8	6.6	8.0
More opportunities for my own personal development	666	76	5.5	6.3	8.0
Better health	561	65	6.0	6.0	7.4
Ability to get more enjoyment out of life; greater capacity to be satisfied with things as they are for me now	663	82	5.6	6.2	8.1
Happier home and family life	531	84	5.5	5.8	7.7
More interesting work; more congenial job	415	66	5.7	6.1	8.0
More exciting life	294	59	5.6	6.2	8.0

*Those who indicated deficiencies but did not state positive or negative expectations are excluded from this table.

† Percent of those indicating deficiencies.

TABLE 55

LADDER RATINGS OF PEOPLE INDICATING DEFICIENCIES
BUT NOT EXPECTING TO ALLEVIATE THEM*

Deficiency	Card units	Percent†	Personal ratings		
			Past	Present	Future
Greater economic or financial security	309	22%	6.1	6.0	6.2
Better education than I now have	781	61	6.0	6.4	7.3
More pay; larger income	250	6	7.0	6.1	6.2
Greater faith in God or religion	67	6	5.8	6.5	7.2
Being of more service to other people	106	10	6.1	5.7	5.4
Better home to live in	157	14	6.7	5.5	5.6
More leisure time and chance to enjoy leisure	214	22	5.5	5.7	6.7
More opportunities for my own personal development	213	24	6.4	6.0	6.6
Better health	302	35	6.4	6.1	6.6
Ability to get more enjoyment out of life; greater capacity to be satisfied with things as they are for me now	149	18	6.3	5.7	6.0
Happier home and family life	101	16	6.5	5.6	5.7
More interesting work; more congenial job	210	34	6.4	5.6	6.6
More exciting life	209	41	6.0	5.4	6.7

* Those who indicated deficiencies but did not state positive or negative expectations are excluded from this table.

† Percent of those indicating deficiencies.

Index

About the Author

Hadley Cantril is chairman of the board and senior counselor of the Institute for International Social Research in Princeton, New Jersey.

Mr. Cantril's career has combined the disciplines of sociology and psychology. After receiving his Ph.D. from Harvard in 1931, he taught sociology at Dartmouth and psychology at Harvard and Columbia, and joined the psychology faculty of Princeton University in 1936, to remain until 1955, when he became associated with the Institute for International Social Research.

During World War II Mr. Cantril was an expert consultant to the Secretary of War and the Office of War Information. In 1948 he headed the UNESCO "Tensions Project," and in 1955–56 again served the Government as expert consultant to the Executive Office of the President.

The present volume is Mr. Cantril's fifteenth as author, co-author, or editor and he has contributed close to one hundred articles to scholarly journals in his field.

The typeface used in the composition of this book was Baskerville. Printed by letterpress on 50# Warren's 1854 Plate, the book was bound in Columbia Fictionette with Canco Duplex Endleaf endpapers. It was manufactured by Quinn & Boden Company, Inc., Rahway, New Jersey.